The Whole Widget

E.B Cohen

First edition, 2026

Contents

The Whole Widget

Steve Jobs, Apple, and the Reinvention of the Modern World

E.B Cohen

First edition, 2026.

This is a work of popular history. It stands on the shoulders of the journalists, insiders, and biographers who did the primary work, and on the public record — Apple's own product launches and financial filings, court documents, and the recollections of the people who were in the room. Its narrative spine is the long shelf of Apple literature: Walter Isaacson's authorized *Steve Jobs*; Brent Schlender and Rick Tetzeli's *Becoming Steve Jobs*; Andy Hertzfeld's insider *Revolution in the Valley*; Michael Moritz's early *The Little Kingdom*; Steven Levy's *Insanely Great*; David Price's *The Pixar Touch*; Leander Kahney's studies of Jony Ive and Tim Cook; Ken Kocienda's *Creative Selection;* and Tripp Mickle's *After Steve.* Where accounts conflict — and around Steve Jobs they very often do — this book says so. Where a famous story is too good to be entirely true, it says that too, because the distance between the legend and the ledger is part of the subject. Apple is a company that has always sold a story about itself, brilliantly, and one task of a history is to hold that story up to the light.

For the tinkerers in the garage, and for everyone who ever believed a small team could change the world.

> "Here's to the crazy ones. The misfits. The rebels. The troublemakers. The round pegs in the square holes. The ones who see things differently... Because the people who are crazy enough to think they can change the world are the ones who do." — Apple, "Think Different," 1997

Introduction: The Man Who Sold the Future

On the morning of January 9, 2007, a slight man in a black mock-turtleneck, faded jeans, and gray sneakers walked onto a stage in San Francisco and, in the space of about ninety minutes, made most of the electronics in the world's pockets obsolete. He did it without seeming to try. He paced, he paused, he let the silence work. "Every once in a while," he said, "a revolutionary product comes along that changes everything." Then he told the audience he was going to introduce three of them: a widescreen iPod with touch controls, a revolutionary mobile phone, and a breakthrough internet communications device. He said it again, slower. An iPod. A phone. An internet communicator. And then, as the laughter of recognition began to build, he stopped pretending. "Are you getting it? These are not three separate devices. This is one device. And we are calling it iPhone."

Almost nothing about that scene was accidental. The turtleneck, the jeans, the sneakers were a costume as deliberate as any monarch's robes, worn so consistently that they had become a brand in themselves. The staging, the lighting, the giant clean typography on the screen behind him, the "one more thing" he would hold back for the end of so many of these performances — all of it was theater, refined over thirty years into an instrument for doing the single thing Steve Jobs did better than anyone of his age: making people want the future before they knew it existed. The device in his hand that morning would, within a decade, put a networked computer into the hands of more than half the human species, remake photography and journalism and human attention, mint one of the largest fortunes in the history of commerce, and lock a billion people into an ecosystem so seamless and so total that leaving it came to feel like emigration. He would not live to see most of it. He had four years left.

This book is about how a machine got built — two machines, really. One is the company, Apple, which began as a partnership between two young men in a suburban garage with a sheaf of hand-soldered circuit boards, nearly went bankrupt twice, and grew into the first business in history worth four trillion dollars. The other is the myth, the story Apple tells about itself and that the world tells about Steve Jobs: the college dropout who saw further, the artist among engineers, the rebel who put a dent in the universe. Both machines are real, and neither can be understood without the other. Apple's products succeeded because of engineering and manufacturing and supply chains and pricing; they also succeeded because of a story about individuality and taste and rebellion that Jobs sold as skillfully as he sold hardware. To write the history of the company honestly, you have to take the machinery seriously and take the myth seriously, and refuse to collapse either one into the other.

It is a story with a shape almost too neat for fiction, which is one reason so many people distrust the smooth version of it. A young man co-founds a company, transforms an industry, is thrown out of the company he built, wanders in a decade-long wilderness of expensive failures, returns to rescue the near-dead firm, and in his second act produces the most successful run of consumer products the world has ever seen — before dying, at the summit, of a cancer he had spent years insisting he could manage. If you tried to sell that arc to a studio, they would tell you it was implausible. And yet it happened, and the temptation is to tell it as a fable: the visionary vindicated, the doubters shamed, the genius who was right all along. This book resists that temptation, not because the achievement wasn't real — it was enormous — but because the fable leaves out the parts that make it human and instructive. It leaves out the daughter he denied for years, the colleagues he humiliated, the good ideas that were other people's, the failures that taught him more than the triumphs, and the workers on the other side of the world whose long shifts made the miracle affordable.

It also leaves out everyone else. The cult of Steve Jobs is so powerful that it can make Apple look like the lengthened shadow of one man, and Jobs did nothing to discourage that impression. But there was no Apple without Steve Wozniak, the shy engineering genius who actually designed the machines that started it all and who wanted nothing more than to build beautiful circuits and give them away. There was no rescue without Jony Ive, the British designer who translated Jobs's taste into aluminum and glass. There was no trillion-dollar empire without

Tim Cook, the quiet operations savant from Alabama who built the most sophisticated supply chain on earth and then ran the company for fifteen years after Jobs was gone — longer than Jobs himself ran it. And the story does not end with any of them. As this book goes to press in 2026, Apple is completing another handoff: Cook is stepping back to become executive chairman, and a hardware engineer named John Ternus, who joined the company as a young man and spent a quarter-century inside it, is taking the chief executive's chair. The garage is fifty years in the past. The story is still being written.

The book moves in thirteen parts, roughly chronological with a few thematic pauses. It begins before Apple, in the orchards of the Santa Clara Valley as they turned into Silicon Valley, and with the two very different young men who would meet there. It follows the founding, the Apple II that built an industry, and the Macintosh that defined a design philosophy. It goes into exile with Jobs, to NeXT and to Pixar, and argues that those "lost" years were in fact the making of him. It comes home for the return and the great second act — the iMac, the iPod, the iPhone, the iPad — and it stops, as Jobs's life stopped, at the peak. Then it keeps going, because the company did: through the Cook era of watches and earbuds and services and homemade silicon and trillion-dollar valuations, into the shadows the miracle cast, and out the other side to the question that hangs over every founder-shaped company when the founder is long gone. What, exactly, did Steve Jobs build? And can it outlast him?

He liked to quote a line, attributed variously and probably apocryphally, that a great person tries to "put a dent in the universe." He put one. This is the story of how — and of the many hands, besides his own, that swung the hammer.

Chapter 1 — The Adopted Son

The condition was written into the arrangement before the baby was born: the adoptive parents had to be college graduates. That was what the biological mother wanted, and she was in a position to insist, because she was giving up a child and the agencies of 1955 gave a birth mother that much leverage. Her name was Joanne Schieble. She was a graduate student from a conservative Wisconsin family, and the father of her child was a Syrian-born teaching assistant named Abdulfattah Jandali, whom her own father had forbidden her to marry. So she traveled to San Francisco, arranged a private adoption, and stipulated that her son go to educated, professional people who would give him the life she felt she could not.

The couple first in line to receive him were a lawyer and his wife. At the last moment they backed out; they had decided they wanted a girl. And so, in the small hours of a February morning, a phone rang in a modest house belonging to Paul and Clara Jobs. Would they like a baby boy? They would. There was a complication. Paul Jobs was a machinist, a Coast Guard veteran with a high-school education and grease permanently under his fingernails. Clara had not finished college either. When Joanne Schieble learned that the people taking her son were not the graduates she had demanded, she refused for weeks to sign the final papers. She relented only after Paul and Clara made a solemn promise: the boy would go to college. It was a promise made about a newborn by strangers, and it would take on an almost mythic weight in the family, and be broken, and in the breaking make history.

The man Joanne's father found so objectionable was not, whatever later tellings would suggest, a refugee or a man without prospects. Abdulfattah Jandali had been born in 1931 in Homs, Syria, one of nine children in a prosperous family; his own father had made a fortune in business, and the son had been sent first to the American University of Beirut and then to the University of Wisconsin, where he was working toward a doctorate in political science — the very campus that put him, in the mid-1950s, in the same rooms as a Catholic farm girl named Joanne Schieble, whose own parents ran a mink farm and owned real estate around Green Bay. Decades later, when Jobs had become the most famous entrepreneur alive and the politics of Muslim immigration were convulsing the country, commentators would seize on Jandali's origins to cast Jobs as, in effect, a refugee's son — proof that immigration built Silicon Valley. It was a tidy story and not quite an honest one. Jandali had come to the United States on a student visa, from a family wealthy enough to send him abroad for an education, fleeing nothing; the objection Joanne's father raised was not to Syria as a place but to Islam as a faith, and to a Catholic daughter marrying outside it. Of all the distortions that accumulated around Steve Jobs's origins over the years, this was among the most persistent.

The story did not end with the adoption, though for years neither side knew how it would continue. Joanne's father died only six months after his grandson was given away, and with the objection that had driven the whole arrangement gone, Joanne and Abdulfattah married. They had a second child, a daughter named Mona, born in 1957 in Green Bay — a full biological sister to the boy who had been placed with the Jobses, raised in the same household as the parents who had given him up, with none of them knowing where the other child had gone. The marriage did not last; Joanne and Jandali divorced in 1962, and Jandali drifted out of academic life and into casino management in Nevada, eventually running restaurants in Sacramento and Reno. Mona Jandali grew up to become the novelist Mona Simpson, and it would be her brother's dogged, years-long search for his birth mother, undertaken only after Clara Jobs died in 1986, that finally brought brother and sister together as adults — two people who had spent a childhood in different houses, unaware the other existed, born of the same two parents.

They named him Steven Paul Jobs. He grew up first in San Francisco and then, when he was small, in the new suburb of Mountain View, on the flat sun-struck plain south of the bay where cheap tract houses were multiplying across what had recently been fruit orchards. It was, for a boy of a certain temperament, the best possible place and time to be alive. Steve Jobs later spoke of his father with a reverence that never left him, and the picture he painted was always the same: Paul Jobs at his workbench in the garage, patient, exacting, teaching his son to build things and to care about the parts you could not see. When they built a fence together, Paul insisted the back of it be as finished as the front. "He loved doing things right," Jobs remembered. "He even cared about the look of the parts you couldn't see." A carpenter making a chest of drawers, Paul said, does not use a piece of plywood on the back just because it faces the wall. That idea — that craftsmanship lives in the hidden places, that you build the inside of the box as beautifully as the outside even though no customer will ever open it — would become, decades later, one of the deepest principles of Apple's design, argued over the layout of circuit boards no user would ever see.

There is a paradox at the center of Jobs's beginnings that he himself circled for the rest of his life, and it is worth pausing on, because the temptation to make it simple is strong and the truth resists it. He was, by the terms of his own birth, given up. He knew from an early age that he was adopted, and the neighborhood children, in the casual cruelty of childhood, told him it meant his real parents hadn't wanted him. According to the story he told, he ran home in tears, and Paul and Clara sat him down and said, slowly and emphatically, the sentence that he said reorganized his sense of himself: *You were chosen. You were special.* Some who knew him believed the abandonment left a permanent wound, a lifelong need to prove his worth and a fear of rejection that shaped how he treated people. Others, including Jobs, insisted the opposite — that being chosen made him feel not abandoned but elect, singular, marked out. Both things were probably true at once, and a good biographer should not have to choose. What is certain is that the fact of his adoption was never neutral to him. He would spend a career building an intensely controlled world of objects that did exactly what he wanted, and he would, for years, refuse to acknowledge a daughter of his own, replaying on the other side the very drama in which he had been the abandoned child.

Jobs himself, asked directly by Walter Isaacson decades later whether the adoption had wounded him, gave an answer that undercuts the tragic reading almost entirely. "Knowing I was adopted may have made me feel more independent," he said, "but I have never felt abandoned. I've always felt special. My parents made me feel special." He bristled whenever journalists described Paul and Clara as his "adoptive" parents, insisting they were his parents, full stop, at "1,000 percent," and he reserved a colder, almost clinical vocabulary for Joanne and Abdulfattah — "my sperm and egg bank," he once said of them, "that's not harsh, it's just the way it was." Yet the record of his adult life complicates even that studied indifference. When he finally located Joanne in the mid-1980s, he pursued a real relationship with her and, through her, discovered and grew close to Mona Simpson, who became one of the most important people in his life. His biological father he chose, deliberately, never to meet. He learned, by chance, years later, that he had once eaten at a Sacramento restaurant Jandali managed, that the two men had shaken hands as stranger and customer without either knowing the truth, and that Jandali — who had no idea whom he had been talking to — had mentioned to Mona, unprompted, that a man named Steve Jobs used to come in and was a terrific tipper. Jobs found the story worth telling and retelling, but he never reached out. Whatever he had decided about his origins, he had decided it a long time before, and nothing he learned as an adult moved him to revise it.

Clara Jobs taught him to read before he started school, which turned out to be a mixed blessing. Steve arrived in first grade already bored, and boredom in a bright and willful child looks a great deal like delinquency. He set off explosives, by his own cheerful account, and made a small career of misbehavior, until a fourth-grade teacher named Imogene Hill — "Teddy," the children called her — figured out how to reach him. She bribed him. She offered him money and candy to finish math workbooks, and something clicked; the bribes soon became unnecessary because the pleasure of mastering the material took over. Jobs credited her, ever after, as one of the saints of his life, one of the people who saw what he was and refused to let it be wasted. It is a pattern that recurs in his story: the difficult, arrogant boy who is nonetheless rescued again and again by adults who recognize something in him and decide he is worth the trouble.

The other great teacher of his boyhood was the place itself. The Santa Clara Valley in the late 1950s and early 1960s was a landscape in transition, and a curious child could feel the future arriving. His neighborhood was full of engineers — Mountain View and the towns around it were becoming the residential zone for the electronics firms that fed off the defense contracts of the early Cold War. Fathers up and down the block worked on things Steve had never heard of: lasers, semiconductors, radar. One neighbor, a Hewlett-Packard engineer named Larry Lang, kept a workbench in his garage and let the boy hang around it. It was Lang who introduced him to the Heathkits — mail-order electronics kits that came as a box of components and a manual and let a determined hobbyist build a working radio or amplifier from scratch. Building a Heathkit, Jobs said later, taught him something that no store-bought gadget could: that the objects in the world were not magic, that they had been designed and assembled by people no smarter than you, and that with patience and a soldering iron you could understand them and even make them yourself. It demystified technology. It gave a boy the radical confidence that the built world was intelligible and improvable.

The adoption itself belonged to a system that has largely vanished. In 1955 a closed adoption meant genuinely closed: birth parents and adoptive parents exchanged no names, and Joanne Schieble had every reason to believe the arrangement would remain secret unless she chose otherwise. That kind of permanent anonymity has grown almost impossible to guarantee since. Sealed adoption records, once effectively unbreakable without a court order, are now routinely circumvented by consumer DNA testing services, which can connect a stranger to a biological parent or sibling from a cheek swab in a matter of weeks; Jobs, by contrast, found Joanne only in the mid-1980s, after years of searching aided by hired investigators, a sympathetic doctor willing to bend the rules, and a fair amount of luck. The world that produced his adoption — discreet, sealed, dependent on paperwork rather than genetics — is not the world adoptees search in today.

The house the Jobses brought him home to, at 286 Diablo Avenue in Mountain View, still stands, one more unremarkable tract house among rows of them built in the late 1950s on land that had recently been orchards. Jobs told

Isaacson it was an Eichler, one of the sleek, glass-walled modernist tract homes the developer Joseph Eichler was scattering across California at the time, and said the clean, democratic design of those houses shaped his own aesthetic instincts. Real-estate researchers who later traced the subdivision's actual builder found it was not an Eichler at all but a look-alike put up by a competing firm, Mackay Homes — a small correction, but a telling one, since it suggests that even Jobs's account of his own most ordinary surroundings had, by the time he told it, acquired a more elegant pedigree than the facts quite supported.

There is one further story from those Mountain View years that Jobs told so often, in so many interviews and commencement addresses, that it hardened into a kind of personal creation myth, and it deserves to be set down here because it previews, in miniature, the method he would use for the rest of his career. At around twelve or thirteen, working on a school project that needed a piece of test equipment called a frequency counter, he found himself short of parts, and rather than ask his father or a teacher for help, he did something that would have struck most boys in the neighborhood as unthinkable: he looked up the home telephone number of William Hewlett, the co-founder of Hewlett-Packard, in the local phone book, and simply dialed it. Hewlett answered. He was amused, by his own later account of the call, that a boy would have the nerve to telephone a company president at home on a Sunday, and rather than hang up he stayed on the line for the better part of twenty minutes, talking Jobs through the parts he needed and where to find them. Then he did something more consequential than supplying spare components: he offered the boy a summer job on Hewlett-Packard's assembly line, an ordinary teenager suddenly standing at a workbench putting together frequency counters by hand, tightening nuts and bolts onto machines he had, only weeks earlier, been too young and too unconnected to have any business touching.

Jobs told the story for the rest of his life as proof of a principle he held with something close to religious conviction — that most people never tried, that the world was far more open to a confident, direct request than anyone assumed, and that the person who simply picked up the phone and asked would astonish himself at how often the answer was yes. "Most people never pick up the phone and call," he said, describing the lesson he drew from it, and he would repeat some version of that advice to interviewers, students, and young engineers for decades, dressed up as counsel about entrepreneurship but rooted, in fact, in a single Sunday afternoon of a twelve-year-old's nerve and a busy executive's decision to answer his own telephone rather than let it ring through to someone else. It is also, read against the rest of this chapter, a small rebuttal to the idea that Jobs's confidence was purely a defense grown out of the wound of adoption; whatever its psychological roots, by the time he was old enough to need spare parts for a science project, that confidence was already operating exactly as it would when he later cold-called suppliers, engineers, and investors on Apple's behalf — as a tool, wielded with total unselfconsciousness, for getting something he wanted from someone who had no obligation to give it to him.

Put those inheritances together — a machinist father who cared about hidden craftsmanship, a mother who made him a reader, a teacher who saw past his arrogance, a valley humming with the electronics of the coming age, and a private, unhealed knowledge that he had been given away and taken back — and you have the raw materials of the man. What you do not yet have is the machine, or the industry, or the partner. Steve Jobs was a bright, prickly, seeking boy in a suburb of engineers. What turned that into Apple was, first, the ground he was standing on, which was about to become the most concentrated engine of invention in the history of the world. And it was, second, another boy a few years older, living a few miles away, who could do the one thing Steve Jobs never could:

actually design a computer. Before we reach him, though, we should understand the valley — how a place named for its blossoms became named for its silicon.

Chapter 2 — The Valley of Heart's Delight

Before it was Silicon Valley, it was the Valley of Heart's Delight, and the name was not marketing. In the first half of the twentieth century the Santa Clara Valley was one of the largest fruit-producing regions on earth, a flat basin of orchards — prune, apricot, cherry, plum — that in spring turned white and pink with blossom for as far as a person could see. Postcards sold the spectacle. Families drove out from San Francisco to picnic among the trees. As late as the 1940s, a visitor to the towns that would later hold Apple, Google, and Intel would have found canneries and packing sheds and the smell of drying apricots, not the smell of solder. The transformation of that agricultural valley into the densest concentration of technological wealth in human history is the stage on which the whole of this book takes place, and it did not happen by accident or by climate. It happened because of a university, a war, and a professor with a grudge.

The scale of that fruit economy is easy to lose in the telling. At its peak the valley held more than one hundred thousand acres under cultivation, and by 1900 it was producing the majority of California's prunes, packed in wooden crates stamped with growers' names and shipped by rail to markets across the country and by steamer overseas. Thirty-nine canneries ran at once through the summer harvest, employing thousands of seasonal workers — many of them immigrant and migrant families — to pit, peel, and can apricots, cherries, and plums before the fruit could spoil in the heat. As late as 1940, Santa Clara County's orchards alone supplied more than half of the nation's apricots and plums, a fact that quietly undercuts a tidy and commonly repeated myth: that the valley's farms simply vanished the instant the transistor arrived. In truth the fruit economy and the electronics economy overlapped for the better part of a generation. Shockley Semiconductor and the earliest of Fairchild's spinoffs went up in the 1950s while packing sheds a few miles away were still processing that year's cherry crop, and the two worlds — one running on sunlight and irrigation, the other on federal contracts and silicon wafers — coexisted, oddly, for years. What finally ended the orchards was not silicon directly but the housing that silicon's growing workforce needed: a postwar wave of tract subdivisions, built to shelter the engineers and assembly-line workers streaming into the new electronics firms, that consumed the fruit trees acre by acre through the 1950s and 1960s rather than in any single stroke. Of the valley's onetime hundred-thousand-plus acres of orchard, historians and local park authorities now reckon that perhaps five thousand acres survive today.

The university was Stanford, endowed by a railroad baron in memory of a dead son and planted in the valley in 1891. For its first half-century it was a respectable regional school of no particular consequence to world affairs. What changed it was a man named Frederick Terman, an engineering professor who returned to Stanford in the 1920s after studying at MIT on the East Coast and was struck by how his most talented students kept leaving. They graduated, and then they moved east, because the great electronics companies were all in the east and there was nothing to hold them in California. Terman set out, with a patience that spanned decades, to build in the valley the ecosystem that would let his students stay: to make Stanford a place that generated companies, not just graduates. He encouraged two of them, Bill Hewlett and Dave Packard, to start a firm rather than take jobs elsewhere, and in 1939, in a rented garage in Palo Alto, Hewlett-Packard was born. That garage is now a state landmark, sometimes called the birthplace of Silicon Valley, and the pattern it set — the two founders, the garage, the professor's blessing — would be repeated, consciously and unconsciously, for the rest of the century, right down to two young men named Steve building circuit boards in Los Altos.

The war supplied the money. The Second World War and then the long Cold War that followed poured federal defense dollars into electronics — radar, microwave technology, guidance systems, communications — and much of it flowed to the West Coast, close to the Pacific theater and to Stanford's laboratories. Terman ran a wartime research operation and came home determined to capture that funding stream permanently. Stanford created an industrial park on its land, leasing space to electronics firms and binding them to the university in a web of contracts, consulting, and shared talent. By the 1950s the valley had a defense-electronics industry, a research university at its center, and a growing culture of engineers who moved fluidly between the two. What it did not yet have was the material that would give it its name.

That arrived with the professor and his grudge. William Shockley was one of the co-inventors of the transistor at Bell Labs in New Jersey, a piece of work that would earn him a share of a Nobel Prize and change the world: the transistor was a tiny switch with no moving parts, able to amplify or switch electronic signals, and it would replace the hot, fragile, power-hungry vacuum tube in every kind of device. Shockley was a brilliant physicist and, by wide agreement, a difficult and eventually poisonous man to work for. In 1956 he left Bell Labs and moved to Mountain View — partly to be near his aging mother — and founded Shockley Semiconductor Laboratory to commercialize the transistor. He chose to build his devices out of silicon rather than the germanium then in common use, a decision that would give the valley its eventual name. But he could not keep his people. His paranoia and cruelty drove away his most talented recruits, and in 1957 eight of them quit together — Shockley called them "the traitorous eight" — and, with outside financing, founded a rival firm: Fairchild Semiconductor.

The break at Shockley Semiconductor, when it finally came, arrived after months of a management style that swung between genius and paranoia. Shockley was given to suspecting sabotage behind ordinary technical setbacks, and at one point he asked his entire research staff to submit to polygraph examinations to root out a saboteur who did not exist. Eight of his most talented recruits — Julius Blank, Victor Grinich, Jean Hoerni, Eugene Kleiner, Jay Last, Gordon Moore, Robert Noyce, and Sheldon Roberts — eventually went over Shockley's head to Arnold Beckman, the instrument-company owner whose money had funded the lab, and asked him to remove Shockley from day-to-day management. Beckman seemed at first to agree, then reversed course and backed Shockley instead. Their bridges burned, the eight resigned within days of one another and went looking for financing to start a competitor of their own — an act so far outside the button-down corporate norms of the 1950s that Shockley denounced them as traitors, a label they wore ever after, half insult and half badge of honor. They found their backer in Sherman Fairchild, an East Coast industrialist and inventor who advanced them $1.38 million to launch Fairchild Semiconductor in September 1957, taking in return an option to buy the company outright for three million dollars, an option his firm would in fact exercise a few years later. It proved to be one of the shrewder bets in the history of American industry: within a decade Fairchild Semiconductor had grown from a dozen founding employees to roughly twelve thousand, with annual revenues above $130 million, and its own alumni had already begun peeling off to seed the valley with dozens of new companies.

Fairchild is the true taproot of the valley as we know it. Two of the eight, Robert Noyce and Gordon Moore, were figures of the first rank. At Fairchild, Noyce and colleagues developed the integrated circuit — the idea of building many transistors together on a single chip of silicon, wired into a working circuit, rather than assembling components one by one. This was the breakthrough that made the modern computer possible, because it meant that computing power could shrink and cheapen at a staggering, compounding rate. Moore would later articulate that rate as a rule of thumb — that the number of transistors on a chip would roughly double every couple of years — and the observation, dubbed Moore's Law, became the metronome of the entire industry, the drumbeat against which every product in this book would be designed. In 1968 Noyce and Moore left Fairchild in turn and founded a company of their own, which they called Intel. And Fairchild's alumni kept splitting off to start firms of their own, dozens of them, in a branching family tree so dense that they were nicknamed the "Fairchildren." The valley's defining habit was set: talent did not stay put; it spun out, again and again, each departure seeding a new company.

By the early 1970s, then, the ground Steve Jobs walked to school on had become something without precedent. Within a few miles' radius there was a great research university actively trying to birth companies; a defense-funded electronics industry; the world's leading makers of the integrated circuits that were doubling in power every two years; a venture-capital business emerging along a road called Sand Hill to finance the whole churning enterprise; and a culture — this is the part that is hardest to manufacture and easiest to underestimate — that treated leaving your employer to start a competitor not as betrayal but as the natural order of things. A journalist named Don Hoefler gave the place its permanent name in a 1971 trade-paper article, "Silicon Valley USA," and the label stuck to the fruit basin like a decal.

It is worth pausing on that naming, because the tidy version — that Don Hoefler single-handedly invented the phrase out of nothing in 1971 — is not quite true, and the real story says something about how the valley actually worked. Hoefler certainly popularized it, running his series under the banner "Silicon Valley USA" in the trade weekly *Electronic News* and fixing the label in print for good. But engineers and journalists who had worked in the region through the 1960s recalled hearing some version of the phrase years earlier, traded informally among people who moved between the chip firms and the defense agencies that funded them; one account credits a local executive, Ralph Vaerst, with suggesting the specific phrase to Hoefler over drinks before the article ever ran. Like so much else about the place, "Silicon Valley" was less a coinage than a crystallization — an insider's private shorthand that a reporter happened to be the one to put a headline on, at the exact moment the rest of the country needed a name for what was happening there.

There is a coda to this agricultural story that the rest of this book will make clear was not incidental. Decades later, when Apple built its circular headquarters in Cupertino, the company deliberately planted a working orchard inside the ring — thirty-seven varieties of apricot, persimmon, and plum, seventeen more of apple and cherry, the very crops that had once defined Cupertino before a single circuit board existed there. It was not a decorative afterthought: the campus itself sat on land first homesteaded by Scottish immigrant farmers in the nineteenth century, and Apple's landscapers researched the valley's own agricultural past to choose which historic varieties to put back into the ground. A visitor standing in that courtyard today, apricot trees in blossom and a half-mile ring of glass rising behind them, is standing in the one place where the Valley of Heart's Delight and Silicon Valley overlap most literally — the beginning and the end of this chapter's story, planted a few hundred feet apart.

The Shockley-and-Fairchild lineage is the one every history of the valley reaches for, and rightly so, but it is not quite the oldest thread in the fabric, and the thread that predates it belongs to a company nobody associates with Silicon Valley today: IBM. In 1952, four years before Shockley ever packed his bags for Mountain View, IBM opened a small research laboratory on Notre Dame Avenue in San Jose, in what was then still fruit country on the valley's southern edge, and put an engineer named Reynold Johnson in charge of finding a faster way to store and retrieve data than punched cards or reels of magnetic tape allowed. Johnson's team worked in near-total secrecy for years, and what they built, announced in September 1956 alongside the new IBM 305 RAMAC computer, was the world's first commercial hard disk drive — a refrigerator-sized unit called the Model 350 that spun fifty spinning aluminum platters, each two feet across, and could store, by the standards of the day, an almost unbelievable five million characters, retrievable in any order rather than only in the sequence they had been written. It shipped to its first customer, a paper company in San Francisco, that same June. The RAMAC's disk drive did for data storage roughly what the transistor would do for the switch: it took something bulky, slow, and sequential and made it small, fast, and random-access, and every hard drive built afterward, in every mainframe, personal computer, and data center of the following half-century, descended in a direct technical line from Johnson's spinning platters.

The reason this earlier chapter of the valley's history tends to go missing from the Shockley-and-Fairchild story is precisely that IBM was, and remained, an East Coast company with an Armonk, New York, address on its letterhead; the San Jose laboratory was treated, even inside IBM, as a distant outpost rather than a headquarters, valuable for the cheap land and the available engineering talent but never the seat of the corporation's identity the way Fairchild and its offspring became the valley's own. Yet the San Jose plant kept growing through the 1950s and 1960s, manufacturing disk drives by the thousands and training a generation of storage engineers who would, in time, seed disk-drive and storage startups of their own around the South Bay, in much the same branching pattern that Fairchild's alumni would later repeat with semiconductors. By the time Shockley arrived to found his own lab, in other words, the valley already had one thriving, secretive, world-changing electronics operation quietly running a few miles from where he set up shop — a reminder that Silicon Valley's silicon was not the first invention to make the place matter, only the one that gave it a name.

Into that ferment two other currents were flowing, and they mattered as much to Apple as the silicon did. One was the counterculture. The San Francisco Bay Area in the late 1960s was the epicenter of the hippie movement, of psychedelics and communes and a wholesale rejection of corporate, conformist America, and the young engineers of the valley were not sealed off from it — many were steeped in it. The other was a strand of that counterculture that had fallen in love with technology, believing that the same computers the military used to run the Vietnam War could, in the right hands, be tools of personal liberation. Its bible was Stewart Brand's *Whole Earth Catalog*, a fat compendium of tools and ideas for people trying to live self-sufficiently and think for themselves, whose back cover carried the line Jobs would quote at the end of his life: *Stay hungry. Stay foolish.* Out of the collision of the engineer's valley and the hippie's dream came a peculiar and powerful idea, heretical to the mainframe establishment: that a computer should not be a giant machine locked in an air-conditioned room and tended by a priesthood, but a personal thing, small and cheap enough for an ordinary person to own, a "bicycle for the mind." That idea was in the air, unclaimed, waiting for someone to build it. And a few miles from the Jobs house, a boy who could actually do the building was growing up obsessed with electronics — a boy who would become the other half of Apple.

Chapter 3 — Woz

Stephen Gary Wozniak was the kind of boy who would rather understand how a thing worked than be told he was clever for wanting to know. He was born in 1950, five years before Steve Jobs, the son of a Lockheed engineer named Jerry Wozniak who designed missile-guidance systems and who taught his children electronics the way other fathers taught baseball. From the beginning Woz — the nickname would eventually belong to the whole world — was a pure engineer in a way that is rare even among engineers. He did not want to run a company. He did not particularly want to be rich or famous. He wanted to design elegant electronic circuits, to solve the puzzle of doing more with fewer parts, and to show his work to people who could appreciate the beauty of it. Money and power, when they came, would strike him as pleasant but slightly beside the point, and he would give a great deal of both away.

The particulars of that childhood are worth pausing over, because they explain so much of what came later. Wozniak was born on August 11, 1950, in San Jose, and by the time he was old enough to notice such things, his father had moved from a job as an engineer at Electronic Data Systems to a position in Lockheed's missile-systems division, work that came home with him in the form of clutter: resistors, capacitors, and salvaged components scattered across the workbench and garage of the family's house. To an ordinary child this would have been junk. To young Woz it was a catalogue of mysteries, and he pestered his father with the question every parent eventually tires of — what's that? — and got, every time, a real answer. Decades later, in his memoir *iWoz*, Wozniak remembered his father starting from the beginning, working back to atoms and electrons and protons, until an ordinary resistor became a doorway into how the entire physical world was built. He was eight years old, or even younger, when it began to sink in, and he would write that knowing it "made me feel different from all the other kids I knew. I started to feel as if I knew secrets no one else knew." That feeling, more than any single fact his father taught him, was the real inheritance: the conviction that the world was made of parts that could be understood, one patient question at a time.

That curiosity did not stay confined to the house. By the sixth grade, around 1961, Wozniak had built his own radio receiver from spare parts and passed the examination for an amateur operator's license, a rite of passage among the electronics-obsessed boys of that era and his first taste of building something that could reach beyond his own house into the wider world. At Cupertino's Homestead High School he found, for the first time, an institution built to reward exactly what he was good at: he was elected president of the school's electronics club at thirteen, and he won first prize at a science fair for a calculator he had built out of transistors — a small machine that, in miniature, previewed the entire logic of his later career, doing more with fewer parts than anyone expected possible. He graduated from Homestead in 1968 and enrolled at the University of Colorado at Boulder, where out-of-state tuition and a growing restlessness combined to send him home after a single year — the first sign that Wozniak's relationship to formal schooling would be a long, unresolved argument rather than a clean break.

He had two obsessions as a young man, and both fed directly into Apple. The first was minimalism in design. Woz treated the reduction of a circuit's parts count as a form of art. Given a problem that other engineers would solve with a hundred chips, he would find a way to do it with fifty, then forty, then thirty, wringing extra functions out of components by using them in clever, unintended ways. This was not mere thrift, though it happened to save money. It was aesthetic. A design with fewer parts was more beautiful, more comprehensible, closer to some Platonic ideal of the machine, and Woz pursued that ideal with the single-mindedness of a poet counting syllables. When he later designed the Apple II, its famously spare and clever architecture — squeezing color graphics and sound and a disk controller out of a startlingly small number of chips — would be the fruit of a lifetime spent in this discipline. His disk-drive controller, in particular, became legendary among engineers as a piece of design so economical it seemed almost like cheating, a magician's trick performed with a handful of parts.

His second obsession was pranks and, relatedly, the telephone network. Woz loved elaborate technical mischief — jamming televisions, building a fake bomb that got him briefly detained, running a "dial-a-joke" line. And in 1971 he read an article in *Esquire* magazine, "Secrets of the Little Blue Box," that described a subculture of "phone phreaks": hobbyists who had discovered that the entire long-distance telephone network could be controlled by precise audio tones, and who built devices called blue boxes to generate those tones and place free calls anywhere in the world. To an engineer of Woz's temperament this was irresistible: the phone system was the largest machine ever built, a continent-spanning network of switches, and here was a way to reach in and command it with a fistful of components and a deep understanding of how it worked. He set out to build a better blue box than anyone had built, an all-digital one, and he succeeded, and in doing so he pulled off feats of technical audacity that included, according to the cherished legend, placing a prank call to the Vatican in which he claimed to be Henry Kissinger asking to speak to the Pope. That article, and that box, would also be the thing that fused his life to Steve Jobs's.

The pranks were not always so consequence-free, and one of them, in particular, showed the same meticulous mind at work on something considerably less welcome than a circuit board. Not long after winning a math prize at Homestead, Wozniak built a metronome disguised as a bomb, wiring it up with battery labels so that, ticking steadily from inside a classmate's locker, it looked exactly like the countdown timer of a movie explosive — and when jostled, it began ticking faster, as though the fuse were running out. He was summoned to the principal's office expecting, by his own account, to be congratulated for the math prize; instead he found the police waiting, and he spent a night in juvenile hall for it. It was a fitting preview of his whole temperament: the same meticulous, technically accomplished mind that could reduce a phone network or a circuit board to its essential parts could also, with total sincerity, misjudge how the world would receive a joke.

The two Steves had been introduced around 1971 by a mutual friend, Bill Fernandez, who correctly sensed that the older boy who could build anything and the younger one who was mesmerized by electronics and full of intensity might have something to say to each other. On the surface they could hardly have been more different. Woz was gentle, guileless, socially awkward, motivated by the pleasure of the work and almost incapable of self-promotion. Jobs was intense, charismatic, hungry, socially fearless in a way that could shade into ruthlessness, and gifted above all with a sense of what other people might want and how to make them want it. But they shared a wavelength — a love of electronics, a taste for pranks, a countercultural streak, an outsider's disdain for the ordinary — and they shared, crucially, a set of complementary talents that made each one able to do what the other could not. Woz could design a machine. Jobs could imagine it as a product and sell it to the world. Neither of them alone would have made Apple. Together they were, for a few decisive years, a nearly perfect engine.

The blue box was where the partnership first showed its shape. Woz built the boxes for the love of it; Jobs saw that they could be sold. This was the division of labor in miniature, and it is worth being clear-eyed about what it was: the boxes were instruments for committing telephone fraud, and the two young men went around dormitories selling them for about a hundred and fifty dollars apiece, of which the parts cost a fraction. It was illegal, it was risky — they were once robbed at gunpoint during a sale, and phone-company investigators were hunting phreaks — and it was, in its way, the founding act of Apple: the engineer's beautiful creation turned by his partner into a business. Jobs said as much for the rest of his life. "If it hadn't been for the blue boxes," he told his biographer, "there wouldn't have been an Apple. I'm 100 percent sure of that. Woz and I learned how to work together." They learned that Woz could make magic and Jobs could find the market, and they learned the intoxicating feeling of two people building something the establishment did not sanction and could not control.

There is a version of the Apple story, popular and false, in which Steve Jobs is a genius inventor. He was not, and he never claimed to be; he could not design a computer or write meaningful code, and the machines that started the company were, to a first approximation, Woz's. There is an equal and opposite version, popular among engineers who resent Jobs's fame, in which Woz did all the real work and Jobs merely took the credit and the money. That is also false, and it misunderstands what a product is. A brilliant circuit board sitting on a workbench is not a company and does not change anything; it becomes a product only when someone decides what it is for, packages it, prices it, markets it, and persuades the world it is worth buying — and that work is as real and as hard as the engineering, and it was work Woz had no interest in and no gift for. The honest account is that Apple was born from a genuine collaboration between two very different kinds of talent, and that its early greatness came precisely from the friction and fit between them. When they later drifted apart — as they would, once the company outgrew the garage and Jobs's ambitions outgrew Woz's — something was lost that neither man ever quite replaced.

It is tempting, given how the story of the two Steves usually gets told, to assume Wozniak shared Jobs's disdain for finishing what he started — another restless genius for whom college was simply beside the point. The truth is closer to the opposite, and it says something real about the difference between the two men. Wozniak never stopped feeling unfinished about Colorado. In 1986, eighteen years after he had first left for Boulder and long after Apple had made him wealthy beyond any reasonable use for the money, he quietly enrolled as an undergraduate at the University of California, Berkeley, to complete the electrical engineering and computer science degree he had never earned. He did it under an assumed name, Rocky Raccoon Clark — Rocky for his dog, Clark for his wife's surname at the time — because he did not want his fame or his fortune to change how professors graded his work or classmates treated him in a lab section. He graduated that same year, and Berkeley's college of engineering, having by then discovered exactly whose diploma it was signing, invited him back — under his own name this time — to deliver the commencement address.

The artifacts of those early years have, improbably, ended up behind glass. The all-digital blue box Wozniak built and refined until it worked better than anything else on the phone-phreak underground — the device whose sale first taught him and Jobs to work as partners — can be seen today at the Computer History Museum in Mountain View, a few miles from the house where his father's spare resistors once lay scattered on a workbench; another of Wozniak's hand-built boxes belongs to the collection of the Henry Ford Museum in Michigan. What was, in 1972, a tool for defrauding a phone company is preserved now as a founding relic of Silicon Valley, and the instinct behind it — the ability to look at an enormous, intimidating system and find the small number of parts that actually mattered — was the same instinct a Lockheed engineer had first demonstrated to his son with nothing more than a resistor and a patient answer to the question, what's that?

The Berkeley degree was not the only time Wozniak's life took an abrupt detour that the tidy Apple narrative tends to compress into a footnote, and the other one very nearly ended his life rather than merely delaying his diploma. On February 7, 1981, five years after the company he had built in a garage had made him rich, Wozniak was piloting a small single-engine plane, a Beechcraft Bonanza, out of a short airstrip called Sky Park in Scotts Valley, in the hills above Santa Cruz, with his then-fiancée and two of her relatives aboard. He was not yet a fully qualified pilot on that type of aircraft. The plane stalled soon after takeoff, bounced down the runway, tore through two fences, and slammed into an embankment. Everyone aboard survived, but Wozniak suffered serious facial and head injuries, and for five weeks afterward he lived with anterograde amnesia — the inability to lay down new memories at all. He could hold a conversation and then, minutes later, have no recollection that it had ever taken place; each day arrived for him with no memory of the day, or the weeks, before it. By his own later account, one of the things that helped coax his memory back into working order was, of all things, playing games on an Apple II, the machine his own engineering had made possible, as though the company he had built was quietly repaying the debt.

The crash reshaped the rest of his relationship with Apple

as much as any boardroom dispute ever could. Wozniak had already been drifting away from full-time engineering duties inside the company he had co-founded, uneasy with what Apple was becoming as it grew past the scale where one clever designer could shape a whole machine, and the recovery gave him, in his own words, a natural and welcome excuse to step back rather than force the question of when and how to leave. He did not resign outright; he simply receded, spending the early 1980s on side projects, on the two US Festival rock concerts he bankrolled and organized at enormous personal cost, and eventually, in 1986, on the unfinished Berkeley degree he completed under the name Rocky Raccoon Clark. The plane that nearly killed him is a strange, half-forgotten hinge in the story of Apple's second co-founder: an accident that had nothing to do with computers left him, for five weeks, unable to remember anything at all, and it was in the working-through of that fog that he began the long, gradual withdrawal from the company that would otherwise have kept demanding more of him than he any longer wanted to give.

For now, though, in the early 1970s, they were two young hobbyists with a shared history of technical mischief, orbiting each other and the exploding world of Silicon Valley electronics, waiting for the thing that would give their partnership a purpose larger than defrauding the phone company. That thing was coming. The integrated circuit was making it possible, for the first time, to imagine a computer small and cheap enough for one person to own. But before Apple could be founded, its younger, stranger co-founder had some wandering to do — through a college he would abandon, a country he would cross on foot, and a set of ideas about simplicity and enlightenment that would end up designed into every product the company ever made.

Chapter 4 — Blue Boxes

It is worth lingering on the blue box, because it is the single most revealing episode of the years before Apple, and because the smooth corporate history tends to skip past it in one embarrassed sentence. The received wisdom about Steve Jobs and Steve Wozniak is that they were idealists, rebels against the beige conformity of the computing establishment, and that is true. But their first commercial venture together was a device for stealing from the telephone monopoly, and understanding why they built it and what they learned from it tells you more about the DNA of Apple than any number of pieties about thinking different.

The phone network in the early 1970s was, in the United States, essentially one company: American Telephone and Telegraph, the Bell System, the largest corporation in the world, a regulated monopoly that owned the wire in the wall and the phone on the desk and everything in between. To make a long-distance call you paid AT&T by the minute, and the rates were high, and the whole system had the settled, unchallengeable feel of a natural feature of the landscape. It was also, it turned out, controllable by sound. The Bell network used tones sent down the same lines as the voice to route calls between switches — a particular frequency, 2,600 hertz, told a trunk line that a call had ended and it was free to accept new routing commands. A blind teenager named Joe Engressia had discovered he could whistle the tone; a phreak named John Draper found that a toy whistle given away in boxes of Cap'n Crunch cereal produced it exactly, which earned him the handle "Captain Crunch." With the right sequence of tones, played into a phone, you could seize a trunk line and route your own free call anywhere on earth. A blue box was simply a device that generated those tones on demand.

When Wozniak read the *Esquire* article describing all this, he was electrified, and he did what he always did: he called Jobs, who was still in high school, and the two of them drove to a library to find the technical journals — the Bell System's own published papers — that listed the exact frequencies. The phone company, with the confidence of a monopoly that could not imagine being challenged by teenagers, had printed the specifications of its own network in the open literature. Woz built a box, and it worked, and the sheer transgressive thrill of it — reaching into the largest machine ever built and bending it to your will from a bedroom — was something both young men would chase for the rest of their lives, in more legitimate forms. Jobs's contribution was characteristic and decisive: he looked at Woz's marvelous toy and said, in effect, we should sell these. And they did, going dorm to dorm, Woz doing the demonstrations, Jobs handling the pitch and the price. They charged around a hundred and fifty dollars for a device whose parts cost maybe forty.

The venture was dangerous in ways that were not abstract. Phone fraud was a federal crime, and the Bell System had its own security force that pursued phreaks with real determination. On at least one occasion a sale went wrong and the two were robbed at gunpoint in a pizza-parlor parking lot, handing over a box to a man who simply took it and walked away. Draper, the Cap'n Crunch himself, would be arrested and imprisoned. The whole enterprise had the flavor of adolescent recklessness, which is what it was. But Jobs drew from it a set of lessons that he stated plainly ever after, and they are the founding lessons of Apple. The first was that a small team of clever people, working outside the sanctioned channels, could take on an institution of unimaginable size and win — could, in fact, control the largest machine on the planet with a device that fit in a hand. The second was that Woz's genius could be turned into a business, and that turning it into a business was itself a creative act, not a parasitic one. And the third, less often noted, was about the relationship between the two of them: that they could work together, that their talents locked together like gears, and that together they could build and sell a real thing that people wanted.

There is a temptation, from the vantage of Apple's later cathedral-like insistence on doing everything the legal, controlled, official way, to be scandalized by the blue box, or to treat it as a youthful indiscretion best forgotten. That is a mistake, and it flattens the story. The rebellion was real, and it was not a marketing pose grafted on later; it was there at the origin, in the form of two young men deciding that the rules of a monopoly did not bind them and that a beautiful piece of engineering ought to be put to use. What changed over the following decades was not the rebel spirit but its object. The same impulse that built a blue box to defy AT&T would build a personal computer to defy IBM, and then a music store to defy the record labels, and then a phone to defy the wireless carriers — and Apple would, in the process, become an institution as large and as controlling as any it had ever set out to disrupt, which is one of the deep ironies this book will keep returning to. The company that was born in an act of joyful, illegal defiance of a monopoly would end its first fifty years as one of the most powerful and most criticized gatekeepers on earth, sued by developers and governments for the very kind of control it once existed to break.

It is worth being precise about how the story actually reached them, because the details matter more than the legend suggests. Wozniak's mother had mailed him the October 1971 issue of *Esquire*, the one carrying Ron Rosenbaum's article "Secrets of the Little Blue Box," subtitled with a wink as a story so incredible it might make you feel sorry for the phone company. Wozniak did not wait to finish reading before reaching for the phone; he called Jobs partway through the article and read him passages aloud over the line, and the next day the two of them drove not to just any library but to the technical stacks at the Stanford Linear Accelerator Center, a research library built to serve physicists chasing subatomic particles, now repurposed by two young men chasing free long-distance calls. That detail says something about the era in its own right: the same institutional openness that let a pair of outsiders without a university appointment walk into a national laboratory's library and photocopy Bell System technical journals was the openness that made the whole scheme possible in the first place. A decade later such documents would have been locked behind proprietary walls and nondisclosure agreements; in 1971 they were simply sitting on a shelf, filed under the assumption that no one who mattered would bother to look.

The popular version of this story tends to compress the invention into a single afternoon of garage tinkering, as though Wozniak built a box, plugged it in, and it simply worked. The truth is more interesting, and more revealing of the engineer he would become. His first attempt, wired from analog oscillators, was audibly imprecise — the tones drifted with temperature and battery voltage, and Bell's own detection equipment would sometimes reject a call placed with a frequency that had wandered even slightly out of tolerance. Rather than accept a device that worked most of the time, Wozniak spent roughly three weeks designing something far more ambitious: a fully digital blue box, built around digital counting circuits that could hold each tone rock-steady with a precision no analog whistle or oscillator could approach. It was, by most accounts of the phreaking underground, the first digital blue box anyone had built, and it is a preview in miniature of the instinct that would come to define Apple's engineering culture — an unwillingness to ship a hack that merely worked when a version that worked perfectly, every time, was within reach.

Jobs himself, many years later, put the significance of the episode to his biographer Walter Isaacson in strikingly blunt terms: if he and Wozniak had never built the blue boxes, he said, there would have been no Apple. It is tempting to read that as an old man tidying up his own myth, but it holds up under scrutiny. What the blue box proved to both of them, in a way no classroom could have, was that the two of them together could take an idea encountered in a magazine, run it down in a library, turn it into working hardware, and sell it for a profit to strangers — the entire life cycle of a technology company compressed into a few months of a Northern California winter, minus only the part where any of it was legal.

The fate of Captain Crunch himself supplies a strange coda that loops directly back into the company Jobs and Wozniak would go on to found. Draper was arrested for phone fraud in 1972 and again in 1976, and the second arrest produced a wire fraud conviction and time in the Alameda County jail. It did not end his career in computing. In 1979, serving part of his sentence under a work-release arrangement, Draper wrote code by hand on paper during the nights and typed it into an Apple II by day, producing EasyWriter, the first commercial word processor sold for Apple's new machine, which not long afterward also became a launch title for the original IBM PC. The man whose cereal-box whistle had given an entire underground its signature sound ended up, within a few years, writing software for the very computer that Wozniak's engineering had helped make possible.

The 2,600-hertz tone outlived the analog phone network it once commanded, and it is not hard to find its afterlife today. When the hacker magazine *2600: The Hacker Quar-*

terly launched in 1984, its founders named it directly after the frequency, a permanent tribute to the discovery that a plastic whistle from a cereal box could address a continent-spanning monopoly as an equal; the magazine is still published four times a year. The physical blue boxes themselves, meanwhile, became collectors' items in the most literal sense: an original circuit board built by Wozniak and sold by the two of them in a Berkeley dorm sold at a Bonhams auction in 2017 for one hundred and twenty-five thousand dollars, a sum that would have stunned the two young men who once charged a hundred and fifty dollars apiece for the same handful of components. What was once a federal crime, prosecuted with real police and real prison time, is now a museum piece under glass — as good a measure as any of how completely the world Jobs and Wozniak set out to defy has since absorbed their rebellion into its own official history.

The dorm-selling routine itself, apart from the gunpoint robbery, had its own catalogue of close calls, and one of them says as much about Wozniak's improvisational nerve as the blue box's circuitry does about his engineering. Their method for finding customers in the Berkeley dormitories was almost comically informal: they would knock on a random door, ask for a made-up name, and when the baffled resident said no one by that name lived there, one of them would add, as if it were an obvious clarifying detail, "you know, the guy who makes the free phone calls" — and more often than the two of them had any right to expect, the door opened wider rather than closing. The approach worked because the blue box's reputation had already spread through campus by word of mouth faster than either Steve could keep up with, an entire underground economy of dormitory gossip doing their marketing for free. It was a near miss of a different kind, though, that finally frightened them into stopping. Riding in a car that broke down on a public street with a blue box in plain view on the seat, they were approached by a police officer who wanted to know what the odd, humming device was; without missing a beat, one of them told him it was an electronic music synthesizer, a plausible enough lie in an era when synthesizers were themselves a novelty, and the officer, satisfied or simply uninterested, let them go. Wozniak later said it was that encounter, more than the earlier armed robbery, that persuaded them the game had gotten too dangerous to keep playing, and the two of them wound the blue box business down not long afterward.

The estimates of how many boxes they actually built and sold have never quite settled into agreement, and the discrepancy is itself a small window into the different temperaments of the two men. Jobs, retelling the story decades later to interviewers and biographers, sometimes put the total figure sold at over a hundred units, a number that flattered the scale of the operation he had built out of Woz's invention. Wozniak, asked the same question, tended to put the number closer to thirty or forty, a more modest tally that fit his general instinct to undersell his own exploits rather than inflate them. Neither man kept careful books at the time — they were, after all, two students running an illegal side business out of a dorm room, with every incentive to leave as thin a paper trail as possible — so the true number probably lies somewhere between their two recollections, forever unrecoverable and, in its way, a fitting detail for an enterprise that was never meant to be counted or taxed in the first place.

But that is decades away. In the early 1970s the blue box venture ran its course, the two Steves went their separate directions for a while — Woz to college and then to a job designing calculators at Hewlett-Packard, which was for him a kind of paradise, and Jobs to a college he would soon leave and a journey that would take him halfway around the world. What they carried forward was the memory of having built something together, sold it, and gotten away with it, and the knowledge that they made a formidable pair. When the moment came, a few years later, when the integrated circuit finally made a genuine personal computer possible, they already knew how to work together, and they already believed, in their bones, that two people in a bedroom could beat the giants. That belief was the seed. Everything else grew from it. First, though, the younger Steve had to figure out who he was, and he would look for the answer not in a laboratory but in a monastery, an orchard, and the dust of northern India.

Chapter 5 — Reed, India, and the Barefoot Years

The promise Paul and Clara Jobs had made to a birth mother — that their son would go to college — came due in the fall of 1972, and Steve honored it in the most expensive and least practical way available to him. He insisted on Reed College, a small, intense, costly liberal-arts school in Portland, Oregon, known for its bohemian intellectualism and its indifference to conventional career preparation. It strained the family's modest finances badly, and it was, by any sensible measure, a poor use of money, because Steve Jobs dropped out after a single semester. But he did not leave. He stayed on at Reed for another eighteen months as a kind of unofficial ghost, no longer enrolled, sleeping on friends' floors, returning Coke bottles for the deposit to buy food, walking miles on Sundays for a free hot meal at the local Hare Krishna temple, and dropping in on the classes that interested him while ignoring the ones that were merely required. He would later present this as one of the best decisions of his life, and in a famous speech he made the case that it was precisely his freedom from the requirements — his ability to follow curiosity rather than a curriculum — that let him stumble into the one class that would shape Apple.

That class was calligraphy. Reed happened to have one of the finest calligraphy programs in the country, and Jobs, with nothing forcing his schedule, wandered into it and fell in love with the art of beautiful letterforms — with serifs and sans-serifs, with the way the space between letter combinations could be varied to make a line of type sing, with the whole invisible craft of typography that most people never notice and that makes the difference between a page that repels the eye and one that invites it. It was useless knowledge, he cheerfully admitted, with no conceivable practical application for a college dropout. And then, ten years later, when he and his team were designing the Macintosh, all of it came back, and the Mac became the first computer with beautiful typography, with multiple proportionally spaced fonts, because its creator had once sat in a calligraphy class with nothing better to do. "If I had never dropped in on that single course in college," he said, "the Mac would never have had multiple typefaces or proportionally spaced fonts. And since Windows just copied the Mac, it's likely that no personal computer would have them." The claim is characteristically grand and not entirely fair to everyone else who worked on those problems, but the underlying point is sound: a piece of apparently frivolous, beautiful, non-technical knowledge became one of the defining features of the personal computer, because of the meandering path of one restless mind.

The teacher behind that class deserves a sentence of his own, if only because he complicates the story in a way Jobs's own telling of it tended to smooth over. Robert Palladino had spent nearly two decades as a Trappist monk in a New Mexico monastery before he ever stood in front of a classroom, and when he arrived at Reed in 1969 to take over its already well-regarded calligraphy program from its founder, Lloyd Reynolds, he brought a monastic patience to the discipline of letterforms that happened to suit a restless dropout perfectly. Palladino taught calligraphy and the history of writing to roughly eighty Reed students a year, welcomed auditors and enrolled majors with the same close attention, and by his own account never mistook Jobs for anyone special at the time — just a serious, oddly intense young man who kept showing up long after he had stopped paying tuition. What tends to surprise people who assume Palladino must have been some kind of proto-Silicon Valley visionary is that he never owned a computer in his life and had little interest in the machines his most famous student would go on to build; his loyalty was to the pen, the brush, and the disciplined line, not to the screen. Yet open the font menu on any Mac, iPhone, or iPad today and scroll past San Francisco, Helvetica, and the dozens of other faces built into the operating system, and you are looking, at one remove, at the inheritance of a monk's classroom in Portland — proof that Jobs's insistence on typographic beauty was not an isolated eccentricity but a traceable transmission from one teacher, to one wandering student, to hundreds of millions of screens.

The Reed years were also when Jobs's spiritual seeking took the shape it would keep for life. He was reading voraciously in the literature of Eastern religion and the counterculture — Zen Buddhism above all, but also the whole shelf of enlightenment-seeking texts that a Bay Area seeker of the early 1970s would have known. He experimented with psychedelics; he would say later, with complete seriousness, that taking LSD was one of the two or three most important things he had done in his life, that it showed him there was another side to the coin, a bigger picture of what was possible, that could not be seen from within ordinary consciousness. He adopted strict, faddish, sometimes bizarre diets — long fasts, all-fruit regimens, a period of eating only one or two foods — driven by a belief that purity of the body was connected to clarity of the mind, and by a lifelong conviction that the ordinary rules of biology did not quite apply to him, a conviction that would have grave consequences much later. And he became, and remained, a serious student of Zen, forming a decades-long relationship with a Japanese teacher named Kobun Chino Otogawa, who would eventually officiate at his wedding.

That relationship with Kobun deserves more than a passing mention, because it captures the tension this chapter keeps circling back to. Jobs met him at the Los Altos Zen center then known as the Haiku Zen Center, where Kobun had taken over as teacher not long after the death of Shunryu Suzuki, the Zen master whose own book, *Zen Mind, Beginner's Mind,* was already required reading for the era's seekers. Jobs attended sittings there, went on long walks with Kobun to talk through questions of practice and ambition, and at one point grew serious enough about the monastic path that he considered leaving California altogether to enter Eihei-ji, the centuries-old training monastery in Japan that serves as one of the two head temples of the Soto Zen school. It was Kobun himself who talked him out of it — counseling Jobs that he did not need to shave his head and disappear into a monastery to find what he was looking for, that the same discipline could be practiced in the world, building something, as in a meditation hall. Jobs later told his biographer that he ended up spending as much time with Kobun as he possibly could, and the two stayed close for the rest of Kobun's life; seventeen years after those conversations, it was Kobun who stood at the Ahwahnee Hotel in Yosemite, in March of 1991, and presided over Jobs's wedding to Laurene Powell in a small ceremony built around Buddhist ritual. The advice to stay and build rather than withdraw and renounce is easy to read, in hindsight, as the hinge on which the rest of the story turns: had Kobun encouraged the monastery instead of discouraging it, there might never have been an Apple to return to.

The seeking reached its furthest point in 1974, when Jobs, back in California and working briefly at the video-game company Atari, saved his money for a pilgrimage to India in search of a guru and enlightenment. He went with a Reed friend, Dan Kottke, and the trip was nothing like the serene spiritual idyll the phrase "found himself in India" might suggest. It was hot, dysentery-ridden, disillusioning, and hard. The guru he had hoped to meet, Neem Karoli Baba, had died before he arrived. He wandered, he got very sick, he shaved his head, he saw poverty and faith at a scale that shook him. And he came home with a conclusion that was almost the opposite of the one he had gone looking for. India, he decided, had taught him that raw rationalism was not the whole of wisdom, but also that Western action and intuition, married to the contemplative insight he admired in the East, might accomplish more than pure contemplation ever could. "We weren't going to find a place where we could go for a month to be enlightened," he said. "It was one of the first times I started to realize that maybe Thomas Edison did a lot more to improve the world than Karl Marx and Neem Karoli Baba put together." He came back a Buddhist and a builder at once, and the tension between those two things — the seeker who wanted to strip life down to a pure essence, and the operator who wanted to bend the material world to his will — would never fully resolve. It would instead become a design philosophy.

The chronology of that pilgrimage is worth setting down plainly, because the popular memory of it has softened into something far more serene than what actually occurred. Jobs and Kottke reached India in the spring of 1974 and made their way north toward Kainchi Dham, the ashram in the Himalayan foothills near Nainital where Neem Karoli Baba — the same guru whose earlier Western disciple, the Harvard psychologist Richard Alpert, had returned to America as Ram Dass and written the era's best-selling spiritual manual, *Be Here Now* — had drawn a small colony of American seekers. But Neem Karoli Baba had died the previous September, so the object of the whole journey had already vanished before either young man arrived at the gate; they found the ashram nearly empty and, after a long trek up a dry riverbed, ended up instead at an ashram belonging to a different teacher, Haidakhan Babaji. What followed over the next seven months was less a retreat than an ordeal. Jobs wore a lungi, went barefoot, contracted dysentery, and by the time he flew home his skin had darkened to a deep, sun-baked brown, his head was shaved, and he had lost so much weight that his own parents barely recognized him at the airport. It is a useful corrective to the myth — the one in which a young mystic wanders into wisdom under a Himalayan sky — because what Jobs actually brought home was less a guru's blessing than a body worn down by the trip and a mind more skeptical of easy transcendence than the one he had left with. The journey has a strange afterlife in the auction market: a letter Jobs wrote just before he left, describing his plan to attend the Kumbh Mela festival and signed with the Sanskrit word for peace, sold at a Bonhams auction in January 2025 for just over five hundred thousand dollars — a single sheet of a nineteen-year-old's handwriting now worth more than most people's houses, bought by someone chasing the same relic-value that clings to everything Jobs ever touched.

That philosophy is the reason these barefoot years belong in a history of Apple rather than in a separate book about a young man's spiritual life. The Zen ideas Jobs absorbed at Reed and in India were not decoration; they became the aesthetic core of everything the company made. Zen prizes simplicity, the removal of the unnecessary, the single perfect object over the cluttered many, the discipline of subtraction. It teaches attention to the ordinary, reverence for craft, the beauty of empty space. Look at any Apple product Jobs personally shaped — the clean face of the original Macintosh, the single button of the iPod and later the iPhone, the empty white expanse of the Apple Store, the obsessive war against clutter and complexity and unnecessary features — and you are looking at Zen aesthetics rendered in aluminum and glass. The famous Apple insistence that saying no to a thousand good ideas is what makes a great product; the willingness to ship a device with fewer features than competitors because the features it had were perfect; the almost moral horror of visual and functional clutter — all of it descends from a young man's immersion in a tradition that finds enlightenment in emptiness. Jobs's genius, if the word applies, was less invention than taste, and his taste was forged in these years, in a calligraphy classroom and a Zen zendo and the dust of an Indian road.

One figure from the Reed years deserves more attention than the tidy version of Jobs's biography usually grants him, because he supplied not only a name but a temperament. Robert Friedland was a few years older than Jobs, a magnetic, silver-tongued Reed student who had already served time for a drug conviction and who ran the student union with the charisma of a born salesman; the two met through their shared interest in Eastern spirituality and Friedland's enthusiasm for the psychedelic and mystical currents running through the campus. Friedland's millionaire uncle owned a working apple orchard on a rural property outside McMinnville, Oregon, and Friedland, acting as its caretaker, turned it into a commune called All One Farm, where young seekers lived communally, worked the land, and experimented with diets and disciplines not unlike the ones Jobs was already drawn to. Jobs spent stretches of time there, weekends and longer, pruning and harvesting apples alongside the commune's other residents, and he watched Friedland work a room — bending a crowd of strangers to his enthusiasm through sheer force of personality — with the close, admiring attention of a student studying a master. Jobs said later that watching Friedland operate taught him something about the raw persuasive power one person could exert over a group, an early and unacknowledged tutorial in the very skill that colleagues would eventually nickname his "reality distortion field."

The connection between that orchard and the company

Jobs would found two years later is more than a coincidence of timing. When Jobs and Wozniak sat down to choose a name for their new partnership in the spring of 1976, fresh off a period during which Jobs had been strict-fruitarian and had made a return visit to the Oregon farm, "Apple" was the word he proposed, and by his own account it carried with it the memory of that orchard — friendly, unthreatening, and rooted in the same back-to-the-land ideals the commune had tried to embody, a world away from the cold acronyms of the mainframe industry. Friedland's own path afterward diverged from Jobs's as sharply as their years at Reed had once run parallel: he left the counterculture behind entirely and became a mining magnate, building and losing fortunes in gold, copper, and diamonds on several continents, a transformation from psychedelic guru to hard-nosed commodities baron that Jobs, watching from a distance, found almost as instructive as the man's charisma had once been up close. The apple orchard itself, long since sold out of the family that once owned it, would decades later be marketed to buyers explicitly on the strength of its connection to Apple's name — proof of how completely even a rural Oregon farm could be swept up into the mythology of the company that borrowed its fruit.

He came back to California in 1974 a strange and formidable young man: barefoot, often unwashed, given to weeping and to cruelty, convinced of his own specialness, a Buddhist who ate fruit and believed in enlightenment and also in changing the material world. He returned to Atari, where his difficult personality was tolerated because he was useful, and where he pulled Woz into an episode — the design of the game *Breakout* — that foreshadowed the whole future of their partnership and its tensions. And all around him, the thing he and Woz had been unknowingly waiting for was finally arriving. The microprocessor had been invented; whole computers on a chip were becoming cheap; and in garages and clubs across the valley, hobbyists were beginning to build machines that an ordinary person could own. The personal computer was about to be born, and the two Steves were standing exactly where they needed to be, with exactly the skills required, at exactly the right moment. It began, as so much in the valley did, in a club.

Chapter 6 — Homebrew

On March 5, 1975, about thirty electronics hobbyists gathered in a garage in Menlo Park for the first meeting of a club that did not yet have a name. They came because of a machine. The January issue of *Popular Electronics* had put on its cover a boxy blue device called the Altair 8800, a build-it-yourself computer kit from a tiny Albuquerque company called MITS, and for the price of a few hundred dollars a hobbyist could, for the first time, own an actual computer. It did almost nothing useful out of the box — you programmed it by flipping switches on the front panel and read the answers off a row of blinking lights — but that was beside the point. The point was ownership. For anyone who had grown up believing that computers were million-dollar mainframes locked in corporate basements, tended by technicians in white coats and rented out by the minute, the Altair was a revelation and a provocation. You could have one. On your own desk. And you could make it do whatever you were clever enough to make it do.

The two men who organized that first gathering were an unlikely pair, and their partnership says something about how strange and various the club's founding impulse really was. Gordon French, who would chair its first three meetings, was a programmer who held a military security clearance. Fred Moore, his co-founder, was a committed pacifist who had refused to register for the draft in 1965, been convicted for it, and served seventeen months in a federal prison camp before returning to the Bay Area as a fixture of its protest movements; it was Moore who wrote up the club's earliest newsletters and who urged members to think of the club as a gift economy, to bring back more than they took. As one of the thirty-two people crammed into French's garage that rainy evening — the engineer Leonard Shustek, who would go on to help found the Computer History Museum — later recalled, the alliance between a man cleared to build weapons systems and a man who had gone to prison rather than serve in one was itself an odd one, and it produced strange bedfellows all around the room. Six of the thirty-two had already built a computer of their own; nearly everyone else wanted to. The Altair that had drawn them together, fittingly, had not been ordered by any one of them — it was a review unit MITS had shipped to the People's Computer Company, a Menlo Park nonprofit devoted to spreading computer literacy, whose members simply passed the invitation along.

The club that formed around that excitement called itself the Homebrew Computer Club, and it became one of the most consequential hobbyist organizations in history. It met every couple of weeks, eventually moving to an auditorium at the Stanford Linear Accelerator Center, and its meetings followed a loose ritual: a "mapping" period where people announced what they were working on or needed, a main presentation, and then the "random access" session afterward where members swapped parts, schematics, and advice in the parking lot. Its ethos was radically communal and anti-commercial. Designs were shared freely, improvements were passed around, and the animating faith was that computing power in the hands of ordinary people was a liberating force, almost a political one. The club's newsletter and its meetings buzzed with the conviction that the mainframe priesthood was about to be overthrown by a democratic army of tinkerers. It was, in a sense, the counterculture's dream of technology-as-liberation made concrete, in a room full of soldering irons.

That ritual sounds tidier in retrospect than it actually was. The club met in a couple of other venues before Leonard Shustek and a SLAC staff member named Frank Rothacker arranged for it to settle into the SLAC auditorium, where it would stay for years. But SLAC, as a federally funded laboratory, was obligated to prohibit any actual buying and selling on its premises, so the cash-and-parts trading the club's culture depended on spilled out of the auditorium and into the parking lot of the neighboring Sharon Heights shopping center, whose management complained loudly and often about the propeller-heads clogging their spaces. A hard core of regulars kept the night going afterward at the Oasis Beer Garden down the road in Menlo Park, hashing out schematics over pitchers until the small hours. It was an unglamorous, slightly chaotic way to incubate an industry, but it worked precisely because nobody involved thought they were doing anything as grand as that. They thought they were doing what hobbyists have always done: showing each other their toys.

It was also, though its members would have bristled at the word, an incubator. Something like two dozen companies would eventually trace their origins to people who met at Homebrew, and by far the most important of them was Apple. Steve Wozniak attended from early on, and for him the club was transformative. Woz was, by his own account, painfully shy, and Homebrew gave him a community of people who spoke his language and who greeted clever design with the appreciation he craved. It also gave him a goal. He wanted, badly, to own a computer of his own, but the available machines like the Altair used a microprocessor he could not afford, and the whole apparatus of switches and lights struck him as clumsy. So Woz set out to design his own computer around a cheaper microprocessor, one he could actually buy — the MOS Technology 6502, which he obtained for twenty dollars at a conference — and he made a set of design choices that were, in retrospect, visionary. His machine would connect to a keyboard, so you typed commands instead of flipping switches. And it would put its output on a screen — a television set — so you could read the results as text on a display, the way we take utterly for granted now and the way almost no hobbyist machine of 1975 worked.

Woz built this machine essentially alone, in a burst of inspired design, and when it worked — when he typed a character on the keyboard and saw it appear on the screen — he did what the Homebrew ethos demanded: he brought it to the club and shared the design. He handed out photocopies of his schematics to anyone who wanted them, freely, because that was what you did, because the point was the beauty of the design and the joy of showing it, not the money. If Woz had been the only founder of Apple, the machine that became the Apple I might well have been given away to the world for nothing, a gift to fellow hobbyists, and there would have been no company at all. That it became a product instead was entirely because of the other Steve.

Jobs was not a natural fit for Homebrew. He was not, like Woz, an engineer who could design a computer, and the club's members knew it; some of them regarded him with a certain wariness as Woz's pushy friend, the one who was always thinking about angles and money in a room that prided itself on not doing that. But Jobs saw what the others, in their communal high-mindedness, did not. He saw that Woz's design was not merely a clever hobby project but a product — that there were hundreds, maybe thousands of people who wanted a machine like this and who lacked the skill or the patience to build one from a schematic, and who would pay real money for a shortcut. And he saw that the shortcut Woz was giving away for free was worth selling. The idea Jobs brought to Woz was, at first, modest: they would not sell finished computers, but printed circuit boards — the bare green boards, professionally made, onto which a hobbyist could solder the components. Woz would give the design to Homebrew as usual, and they would also sell boards to the people who wanted to save themselves the labor of laying out the circuit. Woz was reluctant; he did not really believe they would make their money back. Jobs pushed. To fund the first run of boards, they sold what they had: Jobs sold his Volkswagen bus, Woz sold his prized Hewlett-Packard programmable calculator. It was, in miniature, the pattern of their whole partnership — the engineer who would have given the thing away, and the salesman who insisted there was a business in it, and who was willing to put his own possessions on the line to prove it.

That gift culture had a cost, and it came to a head within a year of the club's founding, in an episode that had nothing directly to do with Apple but that exposed exactly the fault line Jobs had spotted. In 1975 a paper tape carrying a prerelease copy of Altair BASIC — the programming language a young Harvard student named Bill Gates and his partner Paul Allen had written, and the software their fledgling company was staking its future on — went missing at a MITS event in Palo Alto. It reached a Homebrew member with access to a high-speed tape punch, and at the next club meeting fifty duplicate copies turned up in a cardboard box, free for the taking. By the end of that year MITS was shipping about a thousand Altair kits a month, but licensed copies of the BASIC that ran on them were selling only in the low hundreds — a gap Gates blamed squarely on the hobbyists' habit of sharing. Furious, he responded in February 1976 with what became one of the more notorious documents in the industry's early history, "An Open Letter to Hobbyists," sent directly to the Homebrew club and reprinted in half a dozen other newsletters besides. "As the majority of hobbyists must be aware," he wrote, "most of you steal your software. Hardware must be paid for, but software is something to share. Who cares if the people who worked on it get paid?" It was the precise inverse of the ethos the club had built its identity on, and Homebrew's own members were unmoved; looking back decades later, Lee Felsenstein still defended the club's position, pointing out that it was the very ubiquity of the "stolen" Microsoft BASIC — everyone had a copy, everyone had tested it — that made it the industry standard once hardware companies went looking for a BASIC to license a few years afterward. The gift economy and the market economy had collided in that Palo Alto auditorium, and neither side entirely won; both, as it happened, went on to build some of the largest companies in the world.

The club itself did not outlast the decade that made it famous. Meetings swelled from a few dozen people to several hundred and then thinned out again once the personal computer stopped being a hobbyist's secret and became a retail product, and the newsletter Fred Moore had started published its twenty-first and final issue in December 1977. But it never entirely vanished from memory. In November 2013, thirty-eight years almost to the day after that rainy first meeting, the Computer History Museum in Mountain View — a few miles from French's old garage — hosted a reunion of Homebrew alumni, with Lee Felsenstein once again presiding and Steve Wozniak among the old-timers swapping stories beside vintage machines that, somehow, still ran. When one organizer asked the room how many people had not yet been born in 1975, roughly half the hands went up, a reminder that the club's real afterlife was no longer in the memories of the people who had been there but in the habits it left behind — the conviction that hardware and its schematics should be shared rather than hoarded, visible now every time a hobbyist orders an Arduino board or a Raspberry Pi and builds something nobody asked for, just to see if it can be done. The tally of companies that trace a line back to that club has always varied a little in the telling — Wozniak himself once put the number at twenty-one, other chroniclers count as many as twenty-three — but the exact figure matters less than the fact that a rainy-night meeting of thirty-two strangers in a garage produced, within a generation, an entire industry's founding instinct: that the machines belonged to the people who used them, and not to the priesthood that had once guarded them.

One evening at the club, a few meetings after that first gathering in French's garage, produced a moment that captured better than any manifesto what made Homebrew feel like magic to the people who were there. A member named Steve Dompier, who had bought one of the very first Altair kits and traveled to the MITS factory in Albuquerque to pick it up in person, stood up at the April 1975 meeting with his machine and a small portable radio. The Altair had no sound hardware of any kind — it was not designed to make noise, and it certainly was not designed to make music — but Dompier had noticed that the crude electrical interference thrown off by the computer's operation could be picked up as a series of tones on a radio tuned to the right frequency nearby, if the machine's timing loops were built with enough care. He spent something like thirty hours entering, by hand, on the Altair's front-panel toggle switches, a program that manipulated those timing loops precisely enough to pick out a recognizable melody, and when he switched it on in front of the room, the little radio speaker played, tinny and unmistakable, the Beatles' "Fool on the Hill." The room came apart with delight. Nobody had asked the Altair to be a musical instrument, and nobody had built it to be one; a member of the audience had simply refused to accept that the machine's limitations were the end of the conversation, and had spent thirty hours proving that a blinking box of switches and lights could be made, through sheer bloody-minded cleverness, to sing.

It is a small story, and it involves neither Steve Jobs nor Steve Wozniak directly, but it belongs in this chapter because it distills the club's real gift to the two men who would found Apple: not a technology, exactly, but a demonstrated conviction that the boundary between what a machine was designed to do and what a clever person could make it do was far more porous than any manual admitted. Wozniak, sitting in that same room only a few weeks apart from Dompier's demonstration, was absorbing precisely that lesson as he laid out his own design, wringing color and sound and a keyboard interface out of components nobody else thought to combine in quite that way. Homebrew's members did not think of themselves as founding an industry when they laughed and applauded at a Beatles song wheezing out of a repurposed radio. They thought they were watching a good trick. It took the other Steve, standing a little outside that world of tricks for their own sake, to see that a great many people who could never build such a thing themselves would nonetheless pay for the chance to own one.

Out of that push, in the spring of 1976, came the decision to start a company. The two of them, and briefly a third partner, would take Woz's design and sell it. The name they chose has been explained a dozen ways — that Jobs had recently worked at an orchard commune and liked the fruit, that he wanted something friendly and unintimidating that would come before Atari in the phone book, that it simply sounded good and clean and human in an industry full of cold acronyms. Whatever the reason, the name was Apple, and it was perfect: warm, ordinary, a little countercultural, utterly unlike the IBMs and the DECs and the MITSs of the world. The Homebrew Computer Club had done its work. It had brought together a shy genius who wanted to build and share, put in the same room a hungry salesman who wanted to build and sell, and set them both on fire with the belief that ordinary people should own computers. Everything after this is the working-out of that spark. The garage was next.

Chapter 7 — The Apple I

The Apple I was barely a computer in the sense we mean the word now, and understanding exactly what it was — and was not — is the best way to grasp how far and how fast the industry would travel over the next few years. What Apple actually sold in 1976 was a single printed circuit board, about the size of a sheet of paper, populated with chips. It had no case, no keyboard, no monitor, no power supply. It did not turn on and do anything. To make it into a working computer, the buyer had to supply all of those things himself: find a keyboard, wire up a power transformer, connect a television as a display, and knock together some kind of enclosure, often a wooden box built by hand. What Apple provided was the hard part, the brain — Woz's cleverly designed board with its 6502 microprocessor — and the crucial innovations that made it desirable: it worked with a keyboard and a screen, right out of the design, where its rivals still used switches and lights. For a hobbyist, that was the difference between a toy and a tool.

They built the boards, famously, in the Jobs family home — first in a bedroom, then, as the operation outgrew it, in the garage on Crist Drive in Los Altos, the garage that has become the most mythologized structure in the history of business, the humble cradle from which a trillion-dollar company supposedly sprang. It is worth being honest about the garage, because the myth has hardened into something misleading. Real work did happen there: boards were tested, stuffed with components, packed, and shipped, and family and friends were pressed into service around a kitchen table doing assembly. But Apple was not "invented" in the garage the way legend implies; Woz did his design work at his apartment and at his Hewlett-Packard job, and the garage was more a small logistics-and-assembly depot than a laboratory of invention. Woz himself, years later, gently punctured the balloon, noting that they did not really do much building in the garage and that the story had grown in the telling because it made such a good story. This is a small example of a pattern worth naming early: Apple's history, more than most companies', comes to us pre-mythologized, and part of the work of a real history is to keep asking which of the beloved stories are true, which are true-ish, and which are simply better than the truth.

The first real order came from a man named Paul Terrell, who ran one of the earliest computer retail stores, the Byte Shop in Mountain View. Jobs, in his sandals and with his intensity, walked into the store and pitched him, and Terrell said something that changed the shape of the young company. He was not interested in bare boards that his customers would have to assemble; he wanted fully assembled, working boards — populated with all the components, ready to be dropped into a computer — and he would take fifty of them, at about five hundred dollars apiece. Fifty units at five hundred dollars was, to two young men who had been imagining they might sell a few boards to fellow hobbyists, an enormous order, a real business, and it came with a real problem: they now had to buy hundreds of dollars' worth of parts, on credit they did not have, to fulfill an order they would only be paid for on delivery. Jobs's handling of that cash-flow squeeze — talking a parts distributor into thirty days of credit, getting the boards built and delivered inside the window, and paying the supplier just in time — was an early demonstration of the operational nerve that would define him. The Apple I retailed, when a completed computer was assembled around it, at the memorable price of $666.66, a number Woz chose because he liked repeating digits and found the price easy to type, and which caused a certain amount of comment among the superstitious.

Perhaps two hundred Apple I boards were made and sold, and the machine was, in cold commercial terms, a minor product — a stepping stone, quickly obsolete, that established the company but did not make it. Its importance is almost entirely as a proof of concept and a foundation. It proved that there was a market: that beyond the hardest-core hobbyists who would build from a schematic, there was a larger population of people who wanted a computer and would pay for one that came mostly ready to use. It established the division of labor between the two Steves under real commercial pressure and showed that it worked. It gave the company its first revenue, its first customer relationship, its first taste of the cash-flow tightrope that every hardware business walks. And it taught Jobs a lesson he would apply with escalating ambition for the rest of his career: that the winning move was to remove work and uncertainty from the customer, to take the messy, half-built, hobbyist thing and make it more finished, more complete, more of an appliance you could simply use. The Apple I asked the buyer to supply the case, the keyboard, and the power. The next machine would supply all of them. And each machine after that would take the philosophy further, until Apple was selling sealed objects that could not even be opened, machines finished to a degree that would have been unimaginable to the Homebrew hobbyists who soldered their own boards. The direction of travel — from kit to appliance, from the user does the work to it just works — was set with the Apple I, and it never really changed.

Before there was a Terrell order to finance, there was a

smaller, earlier problem: money to print the very first run of bare boards, back when Jobs and Wozniak were still imagining they might sell a hundred or so to fellow members of the Homebrew Computer Club rather than run a company. To raise it, in the weeks before Apple Computer even existed as a formal partnership, both men sold something they valued. Wozniak parted with his HP-65, the programmable calculator he had used for years and genuinely loved, for five hundred dollars — though the buyer, by Wozniak's own account in his memoir, paid him only half of that and never made good on the rest. Wozniak later said he did not mind terribly, since Hewlett-Packard's next calculator, the HP-67, was about to reach the market, and as an employee he could buy one at a steep discount anyway. Jobs sold his Volkswagen van — accounts differ on whether it fetched seven hundred and fifty dollars or eight hundred — the vehicle he had been using to get around the Bay Area. Between the two sales they raised in the neighborhood of thirteen hundred dollars. It is worth being precise about what that money paid for, because the popular version of the story tends to blur two separate acts of financial nerve into one. The calculator and the van did not bankroll Terrell's fifty-unit order; that order, once it came, was financed on credit from a parts distributor, repaid out of Terrell's own money once the boards were delivered. The thirteen hundred dollars went toward the smaller, earlier print run, before anyone outside their circle of hobbyist friends had shown much interest at all — the initial, entirely unhedged bet that gave them something to sell in the first place.

The distributor Jobs talked into thirty days of credit was Cramer Electronics, and the pitch he made to its credit manager survives almost word for word, because Jobs retold it often enough afterward that it entered the historical record: "I have this purchase order from the Byte Shop chain of computer stores for fifty of my computers and the payment terms are COD. If you give me the parts on net 30-day terms I can build and deliver the computers in that time frame, collect my money from Terrell at the Byte Shop and pay you." It is a small speech, but it contains, in miniature, the whole Jobs method: state the deal as though it were already settled, supply just enough verifiable detail to survive a phone call, and let the other party's own incentive to believe him do the rest of the persuading. The credit manager, unwilling to take it purely on faith, telephoned Terrell directly to check the story; Terrell vouched for it, the credit was extended, and the two Steves and a small crew of friends spent the following weeks building, testing, and delivering fifty working boards inside the window Jobs had promised, with days to spare.

The arithmetic behind the famous retail price is worth spelling out, because it shows a business instinct operating well before there was much of a business to speak of. Terrell's wholesale figure of five hundred dollars per assembled board was not arbitrary; chips, boards, and labor all had to be paid for, and a two-man partnership needs margin simply to survive its own growth. When Apple later sold finished boards directly to hobbyists who came calling after seeing the machine demonstrated at a Homebrew Computer Club meeting in the summer of 1976, Wozniak set the price at $666.66 — a one-third markup over the wholesale figure, and, by his own account, chosen mainly because he liked the look of repeating digits and found the number easy to type, with no thought given to its unfortunate association with the biblical number of the beast until customers started pointing it out to him. In total, something on the order of two hundred Apple I boards were ever built, a production run so small that today it reads less like a mass-market product than a limited-edition art object — which is, in a way, exactly what it has become.

That transformation from workbench curiosity to museum piece is easy to trace today. The Apple 1 Registry, a volunteer-run archive that has spent years tracking down every unit that left the garage, counts roughly sixty known surviving boards worldwide, of which fewer than twenty still power on. The Henry Ford Museum in Dearborn, Michigan, paid $905,000 at a Bonhams auction in 2014 for one of the original fifty units sold through the Byte Shop, and now displays it alongside other artifacts of American industrial history — a strange but not inappropriate neighborhood for a board whose schematics Wozniak once handed out for free at a hobbyist club meeting. It is a fitting endpoint for an object that began as five hundred dollars' worth of chips soldered together in a bedroom: a single board, built to be used and then discarded once something better came along, has instead become one of the most carefully guarded artifacts in the entire history of computing.

The actual labor of building fifty working computers inside Terrell's deadline is worth dwelling on for a moment, because the popular image of the two Steves single-handedly stuffing every board tends to erase the household economy that made it possible. The work happened in phases: the first fifty boards were assembled inside the Jobs family house itself, at the kitchen table and in Steve's old bedroom, before the operation outgrew the space and moved out to the garage for the next batch. Jobs recruited whatever hands were available, and one of the first to be pressed into service was his younger sister, Patty, who sat down to help populate the boards with components. She did not last long at the job. Stuffing chips into a circuit board is unforgiving, repetitive work that punishes a wandering eye, and Patty, by the family's own account, kept half-watching the television while she worked and bent one too many of the delicate chip pins in the process, mangling components faster than the fragile Apple I budget could easily absorb. Daniel Kottke, Jobs's old friend from Reed and from the trip to India, took over the job in her place and turned out to have the patience and the steady hand the work demanded, becoming, in effect, Apple's first production-line employee before Apple was much more than a partnership agreement and a stack of orders.

It is a small, almost domestic detail, but it says something true about the company at this exact moment in its life: a business that would one day obsess over the tolerances of injection-molded plastic and the precise radius of a rounded corner began as a kitchen-table operation where the quality-control problem was a teenager getting distracted by whatever was playing on the family television. The transition from bedroom to garage that followed was not, in other words, a mythic leap into some hallowed birthplace of innovation; it was the same logistical problem that afflicts anyone running a growing operation out of a house — you eventually run out of room on the table, and the overflow goes wherever there is space, which in a modest tract house in Los Altos happened to be the garage. Kottke's steady hands finished what Patty Jobs had started, the fifty boards went out the door in time, and Terrell's order was filled with something to spare, days ahead of the deadline Jobs had promised on nothing but his own nerve. Kottke, notably, was working for a few dollars an hour and no equity at all, a technician's wage for a technician's job, which made him useful in exactly the moment Apple needed hands rather than titles — and which would, a few years later, once the company had gone public and made instant millionaires of dozens of far more peripheral employees, curdle into one of the more uncomfortable grievances of Apple's early history, since the same friend who had bent no pins and made no mistakes ended up, by his own account, no better compensated for his patience than Patty Jobs had been for hers.

Today an original Apple I, one of the few dozen that survive, sells at auction for hundreds of thousands of dollars, occasionally for more than half a million, prized by collectors as a relic of the moment the personal computer became a purchasable thing. The irony would have amused Woz, who designed it for the love of the puzzle and gave the design away to his club, and it captures something true about the whole Apple story: that objects made to be used, cleverly and cheaply, by ordinary people, can become, in time, sacred and expensive precisely because of what they started. But in 1976 there was no thought of relics. There was a garage, a growing pile of orders, two founders who could see the thing was working, and the pressing question of what came next. Woz was already deep in the design of a successor, a real computer this time — with a case and a keyboard and a power supply built in, with color and sound, a machine an ordinary person could take out of a box and turn on and use. It would be called the Apple II, and it would not be a stepping stone. It would build an industry. But to build it, and to sell it at the scale it deserved, the two hobbyists in the garage were going to need something they conspicuously lacked: money, management, and a grown-up. He arrived in a Corvette.

Chapter 8 — April 1, 1976

The partnership agreement that founded Apple was signed on April 1, 1976 — April Fools' Day, a coincidence nobody planned and everybody later enjoyed — and it had three signatures on it, not two. The third belonged to a man named Ronald Wayne, and his brief involvement produced one of the most famous cautionary tales in the history of capitalism, a story so painful in its arithmetic that it has become a kind of parable.

Wayne was older than the two Steves, in his early forties, a draftsman and engineer who worked with Jobs at Atari and whom Jobs respected as a steady, experienced hand. When the company was formed, Jobs brought Wayne in for exactly the qualities the two young founders lacked: maturity, business sense, a calming adult presence who could mediate between the volatile Jobs and the gentle Woz. Wayne was given a ten percent stake to their forty-five percent each, and he made himself useful immediately. He wrote the original partnership agreement. He drew the company's first logo — an intricate pen-and-ink drawing of Isaac Newton sitting under an apple tree, a ribbon banner curling around the border, a scene as ornate and Victorian as the later rainbow logo would be clean and modern. And he wrote the manual for the Apple I.

For about twelve days he was, on paper, the owner of a tenth of Apple.

Then he got out. Wayne was worried, and his worry was not foolish — it was simply, catastrophically, mistimed. A partnership, under the law, meant that each partner was personally liable for the debts of the whole enterprise. Jobs was aggressive about taking on obligations; the Byte Shop order had required buying parts on credit, and Wayne could see the young company was going to keep taking financial risks. If Apple failed and collapsed into debt — the overwhelmingly likely outcome for a computer startup run by two twenty-somethings in a garage — the creditors could come after any partner who had money, and Wayne, unlike the two Steves, actually had some assets and a settled life to protect. He had been through a business failure before and had no appetite for another. So he went to the county office and legally removed himself from the partnership, relinquishing his ten percent. For his stake he was paid eight hundred dollars, with a further fifteen hundred later to formalize the separation — call it a couple of thousand dollars in all.

The arithmetic is the part that makes people wince, and it is worth stating plainly precisely because it is so easy to state cruelly. Ten percent of Apple, had Wayne held it, would eventually have been worth — depending on the year you choose to stop the clock — tens or hundreds of billions of dollars. At Apple's four-trillion-dollar valuation, a tenth of the company is a sum that dwarfs the fortunes of most nations' wealthiest citizens. Ronald Wayne sold it for the price of a used car. And so he has been held up, for decades, as history's unluckiest man, the fool who walked away from the greatest fortune ever created, a punchline in a thousand business-school lectures on the dangers of timidity.

But the punchline is unfair, and the honest version of the story is more interesting and more humane. Wayne did not know he was sitting on a tenth of a four-trillion-dollar company; nobody could have known that, because it was not remotely true at the time and would not be for decades. What he knew was that he had an unlimited personal liability for the debts of a wildly speculative venture run by a mercurial young man, and that if it went bankrupt — as the great majority of such ventures did — he could be personally ruined. He made a rational decision to protect what he had against a real and probable downside. That the venture instead became the most valuable company in the history of the world is not a fact he could have foreseen; it is survivorship bias in its purest form, the trick of memory by which we mock the person who bet against the lottery winner while forgetting the millions who bet the same way and were right. Wayne, for his part, took it with remarkable grace. He lived a modest life, sold stamps and coins, never became bitter, and repeatedly said he had no regrets — that at the time it was the correct decision, that he would probably have died of stress inside Apple's pressure cooker anyway, and that he was proud of having been there at the start. He was, in a way, the sane one. He simply happened to be sane in the presence of an insane, one-in-a-billion outcome.

The logo itself deserves a second look, because it says more about who these three men were than its brief lifespan would suggest. Around the border of Wayne's engraving ran a line of verse — "A mind forever voyaging through strange seas of thought, alone," adapted from Wordsworth's description of a marble statue of Newton at Cambridge — an odd, almost mournful epigraph for a hardware startup, closer to a memorial plaque than a corporate mark. It graced the Apple I's price list and its earliest letterhead, and then, within about a year, it was gone. Jobs wanted a mark that would work equally well silkscreened onto a beige plastic case and shrunk to the size of a postage stamp, and Wayne's Newton, all crosshatching and filigree, could do neither. In 1977, in time for the launch of the Apple II, a young designer named Rob Janoff delivered the rainbow-striped, bitten apple the world would come to know instead — the exact moment, in miniature, when Apple traded a hobbyist's flourish for a consumer brand, and Wayne's engraving slipped into the status of trivia question, remembered mainly by the people who collect old letterhead and price lists.

The figure of four hundred billion dollars — the number that shows up, almost ritually, in every retelling of Wayne's story — is worth pausing on, because it measures something that never actually existed. It is arrived at simply by multiplying Apple's roughly four-trillion-dollar market capitalization by an unchanged ten percent, as though Wayne's original stake could have ridden fifty years of history without ever being touched. It could not have. Markkula's own investment a few months later diluted every earlier share; so did the 1980 public offering, and so did five decades of stock issued to employees and executives — the same dilution that shrank Jobs's and Wozniak's own founding stakes long before Apple was worth its first billion, let alone its four-trillionth. Had Wayne held on through every subsequent round, split, and offering without ever selling a single share along the way — itself a wildly improbable premise for a man who, by his own account, could not afford the risk of holding on for even twelve days — he would almost certainly have become very rich indeed. But the precise, headline-ready sum that circulates in article after article is a thought experiment dressed up as a documented loss, and the true figure, whatever it might have been, was never going to keep ten zeroes.

Wayne has had a great many years to refine his account of that decision, and interest in his side of the story only sharpened as Apple approached the fiftieth anniversary of its own founding. In interview after interview — including a public appearance at the Computer History Museum in Mountain View in March 2026, when he was ninety-one years old, sitting for a retrospective conversation timed to the anniversary itself — he has kept arriving at roughly the same place. "My success has never been defined by money," he told one interviewer. "It's been defined by acting with clarity." It is a strange sentence to hear from a man perpetually introduced as the person who missed out on hundreds of billions of dollars, and it is also, on its own terms, a coherent one: Wayne made the decision he could defend at the time he made it, and fifty years of hindsight have not changed what the facts were on April 12, 1976, only what they turned out to mean to everyone watching from the outside.

If Wayne's spoken account of the story has calcified into a kind of legend, repeated almost word for word from one interview to the next, the physical contract that started it all has led a stranger and more literal life of its own. Wayne kept his personal copy of the agreement for more than a decade after signing it, and then, needing money in the early 1990s, sold it for five hundred dollars — a decision he has said, more than once, is the one he actually regrets, in contrast to the sale of his stake, which he continues to defend to this day. The document resurfaced at Sotheby's in December 2011, where a Miami businessman named Eduardo Cisneros bought it for $1,594,500, ten times its high estimate, in a sale that made international news purely on the novelty of the number. It changed hands again on January 23, 2026, when Christie's sold the same three typed pages — dated April 1, 1976, and signed by Jobs, Wozniak, and Wayne — for $2.5 million, as the centerpiece of an auction of American historical artifacts held to mark the country's semiquincentennial and, incidentally, Apple's own fiftieth year. A piece of paper that once seemed worth less than a used stereo is now, by simple auction-house arithmetic, one of the most valuable documents in American business history — a fact that would probably amuse Wayne more than it torments him, since by his own account the paper, and not the stock, is the only part of this story he has ever said he wishes he had kept.

Wayne has since made a small trade out of being Apple's third man, self-published a 2011 memoir called "Adventures of an Apple Founder," and shown up, again and again, at the fringes of every retrospective the company's fiftieth anniversary produced — not embittered, not quite reconciled either, but present, still willing to explain the arithmetic of the one decision the entire world insists on asking him about.

There is a second, quieter reason Wayne left so quickly, one that gets less attention than the arithmetic of his lost stake but that explains his state of mind more fully than fear of liability alone. Wayne had already lived through one entrepreneurial catastrophe before Jobs and Wozniak ever came calling: in 1971 he had designed and manufactured his own line of coin-operated slot machines, building what was reportedly the first wholly electronic slot machine ever qualified by the Nevada Gaming Commission, only to watch the venture collapse within its first year, leaving him to spend the following year working off the resulting debts. That failure was, by his own description, genuinely traumatic, and it left him with a settled, almost permanent wariness of unlimited personal exposure to a partnership's obligations — precisely the exposure a garage computer venture, however exciting, was asking him to take on again. Layered on top of that financial caution was a second disappointment that had nothing to do with money at all: Wayne had assumed, when Jobs invited him in, that his role would eventually include real product engineering, the kind of original hardware design that had been his actual passion since the slot-machine days. Instead he found himself drafting partnership documents and writing the Apple I's operating manual, useful work but not the work he had hoped for, and he had little reason to believe that Jobs and Wozniak, absorbed as they were in their own division of labor, were about to hand him a project of his own to design from scratch. A man who had already been burned once by entrepreneurial risk, offered a role that did not match the work he actually wanted to do, chose the sober path rather than the speculative one — and did so for reasons that had almost nothing to do with a failure of imagination about what Apple might become.

Wayne's slot-machine venture is worth a sentence more, because it is a small, striking irony that the man remembered for walking away from the most valuable company in history had, only a few years earlier, achieved a small first of his own: Nevada's gaming regulators, who tested and licensed every device that touched their state's casino floors, had certified his machine as the first fully electronic slot machine to pass their scrutiny, a genuine engineering distinction in an industry still dominated by mechanical reels and springs. That the achievement collapsed financially anyway, leaving him with debts rather than royalties, was precisely the kind of lesson that does not fade with time; it is the reason Wayne, alone among the three men who signed Apple's founding papers, read the same set of facts about a promising young company and heard risk where his partners heard opportunity.

With Wayne gone, Apple was a two-man partnership again, and its two men were flat broke and utterly unequipped to run a real company. They could design a computer and hustle an order, but they had no capital to buy parts in volume, no idea how to manage inventory or distribution or marketing, no experience of the machinery that turns a promising product into a scaled business. Woz, moreover, still had his day job at Hewlett-Packard, which he loved and was reluctant to leave, and had to be persuaded — partly by his own father, partly by a friend who pointed out that he could be an engineer and get rich at the same time — that it was safe to bet his career on Apple. What the company needed was someone who understood the world the two Steves did not: the world of venture capital, of marketing, of building an organization, of turning a garage operation into an enterprise. It needed, in the language of the valley, an angel — an experienced investor who could put in money and, more importantly, credibility and know-how.

He came in the person of A. C. "Mike" Markkula, and his arrival is the true hinge on which the early history of Apple turns — more, arguably, than the garage or the Apple I. Markkula was a young retiree, in his early thirties, who had made a small fortune in stock options at Fairchild and Intel and had cashed out to enjoy life. A friend sent him to look at what the two Steves were doing. He drove up to the garage in his Corvette, expecting to spend a few minutes humoring some hobbyists, and instead he saw the future. He saw, in the Apple II design Woz was completing, not a hobby machine but a mass-market consumer product, and he did something that revealed both his judgment and his nerve: he offered to invest a substantial sum of his own money, guarantee a line of credit, and join the company full-time as an equal partner, helping to write a business plan and build a real company. The garage phase of Apple was over. The company phase was about to begin, and it would begin with a document that Markkula wrote — a short statement of principles that would guide Apple, on and off, for the next fifty years.

Chapter 9 — Markkula's Millions

Mike Markkula wrote his principles for Apple on a single page, and the page has become one of the founding documents of Silicon Valley, quoted and taught and pinned to office walls decades after he set it down. He called it "The Apple Marketing Philosophy," and it named three ideas. The first was empathy — that Apple would understand the needs of its customers better than any other company, would truly grasp what people wanted, sometimes before they knew they wanted it. The second was focus — that in order to do a good job of the things it decided to do, the company would have to eliminate all the unimportant opportunities, to say no to the many in order to do the few things excellently. And the third was a word he had to coin, or nearly: impute. People form their opinions of a company and its products, Markkula wrote, based on the signals the company sends. If a product is presented in a slipshod, careless way, people will unconsciously assume it is a slipshod, careless product; if it is presented with elegance and care, they will impute those qualities to the product itself. Present things beautifully, in other words, because people judge the book by its cover whether they admit it or not, and the cover is therefore not superficial but essential.

It is difficult to overstate how completely those three words describe the company Apple would become. Empathy, focus, and impute are not a marketing plan; they are a personality, and they turned out to be Apple's personality for half a century. The obsessive attention to what the customer would feel using a product, down to the animation of an icon or the weight of a laptop lid; the ruthless narrowing of the product line, the willingness to kill beloved projects and refuse whole categories in order to concentrate force; the fanatical care lavished on packaging, on typography, on the retail store, on the unboxing experience, on every surface the customer would touch — all of it is Markkula's page, written in 1977, playing out across the decades. When Steve Jobs returned to a bloated, unfocused Apple twenty years later and slashed its product line to four machines, he was applying Markkula's second principle. When Apple spent as much design effort on the box a phone came in as some companies spent on the phone, it was applying the third. Markkula gave the young company not just money but a philosophy, and the philosophy proved more durable than any product.

The money mattered too, of course. Markkula invested a substantial sum of his own — the figure usually cited is around a quarter of a million dollars, part as an equity investment and part as a loan guarantee — and, crucially, he lent the company his credibility. A retired Intel executive vouching for two long-haired kids in a garage opened doors that would otherwise have stayed shut: to bankers, to suppliers, to the venture capitalists whose money would fuel the Apple II's growth. Markkula helped bring in serious venture backing, including the legendary Arthur Rock and the firm of Sequoia's Don Valentine, though Valentine's initial reaction to Jobs — he found the unwashed, intense young man off-putting and reportedly asked Markkula why he had sent him this "renegade from the human race" — is a reminder that the reverence Jobs now commands was not universal at the time. To many of the valley's grown-ups he was, at first, simply an unpleasant and arrogant young man of uncertain hygiene.

Markkula also did something the two Steves could not do for themselves: he installed adult management. He recruited a man named Michael Scott — "Scotty" — from a semiconductor company to be Apple's first president, on the theory that neither Jobs nor Wozniak was ready to run a real corporation, which was plainly true. Scott's job was to bring order and process to a chaotic startup, to make the decisions the founders were too young or too conflicted to make, and to referee the two Steves. It was a thankless role. Scott clashed with Jobs almost immediately and repeatedly — over Jobs's abrasiveness, over such famously trivial matters as which employees got the low, prestigious badge numbers (Jobs was assigned number 2 and wanted number 1, and there is a whole small comic saga about it) — and the friction between the founder's ego and the professional manager's authority would become a recurring theme of Apple's story, one that would eventually blow up catastrophically with a different executive a few years later. But in the beginning, Scott's steadying, if heavy, hand was part of what let Apple grow up.

The structure that emerged in 1977 — a formal corporation, incorporated in January of that year, with Markkula as chairman and investor, Scott as president, Jobs and Wozniak as the founding technologists and executives — was the machine that would launch the Apple II into the world. It is a structure worth pausing on because it complicates the tidy legend. The story we tell about Apple is a story of two geniuses in a garage, and it is a good story and partly true, but the company that actually succeeded was built by at least four people, and the two who are usually left out — the investor who wrote the philosophy and the president who imposed order — were as necessary as the two who are always remembered. Apple worked, in its first incarnation, because Woz could design a beautiful machine, Jobs could see it as a product and will it into being, Markkula could fund it and give it a soul and a strategy, and Scott could run the plumbing. Take away any one of them and the thing very likely falls apart. The heroic-founder myth, which Jobs did much to cultivate and which the culture loves because it is simpler and more flattering to the idea of individual genius, systematically erases the supporting cast on whom the whole enterprise depended.

It is worth asking why a man like Markkula was even available to write that page in the first place, and the answer says something about how Silicon Valley's money actually worked in the 1970s. Markkula was not a venture capitalist or a professional financier; he was a marketing man who had spent the previous years at Fairchild Semiconductor and then Intel, and who had been given, as part of his compensation at both companies, stock options that turned out to be worth a great deal more than anyone at the time could have guessed. By his early thirties he was, by his own later account, comfortably enough off that he did not need to work again, and when a colleague was promoted over him into the marketing vice-presidency he had wanted at Intel, he simply retired rather than fight for the title. He was still in his early thirties, restless, and looking for something interesting to do with his afternoons — which is how he came to be introduced, through the marketing and public-relations man Regis McKenna, to two young men with a wooden-cased circuit board and an unfinished successor to it. Markkula did not arrive at Apple as a savior with a checkbook and a master plan; he arrived as a retired, financially secure engineer-marketeter curious enough to take a meeting, and only over the following weeks did that curiosity harden into the conviction that this particular garage project was worth his money, his time, and his name.

A popular version of the Apple origin story imagines Jobs and Wozniak walking into that first meeting armed with a slick business plan, precise sales forecasts, and a five-year strategy, the kind of polished document venture capitalists expect. The truth undercuts the myth of the two boy-genius founders as businessmen: neither Jobs nor Wozniak had any real interest in writing one. Jobs wanted to build the company and Wozniak wanted to build computers, and the tedious work of projecting revenue, staffing, and market share fell, by default, to Markkula, who sat down and wrote Apple's first business plan largely by himself. As he worked through the numbers he grew bolder rather than more cautious, and the plan he produced predicted that this company operating out of a suburban garage would reach roughly half a billion dollars in sales within a decade and would qualify for the Fortune 500 within about five years — a claim that must have sounded faintly absurd for an outfit with no factory, no distribution, and only one shipped product to its name. He also wrote, more famously, that he expected personal computers to become as common in American homes as telephones, a sentence that reads today as an accurate prophecy and read in 1977 as a wild guess by an unemployed marketing executive. Apple did eventually crack the Fortune 500, in 1983, faster than almost any company in American business history had done it before — a few years behind Markkula's own optimistic timetable, but not by much, and startlingly close for a forecast written at a card table.

The money that followed the plan was structured in a way that also complicates the simple story of Markkula as a passive investor cashing in on someone else's genius. When Apple Computer, Inc. was incorporated on January 3, 1977, ownership was split so that Markkula held roughly the same twenty-six percent stake as each of the two Steves — not a controlling position bought cheap from desperate founders, but a genuine three-way partnership in which the money man, the engineer, and the visionary were made structurally equal. That equality was itself a kind of vote of confidence: Markkula was not merely lending Apple a quarter of a million dollars in direct investment and bank credit line, he was betting his own hard-won early retirement, publicly and irreversibly, on two men in their early twenties whom most of the valley's actual venture capitalists still would not take a meeting with.

Markkula's name persists today in a place far removed from computers, which is itself a small lesson in how thoroughly his role in Apple's founding has receded from popular memory even as its consequences endure. At Santa Clara University, a short drive from the garage where Wozniak and Jobs did their early work, the Markkula Center for Applied Ethics trains thousands of students and working professionals a year in ethical decision-making for business, technology, and public life, funded initially by Markkula and his wife's philanthropy and named for him decades after his Apple money was made. Business students who cite the center's case studies, or executives who take its frameworks into their own companies, are, mostly without knowing it, drawing on the same fortune that once wrote empathy, focus, and impute onto a single page in a spare bedroom in Cupertino.

The badge saga is worth finishing properly, because its resolution is funnier and more revealing than the mere fact of the dispute. Scott, following the plain administrative logic of a numbering system based on hire date, assigned badge and payroll number one to Wozniak, whose informal association with the company predated Jobs's own, and gave Jobs the number two. Jobs, who regarded himself as Apple's founder in a sense no employee-numbering scheme could adequately capture, argued for reassignment and was refused; Scott was not going to let a numbering convention become a precedent that every subsequent hiring dispute would have to relitigate. Jobs's answer, when he could not win the argument, was to simply decline to accept the premise of it: he began referring to himself, and in some tellings had the company records amended to reflect, employee badge number zero — a number that did not exist in Scott's system at all, invented on the spot to resolve, by fiat, an argument that logic alone had not settled in his favor. It is a small episode, almost a joke, but it is also a perfect miniature of the man: faced with a rule he found unacceptable, Jobs's instinct was never to lose gracefully or to escalate through the ordinary channels of appeal, but to step outside the numbering system entirely and declare a new category that put him back at the head of the line. Decades later, employees who joined Apple long after Scott, Wayne, and the original badge ledger were gone would still hear the story told in the hallways as an origin myth of sorts — proof that even a scheme as trivial as a badge number could not, in the end, contain Steve Jobs's sense of where he belonged.

Markkula himself received badge number three in Scott's system, a detail that is easy to overlook amid the drama of the Jobs-Wozniak dispute but that quietly confirms the company's actual hierarchy in its earliest days: the two young engineers who had built the product came first in the numbering, ahead of the investor who had made the product a company, which was precisely the ordering Markkula, for all his money and his authorship of Apple's founding philosophy, seems to have been content to accept. He was, by every account of those first years, unusually comfortable operating just off center stage, content to let the two Steves and later Scott occupy the visible roles while he worked the quieter machinery of financing, governance, and long-range strategy — a temperament that stands in some contrast to the badge dispute itself, and that perhaps explains why history remembers Jobs's invented zero far better than it remembers Markkula's actual three.

With the philosophy written, the money in, and the management installed, everything was ready for the product that would justify all of it. Woz had spent the intervening months designing what many engineers still consider one of the most elegant computers ever made, a machine that took the ideas of the Apple I — the keyboard, the screen — and completed them, wrapping them in a friendly beige case with a built-in power supply, adding color graphics and sound and, most importantly, expansion slots that would let other people extend the machine in ways its designers never imagined. It was ready to be shown to the world, and the world's first proper look at it would come at a computer fair in San Francisco, at a booth Jobs had insisted, over the objections of people who thought it extravagant for a company this small, be as polished and professional as any giant's. Impute. The Apple II was about to launch, and with it, the personal-computer industry.

Chapter 10 — The Apple II

The Apple II went on public display in April 1977 at the first West Coast Computer Faire in San Francisco, and everything about the presentation was calculated to make a tiny company look large and a hobbyist product look like the future. Jobs insisted on a professional booth at the front of the hall, a proper backlit sign, and machines in sleek molded cases rather than the raw metal boxes most exhibitors showed. He had the founders wear suits. He wanted, in Markkula's language, to impute quality — to signal, through the polish of the presentation, that this was a serious product from a serious company, even though the company was four people and had almost no money. The machine on display looked, next to the bare boards and kit computers of its rivals, like something from a different and more advanced civilization. It was an object you could imagine in a home.

What made the Apple II great, though, was not the case but what Woz had done inside it, and his design deserves to be understood, because it is one of the genuine engineering masterpieces of the era and because its central virtue would shape Apple's fortunes in a way its creator did not entirely intend. Woz built the Apple II with his usual obsessive economy, wringing color graphics and sound out of a startlingly small number of chips through tricks so clever that other engineers studied them like chess games. But his most consequential decision was philosophical: he gave the Apple II eight expansion slots — open connectors inside the case into which anyone could plug a circuit board to add capabilities the original designers had never thought of. This was an act of engineering generosity, an expression of the Homebrew ethos that a computer should be open, extensible, hackable, a platform for other people's creativity rather than a sealed appliance. Jobs, characteristically, had argued against so many slots; he wanted a cleaner, more limited, more controlled machine. Woz won that argument, and the openness of the Apple II turned out to be the single biggest reason it succeeded, because it let an entire industry of other companies grow up around it, making cards and peripherals and, above all, software that Apple never had to build.

The tension in that paragraph — Woz wanting openness, Jobs wanting control — is worth flagging because it is one of the great through-lines of this entire book, the argument that would run through Apple's whole history and never be settled. The Apple II was an open machine, and its openness made it a triumph. Yet Jobs's instinct for the closed, controlled, sealed appliance was not wrong either; it would produce, decades later, the iPhone and the App Store, the most successful products in the company's history, precisely by rejecting the open model. The two philosophies would war inside Apple forever: the open platform that invites the world in and grows through others' creativity, versus the closed system that controls every element and delivers a flawless, integrated experience. In 1977, on the Apple II, openness won, and the machine flourished because of it. The irony is that its success would help fund the company that would later become the most famous champion of the opposite principle.

The thing that turned the Apple II from a successful hobbyist computer into a phenomenon arrived in 1979, and it came from outside Apple entirely. It was a program called VisiCalc, the first electronic spreadsheet, written by Dan Bricklin and Bob Frankston. Before VisiCalc, a spreadsheet was a paper grid on which an accountant or analyst laboriously wrote numbers and, when one number changed, erased and recalculated every figure that depended on it by hand, a task that could take days. VisiCalc did it electronically and instantly: change one number, and every dependent cell updated automatically, so a person could ask "what if?" — what if sales grew ten percent, what if interest rates rose — and see the answer ripple through the entire model in a heartbeat. For businesses, this was not a convenience but a revelation, a genuinely new capability that had never existed, and for a while VisiCalc ran only on the Apple II. That made the Apple II the machine you had to buy if you wanted to run it, and businesses bought Apple IIs by the crate simply to get VisiCalc. The industry coined a term for a program so compelling that people buy the hardware just to run it: the killer app. VisiCalc was the first, and it demonstrated a truth that would govern the computer business ever after and that Apple would relearn again and again — that hardware is often just the thing you have to buy in order to run the software you actually want, and that whoever controls the software people crave controls the platform.

The Apple II became, on the strength of its design and its software, one of the most successful computers of its era and the foundation of Apple's fortunes for years. It sold in the hundreds of thousands and then the millions across its long life; its various models stayed in production, remarkably, into the early 1990s, long after they were technologically obsolete, because schools and businesses had standardized on them and the software library was enormous. For most of Apple's early corporate history, it was the Apple II, not the more famous Macintosh, that actually paid the bills — a fact often lost in the Mac-centric legend. The Apple II was the cash engine that funded everything else, including the expensive failures and the Macintosh itself, and it was almost entirely Woz's creation. When people say Steve Wozniak built the machine that built Apple, this is the machine they mean.

The West Coast Computer Faire itself deserves a closer look, because the event captures, in miniature, how deliberately Apple stage-managed its arrival. Nearly thirteen thousand people crowded into the Civic Auditorium that April weekend, wandering past tables of raw circuit boards and hand-soldered kits, and by nearly every account the Apple II booth was where the crowds gathered thickest and stayed longest. Wozniak himself later remembered the mood with evident pride: "We had this Apple II that we thought was so far ahead of the rest in features — color, graphics, sound, games — the computer was the whole deal." Even the rival companies noticed. Chuck Peddle of Commodore, one of the very few outsiders who had been shown the Apple II prototype back in the garage months earlier, made a point of coming by, sizing up what Jobs and Wozniak had built before his own company's PET went head to head with it in the marketplace. Woz, never entirely serious even at a moment of high commercial stakes, spent part of the Faire handing out a gag flyer parodying the Altair 8800 — a joke so dry that several attendees reportedly mistook it for a real product announcement and asked where they could buy the machine it described.

Woz's engineering economy inside the machine repays a closer look too, because it is easy to praise the slots and forget the sheer cleverness of what filled them. When Wozniak designed the Disk II floppy disk controller, competing disk systems of the era typically required around twenty-two chips to manage the reading and writing of data. Wozniak's controller used two. He achieved this by recognizing that much of the disk drive's timing-sensitive work could be handled in software running on the Apple's own idle processor cycles rather than in dedicated hardware — the same instinct for making software do a hardware chip's job that ran through nearly everything he built, from the video circuitry to the disk controller, and that other engineers, once they understood what he had done, studied the way musicians study a difficult score, marveling that so few components could do so much.

The slots themselves were not a small design flourish but the subject of a real argument inside the young company, and the specifics of that argument are worth knowing because they show how close the Apple II came to being a very different, much more limited machine. Jobs, worried about cost and clutter and wanting a clean, contained product, pushed for as few as two expansion slots — enough, in his view, for a printer interface and perhaps one other card, and no more. Wozniak, who had spent his Homebrew Computer Club evenings watching hobbyists jury-rig extra capability onto whatever machine they owned, held out for eight, arguing that nobody, including its own designer, could predict what people would eventually want to plug into a personal computer. The gap between those two numbers — two slots versus eight — is really a gap between two theories of what a computer company sells: a finished object, or a foundation for other people's ideas. Woz's eight slots won, and they are the specific, countable reason that hard-disk makers, network-card makers, and memory-expansion companies all had a reason to build for the Apple II instead of walking away from it.

That victory for openness still echoes in ordinary experience today, well beyond the museums where original Apple IIs now sit under glass. Every desktop computer with a case you can open and a slot you can fill — a graphics card, a sound card, an extra drive — is, in spirit, a descendant of Woz's insistence that a personal computer should invite modification rather than forbid it. So, in a very different register, is the modern argument over whether phones and tablets should allow their owners to install any software they choose, or whether a manufacturer is entitled to seal its platform and control everything that runs on it. That argument, playing out today in courtrooms and regulatory hearings over app stores, is recognizably the same argument Woz won against Jobs in 1977, simply relocated to a new kind of hardware, and it has never been permanently settled in either direction.

One more piece of Woz's engineering inside the Apple II deserves to be understood in some detail, because it is the single cleverest trick in the entire machine and because it shows his minimalism operating on a problem that had nothing to do with counting chips. Color television in the United States worked, and still fundamentally works in its analog form, on the NTSC broadcast standard, which encodes color as a signal riding alongside the black-and-white picture information at a very particular timing relationship to it. A conventional computer wanting to display color needed dedicated circuitry — an oscillator and supporting chips — to generate that separate color signal correctly. Wozniak, characteristically unwilling to spend chips on a problem he suspected could be solved with cleverness instead, noticed that if he simply repeated and shifted the timing of the ordinary black-and-white video signal the Apple II was already generating, the quirks of how a television set interpreted that signal would themselves produce the illusion of color, entirely as an artifact of the display technology rather than as anything intentionally broadcast. By manipulating the pattern and timing of pixels only two at a time, he could coax a consumer television into displaying black, white, and, depending on the phase shift, purple, green, blue, or orange, all without a single chip devoted to the purpose of generating color. It was not a technique any textbook recommended, because it exploited a side effect of the NTSC standard rather than using the standard the way its designers intended; it worked because Wozniak understood the underlying electronics of an ordinary television set more deeply than nearly anyone building computers around one, and because he was constitutionally incapable of accepting that a feature had to cost what its normal price tag said it should cost.

The trick had a real cost of its own, though it was not one that showed up on a parts list. Because the Apple II's color was, in effect, a side effect of an ordinary television's own imperfections rather than a signal generated to a clean, independent standard, the exact hues a program produced could shift subtly depending on the particular television or monitor displaying them, and software developers writing color graphics for the machine had to learn to work within, and sometimes around, quirks that were really artifacts of consumer video engineering from the 1950s rather than anything Wozniak had designed on purpose. It was, in miniature, an early and instructive example of a tension that would recur throughout computing history: an economical hack that saved money and chips in the short run could leave behind a peculiarity that the rest of an industry had to accommodate for years afterward, long after the original reason for the shortcut had been forgotten by everyone except the engineers still squinting at inconsistent color output on their screens.

Its success carried the company to a milestone that would transform the founders' lives and announce Apple's arrival to the world: a public offering. On December 12, 1980, Apple sold its shares on the stock market for the first time, and the offering was so oversubscribed, the demand so intense, that it created more instant millionaires than any public offering since Ford went public in the 1950s. Woz became wealthy; Jobs, at twenty-five, became worth well over two hundred million dollars on paper, one of the youngest self-made multimillionaires in America. Markkula's bet paid off many times over. The two long-haired kids from the garage were now, on paper, rich beyond any reasonable dream, and the company they had founded four years earlier in a partnership signed on April Fools' Day was a public corporation worth well over a billion dollars. It should have been an unambiguous triumph. But even as the Apple II minted fortunes, Jobs's attention had already moved on, restless as ever, to a machine that would carry his own vision rather than Woz's — a machine with a graphical screen and a pointing device, an idea he was about to see, fully formed and years ahead of its time, in a research lab a few miles away that belonged to a photocopier company.

Chapter 10½ — The Apple III Stumble

Between the triumph of the Apple II and the drama of the Macintosh lies a product that Apple would prefer to forget, and that is precisely why it belongs in an honest history: the Apple III, the company's first real failure, a machine whose troubles taught Apple painful lessons about hubris, engineering discipline, and the danger of letting marketing and ego override the physics of a product. The story of the Apple III is a useful corrective to the myth of Apple as a company that could do no wrong, because in 1980 and 1981, at the very moment of its triumphant public offering, Apple shipped a computer so flawed that it had to recall thousands of units, and the episode reveals a company still learning, still fallible, still capable of the ordinary blunders that afflict every enterprise.

The Apple III was conceived as the company's move upmarket, a more powerful and professional machine aimed at business users, meant to carry Apple beyond the hobbyist and home markets that the Apple II served and into the lucrative corporate world that IBM was about to conquer. It was, in a sense, Apple's attempt to grow up, to build a serious business computer, and the ambition was reasonable. But the execution was botched, and the botching flowed in part from the same impulses that would later, in better-controlled forms, become Apple's strengths. Steve Jobs, involved in the design, insisted on aesthetic and design constraints that the engineering could not accommodate — he wanted the machine to be quiet, and so he opposed including a cooling fan, and he imposed constraints on the size and shape of the case that crowded the components. The result was a computer that overheated. Without adequate cooling, the tightly packed machine ran hot, and the heat caused a specific and notorious failure: chips would work loose from their sockets as the machine expanded and contracted, causing the computer to fail. Apple's official advice to some afflicted customers became a symbol of the whole debacle — the suggestion, apocryphal or not in its exact form but true in spirit, that a user experiencing problems should lift the machine a few inches off the desk and drop it, to reseat the loosened chips. A computer that you fixed by dropping it was not a serious business machine.

The Apple III's failure had several causes beyond the overheating, and together they amounted to a comprehensive lesson in how not to build a product. It was expensive. It was rushed to market before it was ready, driven by business pressure and the desire to have a follow-up to the Apple II. Its problems damaged its reputation so badly that even after Apple fixed the engineering flaws and released improved versions, the machine never recovered; the early failures had poisoned the well, and business buyers, already inclined toward the safe choice of IBM, had no reason to trust a computer that had become a punchline. Apple eventually sold far fewer Apple IIIs than it had hoped, recalled and replaced many units, and quietly discontinued the line, absorbing a significant financial and reputational blow at a time when it could have been consolidating its dominance. The Apple II, the machine the Apple III was meant to supersede, went on outselling its intended successor for years, an embarrassment that underscored how badly the newer machine had failed.

The lessons of the Apple III echo through the rest of this book, and Apple, to its credit, largely learned them, though it would take the discipline of Jobs's second act to fully internalize them. The first lesson was that design constraints cannot override engineering reality — that a beautiful, quiet, elegantly small machine is worthless if it overheats and fails, and that the art of great product design lies not in imposing aesthetic demands regardless of physics but in achieving beauty and function together, within the real constraints of engineering and manufacturing. The mature Apple of the iMac and the iPhone would master exactly this: making products that were beautiful and that also worked, that achieved their elegant forms through manufacturing sophistication rather than by ignoring physical limits. The second lesson was about the danger of shipping before you are ready, of letting business pressure force a flawed product into the market, where its failures do lasting damage to trust. The Apple III taught Apple that it was better to be late and right than early and wrong, a lesson that would inform the company's willingness, in later years, to take its time, to withhold products until they were finished, to endure criticism for being slow rather than ship something broken.

The numbers behind the failure are worth setting down plainly, because they show this was not a minor stumble but a genuine financial wound. Apple recalled and replaced the first fourteen thousand Apple IIIs it had shipped, machines that in some documented cases failed completely — chips working loose from their sockets until the computer simply stopped functioning. By 1982 the company had sold only about ten thousand of the original model, at a moment when the Apple II, the machine it was supposed to replace, had already sold roughly three hundred and fifty thousand units. Even after Apple redesigned the machine and released an improved Apple III Plus, total sales across the whole line reached only around one hundred and twenty thousand units over its life — a respectable number for many products, but a rounding error against the Apple II's millions, and nowhere near enough to justify the investment poured into it. Steve Jobs himself, years later, put a figure on the damage in blunt terms, saying Apple had lost "infinite, incalculable amounts" of money on the Apple III; by one accounting, the losses attributable to the machine exceeded sixty million dollars by September 1985, a staggering sum for a company still finding its financial footing.

Steve Wozniak, who had no hand in designing the Apple III and watched its troubles from a distance, offered a diagnosis that cuts to the heart of what went wrong and that differs slightly from the standard telling of the story. In Wozniak's account, the deeper failure was not simply that Jobs vetoed a cooling fan, but that the Apple III was the first Apple computer designed primarily by the marketing organization rather than by engineers solving engineering problems first — a machine shaped by a list of desired features and a competitive positioning document before anyone had fully worked out whether the case, the board, and the chips inside it could actually coexist. The fan-less design was a symptom of that inversion, not its sole cause. It is a useful corrective to the popular shorthand that blames the Apple III's failure entirely on one man's aesthetic stubbornness; the truth is a broader organizational one, about a company that let the desire to have an answer for the business market get ahead of its own engineering discipline.

The story of Apple's official remedy for overheating Apple IIIs has itself hardened, over four decades of retelling, into something not quite accurate, and it is worth being precise about it. The popularized version holds that Apple's support line advised customers to lift the computer several inches off the desk and drop it, so that the chips that had worked loose from the heat would reseat themselves in their sockets. Whether any Apple representative ever gave that instruction in so many words is not well documented; what is well documented is the underlying phenomenon it dramatizes — that heat-related socket failures were common enough, and reseating chips by hand was a real enough fix, that the drop-it anecdote captured a genuine engineering embarrassment even if its exact wording has been sharpened by years of repetition into something closer to legend than transcript. Either way, a computer whose defining home remedy involved dropping it a few inches onto a desk was never going to win the trust of the cautious corporate buyers Apple most wanted to reach.

The instructive afterlife of the Apple III is visible, if you know to look for it, in the almost obsessive environmental and reliability testing that later became routine at Apple — machines baked in thermal chambers, dropped, vibrated, and stress-tested across extremes of temperature and humidity long before a single unit reaches a store shelf. That discipline did not spring from nowhere; it was purchased, in part, with the humiliation of 1980 and 1981, when a beautifully styled machine failed in customers' homes and offices because no one had reconciled the case design with the heat the electronics inside it actually produced. The company that once sold a computer whose fix was a controlled drop onto a desk would spend the following decades building a reputation for products that, whatever their price, worked reliably out of the box — and that reputation has a great deal to do with a failure the company would much rather have forgotten.

The engineer who actually carried the Apple III through its long, troubled gestation deserves to be named, because his story adds a layer of ordinary human cost to what usually reads as an abstract lesson about hubris. Wendell Sander was Apple's first staff scientist, a formally trained electrical engineer with a doctorate from Iowa State who had joined the company in 1977 after showing Jobs a Star Trek game he had built to run on the Apple I; he became, within a year, the sixteenth employee on Apple's rolls. When the Apple III project began in earnest in late 1978, it ran internally under the code name Sara, after Sander's own daughter, and Sander was given a schedule that assumed the machine could be built from off-the-shelf components in about ten months. It did not work out that way. Rather than leaving Sander and his engineering team to define the machine on their own terms, Apple assigned the specifications to a standing committee of engineers and marketing staff who kept adding requirements as the design proceeded — another expansion slot here, an additional feature there — each addition individually reasonable and collectively ruinous to a schedule that had never had much slack in it to begin with. What was supposed to take ten months took two years, and by the time the Apple III finally reached the market in 1980, the case, the board layout, and the thermal design had all been shaped by a moving target rather than a fixed one. Sander later said, in an interview reflecting on the project's failure, that the Apple III had been rushed to market six to nine months before it was actually ready — an assessment that, read alongside the committee-driven schedule slippage that preceded it, suggests the machine was simultaneously too late in its planning and too early in its shipping, a whiplash of a development process that no individual engineer, however capable, could have fully absorbed. Sander stayed at Apple for two more years after the Apple III's launch, long enough to see the redesigned Apple III Plus reach store shelves, before leaving the company in 1982, his name attached forever to the machine that taught Apple its hardest early lesson.

It is worth remembering, in fairness to Sander, that the code name he gave the project was an ordinary act of personal sentiment rather than any kind of foreshadowing — engineers at Apple and elsewhere routinely named internal projects after their own children, spouses, and friends, a small private pleasure amid the otherwise impersonal work of drafting schematics — and there is no evidence he saw anything but promise in the machine that carried his daughter's name into Apple's internal paperwork. That the finished product would go on to become a byword for corporate overreach and rushed engineering was not a fate anyone could have read into the choice of name itself. If there is a lesson in the coincidence at all, it is only the plain one that afflicts every engineer who has ever named a beloved project after someone they love: the name outlives the design decisions that follow it, for better or for worse, and Sander's daughter's name would go on being attached, in company lore and in the occasional historical footnote, to the most publicly humbled product Apple had yet built.

There is a broader significance to dwelling on the Apple III, and it is the same reason this book has insisted throughout on holding the legend against the ledger. The mythologized Apple is a company of unbroken genius, a succession of insanely great products flowing from visionary founders who saw further than everyone else. The real Apple, especially in its early years, was a company that stumbled, that shipped a badly flawed machine at the height of its early success, that failed in the business market it coveted, and that had to learn its most important lessons through failure rather than through inspiration. Steve Jobs himself, the supposed infallible visionary, contributed directly to the Apple III's flaws through the very design instincts that would later, disciplined by experience and by the humbling of his exile, become his strengths. The young Jobs who insisted on a fanless case that overheated is recognizably the same person as the mature Jobs who insisted on beautiful, sealed, integrated products — but the mature Jobs had learned, through failures like the Apple III and the Lisa and the original Macintosh's flaws and the whole catastrophe of NeXT, how to pursue his aesthetic vision without letting it destroy the product. The genius was not born fully formed; it was educated by failure, and the Apple III was one of its earliest and most instructive teachers.

Chapter 11 — VisiCalc and the IPO

To stand at the end of 1980 and look at Apple Computer is to see a company that had, in less than five years, gone from a partnership signed in a suburban living room to a publicly traded corporation that had made its founders and dozens of its early employees wealthy. The stock offering on December 12, 1980 was one of the defining financial events of the young personal-computer industry, the moment the whole idea of the PC — dismissed only a few years earlier as a hobbyist toy — announced itself to Wall Street as a business worth betting real money on. It is worth pausing here, at this first summit, to take the measure of what had been built and to notice the fault lines that were already running through it, because the very success of the Apple II contained the seeds of the crisis that would tear the company apart within five years.

The scale of the wealth created was genuinely startling for the time. Apple's shares, priced modestly, soared on the first day, and the company's market value leapt past a billion dollars almost immediately. Around three hundred people — employees, early investors, friends and family who had bought in — became millionaires essentially overnight. Steve Jobs, twenty-five years old, held a stake worth more than two hundred million dollars, which made him one of the richest young people in America, a status he wore with a complicated mixture of countercultural disdain for money and evident enjoyment of what it could buy. Steve Wozniak, characteristically, responded to his sudden fortune not by accumulating but by giving away: he sold or gave shares to Apple employees he felt had been unfairly left out of the equity, in a program that came to be called the "Woz Plan," an act of generosity that says everything about the difference between the two founders. Jobs, by contrast, was notably tight-fisted about equity for the people around him, a trait that would leave lasting bitterness — including, painfully, toward Daniel Kottke, his old friend from Reed and India who had helped build Apple I boards in the garage and who received no founder's stock at all, a wound Jobs seems never to have adequately addressed.

The engine of all this wealth, it bears repeating, was the Apple II and the software that ran on it, above all VisiCalc. The spreadsheet had done something no amount of marketing could: it had given people a reason they could not argue with to buy a personal computer, transforming the machine from a curiosity into a tool that paid for itself. A small business could justify the cost of an Apple II purely on the basis of what VisiCalc did for its accounting, and once the machine was on the desk, it turned out to be useful for a hundred other things. This is the pattern by which every successful computing platform has grown — a compelling piece of software drives hardware sales, the installed base of hardware attracts more software developers, the growing library of software drives more hardware sales, and the whole thing spirals upward in a virtuous cycle. Apple, almost by accident, had ridden VisiCalc into the center of that cycle. But there was a lesson in it that the company would have to learn and relearn painfully: the killer app was not Apple's. VisiCalc was made by another company and would, before long, be ported to other computers, including the machine that was about to change everything, and when the software that had driven Apple's sales became available elsewhere, Apple's exclusive advantage would evaporate.

That machine was coming from the one company nobody in the personal-computer world could afford to ignore. In August 1981, less than a year after Apple's triumphant IPO, IBM — International Business Machines, the giant of corporate computing, the very establishment the Homebrew hobbyists had defined themselves against — released the IBM Personal Computer. The significance was less about the machine itself, which was technically unremarkable, than about who was making it. When IBM, the most trusted name in business technology, told corporate America that personal computers were real and legitimate, corporate America believed it, and the floodgates of business purchasing opened in a way they never had for the scruffier startups. IBM had built its PC quickly and openly, using off-the-shelf parts and an operating system licensed from a small company called Microsoft, and that openness meant other manufacturers could and soon did build compatible "clones," creating a vast standardized ecosystem that would come to dominate the industry. Apple's response to IBM's entry was, notoriously, a full-page newspaper advertisement headlined "Welcome, IBM. Seriously" — a piece of bravado meant to position the plucky innovator as unthreatened by the lumbering giant. In hindsight the ad reads as whistling past the graveyard, because the IBM PC and its clones would, within a few years, become the standard platform of business computing and relegate Apple to a minority niche it would occupy for two decades.

The mechanics of the offering itself are worth setting down precisely, because the round numbers that get repeated in the retelling tend to flatten just how extraordinary the day actually was. Apple sold 4.6 million shares at twenty-two dollars each on December 12, 1980, and by the time trading closed that afternoon the stock had jumped nearly thirty-two percent, to twenty-nine dollars, leaving the young company with a market value of roughly $1.778 billion — a valuation reached by a business that had not existed five years earlier. It remained, for years afterward, the largest public offering since the Ford Motor Company had gone public in 1956, and the roughly three hundred instant millionaires it created, of whom around forty were Apple employees and early investors, represented more new millionaires in a single day than any stock offering in American history to that point. The offering was oversubscribed so dramatically that shares intended for ordinary retail investors sold out within minutes, and brokers who had underestimated the demand were left fielding angry calls from clients who wanted in and could not get an allocation.

One detail of the offering captures, better than the headline numbers, just how genuinely unprecedented Wall Street judged Apple's rise to be: securities regulators in the state of Massachusetts, applying the kind of "blue sky" investor-protection laws that many states used to screen offerings they considered too speculative for the general public, initially barred Massachusetts residents from buying Apple stock in the IPO at all, judging the untested young computer company too risky an investment to be sold freely to unsophisticated buyers. It was a strange footnote to a moment now remembered as one of the most successful public offerings in history — regulators in one corner of the country looking at Apple Computer, four years removed from a garage, and deciding it was not yet safe enough for its own citizens to buy.

The uneven distribution of that wealth inside Apple deserves a harder look than the celebratory headlines usually gave it, because it set patterns of resentment that lasted for years. When Daniel Kottke — Jobs's old traveling companion from Reed and India, who had helped hand-assemble the very first Apple I circuit boards for a few dollars an hour before the company had an office — asked about receiving founder's stock ahead of the IPO, Jobs's answer, by Kottke's own account, was blunt: he would give him zero. Kottke held the title of technician rather than engineer, a classification that under Apple's stock-option rules left him ineligible, and Jobs, who controlled enough influence to have made an exception, declined to make one for the friend who had slept on his floor and walked beside him through Indian villages a few years earlier. It was Wozniak, learning of Kottke's exclusion and appalled by it, who acted: in the flush of his own sudden wealth, Woz voluntarily redistributed roughly ten million dollars of his personal Apple stock to employees he felt the company's option plan had unfairly passed over, Kottke included, in a gesture the company came to call the Woz Plan. The two founders' opposite reactions to the same windfall — one man closing his fist, the other opening his — say as much about the difference between Wozniak and Jobs as anything either of them ever built.

Seen from the distance of the company Apple eventually became, the 1980 IPO looks almost quaint: a market capitalization under two billion dollars, achieved by a firm that would, within a few decades, become the most valuable corporation on earth, worth thousands of times what it was worth on that December afternoon. But the template set in 1980 — a young technology company going public and instantly minting a class of overnight millionaires among its rank-and-file employees, not just its founders — became the pattern that Silicon Valley would repeat, with escalating scale, at every major technology IPO for the next four decades, from the dot-com flotations of the late 1990s through Google's and Meta's own generation-defining offerings. Apple did not invent the idea of an initial public offering, but it did more than any single event before it to fix in the public imagination the image of the technology IPO as a lottery ticket that could turn an ordinary engineer into a millionaire before lunch, and that image has never entirely faded.

It is worth going back to VisiCalc's own origin for a moment, because the program that did more than anything else to turn the Apple II into a business machine did not begin with a computer at all — it began with a piece of chalk. In the spring of 1978, Dan Bricklin was a first-year student at Harvard Business School, sitting through a lecture in which the professor was building a financial model by hand on the blackboard, a grid of rows and columns ruled out like accounting paper. Partway through, the professor discovered an error, or wanted to test a different assumption, and had to stop and painstakingly erase and rewrite a whole chain of downstream figures that depended on the number he was changing — the ordinary, laborious tedium of manual bookkeeping that every accountant and analyst of the era simply endured because there was no alternative. Watching the professor's chalk-dusted hands redo the same arithmetic that a single changed number should have propagated automatically, Bricklin had the idea that would become VisiCalc: a program in which each cell of a grid could hold either a number or a formula referring to other cells, so that changing one figure would ripple instantly through every dependent calculation, on a screen, without an eraser in sight. He built the idea with his collaborator Bob Frankston, and the two of them chose to write it first for the Apple II, a decision made partly on the merits of the machine and partly because it was the platform they had access to — a choice that turned an ordinary business-school insight into the single most important piece of software the personal computer industry had yet produced.

There is something almost too tidy about the symmetry of it, but it is documented rather than invented: the entire chain of events that made the Apple II a business necessity rather than a hobbyist's toy runs back to a professor's chalk-and-blackboard exasperation in a Harvard classroom, transmitted through one student's insight into a program that, purely by the accident of which computer its authors happened to own, ended up anointing Apple as the platform where American business first discovered it needed a personal computer. Bricklin and Frankston's own company, Software Arts, never became a hardware giant or a household name the way Apple did, and within a few years VisiCalc's dominance was overtaken by newer spreadsheets on newer machines — but the underlying idea, the grid of cells and formulas that recalculates itself, has never left; it survives today, essentially unchanged in its core logic, in Microsoft Excel and every spreadsheet program that succeeded it, a business-school student's frustration with a blackboard quietly running underneath the accounting of most of the world's companies.

All of this — the wealth, the fault lines, the gathering competitive threat — forms the backdrop against which Steve Jobs was already, restlessly, looking past the Apple II toward the next thing. He had never been the technical author of the Apple II; that was Woz's machine, and Jobs knew it, and some part of him wanted a machine that would be his, that would carry his vision and his taste rather than Woz's engineering. He had been shunted, within the company's growing organization, off the flagship business projects and onto a machine called the Apple III (which would turn out to be a costly, flawed failure) and then onto a more ambitious project called the Lisa. And in 1979, in one of the pivotal episodes of the whole story, Jobs had led a delegation of Apple engineers on a visit to a research laboratory run by the Xerox corporation, where he had seen something that reorganized his entire sense of what a computer should be — a screen full of pictures instead of text, a small device that rolled across a desk and moved a pointer, a way of interacting with a machine that was so obviously, self-evidently the future that Jobs came away, in his own telling, almost unable to think about anything else. What he saw at Xerox PARC would consume the next chapter of his life, produce the two machines — the Lisa and the Macintosh — that define his first act at Apple, and set in motion the conflict that would end with his exile. It is one of the most famous, and most misunderstood, visits in the history of technology, and it is where we turn next.

Chapter 12 — The Raid on Xerox

The Xerox Palo Alto Research Center — PARC — was, in the 1970s, the most extraordinary concentration of computing talent that has ever existed in one building, and it was owned by a company that had almost no idea what to do with it. Xerox made photocopiers, and made them so profitably that in the late 1960s it decided to spend some of its money on a research lab to invent "the office of the future," and, in a rare act of corporate faith, gave the lab money and freedom and left it alone. The result was one of the great flowerings of invention in the history of technology. At PARC, in the space of a few years, researchers invented or perfected a staggering share of the things that define modern computing: the graphical user interface, with its windows and icons and pointer; the mouse, refined into a practical device; the bitmapped display that could show any image or font; the laser printer; Ethernet networking; object-oriented programming; the personal workstation itself, embodied in a machine called the Alto. Almost everything about the way you interact with a computer today was, in some form, sitting in that building by the middle of the 1970s. And Xerox, a copier company run by copier executives who thought in terms of copier markets, was constitutionally unable to turn any of it into a product that ordinary people could buy.

In late 1979, Steve Jobs arranged to get inside. The deal he struck was a piece of shrewd horse-trading: Xerox's venture arm wanted to invest in the hot young Apple before its IPO, and Jobs agreed to let them buy a stake — on the condition that PARC open its doors and show Apple's engineers what it had been working on. Xerox agreed, and so Jobs and a group of Apple's best people were given demonstrations of the Alto and its graphical interface. The visit has become legendary, mythologized into a heist — the story of how Steve Jobs walked into Xerox PARC, saw the future, and stole it. Jobs himself encouraged a version of this narrative, and later loved to quote a line he attributed to Picasso, "good artists copy, great artists steal," to describe Apple's willingness to take great ideas wherever it found them. It is a great story. It is also, in important ways, misleading, and the truer version is more interesting.

The first correction is that it was not theft; Xerox invited Apple in and was paid for the privilege in the form of a lucrative pre-IPO investment. Xerox, in effect, sold Apple a look at the future for a stake that it then largely failed to capitalize on — one of the worst trades in corporate history, but a trade, not a robbery. The second and more important correction is about what Jobs actually saw and what Apple actually did with it. The Alto's interface, brilliant as it was, was in many respects primitive and unfinished: its windows did not overlap smoothly, its mouse had three buttons and was expensive and awkward, many of the interactions we now consider fundamental had not been worked out. What Jobs grasped in a flash — and this was the real act of genius, greater than any act of copying — was not the specific implementation but the paradigm: the overwhelming, self-evident rightness of interacting with a computer through a screen full of pictures and a device you moved with your hand, rather than through cryptic typed commands. He saw, as he put it, that this was the way all computers would work someday, and that the only question was who would get there first. He was reportedly so excited during the demonstration that he could barely contain himself, pacing and exclaiming that Xerox was sitting on a goldmine, that this would change the world, that why weren't they doing anything with it.

And then Apple did the hard part, the part the theft narrative erases: it took the paradigm and, over years of intense work, actually finished it, transformed a fragile research prototype into a shippable consumer product, and in the process invented a great deal that PARC had never had. Apple's engineers, led by brilliant people like Bill Atkinson, added the overlapping windows that could slide over one another like sheets of paper on a desk; the pull-down menus that lived along the top of the screen; the drag-and-drop manipulation of icons; the concept of the trash can; the idea that dragging a file into a folder moved it there. They reduced the mouse from a fussy three-button device to a single button, cheap and simple enough for a novice, obsessing over how it should feel and even how it should be manufactured. They worked out the fundamental grammar of the graphical interface — what happens when you click, double-click, drag, select — that has remained essentially stable for forty years. The distance between the Alto that Jobs saw at PARC and the Macintosh that Apple shipped is the distance between a proof of concept and a product, and closing that distance took thousands of decisions and years of labor and a great deal of genuine invention. To call it theft is to misunderstand what making a product is.

There is a moral in the Xerox story that Jobs drew explicitly and that sits at the heart of Apple's identity: the difference between inventing something and delivering it. Xerox invented the graphical interface and could not deliver it; the machine it eventually built to commercialize the Alto's ideas, the Xerox Star, was so expensive and so aimed at the corporate market that it went nowhere. Apple, and to a lesser extent later Microsoft, delivered it, and reaped the reward. The lesson Jobs took, and preached for the rest of his life, was that invention alone is worth little — that the world is full of great ideas that die in laboratories, and that the real, rare, valuable skill is the ability to take an idea and turn it into a thing that ordinary people can actually buy and use and love. Whether you find this inspiring or self-serving depends on where you sit; the Xerox researchers who watched Apple and Microsoft grow rich on ideas they had originated were entitled to some bitterness, and some of them felt it keenly. But it is hard to argue with the underlying point. Ideas are cheap; execution is everything; and Steve Jobs was, whatever else he was, one of the greatest executors the technology industry has ever produced.

The precise shape of the bargain that got Jobs through PARC's doors is worth spelling out, because it sharpens just how much Xerox gave away and how little it got in return. Xerox's venture capital arm secured the right to buy one hundred thousand shares of Apple stock before the company's public offering — an investment that, once Apple went public a year later, would be worth many times what Xerox paid for it. In exchange, Xerox agreed to open PARC to Jobs and a group of Apple's engineers, and the two sides arranged not one visit but two, the second more detailed than the first, so that Apple's people could study the Alto's interface closely enough to understand what they were looking at. Larry Tesler, one of the PARC researchers who ran the demonstration, remembered Jobs's reaction as almost physically uncontainable: Jobs paced back and forth with his fist clenched under his chin while the mouse moved a cursor around overlapping windows on the screen, and at one point blurted out to the room, "You're sitting on a goldmine. Why aren't you doing something with this technology?" It was not a rhetorical question. Within a few years, several of the PARC scientists Jobs had watched that day — Tesler among them — left Xerox for Apple, taking with them an intimate understanding of the very ideas Jobs wanted to build into a shipping product.

The scale of Xerox's failure to capitalize on its own invention becomes clear once you look at what the company itself eventually tried to sell. In 1981 Xerox brought the ideas from the Alto to market as the Xerox Star, a workstation aimed squarely at large offices, priced at roughly seventy-five thousand dollars for a basic system, with each additional networked workstation costing about sixteen thousand dollars on top of that — a sum that, at a moment when a secretary's annual salary was around twelve thousand dollars, put the machine hopelessly out of reach of the ordinary businesses that might have wanted it. Between its introduction and 1985, Xerox managed to sell only around twenty-five thousand Star systems worldwide, a commercial failure so complete that it barely registered against the personal-computer industry the Star was theoretically positioned to lead. Xerox had, in the most literal sense, been sitting on a goldmine and had built, from it, a product almost no one could afford to buy — the exact outcome Jobs had warned them about, pacing in front of the Alto, years before the Star ever reached a customer.

It is worth being precise, too, about what Apple's engineers actually built once they returned from Menlo Park, because the gap between PARC's prototype and Apple's product is where most of the real invention happened. Tesler and Bill Atkinson, working through the Lisa and then the Macintosh projects, invented or radically reworked the menu bar, the trash can as a place you dragged unwanted files, cut-copy-paste editing across different kinds of documents, and dozens of smaller interaction conventions the Alto had never fully worked out — the specific feel of a double-click, the exact behavior of a window when you dragged its edge, the rules governing what happened when one window overlapped another. None of this appeared in finished form at PARC; it was assembled, argued over, and refined at Apple over the following several years, by people who had seen the Alto for at most a few days and then spent years turning a glimpse into a product.

The paradigm Jobs carried out of that demonstration room has, in the decades since, become so completely the water we all swim in that it takes an act of imagination to remember it was ever a novelty. Every time a person today taps an icon on a phone screen, drags a file into a folder, or drops a document into a trash can to delete it, they are performing gestures that Xerox PARC's researchers invented in a lab that most of them never got to see put to widespread use, and that Apple's engineers spent years turning into something a stranger could pick up and understand without instruction. The touchscreen interfaces of smartphones and tablets are, in a direct genealogical line, the great-grandchildren of the Alto's windows and icons — proof, if any were still needed, that the distance between a research demonstration and a piece of technology used by billions of people is measured not in insight but in years of unglamorous, unrewarded engineering labor.

The mouse itself is a case study in exactly the kind of unglamorous engineering that separated Xerox's invention from Apple's eventual product, and the numbers involved are worth setting down plainly. The mouse Jobs's engineers examined at PARC was a three-button device that cost Xerox something north of four hundred dollars to build — a price that made sense for a machine sold to research institutions and large corporations, and that would have been laughable on a computer meant for ordinary households. When Jobs returned from Menlo Park, he went looking for an outside firm that could solve the problem and found Dean Hovey, a young industrial designer whose small design shop would later grow into the celebrated firm IDEO. Jobs's brief to Hovey was famously blunt and famously specific: Apple needed a mouse, and it needed to be manufacturable for under fifteen dollars — a cost reduction of well over ninety percent from the device he had just watched glide across the Alto's screen. Hovey and his partners spent months chasing that number, building and discarding prototype after prototype, testing shapes and mechanisms against ordinary users in makeshift trials, cutting the Alto's three buttons down to one reliable one, and replacing its complicated, failure-prone mechanical guts with a simpler design built around a rubber-coated ball and a handful of cheap plastic rollers. What emerged was not a copy of the Xerox mouse but a wholly re-engineered object, designed from the ground up to be cheap enough to bundle with a consumer computer and durable enough to survive years of use by people who had never touched a pointing device in their lives.

It is a small, concrete illustration of the larger truth about the PARC visit: Xerox handed Apple a brilliant idea that was, in its actual built form, unaffordable, and Apple's real contribution was the unglamorous, expensive, essential labor of making that idea cheap enough to give away. Every mouse that shipped with a Lisa or a Macintosh in the years that followed — and, eventually, with practically every personal computer sold anywhere in the world — descended not from the three-button device Larry Tesler had demonstrated to a pacing, exclaiming Jobs, but from the stripped-down, cost-engineered object Hovey's team built to Jobs's fifteen-dollar specification. Xerox invented the mouse as a concept; Apple, through Hovey and IDEO, invented the mouse as a product a five-year-old could afford to break, and it was the second invention, not the first, that ended up in tens of millions of homes.

What Jobs saw at PARC would now consume him, and it would flow into two machines. The first was the Lisa, the ambitious, expensive business computer that Apple was already developing and onto which the graphical interface was now grafted. Jobs was deeply involved in the Lisa — and then, in a corporate drama that would prefigure his eventual exile, he was pushed off the project by executives who found him impossible to manage. Wounded and furious, he did what he would do again decades later: he found a smaller, scrappier project on the edges of the company, seized control of it, and poured his whole self into making it the vehicle for his vision. That project was the Macintosh, and it would become the most important computer Apple ever made in its first two decades, the machine that defined the company's soul — and the machine whose troubled birth and disappointing sales would give his enemies the opening they needed to throw him out. He named a river of ideas after a daughter he was, at that very moment, refusing to acknowledge.

Chapter 13 — Lisa

The Lisa was named after a person, and the person was a secret Steve Jobs was keeping from the world and, more painfully, from himself. In 1978, a young woman named Chrisann Brennan, Jobs's on-and-off girlfriend from his high-school and Reed years, gave birth to a daughter and named her Lisa Nicole Brennan. Jobs denied that he was the father. He denied it in the face of the obvious, denied it even after a court-ordered paternity test put the probability of his fatherhood at astronomical odds, denied it while a young company he had co-founded was making him worth hundreds of millions of dollars and the mother of his child was on welfare, taking a small support payment he had contested down to a legally minimal figure. It is the ugliest chapter of his personal life, and it cannot be waved away or explained by the pressures of building a company, because the cruelty of it was gratuitous. And at the same time, in a piece of psychological doubling that no novelist would dare invent, he attached the child's name to the most important project at Apple, the computer meant to carry the future — the Lisa. Officially the name was a backronym, said to stand for "Local Integrated Software Architecture," a phrase so obviously reverse-engineered that even Jobs later admitted the truth: of course it was named for his daughter. The abandoned child and the visionary machine carried the same name, and the man who made both spent years insisting the connection did not exist.

The machine itself was Apple's grand attempt to build a business computer around the graphical interface Jobs had seen at Xerox PARC. The Lisa project predated and then absorbed the PARC influence, and it was, by the standards of 1983, astonishingly advanced: a computer with a graphical user interface, a mouse, windows, icons, pull-down menus, and a suite of well-integrated software, all working together in a way that pointed unmistakably toward how every computer would eventually function. In its ambition and its interface, the Lisa was years ahead of anything else on the market, including anything from IBM. It should have been a triumph. It was, instead, a commercial catastrophe, and the reasons it failed are worth understanding because they taught Apple — and specifically taught Steve Jobs — the lessons that would make the Macintosh, and later the whole second act of his career, possible.

The Lisa failed first on price. It cost nearly ten thousand dollars, an enormous sum, far beyond what most businesses would pay for a single desktop machine and light-years beyond any individual. The graphical interface, wonderful as it was, demanded expensive hardware to run — lots of memory, a powerful processor for the time — and Apple, aiming the machine squarely at corporate buyers, priced it to match its ambitions rather than to reach a broad market. It failed second on speed: the graphical interface was so demanding that the Lisa often felt sluggish, and a beautiful interface that responds slowly is a special kind of disappointment, promising elegance and delivering frustration. And it failed third on timing and positioning: it was too expensive for individuals and too unfamiliar and unproven for the conservative corporate buyers who were, at that very moment, standardizing on the safe, boring, IBM PC. The Lisa fell into the gap between markets and found no home in either. Fewer than a hundred thousand were ever sold, and the model was discontinued within a couple of years, its remaining inventory eventually, and infamously, buried in a landfill in Utah.

Jobs's own role in the Lisa's story is a study in the difference between his early and later selves. He had been a driving force on the project, but his management style — the volatility, the contempt, the impossibility of working with him — had led the company's executives, and specifically President Mike Scott and Chairman Mike Markkula, to a hard conclusion: the founder was too disruptive to lead the flagship project. In 1980 and 1981 Jobs was eased out of the Lisa group, stripped of authority over the machine he had helped conceive. It was a humiliation, and it was also, in a sense, a rehearsal for the far larger humiliation of 1985. The pattern was set: Jobs's vision was real and valuable, but his behavior made him, at this stage of his life, genuinely difficult to keep in a position of operational power, and the adults around him kept trying to contain him. What none of them anticipated was what the wounded, ejected Jobs would do next. Rather than sulk or leave, he went looking through the company for another project — smaller, less prestigious, easier to dominate — that he could take over and turn into the vehicle for his rejected vision. He found one on the margins of Apple, a low-priority research effort to build a cheap, simple computer for ordinary people, run by a thoughtful, idealistic engineer named Jef Raskin who had named it after his favorite variety of apple.

The financial dimensions of the Lisa's failure deserve to be stated plainly, because they show a catastrophe on a scale the company had not experienced before. Apple had poured more than $150 million into the Lisa's development — an enormous sum for the time — and over its roughly three years on the market the machine generated only about $100 million in total sales, a loss so large that it stood, at the time, as the biggest commercial failure in Apple's short history, eclipsing even the trouble of the Apple III. Barely ten thousand units found buyers before Apple discontinued the line in the mid-1980s, a rounding error against the hundreds of thousands of Apple IIs still moving off shelves in the same years. The Lisa's brief afterlife as the Macintosh XL — a version updated to run modified Macintosh software, sold for a couple more years to wring some value out of the unsold inventory — could not rescue the underlying arithmetic.

The most notorious coda to the Lisa's failure came years later and has become one of the strangest, most-repeated stories in Apple's history. In September 1989, having decided it no longer made financial sense to keep supporting or reselling its remaining stock of unsold Lisas and Macintosh XLs, Apple trucked roughly 2,700 of the machines to a landfill in Logan, Utah, and buried them. The company paid the city about $1.95 per cubic yard for some 800 yards of landfill space to bury the crushed computers, and an Apple spokesperson at the time explained the decision in the plainest terms of corporate housekeeping rather than embarrassment: with the fiscal year end approaching, she said, it was simply "a better business decision" to write the inventory off than to keep carrying it on the books or servicing it indefinitely. The burial was not an act of shame so much as an act of accounting — a detail that complicates the tidier legend of Apple quietly hiding a humiliating failure in the ground, since the company's own explanation was almost aggressively unsentimental.

That legend has proven durable enough that people have tried, unsuccessfully, to dig the machines back up. In 2015, an enthusiast attempted to crowdfund an excavation of the Logan landfill, hoping to recover intact Lisas for collectors and to film the search as a documentary, explicitly inspired by a celebrated dig a few years earlier that had unearthed thousands of buried Atari game cartridges from a New Mexico landfill. The Lisa excavation attempt raised only a token sum of money and never happened, but the fact that anyone would try — that grown adults would seriously propose digging through a municipal landfill in search of forty-year-old failed computers — says something about how completely the Lisa's commercial disaster has been transmuted, in the retelling, into a piece of cultural folklore, an object of fascination precisely because it failed so completely and so publicly.

The specifics of the paternity dispute sharpen just how deliberately Jobs worked to disown his daughter, because his objection was never really a matter of doubt so much as a matter of arithmetic performed in bad faith. The court-ordered blood test found an overwhelming probability of paternity — the report placed the odds at 94.1 percent that Jobs was Lisa's father — and rather than accept a number that would have settled the question for any reasonable person, Jobs seized on the residual statistical uncertainty and inflated it into a rhetorical shield. He told at least one interviewer, with a straight face, that the same statistical method used in the test would also implicate roughly twenty-eight percent of all adult men in the United States, as though a one-in-four theoretical possibility for the general population were a meaningful defense against a 94-percent finding naming him specifically. It was not really an argument; it was a performance of doubt, delivered by a man who had the money to contest a modest support payment and chose instead to spend years disputing basic biology rather than simply signing a birth certificate. The episode reveals something about the mind that would later obsess over the ninth decimal place of a font's curve: a capacity for selective, motivated reasoning that could, when it served him, be applied just as rigorously to the question of his own daughter's paternity as to the question of how a trash-can icon should look on a screen.

The Lisa's technical anatomy helps explain some of the sluggishness and unreliability that reviewers complained about at the time, beyond the simple facts of its price. Inside the case sat a Motorola 68000 processor running at five megahertz, a full megabyte of memory — lavish for 1983 — and a twelve-inch screen displaying a crisp

720-by-364-pixel image, more than adequate to render the overlapping windows and icons Apple's engineers had labored over. But the machine's storage was handled at first by a pair of proprietary floppy disk drives nicknamed "Twiggy," developed in-house rather than bought from an established supplier, and the Twiggy drives were notoriously unreliable, prone to eating disks and losing data in ways that undermined confidence in a machine already struggling to justify its price. Apple replaced them within the Lisa's first year with a conventional Sony 3.5-inch drive of the kind that would later ship in every Macintosh, but the early reputation for flakiness, layered onto a price tag near ten thousand dollars, did nothing to help a computer that was already fighting an uphill battle for a market it had priced itself out of.

That project was the Macintosh, and Jobs's seizure of it — his gradual, then total takeover of Raskin's small team, his displacement of Raskin himself, his imposition of his own grander and more expensive vision on what had been conceived as an inexpensive appliance — is one of the founding dramas of Apple's culture. It shows Jobs at his most and least admirable at once: the visionary who saw that Raskin's little machine could be something transcendent, and the ruthless operator who took another man's project, pushed its creator out, and claimed it as his own. The Macintosh that resulted would be flawed, overpriced in its own way, and a commercial disappointment at first, much as the Lisa had been. But it would also be the machine that established Apple's identity for decades, the first mass-market computer with a graphical interface, the object around which the company's entire self-image would organize. And its creation would be the theater in which Jobs first fully displayed the qualities — the perfectionism, the reality distortion field, the capacity to inspire a small team to superhuman effort and to wound them in the same breath — that would define him. He was about to gather a group of brilliant young people, hang a pirate flag over their building, and drive them to build something insanely great.

Chapter 14 — Pirates

Over the building where the Macintosh team worked, Steve Jobs raised a pirate flag — a black skull-and-crossbones with a rainbow Apple logo for an eye patch — and the gesture captured exactly the spirit he was trying to create. "It's better to be a pirate than to join the Navy," he told his team, and he meant it as a whole philosophy. The Macintosh group was to be a band of rebels operating outside the bureaucracy of the larger company, a small elite that would move fast and break rules and build something the rest of Apple was too cautious or too corporate to build. He recruited for it obsessively, hunting across Apple and beyond for the very best young engineers and designers he could find, telling them they had the chance to do the finest work of their lives, to make a dent in the universe, to build not just a product but a piece of art that would change the world. And a remarkable number of extraordinarily talented people believed him and gave him years of their lives at a ferocious pace, working nights and weekends, pushed to the edge of exhaustion and beyond, because Jobs made them feel they were part of something transcendent.

The team he assembled has become legendary in its own right, its members celebrated in Andy Hertzfeld's affectionate memoir and on the website he built to preserve the stories. There was Hertzfeld himself, a brilliant and playful software wizard. There was Bill Atkinson, whose graphics software — QuickDraw, and later the visionary program HyperCard — was some of the most important code in the history of personal computing. There was Burrell Smith, a self-taught hardware genius who designed the Mac's elegant, economical logic board in the tradition of Woz. There was Susan Kare, an artist who designed the Mac's fonts and icons, inventing much of the visual vocabulary — the little trash can, the wristwatch cursor, the smiling computer at startup, the command-key symbol — that would become universally familiar. And there were dozens of others, most of them young, most of them working harder than they ever had or would again, unified by Jobs's conviction that they were building the future and by the pressure of his impossible standards.

Those standards are the second thing the pirate flag stood for, and they were exacting to the point of tyranny. Jobs cared, with an intensity that struck outsiders as insane, about details no customer would ever see. He demanded that the circuit board inside the Mac — a component sealed inside a case that users were actively discouraged from opening — be laid out beautifully, the traces routed elegantly, because a true craftsman, in the lesson his father had taught him at the workbench, makes the back of the cabinet as fine as the front. When engineers protested that no one would ever see the board, Jobs was unmoved: he would see it, and they would know, and that was enough. He obsessed over the shape of the case, insisting it be friendly and approachable, with a face-like arrangement of screen and disk slot; he had the team's signatures engraved inside the case, so that every Macintosh carried the names of its makers hidden within it, a gesture that treated the machine as a work of art to be signed by its artists. He fought over the design of the startup screen, the wording of error messages, the exact shade of the beige plastic, the feel of every interaction. Nothing was too small to be worth a battle, because Jobs believed, in a way that was almost religious, that greatness lived in the accumulation of a thousand details each of which most people would consider beneath notice.

But the pirate flag also flew over a darker reality, and an honest account of the Macintosh team has to hold both truths at once. Jobs's leadership was not only inspiring; it was often cruel. He divided the world crisply into geniuses and "bozos," and he could switch a person from one category to the other in an instant. He told people their work was worthless, that they were worthless, in front of their colleagues; he took credit for ideas that were not his and dismissed as idiotic ideas he would later champion as his own. He created what his own team, half-affectionately and half-desperately, called the reality distortion field — a term coined by the engineer Bud Tribble, borrowed from *Star Trek*, to describe Jobs's uncanny ability to convince himself and everyone around him that the impossible was not only possible but already decided. Told that a task would take months, Jobs would insist it be done in weeks, would refuse to accept the constraints of reality, would browbeat and charm and will his people past what they believed were their limits — and sometimes, astonishingly, it worked, and they achieved things they would have sworn could not be done. But sometimes it did not work, and the field left in its wake burned-out, demoralized people who had been told that reasonable limits were merely failures of will. The Macintosh was built by people operating at the edge of human endurance under a leader who could make them feel like gods one day and garbage the next, and many of them look back on it as the most exhilarating and the most damaging period of their working lives.

Susan Kare's own path onto the team illustrates something important about where the Macintosh's much-praised humanity actually came from: not from computer science but from entirely different disciplines that Jobs, unusually among technology executives, thought were worth taking seriously. Kare had no background in computer graphics at all when she joined the project; her visual instincts came from fine art, from mosaics and needlepoint and the counted-thread embroidery her mother had taught her as a child, crafts built entirely out of discrete colored units arranged on a grid, which turned out to be exactly the right training for designing images out of a tiny grid of pixels. She began the way a hobbyist might, mocking up icon designs on a two-and-a-half-dollar notebook of graph paper from an art-supply store in Palo Alto before ever touching Apple's software, sketching the trash can and the wristwatch cursor and the friendly little bomb icon for a system crash cell by cell before translating them into code. Her business card, only half in jest, read "Macintosh Artist" — a title that would have made no sense at any computer company before Jobs decided that a machine's soul lived as much in its typefaces and icons as in its processor.

A small, telling detail about the team's most famous internal ritual complicates the neat version of the story usually told about it. Sometime in mid-1982 — a year and a half before the Macintosh actually shipped, at a moment when the team believed, wrongly, that production was close at hand — forty-eight members of the Macintosh division had their signatures etched into the mold for the inside of the case, so that every finished machine would carry the names of its makers hidden behind the screen, unseen by any customer but known to the team. Because the mold was signed so early, several people who became indispensable to the finished product — Susan Kare among them, along with Steve Capps — are missing from that roster entirely, having joined the team only after the casting was already fixed. The signatures inside the case, in other words, are not quite the complete roll call of the people who built the Macintosh; they are a snapshot of a moment when the team, not for the last time, believed the work was nearly finished when in truth some of its most essential contributors had not yet arrived.

Andy Hertzfeld's own recollections capture, better than

any secondhand description, what it actually felt like to work under Jobs during the software's final, frantic stretch. After a team of roughly a dozen engineers had gone forty-eight hours without sleep trying to finish the system software, several of them collapsed onto the floor of the office in exhaustion. Jobs walked in, looked at the scene, and rather than sending anyone home, told them, "Get up off the floor. You're not done. I want the Macintosh to be the first computer to announce itself" — a demand, delivered to people who could barely stand, that the machine should be able to speak its own name aloud when it started up. It is a small moment that contains the whole chapter in miniature: the casual cruelty of refusing exhausted people any acknowledgment of what they had already given, fused inseparably with the visionary insistence on a detail — a talking computer, greeting its owner by voice — that would, a year and a half later, become one of the most electrifying seconds of the most famous product launch in the industry's history.

The flag itself, so central to the chapter's opening image, was not sewn by Jobs or bought from a costume shop but assembled by the team's own hands, in keeping with the scrappy, do-it-yourself spirit the pirate metaphor was meant to embody. According to the team's own recollections, the programmer Steve Capps bought a length of black cloth and stitched it into a flag, and Susan Kare — already responsible for the machine's icons and fonts — painted the white skull and crossbones onto it, adding the rainbow-colored eye patch that echoed Apple's own six-stripe logo. It was run up a makeshift flagpole above the Macintosh building on Apple's campus, in full view of the rest of the company, an unmistakable signal to every other division that this group considered itself apart from, and above, the ordinary rules of the business. Jobs distilled the philosophy he wanted the flag to represent into a short list of mottoes that circulated among the team almost like scripture: "It's better to be a pirate than to join the Navy"; "Real artists ship"; and, simplest of all, just the word "Mac," repeated as though the name alone were a complete argument. "Real artists ship" in particular became one of Jobs's most quoted maxims inside the company, a riposte aimed at engineers who wanted to keep polishing a feature forever — a reminder that even the most exquisite, most obsessively refined piece of software or hardware was worthless to the world until it was finished and out the door, and that perfectionism divorced from delivery was not a virtue but a failure of nerve.

The flag outlived the machine it flew over by decades, and its afterlife says something about how completely the pirate metaphor became part of Apple's own foundation myth. In 2016, on the fortieth anniversary of the company's founding, Apple ran a reproduction of the same skull-and-crossbones banner up a flagpole at its headquarters, a piece of corporate self-mythologizing that would have been unthinkable from the buttoned-down, image-conscious Apple of later decades were it not for how deeply the pirate story had become part of the company's own creation narrative. Susan Kare herself, years afterward, revisited the design as a limited-edition art print, selling signed reproductions of the flag she had painted as a young artist working nights on a project she had no way of knowing would become one of the defining machines of the century.

The engineering result of all this was a machine of remarkable elegance and serious flaws. The original Macintosh, when it shipped in 1984, was a triumph of design and a compromised product. It was beautiful, friendly, and revolutionary in its interface; it was also underpowered, with far too little memory to do serious work, painfully slow at many tasks, and lacking the software that would make it genuinely useful. Some of these flaws flowed directly from Jobs's own insistences — his refusal to include expansion slots (the openness Woz had fought for on the Apple II, Jobs rejected on the Mac, wanting a sealed appliance he fully controlled), his obsession with keeping the machine small and cheap enough to reach ordinary people, which starved it of the memory it needed. The reality distortion field could will a machine into existence on an impossible schedule, but it could not repeal the laws of physics or economics, and the gap between the Macintosh as a piece of art and the Macintosh as a practical tool would become painfully apparent once the launch excitement faded. But before the flaws mattered, there was the launch, and the launch was a piece of theater so bold and so brilliant that it is still studied, taught, and imitated four decades later. Steve Jobs was about to introduce his machine to the world during the most-watched television broadcast in America, with a sixty-second commercial that would air exactly once and become the most famous advertisement ever made.

Chapter 15 — Insanely Great

"Insanely great" was Steve Jobs's phrase, and he used it constantly during the making of the Macintosh, as praise and as a demand and as a description of the only acceptable standard. A product was not to be good, or even excellent; it was to be insanely great, so far beyond the competition, so transcendently well made, that it would change how people thought about what a computer could be. The phrase captures the quality that made the Macintosh matter beyond its commercial performance: it was the first computer that was designed, from the inside out, to be an object of desire and delight rather than a tool of work, and in that ambition it established the template for everything Apple would become.

The specific ways the Macintosh embodied that ambition are worth cataloging, because many of them are so thoroughly woven into modern computing that we no longer see them as choices. The Mac put a graphical interface into the hands of ordinary people at a price — around twenty-five hundred dollars — that, while still high, was a fraction of the Lisa's, bringing the future within reach of a much larger public. It came with a mouse as standard equipment, teaching millions of people to point and click. Because of Steve Jobs's calligraphy class at Reed a decade earlier, it was the first personal computer with beautiful typography — multiple proportionally spaced fonts with real names, Susan Kare's elegant designs, so that text on a Mac screen looked like something from a fine book rather than the crude monospaced blocks of other machines. It introduced, or popularized, a whole grammar of interaction: the desktop metaphor, files and folders you could see and move, the trash can, the menu bar, cut and copy and paste, the idea that the same commands worked the same way across every program. It made the computer friendly — it literally smiled at you when it started up, Kare's happy little Mac face — in a deliberate rebellion against the intimidating, technical, unwelcoming character of computing as it had existed. A person who had never touched a computer could sit down at a Macintosh and, within minutes, be doing something, because the machine had been designed around human intuition rather than around the convenience of the engineers who built it.

The bundled software demonstrated the point and, in one case, changed an industry. MacPaint, written by Bill Atkinson, let anyone draw and paint on the screen with the mouse, and it was so delightful and so obviously new that it became, for many people, the thing that sold them on the whole idea of a graphical computer. MacWrite let people see, on the screen, more or less what their document would look like when printed — different fonts, styles, and sizes displayed as they would appear — an approach that came to be called WYSIWYG, "what you see is what you get," and that seems utterly unremarkable now precisely because the Macintosh made it universal. When Apple paired the Mac with a new laser printer and a page-layout program called PageMaker a year or two later, it accidentally created an entire industry — desktop publishing — that let a person produce professional-looking printed material on a desk that would previously have required a print shop. Desktop publishing became, for years, the Macintosh's killer application, the VisiCalc of its generation, the reason designers and publishers and small businesses bought Macs when they bought nothing else from Apple, and it kept the platform alive through the lean years that were coming. It was a vindication of the whole philosophy: because the Mac took graphics and typography seriously when other machines treated them as afterthoughts, it became the indispensable tool for anyone whose work involved making things that looked good on a page.

And yet, for all its beauty and influence, the Macintosh as a business was, at first, a disappointment, and the honesty of this book requires dwelling on that as much as on the triumph. After an initial burst of sales driven by the extraordinary launch and the novelty, demand slumped, and slumped badly. The reasons were the ones already visible in its design: it was too expensive for what it could do, it was too slow, and above all it had too little memory — a mere 128 kilobytes in the first model — to run serious software comfortably or to multitask. It lacked a hard drive. It lacked the expansion slots that would have let users and third parties extend it. There was, in the early going, not enough software to make it genuinely useful for most people, and the machine's very elegance and closed nature made it harder to develop for. Businesses, the buyers with real money, looked at the friendly little Mac with its cartoon face and its inability to run their existing software and bought IBM PCs instead. The Macintosh was, in its first year and a half, a machine that critics adored, that a passionate minority loved, and that most of the market declined to buy in the volumes Apple needed. It was, in short, another Lisa — a visionary machine undone by price, performance, and positioning — and its failure to sell in expected numbers created a crisis inside Apple that would, within a year of the launch, cost Steve Jobs his job.

It is worth correcting, with some precision, the common shorthand that the Macintosh was a flop from the moment it shipped, because the truth is more interesting and more painful than that: the launch itself was a genuine, immediate commercial triumph, and the disappointment came later. Jobs had publicly predicted Apple would sell fifty thousand Macintoshes in the machine's first hundred days on the market; Apple blew past that target by early April, and by May 3, 1984 — day one hundred — the company had sold something like seventy thousand units, a pace so far ahead of supply that Apple's own product marketing manager, Barbara Koalkin, told a reporter, "We could have sold 200,000 Macintoshes if we could have built them." Total sales for the first year came to roughly a quarter of a million machines. None of that reads like a failure. The trouble came afterward, in the second half of 1984 and into 1985, when the launch-driven demand exhausted itself and the underlying weaknesses of the machine — the price, the thin memory, the missing software — caught up with it, and the sales curve that had looked so triumphant at the hundred-day mark bent downward for the rest of the year. The Macintosh was not unloved; it was, more precisely, briefly and spectacularly loved by exactly as many people as Apple could reach with a finite supply of very expensive, underpowered machines, and not nearly enough of the much larger market beyond them.

Susan Kare's typographic and iconographic work, dismissed by some contemporaries as decoration rather than engineering, turned out to have a working life far longer than the machine it was designed for. The Chicago typeface she created for the Macintosh's menus and title bars remained part of the Mac operating system's visual identity for more than a decade, through 1997, but its afterlife did not end there: when Apple built the first iPod in 2001, the small monochrome screen of its early models displayed its menus in a scaled adaptation of the very same Chicago typeface Kare had drawn, pixel by pixel, on graph paper for the Macintosh nearly two decades earlier. A font conceived to make a beige box with a nine-inch screen feel friendly ended up, without much fanfare, riding in the pockets of tens of millions of people who never touched a Macintosh, on a product Kare had no reason to imagine when she was choosing which pixels to fill in 1983 — a small, durable proof that the "insanely great" details Jobs insisted on were not vanity after all, but investments whose value compounded for decades.

The contemporary trade press captured, in real time, the very split between visionary triumph and practical shortcoming that the Macintosh would spend its first years failing to resolve. BYTE magazine, then the most influential publication in the personal-computer industry, put the Macintosh through several rounds of scrutiny within months of its release. In its February 1984 issue, reviewer Gregg Williams praised the hardware and software design so highly that he predicted it would be "imitated but not copied" by the rest of the industry — a backhanded compliment suggesting rivals would borrow its ideas without ever quite matching its execution — while also flagging a very practical complaint that would dog the machine for its first year: it shipped without a standard second disk drive, forcing users into a tedious routine of swapping a single floppy back and forth between the program disk and the data disk. By that May, Williams was reporting on the machine's reception in the wild, and his verdict captured exactly the split reaction that would define the Mac's difficult first eighteen months on the market: initial reaction, he wrote, had been "strongly, but not overpoweringly, favorable," with a minority of traditional computer users dismissing the mouse and the windows and the desktop metaphor as "silly, useless frills," even as most who tried the machine came away genuinely impressed. By August, BYTE ran a longer, more considered assessment under a title that captured the ambivalence perfectly: "The Macintosh: The Many Facets of a Slightly Flawed Gem" — a headline that could serve as a one-line summary of this entire chapter's argument, that the Macintosh was simultaneously a genuine marvel and a compromised, underpowered product whose gem-like qualities did not, on their own, guarantee it a place on enough desks to satisfy Apple's ambitions for it.

Apple's own response to the memory shortage that reviewers kept identifying came within the year. In September 1984, barely eight months after the original machine's debut, Apple released the Macintosh 512K — quickly nicknamed the "Fat Mac" by the trade press and by customers — which quadrupled the original's memory from 128 kilobytes to 512 kilobytes at a stroke, easing, though not eliminating, the constant disk-swapping and program-crashing that had made the first machines so frustrating to use for anything beyond simple tasks. The correction came too late to salvage the sales momentum lost during the second half of 1984, but it was an early demonstration of a pattern Apple would repeat again and again in the decades to come: ship a visionary product with real, identifiable compromises, absorb the criticism, and then quietly fix the most damaging flaws in a second or third revision once the market's verdict had made the deficiencies impossible to ignore.

The tragedy, and the lesson, is that the Macintosh was right and early at the same time, and being right and early is often indistinguishable, in the short run, from being wrong. Everything about the Mac's fundamental approach — the graphical interface, the mouse, the friendliness, the beauty — was correct, and within a decade it would be the way essentially every personal computer worked, once Microsoft's Windows brought the same ideas, less elegantly, to the vast installed base of IBM-compatible machines. But in 1984 and 1985 the hardware was not yet cheap enough or fast enough to deliver the vision at a price the market would pay, and Apple had bet enormous resources on a machine that the market was not yet ready to buy in the quantities its economics required. Jobs had willed into existence a product that was, in the deepest sense, ahead of its time, and he had done it with a theatrical brilliance that made the disappointment all the more acute when the sales failed to match the hype. Because before the sales figures came in, there had been the launch — and the launch had been the most audacious piece of marketing the technology industry had ever seen, built around a single television commercial, aired one time, during the Super Bowl, that portrayed IBM as Big Brother and the Macintosh as the hammer that would shatter its tyranny. To understand how high the expectations were, and therefore how hard the fall, we have to go back to that commercial, and to the two days in January 1984 when Steve Jobs, for the first time, showed the world what he could do on a stage.

Chapter 16 — "1984"

On the evening of January 22, 1984, during the third quarter of Super Bowl XVIII, some ninety million Americans watching the most-viewed television broadcast of the year saw sixty seconds of imagery unlike anything advertising had shown them before. A column of gray, shaven-headed drones marched in lockstep through a tunnel into a vast hall, where they sat in rows before an enormous screen on which a Big Brother figure droned about the "Unification of Thoughts." Into this dystopia ran a young woman in bright red shorts and a white tank top, pursued by helmeted riot police, carrying a large sledgehammer. She hurled it at the screen; the screen exploded in a burst of light and wind that washed over the stunned drones; and a voice-over announced: "On January 24th, Apple Computer will introduce Macintosh. And you'll see why 1984 won't be like 1984." There was no shot of the product. There was no list of features. There was only a myth: the machine as liberation, the individual against the totalitarian mass, Apple against — though the name was never spoken — the gray conformity of IBM.

The commercial, directed by Ridley Scott fresh off *Blade Runner*, is routinely called the greatest television advertisement ever made, and its backstory is nearly as remarkable as the film. Apple's own board of directors hated it. When it was screened for them, several members were appalled;

they thought it was a disaster, off-message, incomprehensible, a waste of the enormous sum Apple had spent to produce it and to buy the Super Bowl airtime. They ordered the agency to sell off the ad slots. The agency, Chiat/Day, dragged its feet and managed to sell only a small portion, and so, largely by a combination of the founders' determination — Jobs and the marketing team loved it and fought for it — and administrative delay, "1984" aired during the Super Bowl as planned, essentially once, nationally. The effect was seismic. Newscasts replayed it. Newspapers wrote about it. It generated a wave of free media coverage worth many times its cost, and it seared into the public mind an image of the Macintosh — and of Apple — as the rebel, the liberator, the cool insurgent against the corporate establishment. It is the founding text of Apple's brand mythology, the purest early expression of the idea that buying an Apple product was not a consumer choice but an act of identity, a declaration that you were one of the individuals, the creative ones, the rebels, against the drones. That mythology would be worth, over the following decades, more than almost any patent.

Two days later, at Apple's annual shareholder meeting, Steve Jobs gave the other half of the performance, and it established a form he would perfect over the next thirty years. Dressed in a suit, in front of an auditorium of the faithful, he built suspense, talked about the stakes, invoked the battle against IBM, and then walked to a small table, pulled the Macintosh out of a bag, and switched it on. The machine did something no computer had done at a product launch before: it introduced itself. Synthesized speech emerged from the little beige box — "Hello, I am Macintosh. It sure is great to get out of that bag" — and it made a few jokes, and it thanked its "father," Steve Jobs, and the crowd went berserk, some people in tears, on their feet, roaring. It was theater, pure and deliberate, and it worked because Jobs understood something most technology executives never grasp: that a product launch is not an information session but a piece of storytelling, an emotional experience, a chance to make people feel that they are witnessing history and that they want, badly, to be part of it. The template established that day — the suspense, the reveal, the demonstration, the sense of unveiling the future, the "one more thing" that would later cap so many of these performances — would be reused and refined at every major Apple launch to come, most famously at the unveiling of the iPhone twenty-three years later. Jobs turned the keynote into an art form, and it became one of Apple's most powerful and least imitable competitive weapons.

One popular detail of the "1984" story is not quite accurate as it is usually told, and correcting it makes the episode more interesting rather than less. The commercial is often described as having aired exactly once, nationally, during the Super Bowl — a single, unrepeatable flash of advertising lightning. In fact it had already run once before, quietly and by design: in the last days of December 1983, Chiat/Day arranged for "1984" to air in the middle of the night on a small television station in Twin Falls, Idaho, specifically so that the ad would qualify, under contest rules requiring the previous calendar year's airing, for that season's advertising industry awards. Almost no one saw it. The agency was not trying to build buzz with that airing; it was quietly satisfying a technicality so the commercial could later be entered for a Clio, while saving the real unveiling — the one meant to be seen by the entire country — for the Super Bowl three and a half weeks later. The Super Bowl broadcast really was the ad's only national showing, but the claim that it aired only once, anywhere, was never quite true.

The fight over whether the commercial would air at all deserves to be remembered in more detail than the sanitized version usually allows, because Apple came startlingly close to killing its own most famous advertisement. When Jobs and Sculley screened "1984" for Apple's board of directors in December 1983, the reaction was not lukewarm skepticism but open hostility: several board members called it the worst commercial they had ever seen, alarmed above all by its bare-knuckled attack on IBM, and Mike Markkula, the very board member who had once written Apple's founding marketing philosophy, suggested the company fire its ad agency outright. Sculley, unnerved, instructed Chiat/Day to sell back both the thirty-second and sixty-second slots Apple had already purchased from CBS for roughly a million dollars. Jay Chiat, believing in the ad, slow-walked the instruction and managed to unload only the thirty-second slot, letting the sixty-second version run essentially by bureaucratic delay as much as by conviction. Had Chiat/Day done exactly as told, one of the most consequential pieces of advertising in American business history would have vanished before anyone outside a Boise-area television market ever saw it.

The spectacle Jobs and Chiat/Day created that January afternoon did more than sell computers; it helped invent the entire modern idea of the Super Bowl commercial as a cultural event unto itself, a piece of programming people watch as attentively as the game surrounding it. That transformation is easy to measure in dollars: a single thirty-second slot during the broadcast, which cost Apple a few hundred thousand dollars in 1984, now routinely sells for seven or eight million dollars, with the very top slots fetching more than ten million — a testament to an industry that "1984" helped teach to think of the Super Bowl broadcast not as an interruption to sell products, but as the single biggest stage in American culture on which to tell a story. Every company that now saves its splashiest, most cinematic commercial of the year for that one Sunday in February is, whether or not its marketing department realizes it, working in a tradition Steve Jobs and a group of skeptical, frightened board members nearly extinguished before it began.

And then reality arrived, in the form of sales figures, and the reality was harsh. The initial surge of Macintosh sales, driven by the launch frenzy, faded within a few months, and the underlying weaknesses of the machine — the price, the sluggishness, the crippling shortage of memory, the thin software library — reasserted themselves. By late 1984 and into 1985, Macintosh sales were falling well short of Apple's projections, inventory was piling up, and the machine that had been launched as a world-changing revolution was, in the cold arithmetic of the market, underperforming badly. The Apple II was still the company's real breadwinner, quietly generating the profits that the glamorous, struggling Macintosh was consuming. The gap between the myth Jobs had sold — the Macintosh as the hammer that would shatter the old order — and the mundane commercial disappointment was enormous, and inside Apple that gap became a crisis, and the crisis became a search for someone to blame. There was an obvious candidate.

The woman wielding the sledgehammer very nearly wasn't cast at all, and the search for her says something about how literally Ridley Scott insisted on staging what was, in effect, a piece of action filmmaking rather than a conventional commercial. Scott auditioned a series of actresses and models for the role of the unnamed heroine, but when it came time to actually throw a full-sized sledgehammer at a movie screen with the force and follow-through the shot required, most of them could not manage it safely — on at least one occasion, according to accounts of the shoot, a hammer flew out of a would-be actress's hands and went sailing into a London park, missing an elderly woman out for a walk by an alarmingly narrow margin. Scott's production team eventually turned to Anya Major, a young British athlete with a background in discus throwing, who could hurl the hammer with the accuracy and control the stunt demanded. It is a small, almost absurd detail, but it underlines how seriously Scott treated the commercial as cinema rather than advertising — he was not staging a metaphor so much as choreographing a real athletic feat, with a real thrower's arm standing in for an action star, because anything less convincing would have undercut the sixty seconds of myth-making he and Apple were selling.

The commercial's afterlife in the advertising industry itself validated the gamble Apple's board had so nearly refused to take. Later in 1984, "1984" won the Grand Prix at the International Advertising Film Festival in Cannes — the festival's highest honor — a recognition from the advertising profession's own peers that the ad Apple's directors had once dismissed as a disaster and tried to sell back to the network was, by the unanimous judgment of the people who made commercials for a living, the best one made that year. Decades on, Ridley Scott's Orwellian nightmare-turned-liberation fantasy is still cited, in surveys of advertising professionals and in the trade press alike, as among the greatest television commercials ever produced — a verdict that makes the board's initial revulsion, and Jay Chiat's quiet refusal to fully carry out their instructions to sell back the airtime, look, in retrospect, like one of the more consequential acts of institutional disobedience in corporate history.

Steve Jobs, in 1985, was thirty years old, the co-founder and public face of the company, the impresario of the greatest product launch in the industry's history, and, increasingly, a problem that Apple's leadership no longer knew how to contain. The Macintosh's poor sales had stripped away the protection that success confers; his abrasiveness, his tantrums, his division of colleagues into geniuses and bozos, his meddling and his volatility, which might have been tolerated in a triumphant leader, became intolerable in one whose flagship was faltering. He was running the Macintosh division as a fiefdom, feuding openly with the Apple II division whose profits were keeping the company alive, and clashing with the very executive he had personally recruited two years earlier to be Apple's chief executive — a marketing genius from the world of soft drinks named John Sculley, whom Jobs had lured to

Apple with one of the most famous sentences ever spoken in a job interview. Jobs had brought Sculley in to be his ally, his partner, the professional manager who would let him focus on products. Instead, over the course of 1985, the two men would turn on each other in a struggle for control of the company, and Jobs would lose — would be stripped of his power, pushed out of the company he had co-founded, and sent into an exile that felt, at the time, like the end of his story. It was, instead, the interruption that would remake him. But it began with a betrayal, and the seeds of the betrayal had been planted at the moment of recruitment, when Jobs asked a question he would come to regret.

Chapter 17 — Sugared Water

The sentence that brought John Sculley to Apple has become the most famous recruiting line in business history, and like most famous lines it is quoted more often than it is understood. In 1983, Apple needed a chief executive — a seasoned corporate leader to run the growing company, since neither Jobs nor Markkula wanted the job long-term and Mike Scott had been pushed out after a rocky tenure. Jobs set his sights on John Sculley, the president of PepsiCo, a marketing prodigy who had masterminded the "Pepsi Challenge" campaign and driven Pepsi's rise against Coca-Cola. Sculley was everything Jobs, at that moment, thought Apple needed: a polished, experienced executive who understood mass-market consumer marketing, branding, and the machinery of a large organization — precisely the domains where the young founder felt Apple was weak. Jobs courted him for months, flattering him, dazzling him, painting a picture of changing the world. And when Sculley hesitated, worried about leaving the security of a giant corporation for a volatile computer company, Jobs delivered the closer. "Do you want to spend the rest of your life selling sugared water," he asked, "or do you want a chance to change the world?"

It worked. Sculley, stung and inspired in equal measure,

took the job, and for a time the partnership between the visionary founder and the professional manager looked like a model of complementary strengths. The two men were, for a while, genuinely close; Jobs spoke of Sculley as a mentor and a friend, and Sculley admired Jobs's brilliance and threw himself into learning the technology business. The press celebrated the "dynamic duo." But the fit was, in retrospect, doomed from the start, because it rested on a misunderstanding of what each man wanted. Jobs believed he was hiring a marketing expert who would handle the business side and defer to him on products and vision — that Sculley would run the plumbing while Jobs ran the soul of the company. Sculley believed he was being hired to be the chief executive, the actual leader of the company, with the authority that title implies. Those two understandings could coexist only as long as the company was succeeding and Jobs's judgment was being vindicated by results. The moment the Macintosh faltered, the moment Jobs's decisions started producing losses instead of triumphs, the two understandings collided, and there was room in the collision for only one of them to prevail.

The deeper problem was that Sculley did not, and perhaps could not, actually understand the technology or the product vision at the level Jobs did, and Jobs came to see this and to lose his respect for the man he had recruited. Sculley was a consumer-marketing executive; he understood positioning and pricing and advertising and distribution, and he made real contributions in those areas. But he did not have the instinct for what a computer should be, the feel for the product that was Jobs's genius, and as the relationship soured Jobs increasingly regarded him as a suit who did not get it, a "bozo" who had wandered in from the beverage industry and did not belong in a company that was trying to change the world. For his part, Sculley came to see Jobs as an uncontrollable, destructive force — a brilliant but dangerous manager whose division was hemorrhaging money, who bullied and demoralized employees, who feuded with the rest of the company, and whose famous product judgment had just produced an expensive commercial flop. Both assessments contained truth, which is what made the conflict so bitter and so hard to resolve. Jobs really was, at this stage of his life, a genuinely difficult and often destructive executive. Sculley really did lack the vision the company most needed. Apple had, at its head, two men each of whom was half right about the other and half wrong about himself.

By early 1985 the situation had become untenable. Macintosh sales were poor, the company was heading toward its first losses and layoffs, and the relationship between the founder and the CEO had curdled into open antagonism. Jobs, running the Macintosh division, was undermining Sculley, second-guessing him, and — in the maneuver that would prove fatal — beginning to plot to remove him. Jobs concluded that Sculley was the problem, that the company needed to be rid of the CEO he had himself installed, and he set out to persuade the board of directors to remove Sculley and give Jobs real operational control. It was an audacious gamble, and it rested on a catastrophic misreading of his own standing. Jobs believed that as co-founder and visionary he commanded the loyalty of the board and the company; he believed that in a contest between himself and the beverage executive, the board would naturally side with the founder. He was wrong, and the wrongness of it would be one of the hardest lessons of his life. When the confrontation came, the board — the very people Jobs thought were his — looked at the numbers, looked at the chaos in the Macintosh division, looked at the volatile thirty-year-old who could not get along with anyone, and looked at the steady, experienced CEO, and they made the choice that boards make. They backed Sculley.

It is worth understanding exactly what Sculley's reputation at Pepsi actually rested on, because it illuminates precisely the gap that would later open between the two men. Sculley had joined PepsiCo as a trainee in 1967, risen to vice president by 1970 and to the presidency of the Pepsi-Cola division by 1977, and made his name chiefly through the Pepsi Challenge, a national advertising campaign begun in 1975 built around televised blind taste tests in which longtime Coca-Cola drinkers, sipping unmarked cups, frequently chose Pepsi. It was a brilliant piece of marketing theater — and, as critics pointed out even at the time, a somewhat misleading one, since the preference the tests reliably captured had more to do with Pepsi's greater sweetness biasing a single small sip than with any considered judgment about which cola a person would actually want to drink through a whole can. Sculley's genius, in other words, was for the perception of a product rather than the substance of it, for the theater of choice rather than the engineering of the thing being chosen — a set of instincts that served Pepsi well and that would prove almost exactly wrong for managing a company whose founder believed, to his core, that the substance had to be right before any theater mattered at all.

The rupture between the two men, once it happened, proved permanent in a way that neither seems to have wanted at the time, and Sculley's own later reflections on it are more revealing than any outside account. Years afterward, in interviews given long after Jobs's death, Sculley described the two of them as having been genuinely close before the 1985 conflict — friends, not merely colleagues — and said that his greatest regret was never approaching Jobs to say, in effect, let's find a way for you to come back and lead what you created. "It was never repaired," Sculley said of the friendship, "which was such a shame — I look back and think what a mistake on my part." He admitted that he had not understood, coming from the executive culture of a large consumer-products company, what it meant to a founder to be stripped of authority over the very thing he had built from nothing. The two men never reconciled; by Sculley's own account he did not speak with Jobs again for more than twenty years, an estrangement that lasted, in effect, for the rest of Jobs's life.

The financial terms Apple offered to close the deal are worth setting down, because they show just how badly Jobs wanted Sculley and how starkly the arrangement was tilted to protect the executive rather than the company recruiting him. To lure Sculley away from a job paying roughly half a million dollars a year at PepsiCo, Apple offered a compensation package of about a million dollars annually, split between salary and bonus, together with a million-dollar signing bonus simply for accepting the offer, a further million-dollar severance guarantee — a golden parachute — should the arrangement not work out, an allotment of some 350,000 shares of Apple stock, and financial assistance to help him purchase a home in California comparable to the one he was leaving in Connecticut. It was, in other words, a deal constructed to make Sculley's downside as close to riskless as Apple's lawyers could make it, which is precisely why the ultimate collapse of the relationship reads so differently depending on whose ledger you consult: Jobs walked away from Apple in 1985 with nothing but his own stock, sold off in anger, while Sculley's contract had been built, from the very first negotiation, to ensure that whatever happened to the founder who recruited him, the professional manager would land safely. That template — enormous guaranteed compensation, signing bonuses, and golden parachutes offered to convince an outside executive to gamble a secure corporate career on an unproven upstart — was, in 1983, still a relative novelty in the technology industry, and Apple's willingness to write those terms into Sculley's contract reflected just how urgently Jobs believed the young company needed adult supervision from outside its own ranks. It would become a far more common pattern in Silicon Valley in the decades that followed, as one growing technology company after another borrowed the same basic playbook — extravagant guarantees dressed up as confidence in a shared future — to pry seasoned executives loose from the safety of established corporations. The asymmetry in Sculley's deal was baked in before either man had any idea it would matter, and it is a small, telling detail about how differently the two of them approached risk from the very beginning of a partnership that both later described, in their more reflective moments, as having started in genuine mutual admiration.

The showdown played out over a tense stretch of weeks in the spring of 1985, with Jobs attempting to organize his coup while Sculley, learning of it, moved to defend himself and forced the issue into the open before the board. The board sided decisively with Sculley and against Jobs. Jobs was not fired outright — that would have been too naked a repudiation of a co-founder — but he was stripped of all operational responsibility, removed from the Macintosh division, given a grand-sounding but empty title, and left with no real role in the company he had created. He was, in every way that mattered, exiled to the margins, a chairman without a portfolio, allowed to keep an office but given nothing to do. For a man whose entire identity was bound up in building products and running the company, it was a devastation more complete than a simple firing would have been: he was kept on as a figurehead precisely so that his removal would not look like a removal, and he was left to wander the halls of Apple with no power and no purpose, watching other people run the thing he had built. He lasted a few months in that limbo before he could bear it no longer. In September 1985 he resigned, sold nearly all his Apple stock in fury and grief, and set out to prove that the company had been wrong to cast him aside. The exile had begun, and it would last eleven years.

Chapter 18 — The Coup

The removal of Steve Jobs from Apple in 1985 is often told as a tragedy — the visionary founder betrayed and cast out by lesser men who could not see his greatness — and there is truth in that telling. But it is a partial truth, and the fuller story, the one that does justice to everyone involved, is more uncomfortable and more instructive. The uncomfortable part is that the board was not wrong to do what it did. The Steve Jobs of 1985 was, by nearly every account including his own later reflections, a genuinely poor executive to have running a large and struggling company. He was brilliant and he was destructive, and at that moment the destruction was outweighing the brilliance, and the people responsible for the survival of a company employing thousands of people made a defensible, even a correct, decision to remove him from operational power. The tragedy is not that they were wrong. The tragedy, if it is one, is that a company can be right to remove the very person it most needs — that Jobs's flaws were real and disqualifying in 1985, and that his gifts were also real and would prove, a decade later, to be the only thing that could save the company from death.

To understand the board's decision, you have to see Apple as it looked from the boardroom in the spring of 1985, not as it looks in the golden haze of the legend. The Macintosh, launched with world-historical fanfare a year earlier, was selling far below projections. The company was heading into a quarter of losses and its first major layoffs, wrenching for a firm that had known only growth. The Macintosh division, run by Jobs, was consuming enormous resources while feuding openly and destructively with the Apple II division, whose profits were the only thing keeping the company afloat — and Jobs treated the Apple II people, the ones actually earning the money, with open contempt, as second-class citizens working on yesterday's machine. Employees were demoralized by his management; talented people were threatening to leave rather than endure his abuse. And the founder himself, rather than helping to steady the company through a hard patch, was spending his energy plotting to overthrow the chief executive. Put yourself in the board's chair, responsible to shareholders and employees for the survival of the enterprise, and the choice between the volatile thirty-year-old who was creating chaos and the steady executive trying to impose order does not look like a betrayal. It looks like fiduciary duty.

And yet the board's decision was also, in a way it could not have known, a catastrophic mistake — not because removing Jobs from operational control in 1985 was unreasonable, but because the company then spent a decade without the one quality only he could provide, and nearly died for lack of it. Sculley and his successors were competent managers, and under them Apple did some things well; the company remained profitable for years after Jobs left, riding the Macintosh's eventual maturation into a viable product and the growth of desktop publishing. But without Jobs, Apple slowly lost the thing that had made it special: the relentless product vision, the taste, the willingness to bet everything on a insanely great idea and to say no to everything else. Over the following decade the company would drift, proliferate a confusing sprawl of mediocre products, lose its design edge, watch its market share erode under the relentless advance of Microsoft Windows, and stumble from one strategic misstep to another until it stood, in 1996 and 1997, on the actual brink of bankruptcy. The board that removed Jobs to save the company had, in the long run, deprived it of its soul, and it would take his return, eleven years later, to restore it. Both things are true. The removal was defensible in the moment and disastrous over the arc, and holding those two judgments together is the only honest way to understand what happened.

For Jobs himself, the exile was, at the time, an unambiguous catastrophe, and it is worth taking seriously how much it wounded him, because the pain of it shaped the man who eventually returned. He had co-founded Apple at twenty-one, made it one of the most famous companies in the world, put his entire identity into it, and then been thrown out of it at thirty by people he had trusted, in a public humiliation that the whole industry watched. He was, by his own later account, devastated — publicly rejected, his life's work taken from him, uncertain who he even was if he was not the man building Apple. He would later describe this period, with the benefit of enormous hindsight, as the best thing that could have happened to him, a claim we will examine skeptically in the coming chapters. But in the moment there was no silver lining visible, only the raw fact of failure and rejection. He sold nearly all his Apple stock — keeping a single share so he could still attend shareholder meetings — in an act of finality and anger, cutting his financial ties to the company he had built. And then he did the thing that defines him, the thing that separates him from the many talented people who are broken by a failure of this magnitude: he refused to disappear. He did not retire on his fortune, did not sink into bitterness, did not spend his life litigating the injustice. He immediately started building again.

The mechanics of the ouster, stripped of the legend's compression, unfolded more slowly and more procedurally than the popular telling allows, and getting the sequence right corrects a widespread misconception: Steve Jobs was not fired from Apple in a single dramatic stroke in 1985. What actually happened was a two-stage unraveling spread across five months. At a marathon board meeting on April 10 and 11, 1985, Sculley forced the issue directly, telling the assembled directors, in words he would recount many times in later years, "I'm asking Steve to step down and you can back me on it and then I take responsibility for running the company, or we can do nothing and you're going to find yourselves a new CEO." It was an ultimatum rather than a dismissal, and it worked: the board sided with Sculley, ordered a reorganization of the Macintosh division, and quietly stripped Jobs of his operating authority while leaving him the empty title of chairman. Jobs did not accept this quietly. Over the following months he lobbied board members and executives to reverse the decision and remove Sculley instead, attempting a counter-coup of his own — and when the board was asked a second time to choose between them, it chose Sculley again. Only after that second defeat, in September 1985, did Jobs resign outright. The single dramatic firing that lives in popular memory was, in reality, a war of attrition that Jobs fought over the better part of a year and lost twice.

The most persistent distortion in the popular retelling, in fact, involves Sculley himself, who spent much of his later life trying to correct a record that had cast him as a small man who felled a giant out of jealousy or incomprehension. In interviews given decades afterward — as late as 2012 and 2013, when he sat for extended, detailed accounts of the episode — Sculley insisted that he had not wanted to force Jobs out at all, that the board's action was a reluctant response to a genuinely unworkable situation rather than a coup he had engineered for his own benefit, and that he had tried and failed to find another way to keep Jobs meaningfully involved in the company. Whether or not one credits every detail of his account, its persistence is itself revealing: nearly thirty years after the fact, the man most identified with Jobs's ouster still felt the need to explain himself in public, which tells you something about how completely the later legend of the martyred visionary had swallowed the more complicated reality of 1985, and how uncomfortable it remained, even in old age, to be remembered as the villain of somebody else's origin story.

That refusal to collapse into a simple story of villainy or vindication is exactly why the episode has endured as a fixture of corporate-governance teaching, cited for decades in business-school case studies as the canonical instance of a board forced to choose between an organization's most gifted person and the stability it needed simply to survive. The lesson instructors draw from it cuts against whichever side a given student wants to root for: it is not a parable about founders always knowing best, nor one about boards always being right to rein them in, but a demonstration of how genuinely hard the tradeoff can be when brilliance and dysfunction arrive in the same person, and of how a decision can be procedurally sound, unanimously supported, and still turn out, years later, to have been a near-fatal misjudgment. Few corporate case studies manage to be right and wrong at the same time this cleanly, which is why Jobs's ouster is still taught alongside the far more recent boardroom dramas it anticipated, at companies whose founders would later be pushed out by boards facing an eerily similar calculus.

The human cost of the defeat, meanwhile, is easy to understate if you read only the ultimatum and the vote and skip the man living through it. Jobs was thirty years old, and by every account he had built more of his identity around Apple than any other single fact of his adult life; losing it was not merely a career setback but something closer to an amputation. That fear of an eerily similar fate has since left a concrete mark on how technology companies are built. A generation later, when Larry Page and Sergey Brin took Google public, and when Mark Zuckerberg took Facebook public, both companies adopted dual-class share structures that let their founders keep voting control far out of proportion to their equity — a structural innovation designed, in no small part, so that no board could ever again do to a company's founder what Apple's board did to Jobs in 1985. It is a strange kind of legacy for an ouster to leave: the decision that removed Steve Jobs from power became, twenty years on, the cautionary tale that let the next generation of founders make sure it could never happen to them.

The plot's collapse turned on a single miscalculation that Jobs, of all people, should not have made: he tried to enlist an ally who was not actually on his side. In May 1985, with Sculley away on a business trip to China, Jobs moved to execute his counter-coup, and in building support for it he approached Jean-Louis Gassée, the head of Apple's French operations and a Macintosh-division executive Jobs believed he could count on. Gassée, instead of joining the plot, went straight to Sculley and told him what Jobs was planning — a warning that handed Sculley the chance to move first and decisively once he returned. It is a detail that recasts the famous board ultimatum: the confrontation was not simply the board turning on Jobs unprompted, but the culmination of a plot that failed at the recruiting stage, undone by a lieutenant who judged, correctly as it turned out, that his own future lay with the CEO rather than the founder.

The reorganization that followed the vote shows just how completely and how quickly Jobs's authority was dismantled, piece by piece, once the board had made its choice. Del Yocam, an Apple veteran, was elevated to chief operating officer, taking over the operational functions that had once run through Jobs's Macintosh division. Bill Campbell, who would go on to become one of Silicon Valley's most celebrated executive mentors, was put in charge of sales and marketing. And Gassée himself — the man whose warning had made the whole reorganization possible — was rewarded with control of product development, the very domain of hardware and software vision Jobs had once considered his personal fiefdom, reporting now to Yocam rather than to Jobs. Every piece of authority Jobs had accumulated as head of the Macintosh division was redistributed to other executives within weeks, so that by the time he actually resigned in September, there was, in the most literal organizational sense, almost nothing left of his old job for him to walk away from. There is a coda to Gassée's role that the standard telling of the coup usually omits, and it complicates any temptation to cast him as simply Sculley's loyal instrument: within five years Gassée himself fell out with the very CEO he had helped save, clashing with Sculley over product strategy and Apple's direction until he, too, left the company in 1990 — a reminder that the boardroom politics Jobs lost in 1985 did not resolve into stable loyalty for anyone involved.

Within months of resigning he had founded a new company, taking several of Apple's best people with him — an act that provoked a lawsuit from Apple and further poisoned the relationship — and set out to build a computer so advanced that it would humiliate the company that had cast him out. The new venture was called NeXT, and it would become the vehicle for the next decade of his life: a beautiful, brilliant, wildly overambitious, commercially doomed machine that would nearly bankrupt him, teach him more than any of his successes had, and — in the twist that makes the whole story cohere — become, through a chain of events no one could have predicted, the technological foundation on which Apple's entire resurrection would be built. The operating system Jobs built in exile, at the company he founded out of spite, would be the software running inside every Mac and every iPhone Apple would ever sell. His revenge, when it came, would arrive not as a conqueror but as a Trojan horse: the exiled king would sell his old kingdom the very thing it needed to survive, and ride back in on it. But first came the wilderness, and the wilderness was long, and for most of it there was no sign that it would end in anything but failure.

Chapter 19 — NeXT

NeXT was Steve Jobs's chance to do everything he had wanted to do at Apple with no one to tell him no, and the result was a case study in what happens when a perfectionist visionary is given complete control and unlimited ambition and no adult supervision. It produced one of the most beautiful and technically advanced computers ever built, and it nearly destroyed him, and both outcomes flowed from the same source: the absence of any constraint on his perfectionism.

The company was founded in 1985 with a mission that flattered Jobs's self-image as a world-changer: it would build a powerful workstation for higher education and research, a machine that would give university scientists and students computing power previously available only on far more expensive systems. Jobs poured himself and his money into it, and he poured in an enormous amount of both. He hired brilliant engineers, several lured from Apple. He commissioned the famous graphic designer Paul Rand to create the NeXT logo — a perfect black cube with the letters arranged just so — reportedly paying a hundred thousand dollars for the single design, and treating the result as a work of art. He built, to manufacture the machines, an automated factory of stunning sophistication and cost, a showpiece of robotic assembly that could produce far more computers than NeXT would ever manage to sell. He obsessed, as always, over details invisible to any user: the NeXT Computer was housed in a perfect one-foot magnesium cube, and Jobs insisted that even the inside of the case, the parts no customer would ever see, be finished beautifully, the internal screws and surfaces held to standards of appearance that added cost and difficulty for no functional reason except that he could not tolerate ugliness anywhere, seen or unseen. The machine that emerged, the NeXT Computer, unveiled in 1988, was gorgeous, powerful, and staggeringly expensive — priced around six thousand five hundred dollars for the base configuration, far beyond what most of its intended student market could pay, and requiring extra hardware that pushed the real cost higher still.

It did not sell. The reasons were the ones that had sunk the Lisa, magnified: it cost too much, it was aimed at a market (students) that could not afford it, it initially used a novel optical-disk storage system that was slow and finicky, and it lacked the software and the installed base that would have justified the price. NeXT sold its machines in the thousands when it needed to sell them in the hundreds of thousands, and the beautiful automated factory sat mostly idle, a monument to demand that never materialized. Year after year the company lost money, burning through Jobs's fortune and through investments from partners including the businessman Ross Perot, who put in millions and later admitted it was one of the worst investments of his life. By the early 1990s NeXT's hardware business was clearly failing, and in 1993 Jobs made the painful decision to abandon hardware altogether — to stop making the beautiful cubes, close the gleaming factory, lay off much of the staff, and pivot the company to selling software alone. It was a humbling retreat for a man who had defined himself by making objects, an admission that the physical machine, the thing he cared about most, had failed in the market.

But here is where the NeXT story turns, and where its

apparent failure begins, in retrospect, to look like the most important work of Jobs's exile. The software that ran on the NeXT machine — the operating system, called NeXTSTEP — was genuinely, profoundly ahead of its time, and it was NeXT's true and lasting achievement. NeXTSTEP was built on a stable, sophisticated foundation (a Unix core) and, crucially, it was designed around object-oriented programming, a way of building software out of reusable, modular components that made it dramatically faster and easier to create powerful, complex applications. Developers who used NeXTSTEP's tools found they could build in weeks what took months on other systems, and the elegance of the whole environment inspired a small but fervent following among programmers who understood what they were looking at. NeXTSTEP was, quite simply, one of the best operating systems in the world, years ahead of anything Apple or Microsoft was shipping, and its object-oriented frameworks were a glimpse of how software would be built for decades to come.

The proof of NeXTSTEP's quality came from an unexpected direction and would change the world in a way that had nothing to do with Jobs. In 1990, at the CERN physics laboratory in Switzerland, a British scientist named Tim Berners-Lee needed a powerful, flexible machine on which to build an idea he had for linking documents across a network, and the machine he chose was a NeXT Computer. On that black cube, using NeXTSTEP's advanced development tools, Berners-Lee wrote the first web browser and the first web server, and invented what he called the World Wide Web. The single most transformative software system of the coming age was born on Steve Jobs's exiled, commercially failed machine, because that machine's software was so far ahead of everything else that it was the natural tool for a person trying to build something genuinely new. It is one of history's quiet ironies: the computer that could not find customers became the birthplace of the technology that would define the next half-century, and the operating system that lost money for a decade would, through two separate channels — the Web, and Apple's eventual rescue — reshape the entire world of computing. The Paul Rand commission is worth dwelling on, because it is one of the purest expressions of how completely design obsession structured Jobs's thinking even in a company that had, as yet, sold nothing. Rand was already the most famous corporate-identity designer in America — the creator of the logos for IBM, UPS, and ABC — and Jobs approached him not for a set of options to choose among but for a single, finished answer, the way a client commissions a painting rather than shopping a mood board. Rand's terms were unusual and, by the standards of corporate branding, almost imperious: he would study the company, design one logo, present it once, and Jobs would either accept it or pay for the work and walk away, with no rounds of revision offered in between. He delivered a lush, twenty-page brand presentation explaining every decision, down to the precise twenty-eight-degree tilt at which the letters NeXT — spelled with a lowercase e nestled among capitals — were angled inside a perfect cube, and he charged a hundred thousand dollars for it. Jobs, who could easily have balked at paying six figures for a company that did not yet have a product, loved it instantly and used it exactly as delivered. Design students still study that presentation today, in the same courses that study Rand's IBM and UPS work, as one of the rare documented cases of a client surrendering total creative control to a designer and being rewarded for the surrender — a preview, in miniature, of the trust Jobs would later extend to Jony Ive.

The company's early finances also complicate the easy retrospective verdict that NeXT was obviously doomed from the start. In November 1986, the Texas billionaire Ross Perot happened to watch a PBS documentary called *Entrepreneurs* that featured Jobs and his new venture, and he was sufficiently impressed to invest twenty million dollars for a sixteen percent stake, calling NeXT, in a remark that reads very differently in hindsight than it must have sounded at the time, one that "in terms of a startup company... carries the least risk of any I've seen in twenty-five years in the computer industry." Perot was not a naif; he was one of the shrewdest dealmakers in America, and his willingness to bet heavily on NeXT is a reminder that the company's eventual failure was not preordained or obvious to contemporaries — it looked, to a serious investor doing serious diligence, like one of the safer technology bets of the decade, precisely because it carried the Steve Jobs name and the NeXTSTEP technology that even skeptics conceded was extraordinary. Perot stayed on NeXT's board for nearly five years before resigning in June 1991 to focus on his own company, quietly exiting before the hardware business collapsed entirely two years later, and by his own later account the investment ranked among the worst he ever made — not because the diligence had been careless, but because even careful diligence could not have priced in just how badly a six-thousand-dollar workstation aimed at cash-poor graduate students would fail to sell.

None of this is to rehabilitate NeXT as a secret commercial success — it was not, and Jobs's own later assessments of the venture were unsentimental about how badly it had underperformed his ambitions for it. But the Rand logo and the Perot investment together complicate the tidy narrative in which NeXT reads, from its first day, as an obvious folly that only Jobs's ego failed to see coming. Sophisticated outsiders — a legendary designer, a billionaire investor — looked at the same company in the middle of its life and saw something worth an enormous bet. That they were both eventually proven wrong about the market does not mean they were foolish to have been convinced; it means that NeXT's failure was a market failure of pricing and timing, not a failure of the underlying technology or of Jobs's ability to persuade serious people that something remarkable was being built.

That lineage did not end when the hardware business did,

and it survives, oddly, in a detail visible to any software developer working on an Apple product today. When Apple eventually bought NeXT and adopted its technology as the foundation of its modern operating systems, it carried over NeXTSTEP's programming frameworks essentially intact, and with them a naming convention Apple never bothered to change: the basic building-block classes that iPhone and Mac programmers use every day — NSString for handling text, NSArray for handling lists, NSObject as the root of nearly everything — all carry the prefix NS, standing for NeXTSTEP. It is a small thing, invisible to any ordinary user, but it means that every app on every iPhone in the world today is assembled, at the code level, out of components whose names still silently credit the failed six-thousand-dollar cube that almost bankrupted Steve Jobs. The revenge machine left its fingerprints in the literal vocabulary of the software that succeeded it.

The company's most important later financing round illustrates both how seriously outside investors continued to take NeXT even as its hardware struggled, and how directly the Japanese electronics industry ended up bound into the company's fortunes. In June 1989, the Japanese camera and electronics giant Canon invested one hundred million dollars in NeXT in exchange for roughly a sixteen-and-a-half-percent stake, a sum that instantly valued the whole company at around six hundred million dollars despite NeXT employing only about two hundred people at the time and having sold hardware in the low thousands of units. Canon's commitment went beyond a passive check: the company agreed to install NeXTSTEP on its own line of workstations, extending the software's reach into the Japanese market, and Canon was already an intimate technical partner of NeXT in another sense, having supplied the optical disk drive built into the original NeXT Computer's magnesium cube — the same finicky storage technology that had done real damage to the machine's early reputation for reliability. The investment kept NeXT solvent through some of its most difficult years and gave

Jobs, at a moment when his fortune and his standing in the industry were both under serious strain, a fresh infusion of both capital and credibility from one of the most respected manufacturers in the world. Canon's bet also produced one of NeXTSTEP's more obscure commercial afterlives: for several years the operating system shipped, in modified form, on Intel-based workstations Canon sold in Japan under names like the object.station line, machines aimed at exactly the kind of technical and creative professionals NeXT itself had never quite managed to reach in sufficient numbers in the United States — a small, almost invisible extension of Jobs's software into a market his own sales force had never cracked, achieved not by NeXT's own marketing but by the deep pockets and manufacturing reach of a partner who believed, even after the hardware business collapsed in 1993, that the software underneath it all was still worth building a product around.

Jobs did not know any of this yet. What he knew, in the early 1990s, was that his revenge machine had failed, that his fortune was dwindling, that the company he had left Apple to build was a commercial disappointment kept alive on software sales to a niche market. He was, by the standard measures, a fallen figure, a has-been whose second act had flopped. And then, in a move that most people at the time regarded as a bizarre and doomed distraction, he sank a large chunk of what remained of his money into a tiny company that made computer graphics and had never turned a profit — a company that would, against all odds, make him a billionaire, teach him how to lead, and hand him the confidence and the credibility to return.

Chapter 20 — The Web on a Black Box

It is worth stopping the narrative for a chapter to sit with the strangeness of what happened at CERN in 1990, because it illuminates a truth about technology and about Steve Jobs that the triumphant later story tends to obscure. The truth is that the value of a thing is not always visible in its commercial performance, that a product can fail utterly in the market and succeed profoundly in history, and that Jobs, during the years everyone regarded as his wilderness, was building something whose worth would not be measured for decades. NeXTSTEP was a commercial failure and one of the most important pieces of software ever written, and both of those statements are true at the same time, and the tension between them is the tension at the heart of Jobs's whole exile.

Tim Berners-Lee was a software engineer working at CERN, the European particle-physics laboratory, an institution that generated staggering quantities of information and where researchers from around the world struggled constantly to share and find one another's documents. Berners-Lee's idea was elegant and, in hindsight, world-altering: a system of documents that could contain links to other documents, so that a reader could move from one to another by following the links, across different computers and different institutions, over the network — a web of information with no center and no hierarchy, in which any document could point to any other. He called it the World Wide Web, and to build the first version of it he needed a development environment powerful and flexible enough to let one person create a genuinely new kind of software quickly. He chose a NeXT Computer, and NeXTSTEP's object-oriented tools were exactly suited to the task. On that machine, in a matter of months, he wrote the first web browser (which he called WorldWideWeb), the first web server, and defined the basic protocols and formats — the addresses, the markup language, the transfer protocol — that still underpin the entire Web today. The original NeXT cube on which he did this work still exists, preserved as one of the most important artifacts in the history of computing, with a hand-written label on it reading: "This machine is a server. Do not power it down."

The reasons Berners-Lee chose a NeXT are the whole point. He did not choose it because it was popular — it was not; it was an obscure, expensive machine used by almost no one. He chose it because it was the best tool for the job, because NeXTSTEP let him build something new faster and more elegantly than any other system available, because its development environment was, quite simply, years ahead of everything else. The machine's commercial obscurity was irrelevant to its technical superiority, and it was the technical superiority that mattered when a person needed to invent the future. This is a pattern worth naming, because it recurs throughout the history of technology and throughout this book: the tools that shape the future are often not the ones that win the market of the moment, and commercial success and historical importance can diverge completely. NeXT lost the market and won a piece of history that dwarfs the market it lost.

For Jobs, the deeper significance of NeXTSTEP would not become clear for several more years, and it is one of the most satisfying reversals in his story. The operating system he had built in exile, the one that lost money for a decade, contained something Apple would eventually need so badly that the need would bring him home. By the mid-1990s, Apple was in desperate trouble in a specific and technical way: its Macintosh operating system, the classic Mac OS, had grown old and creaky, unable to do the things a modern operating system needed to do — run multiple programs robustly without one crashing all the others, manage memory properly, provide the stable foundation that serious computing required. Apple had spent years and enormous sums trying to build a modern replacement, a next-generation operating system, and had failed repeatedly and expensively; project after project collapsed, and by 1996 the company had essentially given up on building its own future operating system and had begun, humiliatingly, to shop for one to buy. And there, available for purchase, was NeXTSTEP — a mature, modern, elegant operating system, exactly the kind of foundation Apple needed, built by Apple's own exiled founder. The machine had failed, but the software had become the thing that could save the company that had cast its maker out.

It is worth pausing to correct a conflation that even careful readers often make, because it changes what Berners-Lee actually accomplished on that NeXT cube. He did not invent the internet. The internet — the underlying global network of connected computers, speaking a common protocol to pass data between machines — had existed for decades before 1990, built up through government and university research going back to the 1960s and standardized in the early 1980s. What Berners-Lee invented was a layer on top of that existing network: a system of documents connected by clickable links, addressed by a standard naming scheme, and transmitted by a standard protocol, all of which together make up the World Wide Web. The internet is the road; the Web is one particular thing you can drive on it, invented decades after the road itself, on a machine built by a man who had nothing to do with either the internet's invention or, until that moment, its history. Conflating the two erases the specific, nameable act of invention that happened at CERN in 1990, and it erases the surprising fact that the world's information network and the world's information web are separate technologies, invented at different times by different people for different reasons, that happen now to be inseparable in most people's minds.

The invention itself proceeded with unglamorous speed once Berners-Lee had NeXTSTEP's tools in hand. He had circulated a memo in 1989, titled with deliberate modesty "Information Management: A Proposal," outlining the idea to CERN management, who approved it as a low-priority side project rather than a landmark undertaking — his supervisor's now-famous notation on the memo was simply "vague, but exciting." Working with a Belgian colleague, Robert Cailliau, Berners-Lee spent 1990 building the three technologies that still define the Web today: HTML, the formatting language for pages; HTTP, the protocol for transmitting them; and the URL, the addressing scheme that gives every page on the Web a unique location. The world's first website went live on the NeXT cube on December 20, 1990, at an address — info.cern.ch — that functioned simultaneously as the first page ever published and as a manual explaining what a website even was, since no one reading it had ever encountered one before. It remained a curiosity used mostly by physicists for the better part of a year before CERN made it available to the wider public in August 1991, at which point the rest of the world could begin, slowly at first, to discover what had been built.

CERN's decision about what to do with the invention, once it existed, turned out to matter almost as much as the invention itself. In April 1993, the laboratory formally released the World Wide Web's underlying code into the public domain, placing no patents, licensing fees, or restrictions on anyone who wanted to build a browser, a server, or a website of their own. It was a choice made by a nonprofit physics laboratory with no commercial stake in the outcome, and it is the reason the Web grew, in the following years, into an open commons that anyone could build on rather than a proprietary platform controlled by a single company charging for access — the opposite, in a pointed irony, of the tightly controlled hardware-software ecosystems that Jobs himself would spend the rest of his career building at Apple. The most important software platform in history was given away for free by an institution that wanted nothing from it, on a machine made by a man whose entire business philosophy was the careful, profitable control of exactly that kind of platform.

That first page is not merely a historical curiosity gathering dust in an archive, either. CERN has kept the original address alive and has worked, for its anniversaries, to restore the site as closely as possible to how it looked and behaved in 1990 and 1991, so that a visitor today can load a page that is, in its content and structure, substantially the same one the first web browser in history ever displayed. It is a strange kind of monument — not a plaque or a preserved building, but a live, loadable, clickable web page, still running on the network it created, still answering requests from anywhere in the world, a working artifact rather than a retired one. Few inventions of comparable importance remain so directly and literally accessible to anyone curious enough to type in the address, which means that the single strangest fact about the Web's origin — that it was built to solve a document-sharing problem for physicists, on a failed businessman's failed computer — is one that anyone can go verify firsthand, in about the time it takes to load a page.

Berners-Lee did not build the Web entirely alone, and giving the Belgian engineer Robert Cailliau his due corrects a common oversimplification of the invention's early history. Cailliau, a systems engineer at CERN, joined the effort in 1990, and it was the two men working together who turned Berners-Lee's original 1989 proposal — the one his supervisor had scrawled "vague, but exciting" across — into a formal management document later that year, giving the project the institutional backing it needed to move from an unofficial side effort toward something CERN would actually support with time and resources. Cailliau also pushed, from very early on, for the project to reach beyond the NeXT machines that only a handful of CERN staff owned, and that effort produced one of the more important and least glamorous pieces of the Web's early history: a stripped-down "line-mode" browser, released to CERN's central computer users by March 1991, which sacrificed the graphical elegance of Berners-Lee's original NeXTSTEP application in exchange for something the original could never offer — the ability to run on almost any computer connected to CERN's network, not just the small number of expensive black cubes capable of running NeXTSTEP. Without that unglamorous compromise, the Web might have remained, for years longer, a beautiful demonstration confined to a technology most of the world's computer users could never touch; the line-mode browser was the bridge between an elegant invention built for one exclusive machine and a genuinely universal system that anyone, on any hardware, could eventually use.

Cailliau's contributions did not end with engineering. In May 1994 he organized the first International World Wide Web Conference at CERN, bringing together, for the first time in one room, the small community of programmers and researchers who had spent the previous three years building browsers, servers, and websites on top of Berners-Lee's original protocols. It was a modest gathering by the standards of the technology conferences the Web would later spawn, but it marked the moment the invention stopped being the private project of a physics laboratory and became the shared property of a rapidly growing community that neither Berners-Lee, nor Cailliau, nor the NeXT computer that had started it all, could any longer claim to control.

We will come to that rescue and its consequences, because they are the hinge of the entire book. But it is worth registering, here at the low point of Jobs's fortunes, the shape of what was coming, because it transforms how we read the exile. The conventional story treats NeXT as a failure and Pixar as a lucky side bet, the years between Apple and Apple as a wilderness to be endured. The truer story is that the exile was the most productive failure in the history of technology: at NeXT, Jobs built the operating system that would run every Apple product of the twenty-first century, and would also, in the hands of a physicist he never met, birth the World Wide Web; and at Pixar, which we turn to next, he would build a company that reinvented an art form, make himself a billionaire, and — most important for what came after — learn, finally, how to lead. The man who returned to Apple in 1997 was not the man who had been thrown out in 1985. He had been humbled by NeXT's commercial failure, seasoned by having to make hard, unglamorous decisions, and transformed by his experience running Pixar into a leader who understood how to nurture talent rather than merely dominate it. The wilderness did not just interrupt his story. It made the second act possible, because it made him into someone capable of the second act. And a great deal of that making happened not in the beautiful failing computer company, but in an animation studio full of people who told stories, where Steve Jobs learned patience.

Chapter 21 — The Wilderness

The years between 1985 and 1996 are usually compressed, in the telling of Steve Jobs's life, into a brief interval between the two Apple acts — the wilderness he wandered before his triumphant return. But eleven years is a long time, more than a third of his adult life, and it deserves to be understood on its own terms and not merely as a prelude. For most of it, Jobs was, by the measures the world uses, a failure and a diminished figure. NeXT was losing money and going nowhere; Pixar, for years, was a bottomless money pit that consumed his fortune with no return in sight; and the technology industry, which had once hung on his every word, had largely written him off as a burnout, a one-hit founder whose moment had passed, a man whose arrogance had cost him his company and whose subsequent ventures were flopping. There were long stretches in this period when Steve Jobs looked, to any reasonable observer, like a cautionary tale rather than a hero — the brilliant young man who peaked at thirty and spent the rest of his life failing to recapture it.

The financial reality of the wilderness was genuinely precarious for a time, which is easy to forget given how the story ends. Jobs had sold his Apple stock in 1985 and had a fortune, but he was pouring it into two companies that were both losing money, and by the early 1990s the outflow was serious enough that his wealth was declining rather than growing. He was subsidizing Pixar out of his own pocket, year after year, as it failed to find a profitable business — it tried selling expensive graphics computers (which failed), tried selling animation software, tried making commercials — and the cumulative losses ran into tens of millions of his own dollars. There were moments when he considered giving up on Pixar, when the drain seemed unsustainable, when the sensible financial move would have been to cut his losses and walk away. That he did not, that he kept funding a company most people would have abandoned, is sometimes told as a story of visionary faith, and there is some of that in it; but it was also stubbornness, an unwillingness to admit defeat, and a good deal of luck that the bet eventually paid off. Many equally stubborn people fund their failing companies straight into personal bankruptcy. Jobs happened to be funding one that turned out to have Ed Catmull and John Lasseter inside it, and a deal with Disney waiting in the future, and so his stubbornness looks like vision. Had *Toy Story* flopped, it would look like folly.

What is genuinely true, and important, is that the wilderness changed Jobs as a person and as a leader, and the change is the reason the second act succeeded where the first act had ended in disaster. The Jobs of 1985 was a prodigy who had never had to grow up professionally — who had ridden a rocket from the garage to the cover of magazines without ever learning the patient, humbling craft of actually running an organization through hard times, of managing people he could not simply bully, of making decisions whose consequences he had to live with. The wilderness taught him those things, slowly and painfully. At NeXT he learned what it felt like to have his product judgment fail in the market, to watch a beautiful machine that he was certain was great be rejected by customers, to have to abandon hardware and admit he had been wrong — an experience of failure he had never really had before and that punctured, at least somewhat, the invulnerable arrogance of his youth. And at Pixar, crucially, he learned a different model of leadership from the one he had practiced at Apple.

Pixar taught him patience, and it taught him to trust and nurture creative talent rather than to dominate it, and these lessons came from being, for once, not the smartest person in the room about the core work. Jobs knew computers; he did not know how to make an animated film, and he had the wisdom, at Pixar, to recognize that Ed Catmull and John Lasseter did, and to protect and fund and enable their work rather than to override it. He watched Catmull build a creative culture based on candor and mutual respect, a culture designed to let talented people do their best work and to give honest feedback without crushing the people receiving it — almost the opposite of the genius-or-bozo brutality Jobs had practiced at Apple. He watched Lasseter labor over stories, iterating patiently, understanding that a great film could not be willed into existence on an impossible schedule the way Jobs had tried to will the Macintosh. He learned that some things take the time they take, that a reality distortion field cannot rush a story into being, that the leader's job is sometimes to create the conditions for others' greatness rather than to impose his own. None of this made Jobs a gentle man — he remained capable of cruelty and impatience to the end of his life — but it tempered him, gave him a second register, taught him a kind of strategic patience and a respect for talent that the young Jobs had lacked. The man who would return to Apple could still be a tyrant, but he had also learned when not to be, and that difference was worth billions.

The wilderness years were not only a professional trial; they were also the period in which Jobs's most painful personal failure began, slowly and imperfectly, to be repaired, and the repair is worth including here because it complicates the redemption narrative in ways that are instructive rather than merely biographical. Jobs had a daughter, Lisa, born in 1978 to his former girlfriend Chrisann Brennan, and for years afterward he had denied paternity in the face of a paternity test that confirmed it, forcing Brennan to raise their daughter largely alone while he built Apple — even as he named the company's most ambitious early computer, with a coldness that later struck him as unbearable, Lisa. A court eventually ordered him to pay child support of three hundred and eighty-five dollars a month and to reimburse the state for the welfare payments Brennan had needed in the meantime, a settlement so far beneath what a young multimillionaire could plainly have afforded that it reads, in retrospect, less as a financial arrangement than as a measure of how completely he had chosen to look away.

What changed, during the exile, was that Jobs found his biological mother and, through her, discovered he had a biological sister he had never known existed: the novelist Mona Simpson. The two formed a close bond, and Simpson, by later accounts, worked patiently to draw her brother back toward the daughter he had spent years refusing to claim. The reconciliation that followed was neither sudden nor complete — Jobs remained, by every honest account including his daughter's own later memoir, a difficult and inconsistent father, capable of great warmth and great coldness sometimes within the same visit — but it was real. By the time Lisa was nine, Jobs had formally added his name to her birth certificate, changing her legal name to Lisa Brennan-Jobs, and she spent stretches of her adolescence living with him, an arrangement that would have been unthinkable during the years he was refusing even to acknowledge the test that had already proved what everyone around him already knew.

Alongside this slow, partial repair, Jobs was also building the family life that would anchor the rest of his years. In March 1991, in the same stretch of his life when NeXT was floundering and Pixar was still bleeding money, he married Laurene Powell in a small ceremony at the Ahwahnee Hotel in Yosemite, conducted by his longtime Zen teacher; the marriage would last the rest of his life and produce three more children, giving him, for the first time since founding Apple, a stable domestic center that did not depend on the fortunes of either company he was struggling to keep alive. It is easy to read the wilderness years purely as a chronicle of professional failure redeemed by two improbable successes, NeXT's software and Pixar's films, but the deeper transformation running underneath both was personal: a man who had spent his twenties disowning a daughter and defining himself entirely through his company was, by his late thirties, raising a family and beginning, however imperfectly, to take responsibility for the people his ambition had once let him ignore.

The popular version of Jobs's biography tends to treat the reconciliation with Lisa as a minor, mostly resolved footnote to the main story of professional exile and comeback, and that is a misreading worth correcting. It was not resolved so much as it was, like the man himself, left permanently unfinished — a wound that scarred over without ever fully healing. Lisa Brennan-Jobs made this plain to a wide audience decades later, in 2018, when she published a memoir, *Small Fry*, describing in unsparing detail a childhood spent orbiting a father who could be tender one week and coldly withholding the next. That a book reopening these wounds could still generate headlines and extended public discussion so long after Jobs's death is itself a measure of how incompletely the tidy redemption story accounts for the man; the wilderness gave Steve Jobs the professional patience that saved Pixar and, eventually, Apple, but it bought him only a partial and complicated peace with the daughter he had spent his twenties refusing to see.

The "longtime Zen teacher" who married Jobs and Laurene Powell at the Ahwahnee Hotel deserves to be named, because his influence over Jobs's inner life during the wilderness years ran far deeper than a single ceremony. He was Kobun Chino Otogawa, a Zen Buddhist priest Jobs had first sought out as a young man exploring meditation at the San Francisco Zen Center, and the relationship endured, on and off, for the rest of Jobs's life. During the exile years, Jobs periodically retreated to Tassajara, a Zen mountain monastery in the hills above the Carmel Valley, seeking in silence and long stretches of meditation some of the clarity his very public professional failures had stripped away. When Jobs proposed to Powell on New Year's Day of 1990, it set in motion a wedding that looked nothing like the corporate world he was fighting to reenter: a vegan cake shaped like Yosemite's Half Dome, Buddhist rites led by Kobun Chino Otogawa, and, once the ceremony ended, a hike into the surrounding mountains with Laurene's brothers rather than a conventional reception. It was a wedding built around the interior life Jobs had been quietly cultivating throughout the very years the business press was writing him off as a washed-up founder.

The domestic side of the wilderness had a physical setting, too, and it says something about Jobs's relationship to material things that the setting was, for years, almost deliberately unfinished. In 1984, flush with Apple stock and still near the peak of his first run at the company, Jobs had purchased the Jackling House, a sprawling seventeen-thousand-square-foot Spanish Colonial mansion in Woodside, California, designed decades earlier by the architect George Washington Smith. He lived in it for nearly ten years, through the worst of the NeXT and Pixar struggles, but by most visitors' accounts kept it strikingly, almost comically underfurnished — vast rooms with little more than a mattress and a lamp, the trappings of wealth acquired but never actually installed, as though furnishing the house properly would have been an admission of a settled, finished life that Jobs, still fighting his way back from professional disgrace, was not yet ready to claim. Decades later, after a long fight with preservationists who wanted the historic estate saved, Jobs had the mansion demolished — a coda that fits the man's exacting, often uncompromising relationship to his own surroundings: he would rather see a building he had stopped caring for erased entirely than preserved in a state he considered wrong.

There is a version of Steve Jobs's later self-mythology in which he claims the wilderness was a gift, that getting fired from Apple was the best thing that ever happened to him, that it freed him to enter one of the most creative periods of his life. In his famous Stanford commencement address, delivered near the end of his life, he made exactly this case, telling the graduates that the heaviness of success had been replaced by the lightness of being a beginner again, less sure of everything, and that this freedom let him do his best work. It is a beautiful and inspiring formulation, and there is real truth in it — the wilderness did make him, did teach him, did lead through an improbable chain to his return. But it is also, like much of Jobs's self-presentation, a retrospective smoothing of a much messier reality, the triumphant man rewriting the humiliation as a blessing because he happened to survive it and come out the other side on top. In the actual years, there was no serene confidence that it would all work out; there was a fallen prodigy pouring his fortune into two struggling companies, uncertain whether either would ever succeed, watching the industry that had once adored him move on without him. What turned that wilderness into a prologue rather than an ending was a single film, released in November 1995, about a cowboy doll and a space ranger, that would become the most successful movie of the year and make Steve Jobs, at last, spectacularly right. To understand how a struggling maker of graphics computers became the studio that reinvented animation, we have to go back to 1986, to a small division of a film company that George Lucas wanted to sell.

Chapter 22 — The Graphics Group

In 1986, Steve Jobs bought a company that made no money and had no clear path to making any, for reasons that even he could not fully articulate at the time, and it turned out to be the best investment of his life. The company was the computer-graphics division of Lucasfilm, the film company of *Star Wars* creator George Lucas, who was selling it off partly to raise cash in the wake of an expensive divorce and partly because he had no idea how to make it profitable. The division was a collection of brilliant technologists who had been building specialized computers and software for generating high-end computer graphics, and it was, in commercial terms, a burden — a research operation with a small, unprofitable business selling costly image-processing machines. Lucas wanted around thirty million dollars for it; when no buyer at that price appeared, the price fell, and Jobs eventually acquired it for around five million dollars in cash, plus a commitment to invest several million more in capital. He set it up as an independent company, and it took its name from the imaging machine it was then trying to sell: Pixar.

What Jobs thought he was buying is a matter of some dispute, and the honest answer is that his own understanding of it evolved. At the outset, he seems to have seen Pixar primarily as a hardware company — a maker of powerful graphics computers, the Pixar Image Computer, which could process visual data in ways ordinary machines could not and which he imagined selling to industries like medicine and government and film. This was consistent with who Jobs was: a builder of computers, seeing another computer company. And by that measure Pixar was, for years, a failure, because the Image Computer was expensive and specialized and sold in tiny numbers, never remotely justifying its costs. If Pixar had been only the hardware company Jobs initially thought he was buying, it would have been a straightforward disaster, another NeXT, and he would have been right to cut his losses. What saved it — what made it, eventually, one of the most beloved and valuable creative enterprises in the world — was the part of it that Jobs had not particularly valued at the purchase: the handful of people inside it who wanted to make not graphics hardware but movies.

Two of those people were the heart of everything Pixar became, and they deserve to be understood as fully as Jobs himself, because Pixar was their achievement far more than his. The first was Ed Catmull, a soft-spoken computer scientist who had dreamed since childhood of making a computer-animated film and who had spent his career pushing the boundaries of what computers could render — a technologist of the first rank, but also, unusually, a gifted and humane leader of creative people, a man who thought deeply about how to build an organization in which talented individuals could do their best work without being crushed by ego or fear. The second was John Lasseter, an exuberant animator who had been trained in the classical Disney tradition, had been fired from Disney for being too enthusiastic about the potential of computer animation, and had found a home at Pixar where he could pursue his conviction that computers were not a threat to the art of animation but a new medium for it. Lasseter understood, more clearly than almost anyone, that the technology was never the point — that no amount of rendering power mattered if the story did not make you feel something, that the audience would forgive any technical limitation for a character they loved and forgive nothing for a character they did not. Catmull provided the technology and the culture; Lasseter provided the storytelling and the soul; and together, over years, they built the capability to do something no one had ever done: to make a feature-length film entirely with computer-generated animation.

For a long time, though, this capability was a promise rather than a business, and Pixar survived on a combination of Jobs's money and small revenue streams while it figured out what it was for. It made short animated films — Lasseter's *Luxo Jr.*, a charming two-minute piece about a pair of desk lamps that became Pixar's mascot, and *Tin Toy,* which won an Academy Award for animated short — that demonstrated the artistic potential of the medium and won acclaim but earned nothing. It sold animation software. It made television commercials with its animation tools to bring in cash. And through all of this it lost money, year after year, kept alive only because Steve Jobs kept writing checks, tens of millions of dollars of his own diminishing fortune, funding a company that by any conventional analysis he should have abandoned. His reasons for continuing were mixed — genuine belief in the people, stubbornness, ego, an unwillingness to be seen to fail again after NeXT — but the effect was that Pixar survived long enough for the technology and the talent to converge on the thing they had always been building toward.

John Lasseter's path to Pixar deserves to be told in more than a single clause, because the popular shorthand — fired from Disney for being too enthusiastic about computer animation — makes it sound like a single dramatic clash of ideas, and the fuller picture is messier and more forgivable to everyone involved. Lasseter had joined Disney's animation department in 1979, fresh out of the California Institute of the Arts, and became captivated by the potential of computer graphics after seeing early test footage for the effects-heavy film *Tron*. He pitched Disney executives on adapting a children's book as a computer-assisted animated feature, and kept pushing the idea — but Disney's animation division in the early 1980s was contracting, unprofitable, and deeply skeptical of the new medium, and when a round of layoffs came in 1984, Lasseter, whose passion project had made him a visible advocate for a technology the studio's leadership did not yet believe in, was let go along with many others. It was less a firing over a single bad idea than an ordinary layoff that happened to fall on a man whose enthusiasm had made him conspicuous — a distinction that matters, because it means Disney did not so much reject Lasseter's talent as fail, for a few more years, to recognize what it was looking at.

The accident of that layoff produced one of the more improbable hinges in the whole Pixar story. Unemployed and uncertain what to do next, Lasseter attended a computer-graphics conference in November 1983 aboard the retired ocean liner Queen Mary in Long Beach, where he met Ed Catmull and Alvy Ray Smith, then running Lucasfilm's computer graphics research group — the very division Jobs would buy three years later. The two men, who had spent years trying to attract a real animator to their purely technical operation, recognized immediately what they had found, and brought Lasseter on. Within a year the group produced *The Adventures of André and Wally B.*, a two-minute short combining Lasseter's classical animation instincts with Catmull's rendering technology, and though it is little remembered today next to *Luxo Jr.* or *Toy Story*, it was the first piece of computer animation to attempt real character performance rather than mere technical demonstration — the moment the tools Catmull had spent his career building finally had a storyteller behind them worth building for.

The short's premiere reinforced the pattern. Debuted at SIGGRAPH, the computer-graphics industry's annual conference, in the summer of 1984, *André and Wally B.* reportedly drew gasps and a standing ovation from an audience of technologists who had never before seen computer-generated characters move with anything like comic timing or personality — a reaction that had less to do with the short's technical polish, which was primitive by any later standard, than with the sheer novelty of watching a computer produce something that felt alive rather than merely rendered. SIGGRAPH remains, four decades later, the venue where the computer-graphics and animation industries unveil their most significant new techniques each year, and the reception that greeted a two-minute short about a bee chasing a man out of bed is now remembered as the moment the wider technical community first understood that the Lucasfilm group had assembled something unprecedented: not just better rendering, but performance.

The episode is worth holding onto because it undercuts a comforting myth that Pixar's later biographers, and Jobs himself, sometimes let stand: that everyone involved could see the destiny of computer animation clearly from the start, that Lasseter's genius and Catmull's technology were an obviously perfect match waiting to happen. In fact the match happened because a struggling studio laid off an animator it did not know what to do with, at almost exactly the moment a struggling research group needed exactly the animator it did not yet know it was looking for. Neither institution planned the collision; both simply failed to recognize, until after the fact, what they had lost and gained. It is the same lesson this book keeps returning to in different forms — that the people who eventually look, in hindsight, like inevitable partners were, in the moment, accidents that could very easily not have happened, saved from oblivion by luck and by the particular curiosity of a handful of people willing to take a meeting with someone whose résumé did not obviously fit.

The hardware business that had originally justified Jobs's

purchase came to an ignominious and almost comically small end, a detail that sharpens just how completely the company's identity shifted away from the machines Jobs had first imagined selling. The Pixar Image Computer never found the broad commercial market Jobs had envisioned — it found niche use in specialized fields like medical imaging, where its ability to process large volumes of visual data, such as CAT scan output, proved genuinely useful to a small number of institutions — but the numbers never came close to justifying the investment, and in 1990 Jobs sold the entire hardware division to a company called Vicom Systems for a mere two million dollars, a fraction of what had been poured into it and a formal acknowledgment that Pixar's future, if it had one, would not involve manufacturing computers at all. What remained after that sale was smaller, more focused, and, it turned out, exactly positioned to become what Pixar is remembered for today: a software and storytelling operation built around Ed Catmull's rendering technology and John Lasseter's animation talent, unencumbered by a hardware business that had never worked.

That rendering technology had a name and a price tag worth recording. RenderMan, the proprietary software Pixar had developed to translate three-dimensional computer models into the finished, photorealistic frames of a movie, represented an investment on the order of fifteen million dollars by the time it was mature enough to carry the visual weight of a full feature film — money spent, like so much else at Pixar, years before there was any certainty the company would survive long enough to use it on anything but a two-minute short. When *Toy Story* finally reached theaters at Thanksgiving in 1995, it had been made for a production budget of around thirty million dollars, modest by the standards of a major studio release but an enormous gamble on an unproven medium and an untested feature-length production pipeline. The film went on to earn roughly three hundred seventy-four million dollars at the worldwide box office, a return that instantly reframed computer animation from an interesting experiment into a commercially proven category worth every major studio's attention, and that turned Pixar's subsequent public stock offering, coming barely a week after the film's release, into one of the most successful initial public offerings of the decade — the event that would make Steve Jobs, for the first time in his life, a billionaire.

The turning point was a deal with Disney. In 1991, Pixar signed an agreement with the Walt Disney Company — the studio that had defined animation for half a century and that Lasseter had once been fired from — to produce a computer-animated feature film, with Disney funding and distributing it and Pixar creating it. The terms were, from Pixar's side, not especially favorable; Disney held most of the power and most of the potential profit, as the established giant dealing with an unproven upstart. But the deal gave Pixar what it needed above all else: the resources and the mandate to finally make the feature film that Catmull and Lasseter had spent their whole careers preparing for. The film would be about toys — about what toys do when their owner is not watching, about a cowboy doll named Woody whose place as a boy's favorite is threatened by a flashy new space-ranger toy named Buzz Lightyear. It would take years of grueling work, would nearly collapse more than once, would require Pixar to invent not just the technology but the entire craft of computer-animated storytelling as it went. And when it was released, at Thanksgiving in 1995, it would change animation forever, become the highest-grossing film of the year, and set in motion the events that would make Steve Jobs a billionaire and hand him the standing to return to Apple. It was called *Toy Story*, and its making is one of the great creative adventures of the late twentieth century.

Chapter 23 — Catmull and Lasseter

To understand why Pixar succeeded where so many technically gifted companies fail, you have to understand the culture that Ed Catmull built, because Pixar's real invention was not a rendering algorithm but a way of making creative work together — and it was a way of working that stood in deliberate, instructive contrast to the culture Steve Jobs had built at Apple, and that Jobs, to his lasting credit, had the wisdom to protect rather than override.

Catmull's central insight, refined over decades and eventually written up in a book that became required reading in creative industries, was that the enemy of good creative work is not a shortage of talent but the fear and ego that prevent talented people from being honest with one another. Every creative project, he observed, begins as something bad — a first draft, a rough cut, an early version that is clumsy and wrong in a hundred ways — and the only path from bad to good runs through candid, unsparing, but non-threatening feedback, through many rounds of people telling each other the truth about what is not working. The problem is that honesty of this kind is psychologically dangerous: people are afraid to criticize, afraid to be criticized, afraid that admitting a problem will be taken as an admission of failure, and this fear, in most organizations, causes problems to be hidden until they become catastrophes. Catmull designed Pixar's culture specifically to defeat that fear. He created structures — most famously the "Braintrust," a group of the studio's best storytellers who would watch a film in progress and give the director brutally honest feedback — in which candor was expected and safe, in which the feedback was about the work and never about the person, and in which the director retained final authority so that criticism was advice rather than command. The goal was to make it possible for smart, passionate people to tell each other hard truths without the exchange curdling into ego and defensiveness.

This was, in an important sense, the opposite of how Steve Jobs operated. Jobs's method was to divide people and ideas into brilliant and worthless, to deliver criticism as devastating personal verdict, to create through fear and charisma and the sheer force of his conviction. Catmull's method was to build a system in which the fear was engineered out, in which honesty flowed because it had been made safe. And one of the most interesting facts about Steve Jobs's time at Pixar is that he largely respected Catmull's culture and did not try to remake it in his own image. He could have; he owned the company, he funded it, he had every ability to impose himself. But Jobs, at Pixar, understood something he had not understood at Apple: that he did not know how to make animated films, that the people who did were doing something he could not do and did not fully understand, and that his job was to protect and enable them rather than to override them. He handled Pixar's business — its finances, its deals with Disney, its eventual public offering — with characteristic aggression and skill, but he left the creative culture to Catmull and Lasseter, and he learned from watching it. This restraint, this capacity to recognize the limits of his own expertise and to defer to others within their domain, was new in Jobs, a fruit of the humbling wilderness, and it was one of the ways Pixar made him a better leader.

John Lasseter, for his part, supplied the thing that all of Catmull's careful culture existed to serve: story. Lasseter's conviction, which became Pixar's founding creative principle, was that technology must always serve story and never the reverse — that the point of computer animation was not to show off what computers could do but to tell tales that made audiences laugh and cry, and that a technically dazzling film with a hollow story was worthless while an emotionally true story would triumph even with primitive tools. This sounds obvious and is anything but; the history of computer graphics is littered with technically impressive, emotionally dead work made by people who fell in love with the tools. Lasseter kept Pixar oriented, relentlessly, toward feeling. He insisted that Pixar's films be about something real — *Toy Story* about the fear of being replaced and the meaning of loyalty, later films about grief, aging, memory, the passage of time — and that the characters be people (even when they were toys or fish or robots) whom the audience genuinely came to love. This insistence, more than any rendering breakthrough, is why Pixar's films succeeded, and it is a principle with a direct echo in Jobs's own philosophy of products: that the technology is never the point, that people do not care about specifications or engineering elegance for its own sake, that what matters is how the thing makes them feel. Jobs believed this about computers and phones; Lasseter believed it about films; and their shared conviction that emotion trumps technical achievement is one of the deep affinities that made Pixar and Apple, in their very different domains, expressions of the same worldview.

Catmull's account of this culture-building, when he finally set it down in writing, became required reading well beyond the world of animation, and it is worth quoting directly because his own words capture something the polished, decades-later telling can lose: the sheer discomfort of the process even when it works exactly as designed. In *Creativity, Inc.*, the book he published in 2014 with the journalist Amy Wallace, Catmull wrote of Pixar's films with a bluntness that surprised many readers expecting a celebratory account of the studio's golden run: "Because early on, all of our movies suck," he wrote, adding that he chose the blunt phrasing deliberately because "saying it in a softer way fails to convey how bad the first versions really are." It is a striking admission from the head of a studio then responsible for some of the most beloved films of a generation, and it is also the whole philosophy in miniature: the Braintrust existed not to catch occasional mistakes in otherwise strong films but to walk every single Pixar production, without exception, from an embarrassing, unworkable first draft to something audiences would eventually love, and the culture's entire design was built around making that walk survivable for the people whose work was being picked apart.

A common misunderstanding of the Braintrust, repeated in many business articles that borrow the concept without fully understanding it, is that it functioned as a kind of committee with the power to order changes — a creative oversight board that directors had to satisfy. This gets the mechanism exactly backward, and the distinction is the entire point. The Braintrust could say anything it wanted about a film in progress, however blunt, but it had no authority to compel a single change; the director retained complete and final say over every decision, and was free to ignore every note if their own judgment disagreed. What made the Braintrust work was precisely this absence of enforcement power: because directors knew they could not be overruled, they could afford to hear the harshest feedback without feeling cornered into defending territory, and because the feedback carried no threat of a mandate, it could be delivered with a bluntness that would have felt like an attack in almost any organization where the critic also held the power to force compliance. Strip away the enforcement and, paradoxically, you get more honesty rather than less.

Catmull institutionalized the same philosophy in more literal form as well, through what the studio still calls Pixar University: an ongoing, voluntary internal program open to every employee regardless of job title, offering classes taught by Pixar's own artists and outside instructors in subjects ranging from drawing and sculpture to the history of cinema, on the theory that a company whose entire business depended on creative judgment needed to keep cultivating that judgment in people whose day jobs, on paper, had nothing to do with storytelling. It is another way the same underlying belief shows up in practice: that creativity is not a fixed trait possessed only by a designated few artists but a capacity an organization can deliberately keep feeding, the same conviction that animates the Braintrust's insistence that anyone in the room, regardless of rank, might be the person who sees the fix a film needs.

The idea traveled far beyond Pixar's animation studios in the years after Catmull's book appeared, cited approvingly in business publications, adopted in modified form by software companies and design firms trying to build feedback cultures of their own, and referenced constantly in the broader vocabulary of management writing, where terms like "radical candor" and "psychological safety" became shorthand for versions of the same basic insight Catmull had spent decades refining inside a single animation studio. That a set of internal practices developed to fix a specific problem in feature-film storytelling should end up as assigned reading in business schools and engineering organizations with no interest in animation at all is itself a kind of vindication of Lasseter's founding conviction that Pixar's real innovations were never really about computers — the studio's most exported product, in the end, may not be any single film but the theory of how creative people can tell each other the truth without breaking each other.

The road to that culture ran through a company that, for its first several years, was not really in the movie business at all. Pixar began as a hardware operation, spun out of Lucasfilm's computer division and purchased by Jobs in 1986 specifically because he believed its rendering technology and its graphics hardware, not its handful of animators, were the real opportunity; the little animation unit under Lasseter existed initially to produce short demonstration films that would show off the company's expensive Pixar Image Computer to potential buyers in medicine, government, and industry, rather than to make art for its own sake. That mercantile origin makes what happened next more remarkable rather than less: even while Pixar's founders were struggling to sell computers that nobody much wanted, Lasseter's demo shorts kept overshadowing the machines they were supposed to be selling. In 1988 one of them, a two-minute film called *Tin Toy*, about a wind-up toy fleeing a destructive baby, won the Academy Award for Best Animated Short Film — the first time an Academy Award had ever been given to a film made substantially with computer animation, seven years before *Toy Story* existed even as an idea. It was a small trophy for a division that was, financially, a rounding error inside a struggling hardware company, and yet it was the first hard, external, unimpeachable evidence that Lasseter's storytelling instincts and Catmull's rendering technology, combined, were capable of something the rest of the industry recognized as genuine art rather than a technical curiosity.

Catmull's tenure at Pixar was not, however, free of the very ego and conflict his later culture-building was designed to guard against, and one of the company's earliest and most consequential ruptures involved Jobs directly. Alvy Ray Smith, who had co-founded the graphics group with Catmull at Lucasfilm and helped bring it to Pixar as an equal partner in the technology, left the company in 1991 after a shouting match with Jobs during an executive staff meeting — an argument, by later accounts, that began over something as small as who was allowed to write on a whiteboard and escalated, in the way disputes with Jobs often did, into a much larger confrontation over authority and respect within the company he had funded and now controlled. Smith's departure meant that one of Pixar's two principal technical founders was gone years before *Toy Story* ever reached a theater, a reminder that even inside the company whose whole later fame rested on teaching Hollywood how to disagree productively, its own founding partnership had, at least once, failed to survive the very kind of raw personal confrontation the Braintrust was later built to prevent.

The partnership of Catmull and Lasseter, funded and protected and business-managed by Jobs, produced over the following decades one of the most extraordinary runs in the history of film — a string of critical and commercial triumphs, *Toy Story* and its sequels, *A Bug's Life, Monsters, Inc., Finding Nemo, The Incredibles, Ratatouille, WALL-E, Up,* that reinvented feature animation, made Pixar the most respected name in the medium, and generated billions of dollars. But that run was still in the future in the early 1990s, unproven and uncertain, riding entirely on a single film that was proving agonizingly difficult to make. *Toy Story*'s production was troubled — at one low point Disney executives, unhappy with the direction, forced a reworking that nearly broke the film and the team — and its success was very far from guaranteed. Everything Pixar had built, all of Catmull's culture and Lasseter's storytelling and Jobs's years of funding, was staked on whether audiences would fall in love with a computer-animated cowboy doll. To understand what was riding on that gamble, and how completely it paid off, we turn to the making and the triumph of the film that started it all.

Chapter 24 — To Infinity

Toy Story opened in American theaters on November 22, 1995, and by the end of its run it had become the highest-grossing film of the year and one of the most acclaimed, the first feature-length film made entirely with computer animation and, more importantly, a genuinely great movie — funny, moving, beautifully constructed, beloved by children and adults alike. Its success was total and it was transformative, and it vindicated, in a single stroke, nearly a decade of Steve Jobs's stubborn funding and Ed Catmull's and John Lasseter's lifelong faith that computers could tell stories that made people feel. But the smooth triumph of the finished film conceals how close it came to disaster, and the story of its troubled making is a lesson in the very patience and creative discipline that the young Steve Jobs had lacked and that Pixar embodied.

The film nearly collapsed partway through production, in an episode that has become legend in the animation world. Disney, which was funding and would distribute the film, had considerable creative authority over it, and Disney executives pushed Pixar to make the story edgier, the characters more sarcastic and adult, in line with what they thought audiences wanted. Lasseter and his team complied, reworking the film to make Woody, the cowboy protagonist, sharper and more cynical — and the result, screened in a rough version at the end of 1993, was a disaster. Woody had become genuinely unlikeable, mean-spirited and cruel, and the whole film curdled around him; the screening was so bad that Disney halted production entirely, shutting the project down and putting Pixar's future in jeopardy. It was a moment of real crisis: the company's one shot at a feature film had produced something that did not work, and the funding partner had pulled the plug. What saved it was the response of the Pixar team, which reveals the culture Catmull had built. Rather than despairing or defending the failed version, they treated the shutdown as an opportunity to fix the fundamental problem, went back to the story, restored Woody's warmth and made his flaws sympathetic rather than repellent, and rebuilt the film around a character audiences could love. They took the honest, brutal feedback that the film was not working, absorbed it without ego, and used it to make the film great. It is exactly the process — bad first version, candid feedback, patient iteration toward good — that Catmull had designed the whole culture to enable.

The technical achievement of *Toy Story* was staggering and is easy to underappreciate now that computer animation is everywhere. In 1995, rendering a feature-length film entirely in the computer was at the absolute edge of what was possible; every frame had to be computed by banks of processors laboring for hours, the total computation running to millions of processor-hours, the technical problems of simulating light, texture, motion, and form solved essentially from scratch. Pixar had to invent much of the craft as it went — how to make computer-generated characters move with life and weight, how to light a digital scene so it felt real, how to give plastic and fabric and skin their proper texture. That the film's world was made of toys was itself a shrewd choice, because plastic toys were exactly the kind of smooth, hard-surfaced objects that 1995's computer graphics could render convincingly, where realistic humans or animals or organic textures would have looked wrong. Lasseter and Catmull matched their story to their technology's strengths, telling a tale that computers could render beautifully rather than one that would expose their limitations — a discipline that, again, echoes the whole Pixar and Apple philosophy of working within real constraints to produce something that feels flawless rather than reaching beyond them and producing something that feels broken.

But the technology, as Lasseter never tired of insisting, was not why *Toy Story* succeeded. It succeeded because it was a wonderful story about recognizable emotions — jealousy, loyalty, the fear of being replaced, the discovery that a rival can become a friend — carried by two characters, Woody and Buzz Lightyear, whom audiences fell completely in love with. Buzz's delusion that he is a real space ranger rather than a toy, and his devastating discovery of the truth, is a genuinely affecting piece of storytelling that has nothing to do with computers and everything to do with the universal experience of confronting who you really are. Children delighted in the adventure; adults recognized, underneath it, real feeling about identity and change and letting go. The film worked on every level at once, and it proved Pixar's founding thesis beyond any argument: that computer animation was not a gimmick but a new medium for the oldest of arts, and that a company built around story and protected by a healthy creative culture could produce work of lasting greatness. *Toy Story* was not just a hit; it was the beginning of a golden age, the first of a run of films that would make Pixar synonymous with quality and would reinvent an entire art form.

The scale of what *Toy Story* achieved is easier to grasp in hard numbers than in any description of technique or emotion. Pixar made the film for roughly thirty million dollars, a modest budget even by the standards of 1995, and it went on to return nearly three hundred seventy-four million dollars in worldwide ticket sales — a multiple that would have been remarkable for any film and was almost unthinkable for one whose entire cast, sets, and props existed only as numbers inside a render farm rather than actors and physical sets. Its opening weekend alone brought in a little over twenty-nine million dollars, nearly matching the film's entire production cost in three days, a fact that told Disney and Pixar both, immediately and unambiguously, that they had underestimated what a genuinely good story, rendered in an unfamiliar medium, could do at the box office. Set against the years of risk Jobs had absorbed simply keeping Pixar's lights on through a decade in which the company had produced nothing resembling a hit, the return on investment was staggering, and it retroactively justified every dollar of patience that had, at the time, looked like stubbornness rather than foresight.

The film also planted something smaller and stranger that would long outlive its opening-weekend records: a shot of a minivan bearing the license plate A113, a nod to the classroom number at the California Institute of the Arts where Lasseter and several future Pixar and Disney directors had studied animation together as students before any of them had ever touched a computer. It was such an unassuming little joke, tucked into a single background frame, that almost no one watching the film in 1995 registered it at all — and yet the studio's animators liked it enough to slip the same four characters onto a sign, a badge, or some stray prop in every Pixar film that followed, a private, recurring signature of the classroom where much of the studio's creative leadership had first learned to tell stories on paper, long before Catmull's machines gave them a way to tell them in three dimensions. It is a small detail, but a telling one: for all the emphasis, in Pixar's own telling of its history, on computers and rendering and technical firsts, the joke its own animators chose to bury in every subsequent film pointed backward, not to a laboratory, but to an art school classroom — a quiet acknowledgment, repeated without fail for decades, of exactly where the storytelling instincts that made the machines worth building had actually come from.

The near-collapse deserves more than a passing mention, both because its specifics are more dramatic than the polished retrospective suggests and because it is one of the clearest illustrations in Pixar's history of a principle the studio would spend the rest of its existence proving: that a computer-animated film lives or dies on story, not rendering. On November 19, 1993, Pixar screened what its own staff came to call the "Black Friday reel" for Disney executives, including animation chairman Jeffrey Katzenberg, who had spent months pushing the production toward a sharper, more cynical, more adult sensibility than Lasseter's team had originally intended. The version they screened delivered exactly what had been requested, and it was a disaster: Woody, reimagined as a status-anxious bully rather than a beloved leader, spent much of the reel behaving with open cruelty toward the other toys, at one point shoving Buzz Lightyear out of a window in a fit of jealous spite and showing no remorse afterward. Even Tom Hanks, who had already recorded Woody's dialogue, reportedly disliked what the character had become. Disney executives were appalled, and rather than requesting further notes, they halted the production outright — an almost unthinkable outcome for a studio's first feature film, one that put Pixar's entire future, and years of Jobs's money, in immediate jeopardy.

What makes the episode instructive rather than merely dramatic is what it reveals about where the crisis actually lived. The rendering, the lighting, the technical machinery Pixar had spent years inventing were never the problem; the animation looked exactly as intended, the toys moved and looked precisely the way the technology allowed. The entire catastrophe was one of character and story — a sympathetic hero had been rewritten, under outside pressure, into someone audiences could not love — and it could only be fixed by going back to the writing, not the code. Pixar was given roughly two weeks to prove the film could be saved, and the team used the time to strip out the cynicism and rebuild Woody as a character whose flaws were rooted in insecurity rather than malice, so that his jealousy of Buzz became understandable rather than repellent. Production resumed in February 1994, more than a year behind where Pixar had hoped to be, on essentially the same technology and the same computers as the version that had just been shut down for failure — proof, if any were needed, that the difference between the film that flopped in the screening room and the film that would go on to become a phenomenon was entirely a matter of story, exactly as Lasseter had always insisted it must be.

The Black Friday reel itself still exists in Pixar's archives, and though it has never been officially released, footage and detailed descriptions of it have circulated for years in documentaries and retrospectives about the studio, treated by animation historians as a kind of cautionary artifact — the film *Toy Story* could have been, preserved specifically as a reminder of how close the whole enterprise came to failing for reasons that had nothing to do with technology. It is a small but sharp irony that the lesson which saved the film — that audiences forgive technical limits but not emotional falseness — was exactly the lesson the young Steve Jobs of the first Apple act had never quite learned, and exactly the one the Pixar years were teaching him in real time, on someone else's film, in preparation for the moment he would need to apply it to computers again.

That near-miss makes the triumph that followed two years later all the more striking. When Pixar went public on November 29, 1995, floating just under seven million shares a week after *Toy Story*'s release, the stock closed its first day of trading at thirty-nine dollars a share, giving the young company a market valuation of roughly a billion and a half dollars and Jobs, who still held the great majority of its stock, a personal fortune to match. By most accounts, one of the first calls he made afterward was to his friend Larry Ellison, the Oracle co-founder who was already a billionaire — a small, telling detail, since it meant that Jobs's first instinct upon finally reentering the ranks of the spectacularly wealthy was to share the news with one of the only people he knew who could fully understand what it meant to have just crossed that particular threshold.

For Steve Jobs, the film's success was also, and immediately, a financial and personal transformation of the first magnitude, and he moved to capitalize on it with characteristic decisiveness. He had spent years and much of his fortune keeping Pixar alive, holding the overwhelming majority of its stock; now, with a blockbuster film and a relationship with Disney, Pixar had a real business at last, and Jobs took it public. The Pixar initial public offering, timed to occur just after *Toy Story*'s triumphant release in late 1995, was a sensation; the stock soared, and Steve Jobs's stake in the company he had bought for a few million dollars and subsidized for a decade was suddenly worth well over a billion dollars. In a single week, the fallen prodigy of 1985 — the man the industry had written off, whose NeXT was failing, who had poured his money into an animation company most people thought was folly — became a billionaire, richer than he had ever been at Apple, vindicated in the most spectacular and public way possible. The wilderness was over, though he did not yet know how completely. He had a fortune again, a triumphant company, and something he had lacked since 1985: the standing and the confidence of a winner. And he was about to need all of it, because the company that had cast him out was dying, and it was about to come, desperate and humbled, to ask for his help.

Chapter 25 — Billionaire

Before we follow Steve Jobs back to Apple, it is worth completing the Pixar story, because its later chapters reveal how much the company had changed him and how the wilderness had, in the end, made him whole. The relationship between Pixar and Disney, which had begun with the underdog Pixar signing an unfavorable deal with the mighty Disney, would over the following decade completely reverse, until it was Pixar that held the power — and the reversal would culminate in a transaction that made Steve Jobs the largest individual shareholder of the Walt Disney Company and placed him on its board, a resolution so improbable that it reads like fiction.

After *Toy Story*, Pixar's run of success continued and accelerated. Film after film — *A Bug's Life*, *Toy Story 2*, *Monsters, Inc.*, *Finding Nemo*, *The Incredibles* — earned both critical acclaim and enormous box-office returns, and with each success Pixar's leverage grew and Disney's grew relatively weaker. Disney's own in-house animation, meanwhile, was struggling; the studio that had defined the art form was producing a string of underperforming traditional films even as its partner Pixar produced hit after hit. By the early 2000s the balance of creative power in animation had shifted decisively: Pixar was the golden studio, the one that could not seem to make a bad film, and Disney needed Pixar far more than Pixar needed Disney. Jobs, negotiating on Pixar's behalf, drove increasingly hard bargains, and the relationship between him and Disney's chief executive, Michael Eisner, deteriorated into open hostility. At one point Jobs publicly threatened to take Pixar elsewhere when its distribution deal with Disney expired, a threat that carried real weight given Pixar's track record and that put enormous pressure on a Disney whose own animation had faltered.

The impasse broke when Eisner was pushed out of Disney and replaced by Bob Iger, a more conciliatory and strategically shrewd executive who understood two things clearly: that Disney's animation crown had passed to Pixar, and that the smartest move was not to fight Pixar but to acquire it. In 2006, Iger negotiated Disney's purchase of Pixar for around seven and a half billion dollars in stock. The deal was a triumph for everyone: Disney got the best animation studio in the world and, crucially, got Ed Catmull and John Lasseter installed to revitalize Disney's own moribund animation division (which they did, spectacularly, presiding over a Disney animation renaissance). Pixar's people got the resources and stability of Disney with, at least in principle, protection for their culture. And Steve Jobs, whose Pixar stock was the bulk of the purchase price, received Disney shares that made him the single largest individual shareholder of the Walt Disney Company — the company whose animator John Lasseter had once been fired, the entertainment giant that Pixar had begun its life as a junior partner to — and a seat on Disney's board. The underdog had, in twenty years, quietly swallowed the giant, or been swallowed on the underdog's own terms, and its owner had become a media mogul on top of being a technology titan.

The mechanics of the 2006 deal are worth setting down precisely, because the numbers capture just how completely the balance of power had reversed since Pixar signed its first, unequal contract with Disney in 1991. Disney paid roughly seven and a half billion dollars in stock — about six billion three hundred million dollars net of the cash sitting on Pixar's own balance sheet — exchanging two-point-three Disney shares for every Pixar share outstanding. Jobs, who by then owned just under half of Pixar's stock outright, emerged from the transaction holding roughly seven percent of Disney, a stake worth nearly four billion dollars, which made him not merely rich from the deal but the single largest individual shareholder in one of the most storied entertainment companies in American history — a strange culmination for a man whose only prior connection to Hollywood had been buying a struggling special-effects division nobody else wanted.

The deal's terms extended beyond stock and cash in ways that mattered more, in the long run, than the price. As part of the agreement, John Lasseter became chief creative officer of both Pixar and Walt Disney Animation Studios at once, while Ed Catmull took the equivalent role as president of both organizations — meaning the two men who had spent two decades building Pixar's culture from nothing were handed direct authority over the very animation department that had once fired one of them and treated the other's technology as a curiosity. They used the authority to import Pixar's methods, including the Braintrust, into Disney's own famous but faltering animation studio, and the results showed up within a few years in a string of Disney films that recaptured a commercial and critical success the studio had not consistently managed since its own earlier golden age — an outcome that would have seemed almost too neat to believe in 1984, when Lasseter had been shown the door for caring too much about the very medium he eventually used to help save the company that fired him.

By Bob Iger's own later account, he broached the idea to Jobs directly and simply, framing it, in a phrase Iger would later use as the title of his own memoir, as having "a crazy idea" — buy Pixar outright rather than continue fighting over distribution terms — a pitch remarkable mainly for how little salesmanship it required once Iger had correctly read that Jobs, tired of an increasingly personal feud with Eisner, wanted a partner who would let Pixar's culture remain intact rather than a rival determined to out-negotiate it. That reading proved correct, and the acquisition is still cited, in business-school treatments of corporate dealmaking, as a rare case of a giant company essentially agreeing to be led, in the specific and narrow domain of animation, by the much smaller studio it had just purchased.

The renegotiation of Pixar's contract with Disney did not wait for the 2006 acquisition; it began years earlier, in the middle of production on *Toy Story 2*, in an episode that shows how quickly the balance of power had already begun shifting even before Pixar's string of hits made the imbalance undeniable. Under Pixar's original, lopsided 1991 agreement, Disney held the right to make sequels to Pixar's characters without Pixar's involvement at all, and its plan, initially, was to send Woody and Buzz straight to the direct-to-video market that had proven lucrative for Disney's other sequels — a lower-budget, lower-prestige release that would have kept *Toy Story*'s characters alive commercially without costing Disney a theatrical marketing budget or counting against the small number of feature films Pixar was contractually obligated to deliver. Jobs, who by 1997 had Pixar's finances and *Toy Story*'s success behind him, pushed to renegotiate the entire arrangement, seeking a deal that would let Pixar finance its own films and split profits far more evenly than the original contract allowed. Disney agreed to a new five-picture deal that shared costs and profits close to equally, a startling concession from a studio that, six years earlier, had dictated terms to a Pixar with essentially no leverage at all.

Toy Story 2's own fate settled the direct-to-video question in a way that had nothing to do with contracts and everything to do with quality. In late 1997, Disney executives

Joe Roth and Peter Schneider sat down at Pixar to review story reels and early animation from what was still, on paper, a modest sequel destined for video store shelves, and what they saw changed their minds entirely: the work was strong enough, and the economics of producing it were expensive enough, that a direct-to-video release no longer made business sense. Disney reversed course and gave *Toy Story 2* a full theatrical release, and the film that had begun life as a contractual afterthought went on, in 1999, to match and in some respects exceed the achievement of the original — proof, once again, of the same lesson Pixar's whole history kept teaching in different forms, that quality made on its own terms had a way of overturning whatever modest commercial plans had been drawn up for it in advance. The irony was not lost on Pixar's own staff, several of whom recalled watching the same Disney executives who had proposed shelving the film to video return, weeks later, treating it as prestige work worthy of a full theatrical campaign — a reversal of opinion that had cost Disney nothing to make and that cost Pixar nothing to accept, but that told everyone involved, plainly, which side of the partnership now held the leverage.

It is worth resisting, however, the temptation to leave the story here as an uncomplicated fairy tale in which the underdog triumphs and everyone lives happily ever after inside a newly harmonious creative empire. Lasseter's tenure atop both studios ended in 2017, when he took a leave of absence and then departed the company altogether the following year after Disney received complaints about inappropriate workplace conduct — a coda that Jobs, who had died in 2011, never lived to see, and one that complicates any reading of the Pixar-Disney merger as a purely triumphant capstone to the partnership Jobs, Catmull, and Lasseter had built. The technology and the culture Catmull had spent decades designing outlived the specific men who built it, for better and for worse, which is itself an unglamorous but honest coda to a chapter that could otherwise read like an uninterrupted victory lap.

The Pixar experience is essential to the story of Apple because of what it did to Steve Jobs as a leader and a person, and the change is measurable in the difference between his first and second acts at Apple. At Pixar he had learned patience — the patience to let a film take the years it needed, to let Catmull and Lasseter work in their own way, to build something great slowly rather than willing it into existence overnight. He had learned to trust and protect creative talent rather than merely to dominate it, to recognize the limits of his own expertise, to lead by enabling others' genius as well as by imposing his own vision. He had experienced, at NeXT, the humbling of real failure, and at Pixar the vindication of patient faith, and the combination had matured him in ways that the meteoric young founder of the first Apple act had never had the chance to mature. He had also, not incidentally, become wealthy and successful on his own terms, independent of Apple, which meant that when he did return to Apple he would return not as a supplicant desperate for the job but as a proven winner who did not need it — a position of strength that would shape everything about how he handled the rescue.

There is a temptation to tidy all this into a redemption arc: the arrogant young man is humbled, learns his lessons, and returns wise and whole. The reality was more partial, as reality always is. Jobs remained, to the end of his life, capable of stunning cruelty, of dividing the world into geniuses and bozos, of humiliating employees and denying credit and behaving in ways that damaged the people around him. The wilderness tempered him but did not transform him into a gentle or an easy man; the reality distortion field never switched off; and the same intensity that made him a great builder made him, often, a painful person to be near. What changed was not his fundamental nature but his range and his judgment: he had acquired a second register, a capacity for patience and for trusting others that he could deploy when it served him, and a hard-won understanding of failure and of the limits of pure will. He was still Steve Jobs. But he was a more complete version, one who had learned, in eleven years outside the company he had founded, the things he had needed to know and had been too young and too triumphant to learn the first time. And now, in late 1996, the moment was arriving for those lessons to be tested, because Apple — the company that had cast him out, that had spent a decade proving it could not thrive without him — was on the edge of collapse, and its desperate leadership was about to make the decision that would bring Steve Jobs home.

Chapter 25½ — The Lost Decade

While Steve Jobs wandered his wilderness at NeXT and Pixar, the company he had co-founded lived through a slow-motion decline that is worth examining in its own right, because it is the necessary dark background against which his return shines, and because it is a case study in how a great company loses its way. The Apple of 1985 to 1996 — the decade between Jobs's exile and his return — is the forgotten Apple, the Apple most histories skip past on the way from the Macintosh to the iMac, and yet it is essential to understanding both what Jobs restored and what a company becomes when it loses the thing that made it special. For eleven years Apple was run without its founder, by a succession of professional managers, and it declined from the most exciting company in technology to a struggling also-ran on the edge of bankruptcy, and the story of how it happened is instructive.

The decline was not immediate, and this is part of the lesson. For several years after Jobs left, Apple prospered — indeed, under John Sculley it enjoyed a period of strong growth and profits, riding the Macintosh's maturation into a genuinely useful machine and, above all, riding the desktop-publishing revolution that made the Mac indispensable to designers, publishers, and creative professionals. The Macintosh, freed of its original crippling limitations as later models added memory and hard drives and expansion, became a real and valuable product, and Apple made good money selling it to the creative markets where its graphical strengths mattered most. By some measures, the Apple of the late 1980s was doing well. But beneath the prosperity, the company was losing the qualities that had made it distinctive, and the losses would prove fatal. Without Jobs's product vision and his ferocious discipline of focus, Apple began to drift, to proliferate products, to lose the clarity about what it was and what it should make. The company grew complacent and bureaucratic, its margins fat, its culture increasingly corporate and cautious, its sense of mission fading into the ordinary business of maximizing quarterly results.

The strategic failures compounded over the decade, and several stand out as decisive. Apple failed, catastrophically, to respond to the rise of Microsoft Windows, which brought a graphical interface — cruder than the Mac's but adequate — to the vast installed base of cheap IBM-compatible computers, steadily eroding the Mac's key advantage and its market share. Apple's response was slow, defensive, and legalistic; it sued Microsoft over the interface, lost, and meanwhile watched Windows conquer the world. It clung to its premium prices and its closed model even as the market moved decisively toward cheap, open, commodity computing, and it failed to find a way to compete. It launched a confusing proliferation of products — dozens of Macintosh models with baffling names, plus ventures into printers, cameras, and the ill-fated Newton handheld — spreading its resources thin and losing the focus that had been Markkula's founding principle. It burned through its lead in the graphical interface, its head start in ease of use, its brand's association with innovation, until by the mid-1990s Apple was a company living on past glories, its market share shrinking, its products increasingly undistinguished, its future in doubt.

The leadership churn of the period reflected and accelerated the decline. Sculley, having won the company from Jobs, presided over both the good years and the beginning of the bad, and was himself ousted in 1993 as problems mounted. He was succeeded by Michael Spindler, an executive who struggled to stem the decline and who explored, unsuccessfully, selling the company. Spindler gave way in 1996 to Gil Amelio, brought in as a turnaround specialist, who found a company in far worse shape than he had imagined — hemorrhaging money, its operating system obsolete and its replacement a failure, its product line a mess, its market share in free fall, its very survival in question. Amelio made some necessary hard decisions, but the company was in a death spiral, posting enormous losses, and the business press had begun writing Apple's obituary in earnest. It was Amelio who, searching desperately for a modern operating system to replace the failed in-house efforts, made the decision that would inadvertently save the company and end his own tenure: he bought NeXT, and brought Steve Jobs back through the door.

The lawsuit against Microsoft over the Macintosh interface, mentioned only in passing so far, deserves its specific shape recorded, because losing it as badly as Apple did was one of the clearest signals of the company's declining fortunes during these years. Apple filed suit in 1988, arguing that Microsoft's Windows had copied the "look and feel" of the Macintosh's graphical interface beyond what its original licensing agreement permitted. The case dragged on for six years, and when the Ninth Circuit Court of Appeals finally ruled in 1994, Apple lost almost every claim; the court held, in effect, that copyright law could not grant Apple something close to a patent on the general idea of a graphical desktop, windows, and icons, and Apple's own earlier licensing deal with Microsoft undercut its position further. Apple won only a narrow, almost consolation-prize ruling concerning icons borrowed from a Hewlett-Packard product. The company that had once been so certain of its interface's uniqueness that it sued a competitor for imitating it could not, in the end, convince a court that the imitation was even illegal — a legal defeat that mirrored, almost too neatly, Apple's broader commercial defeat at Microsoft's hands during the same years.

The Newton handheld, mentioned earlier as one of the decade's expensive distractions, deserves a fairer hearing than the era's popular mockery gave it, because the common memory of the device — a punchline about garbled handwriting recognition, immortalized in a *Doonesbury* comic strip and later a *Simpsons* joke — obscures how technically consequential the project actually was. To build the processor the Newton needed, Apple, in 1990, joined a small British firm called Acorn Computers and the chip maker VLSI Technology to spin off a joint venture called Advanced RISC Machines, contributing roughly three million dollars for its share; the new company's first product was the processor that shipped inside the Newton MessagePad in 1993. The Newton itself was a commercial failure, killed a few years after Steve Jobs returned to Apple in 1997. But the chip architecture built to power it was not: renamed simply ARM, the company Apple had helped seed went on to design the low-power processor architecture that today runs the overwhelming majority of the world's smartphones, including, in its modern Apple Silicon form, the iPhone and the Mac. Apple spent the 1990s mocked for a handwriting-recognition joke and, almost as a byproduct, helped plant the seed of the chip technology its entire product line would run on three decades later.

Gil Amelio, arriving as the decade's last pre-Jobs chief executive, inherited both of these legacies and mostly could not fix either. Advisers urged him to shut the money-losing Newton division outright; he instead spun it into a stand-alone unit in 1996, a hedge that satisfied no one and delayed rather than avoided the product's eventual cancellation. His broader numbers told the same story of a company in genuine crisis rather than mere stagnation: Apple's revenue fell roughly fifteen percent in fiscal 1996 alone, at a moment when the rest of the personal-computer industry was growing by nearly eighteen percent, a divergence stark enough that it was no longer possible to describe Apple's troubles as an industry-wide downturn the company happened to be caught up in. It was losing, specifically and severely, to competitors who were otherwise thriving. Amelio would be gone within eighteen months, forced out by the board in July 1997, but not before making the one decision that mattered more than anything else he did or failed to do: buying NeXT, and with it, Steve Jobs.

It is worth pausing on that ARM detail specifically, because it undercuts the tidy notion — convenient both to the era's critics and to Apple's later triumphant self-mythology — that the lost decade produced nothing of value at all. The company's culture, focus, and morale were genuinely broken during these years, and its products were genuinely mediocre by its own historic standard. But the underlying research and hardware investments made during the depths of the decline did not vanish when the company's fortunes did; some of them simply waited, dormant, for a future that the executives who funded them never got to see, in exactly the way NeXTSTEP waited in obscurity for the operating-system crisis that would make it valuable again. Apple's worst decade was not, in every sense, wasted. It was simply investing in a future its own leadership at the time could not have described, one product generation and one processor architecture ahead of where anyone in 1990 was looking.

The operating-system disaster deserves a fuller accounting than the mere mention of Copland's failure allows, because Apple did not simply try once and fail; it tried, at enormous expense, in overlapping and increasingly desperate ways for nearly a decade before finally admitting it would have to buy a solution from outside. As early as 1988, while the Macintosh was still selling well and the crisis was not yet visible to most of the company's own executives, Apple began an ambitious internal effort, code-named Pink, to design an entirely new, modern, object-oriented operating system meant to replace the aging Mac OS at its foundations. By 1991 Sculley was telling the press that Apple had already written a million and a half lines of code toward it, but Pink kept expanding in ambition and slipping in schedule, and in 1992 Apple folded the effort into a new joint venture with IBM, and later Hewlett-Packard, called Taligent — a separate company, staffed with hundreds of engineers, built for the sole purpose of finishing what Pink had started. Taligent never shipped a product that mattered. By some estimates, its three corporate parents spent more than a hundred million dollars on the venture before quietly dissolving it into IBM in 1998, a sum that bought Apple nothing except further proof that the operating system it needed could not be willed into existence by committee, however well-funded. Even as Taligent limped along, Apple hedged its bets with a second, parallel, in-house effort — the project that would become Copland, intended for release as the next major version of the Mac OS — and that project, too, collapsed under the weight of its own ambition and Apple's institutional dysfunction, canceled in 1996 without ever reaching customers. Two entirely separate, richly funded attempts to solve the same problem, pursued for the better part of a decade, produced nothing that Apple could ship, which is the specific, concrete shape that the company's larger loss of focus and discipline took at the engineering level.

The human cost of the drift showed up just as clearly at the top of the org chart. When Apple's board finally moved against John Sculley in the summer of 1993, the proximate trigger was a dismal first quarter set against a brutal industry-wide price war, but the deeper frustration, among directors and executives alike, was that Sculley had by then become visibly more absorbed in the Newton — the handheld project he had personally championed and unveiled with great fanfare in 1993 — than in the unglamorous business of running a computer company whose core product line was losing ground every quarter. Sculley resigned as chief executive that June, kept the chairman's title for a few more months, and left the board entirely by October, and it is one of the era's small, sour ironies that the leader ousted partly for over-investing his attention in the Newton would depart just as the device he had bet so much personal credibility on arrived to the derision that would follow it for years. His successor, Spindler, inherited both the price war and the Newton's disappointing debut, and had no more success reconciling the two than Sculley had.

The lost decade is, in the end, the strongest possible argument for the thing this book has been careful not to overstate — the indispensability of Steve Jobs — and it is worth being precise about what it proves and what it does not. It does not prove that Apple was nothing without Jobs, because Apple did survive and even prosper for years after he left, and because the company's eventual revival depended on many people besides him. But it does prove that the particular magic that made Apple extraordinary — the product vision, the design obsession, the discipline of focus, the willingness to make bold bets and to say no, the sense of mission and identity — was, to a remarkable degree, bound up in Jobs, and that without him the company drifted toward the mediocrity and eventual crisis that afflicts most firms that lose their distinctive edge. The Apple of the lost decade was a competently managed company that had forgotten what it was for, and it declined accordingly, until it stood at the brink of death. What Jobs restored, when he returned, was not just good management — the company had had that — but the soul, the vision, the focus, the identity that competent management alone could not supply. The lost decade shows what Apple was without those things, and it makes the second act, when it came, look less like a lucky turnaround and more like the restoration of something essential that had been missing for eleven years.

Chapter 26 — Buying NeXT

By 1996, Apple Computer was dying, and everyone in the industry could see it. The company that had once defined personal computing had spent a decade losing ground to Microsoft Windows, which had brought a graphical interface — cruder than the Mac's, but good enough, and running on cheap, standardized, IBM-compatible hardware made by dozens of competing manufacturers — to the vast majority of the world's computer users. Apple's market share had dwindled to single digits and was still falling. Its products had lost their edge, proliferating into a bewildering, incoherent line of dozens of barely distinguishable models with confusing names. Its finances were bleeding red; it was posting enormous losses and burning through cash. Its executives had cycled through failure after failure — Sculley had been pushed out in 1993, his successor Michael Spindler had floundered, and now Gil Amelio, brought in to turn things around, was presiding over a company that many observers frankly expected to go bankrupt or be sold for parts. Business magazines ran cover stories on Apple's imminent death. Michael Dell, asked what he would do if he were running Apple, famously said he would shut it down and give the money back to the shareholders. The company that had launched the personal-computer revolution was, by any sober measure, circling the drain.

At the technical heart of Apple's crisis was a problem that would, with beautiful irony, become the door through which Steve Jobs walked back in. Apple's operating system, the software that made the Macintosh a Macintosh, had grown dangerously obsolete. The classic Mac OS was old, and it lacked the fundamental capabilities that a modern operating system required — it could not properly run multiple programs at once without them interfering with each other, it managed memory primitively so that a single misbehaving program could crash the entire machine, it had none of the robust foundations that serious computing in the late 1990s demanded. Apple knew it needed a modern replacement, and had known for years, and had tried repeatedly and expensively to build one. Project after project — a next-generation operating system codenamed Copland chief among them — had consumed vast resources and collapsed under its own weight, defeated by the difficulty of the task and the dysfunction of the company. By 1996, Apple had essentially admitted defeat: it could not build the modern operating system it needed, and so it would have to buy one from someone else. Amelio put out the word that Apple was shopping for an operating system to serve as the foundation of its future, and the search became one of the pivotal decisions in the company's history.

Two main candidates emerged. One was a company called Be, founded by a former Apple executive named Jean-Louis Gassée, which had built an elegant modern operating system called BeOS. The other was NeXT, and NeXTSTEP — Steve Jobs's operating system, the one built in exile, the one that had failed commercially but was, technically, one of the best operating systems in the world, mature and modern and exactly the kind of foundation Apple needed. The competition between Be and NeXT for Apple's rescue contract is a wonderful piece of business drama, complete with Gassée reportedly overplaying his hand on price, believing Apple had no alternative and could be squeezed. But the deeper truth is that NeXT offered Apple something Be could not: not just an operating system, but Steve Jobs. And in late 1996, Apple chose NeXT. It agreed to acquire NeXT for a sum in the neighborhood of four hundred million dollars, bringing NeXTSTEP in-house to become the foundation of Apple's next-generation operating system — and bringing, with it, the company's exiled co-founder, back through the door eleven years after he had walked out.

The elegance of this reversal is almost too perfect, and it is worth savoring because it is the structural keystone of the entire Steve Jobs story. The man who had been humiliated and cast out of Apple in 1985 returned in 1996 not as a beggar asking for his old job back, but as the owner of the thing Apple most desperately needed, selling his old company its own salvation at a price of hundreds of millions of dollars. The operating system he had built out of spite, in a venture everyone considered a failure, turned out to be the one asset that could save the company that had rejected him — and so his return was not a favor granted to him but a purchase made by a desperate Apple, on terms that reflected Apple's need and Jobs's leverage. NeXTSTEP would become, over the following years, the technical basis of Mac OS X, and its DNA would run inside every Macintosh, and later inside every iPhone, iPad, Apple Watch, and Apple TV — every product Apple would ever ship in the twenty-first century would be, at its software core, a descendant of the operating system Steve Jobs built during his exile. His revenge on the company that fired him was to become the foundation it could not live without. No screenwriter would dare it.

The precise terms of the deal are worth pausing on, because they are more interesting than the round number usually quoted. When Apple's board signed off in December 1996, the agreement called for $429 million in cash plus roughly 1.5 million shares of Apple stock — not, as it is often simplified, an even four hundred million — and the transaction closed on February 7, 1997, formally folding NeXT's engineers and technology into Apple. Before the papers were signed, Apple ran what insiders called a "bake-off," setting BeOS and NeXTSTEP side by side and asking its own engineers to judge which could be shaped into the Mac's future operating system fastest and most reliably. Jean-Louis Gassée, believing Apple had nowhere else to turn, is said to have priced Be's technology aggressively, confident he held the stronger hand. NeXT's team, by contrast, could offer something Be could not match at any price: a complete, mature, already-shipping operating system, battle-tested for a decade — and the man who had built it.

The bake-off itself has a specific date and a considerably more lopsided texture than the phrase suggests, and both are worth setting down. Apple's senior executives gathered on December 10, 1996, to watch Gassée and Jobs each make a final case for their technology, and by multiple accounts the meeting was hardly a contest at all by the time it ended. Gassée, apparently convinced that Apple had no real alternative and that the deal was already his to close, gave what witnesses later described as a perfunctory presentation that offered the assembled executives little they had not already heard; Jobs, by contrast, arrived with Avie Tevanian in tow to walk through NeXTSTEP's technical merits in detail and made, by every surviving account, an unmistakably more compelling case. Gassée compounded the miscalculation on price: he reportedly held out for something in the neighborhood of two hundred seventy-five million dollars for Be, while Apple was unwilling to go beyond roughly two hundred million, a gap that a company genuinely desperate for a modern operating system might have been expected to close quickly if BeOS had truly been the stronger technical option. It never closed, and NeXT — priced, in the end, higher than Be's own asking figure — got the deal anyway, because Apple's engineers were persuaded that NeXTSTEP was simply the better foundation to build on, whatever the price difference implied about relative confidence.

Amelio's own account of what he told Apple's board when he brought them the NeXT recommendation captures, better than any retrospective gloss, just how little romance was actually involved in the decision at the moment it was made. He did not sell the acquisition to his directors as a visionary masterstroke; by his own later description, he told them bluntly that he was not going to stand there and claim the deal was worth the price Apple was about to pay, but that Apple had let its operating-system strategy collapse so completely that the company was nearly out of options, and NeXT was the least bad one available. It is a useful corrective to any telling of this moment that casts Amelio as either a fool who stumbled into rescuing Apple or a visionary who saw Jobs's genius coming — the man who actually sat in the room describes a far more ordinary and more believable calculation, a board approving an expensive purchase not because it promised salvation but because the alternative, doing nothing, promised something considerably worse. That the same meeting also happened to reunite Jobs with the company that had cast him out eleven years earlier was, by every contemporary account, incidental to the business logic in the room — a coincidence of timing that only looks inevitable in hindsight.

It is tempting, in hindsight, to imagine Jobs plotting his triumphant return from the moment the acquisition talks began, but the contemporary record resists so tidy a script. Gil Amelio, who personally negotiated the NeXT purchase and who would be gone from Apple within eight months of signing it, always maintained that he saw Jobs's advisory role exactly as it was billed to the public — a technical consultant brought in to help NeXTSTEP graft cleanly onto the Mac, not a shadow chief executive quietly waiting for his moment. Amelio later wrote his own account of those months, and his evident astonishment at how quickly the ground shifted beneath him in the summer of 1997 is part of what makes the episode so striking: a company that believed it was hiring a consultant discovered, within a matter of months, that it had hired its next chief executive, largely because its board looked at the two men in the room and could no longer see a reason to keep the one whose name was not on the building he had co-founded. The myth worth retiring, then, is not that Jobs wanted to come back — of course he did — but that the NeXT deal was a chess move he alone orchestrated from exile. It was, more accurately, a rescue that Apple's own executives designed and negotiated because they were out of better options, and Jobs's ascension to the top job followed from Apple's continuing collapse under Amelio rather than from any clause written into the NeXT purchase agreement.

There is a stranger footnote buried in NeXT's own history that makes the eventual reversal even richer. Years before Apple came calling, in 1990, a British researcher named Tim Berners-Lee sat down at a NeXT workstation in a physics laboratory in Switzerland and used it to write the software for the world's first web server and the first web browser — meaning that the very same NeXTSTEP operating system Apple would later buy as a rescue plan had already, quietly, midwifed the invention of the World Wide Web. NeXT's commercial failure as a hardware company had obscured just how much serious, foundational computing had been done on its machines by people who valued its engineering long after the wider market had written NeXT off as a boutique curiosity for university labs and Wall Street trading desks.

The deepest proof of how completely NeXTSTEP became Apple's operating system is not a boardroom fact but a coding one, and it survives in plain sight in the work of every Apple software developer today. Open the reference documentation for macOS or iOS and the foundational classes are still wrapped in a two-letter prefix: NSString,

NSArray, NSObject, NSDictionary. That "NS" is not decorative — it stands for NeXTSTEP, a fossil of the 1996 acquisition preserved in the source code running inside the iPhone in your pocket, more than a quarter-century after the company that built it was absorbed into Apple. Alongside the software came key people who would prove just as durable an inheritance: Avie Tevanian, NeXT's head of software engineering, and Jon Rubinstein, who had also worked with Jobs at NeXT, both crossed over to Apple and became central architects of Mac OS X and, in Rubinstein's case, of the hardware engineering that would soon produce the iMac and the iPod. Every app on the App Store, whether written by a lone hobbyist or an engineer at a trillion-dollar company, still calls out, in its very syntax, to the operating system Steve Jobs built during the years everyone assumed he was finished.

At first, Jobs returned in a limited capacity — as an adviser to Amelio, brought in as part of the NeXT acquisition to help with the transition, with no formal executive authority and, ostensibly, no intention of taking over. But anyone who knew Steve Jobs, and anyone who understood the dynamics of the situation, could see what was coming. Apple was failing, Amelio was not turning it around, the board was losing faith, and here, back inside the company, was its charismatic co-founder — a man who now had the credibility of Pixar's triumph behind him, the standing of a proven winner, and an intimate understanding of what had made Apple great and what had been lost. It was only a matter of time. Over the first half of 1997, as Apple's losses mounted and Amelio's position crumbled, Jobs maneuvered — quietly, deniably, but unmistakably — and in the summer of 1997 the board removed Amelio and turned to Jobs, who agreed to step in as interim chief executive. He gave himself the mocking title "iCEO," and he took no meaningful salary, famously accepting one dollar a year, positioning himself as the reluctant savior rather than the ambitious returnee. The exile was over. Steve Jobs was, once again, running Apple, twelve years after being thrown out of it — and the company he had come back to was, by many estimates, ninety days from insolvency. What he did in those first ninety days, and the years that followed, would become the most celebrated corporate turnaround in the history of business.

Chapter 27 — iCEO

When Steve Jobs took control of Apple in the middle of 1997, the company was, by his own later account, perhaps ninety days from bankruptcy, and the actions he took in his first months back are a master class in focus, nerve, and the willingness to make brutal decisions fast. The turnaround he engineered is one of the most studied episodes in modern business, and its lessons come down, again and again, to a single principle that Mike Markkula had written on a page twenty years earlier and that Jobs now applied with ferocious discipline: focus. To save Apple, Jobs did not add; he subtracted. He cut, and cut, and cut, until what remained was small enough to be excellent.

The most famous of his cuts was to the product line, and it captures his whole method. Apple in 1997 made dozens of different computer models, a sprawling, incoherent tangle of Performas and Power Macs and PowerBooks with overlapping capabilities and baffling names, so many that Jobs, by his own account, could not figure out which one to recommend to his own friends. He found this intolerable and clarifying at once. He drew, on a whiteboard, a simple two-by-two grid: two columns, Consumer and Professional; two rows, Desktop and Portable. Four boxes. Apple, he decreed, would make four great computers — one for each box, one superb machine for each of the four kinds of customer — and it would kill everything else. It was a staggering reduction, the elimination of the overwhelming majority of the company's products in a single stroke, and it terrified people inside Apple who could not imagine the company surviving on four machines. But the logic was Markkula's logic and it was correct: a small company bleeding to death could not afford to spread its limited talent and resources across dozens of mediocre products; it had to concentrate everything on making a few products great. The four-quadrant strategy focused Apple's engineering, its marketing, and its manufacturing, and it made possible the string of hit products that followed. Saying no to a thousand things, Jobs said, is what focus means, and focus is what he brought back to a company that had lost it.

He cut far more than products. He killed the licensing program under which Apple had allowed other manufacturers to build "clone" Macintosh computers — a strategy Apple had adopted in a doomed attempt to imitate the Windows model of spreading its software across many hardware makers, and which Jobs regarded as suicidal because the clones cannibalized Apple's own hardware sales without expanding the market, and because they violated his deepest conviction that Apple must control both the hardware and the software, the whole widget, to deliver a great experience. He ended the clone program abruptly and expensively, buying out the largest cloner, and reclaimed Apple's exclusive right to make Macintosh computers. He canceled projects, killed the Newton handheld (a product he had personal contempt for, associated with the Sculley era), slashed research efforts, and reduced the company to a tighter, more focused, more controllable organization. He reorganized ruthlessly, pushed out people he regarded as second-rate, and installed his own leadership, including, crucially, an operations executive he would soon recruit named Tim Cook, whose mastery of manufacturing and supply chains would clean up Apple's bloated, money-losing operations and become one of the pillars of the company's revival.

The scale of the human cost behind these cuts is easy to lose in the celebratory shorthand of "focus," and it is worth stating plainly. In the spring of 1997, months before Jobs formally took the reins, Apple laid off roughly three thousand employees, close to a quarter of its total workforce, in response to a disastrous quarterly loss — a wrenching reduction that fell across engineering, marketing, and administrative staff alike and that set the tone for the ruthlessness with which Jobs would continue paring the company down once he was fully in charge. Among the projects that did not survive the following year's continued cuts were two that had once been treated, inside Apple, as strategically important: OpenDoc, an ambitious and expensive effort to let users build documents out of interchangeable software components as an alternative to Microsoft's own document technology, and Cyberdog, an OpenDoc-based suite of internet applications that Apple had introduced with some fanfare only a year earlier. Jobs killed both without ceremony in 1997, reportedly telling the engineers responsible for OpenDoc, in characteristically blunt language, that Apple's previous management had effectively "put a bullet through its head" — a line that captured, better than any strategy memo could, his contempt for projects that consumed engineering talent on ambitious technical ideas with no coherent path to a product people would actually buy. The Advanced Technology Group that had incubated OpenDoc and much of Apple's other blue-sky research was itself largely dismantled in the same purge, on the theory that a company fighting for survival could not afford research divisions pursuing interesting problems disconnected from products.

What makes this round of cuts worth dwelling on, beyond the raw numbers, is how directly it enacted the same philosophy that produced the four-quadrant product grid, at a level far less visible than a whiteboard presentation to the press. Killing OpenDoc and Cyberdog did not generate headlines the way discontinuing entire computer lines did, and neither project was widely known outside the industry press that covered Apple closely. But the logic was identical: a struggling company with finite engineering talent could not simultaneously build four great computers, rebuild an operating system around NeXTSTEP, and sustain a set of ambitious, unproven middleware technologies that had failed to attract meaningful outside developer support in the years since their introduction. Something had to give, and Jobs showed no more sentimentality toward internal engineering projects that had absorbed years of other people's work than he did toward whole product lines carrying his own company's name. The willingness to kill ambitious, technically interesting work that did not serve a clear, sellable purpose was, in its way, as important to the turnaround as anything that happened on stage.

Cook's recruitment is itself a small case study in Jobs's persuasive power, and Cook has told the story many times in the years since, including in a widely quoted 2010 commencement address at his alma mater, Auburn University. Cook was, at the time, a rising operations executive at Compaq, then one of the most successful computer companies in the world, while Apple was a byword for corporate failure; by his own account, "any purely rational consideration of cost and benefits lined up in Compaq's favor." And yet, Cook said, "no more than five minutes into my initial interview with Steve, I wanted to throw caution and logic to the wind and join Apple," because his intuition told him this was a once-in-a-lifetime chance to work alongside a creative genius and help resurrect a great American company. Cook joined in March 1998, at thirty-seven, as senior vice president of worldwide operations, and within a few years he had done for Apple's factories and warehouses what Jobs was doing for its products: eliminated almost all of its inventory, closed plants, and turned a company that assembled its own computers into one that outsourced manufacturing with a discipline rivaling the best in the industry.

The numbers behind the turnaround, once they arrived, were as dramatic as the rhetoric that preceded them. Apple's fiscal year 1997 — the year that ended just weeks after Jobs took the interim chief executive title — closed with a net loss of just over one billion dollars, one of the largest in the company's history and the culmination of the losses that had piled up under Spindler and Amelio. Fiscal 1998, Jobs's first full year back in charge, closed instead with net income of roughly three hundred million dollars: a swing of well over a billion dollars in a single year, achieved not through some new blockbuster product — the iMac had only just shipped, in August of that fiscal year — but overwhelmingly through the unglamorous work of cutting costs, killing products, ending the clone program, and forcing a chaotic company into a small number of coherent priorities. It remains one of the fastest corporate reversals of fortune in American business history, and it happened before most of the products people now associate with Apple's revival had even reached store shelves.

It is worth correcting a version of this story that has calcified into myth: that Jobs single-handedly and instantly transformed Apple through sheer force of charisma, waving away complexity with a whiteboard and a speech. The truth is less magical and, in its way, more instructive. The four-quadrant strategy took months of internal argument and painful layoffs to execute; the clone buyout required protracted negotiation and a large cash payment; and the operational discipline that actually stopped the bleeding — squeezing suppliers, slashing inventory, renegotiating contracts — was largely the unglamorous work of operations people like Cook, brought in and empowered by Jobs but not personally performed by him. Jobs's genius in this period was less about doing every job himself than about ruthlessly identifying the few things that mattered, hiring people who could execute relentlessly on each one, and refusing to be talked out of unpopular decisions by an organization accustomed to compromise. The whiteboard moment made for a better story than the eighteen months of hard, patient management that actually followed it, but it was the eighteen months that saved the company.

Jobs also grasped, in his first months back, that Apple's problem was not only operational but psychological and strategic — that the company had lost its identity, its story, its sense of what it was for — and he moved to restore that as forcefully as he cut costs. He understood that Apple could not win by competing with Windows on Windows's terms, by being a cheaper or faster maker of commodity boxes; it could only survive by being different, by being the company for the people who wanted something better and more beautiful and more human, the creative ones, the rebels. This conviction produced, within his first months back, one of the most important marketing campaigns in corporate history — "Think Different" — which we will come to in its own chapter, and which was less an advertising campaign than an act of collective self-definition, a reminder to Apple, its customers, and the world of who Apple was supposed to be. Jobs's turnaround was as much about restoring belief as about cutting costs. He had to convince a demoralized company that it could win, a skeptical public that Apple was not dying, and a wary developer community that it was worth continuing to make software for the Mac. His genius for storytelling, for making people believe in a vision, was as essential to the rescue as his willingness to slash the product line.

The financial results came faster than almost anyone expected. Within a year, Apple had returned to profitability; the losses that had threatened to sink it turned to gains, the cash bleed stopped, and the company that had been given up for dead was, suddenly, alive again and growing. The turnaround was real and rapid, and it established, beyond any argument, that the thing Apple had been missing for twelve years was exactly the thing the board had removed in 1985: Steve Jobs's product vision, focus, and force of will. But before we reach the products that would make the revival spectacular — the iMac, and then the whole cascade of the digital hub — we have to understand one more decision from these desperate early months, a decision so counterintuitive, so seemingly self-humiliating, that Jobs was booed for it on stage by Apple's own faithful, and that nonetheless may have been the single move that most ensured Apple's survival. He made peace with the enemy. He stood in front of a hall full of Mac loyalists and told them that Apple's great rival, the company they had defined themselves against for two decades, the maker of the Windows they despised, was going to invest in Apple and keep making software for it — and that the era of thinking Apple could only win if Microsoft lost was over. It was one of the bravest and most clear-eyed things he ever did.

Chapter 28 — The Microsoft Truce

At the Macworld Expo in Boston in August 1997, Steve Jobs stood on a stage before an audience of Apple's most devoted followers and announced that he had made a deal with the devil. Apple, he told them, would be entering into a partnership with Microsoft — the company that Apple loyalists regarded as the great enemy, the maker of the inferior Windows that had stolen the Macintosh's ideas and conquered the world with them, the corporate villain against which Apple's entire identity was defined. And when Bill Gates's face appeared, enormous, on a screen above the stage, beamed in by satellite to explain the deal in his own words, the audience did something that has become one of the iconic moments of Apple history: they booed. They booed Bill Gates, and by extension they booed the deal, and Jobs stood there absorbing the hostility of his own most loyal customers, because he understood something they did not: that this humiliating-looking truce was, in cold strategic terms, one of the smartest and most necessary things Apple could possibly do.

The specifics of the deal were these. Microsoft would invest one hundred and fifty million dollars in Apple, buying non-voting stock — a vote of confidence, and cash, for a company that badly needed both. More importantly, Microsoft committed to continuing to develop its software for the Macintosh, and specifically to keep making Microsoft Office — the suite of Word, Excel, and PowerPoint — for the Mac for a period of years. The two companies settled a long-running set of patent disputes, agreeing to a cross-licensing arrangement that ended their legal warfare. And Apple agreed to make Microsoft's Internet Explorer the default web browser on the Macintosh, a concession that mattered in the browser wars of the era. On its face, to an Apple loyalist, it looked like surrender — like Apple crawling to its enemy, taking its money, and giving up ground. That is why they booed.

But Jobs understood the real situation with a clarity his booing fans lacked, and the clarity is a lesson in strategic maturity that the younger, more ideological Jobs might not have possessed. The truth was that Apple in 1997 could not survive without Microsoft's software. Microsoft Office was essential; the ability to run Word and Excel and to exchange files seamlessly with the Windows world was not a nice-to-have but a requirement for the Macintosh to be a viable business and personal computer. If Microsoft had decided to stop making Office for the Mac — and there were people at Microsoft who wanted to, and it was a real possibility given how small and troubled the Mac market had become — the Macintosh would have lost its most important software and might well have died. Apple needed Microsoft's continued commitment to the platform far more than Microsoft needed anything from Apple. Jobs's genius was to recognize this dependency clearly, to stop treating Microsoft as an enemy to be vanquished and start treating it as a partner whose cooperation Apple required, and to secure that cooperation, plus a badly needed cash infusion and a settlement of the patent disputes, in a single deal. It was the act of a leader who could set aside ego and ideology to do what the company's survival required.

There was also a deeper strategic insight embedded in the moment, one Jobs articulated on the stage as he tried to calm his booing audience, and it marked a genuine break from the zero-sum thinking that had characterized Apple's culture. The idea that Apple could only win if Microsoft lost, Jobs said, was a destructive fantasy that Apple had to abandon. "We have to let go of this notion that for Apple to win, Microsoft has to lose," he told them. Apple did not need to destroy Microsoft to succeed; it needed to make great products and build a healthy business, and it could do that in a world where Microsoft also thrived. The two companies served overlapping but distinct needs, and the market was large enough for both. This was a profound reframing for a company whose entire self-image had been built on being the rebel against Microsoft's empire, and it reflected the matured Jobs, the one who had learned from Pixar and NeXT that survival and success came from building great things rather than from defeating enemies. He was asking Apple to grow up, to stop defining itself by opposition and start defining itself by what it made.

The scene itself is worth reconstructing in a little more detail, because the theater of it tells you as much as the substance. Jobs, only weeks into his role as interim chief executive, walked onto the Macworld Boston stage in August 1997 to deliver his first major keynote, and partway through it he told the crowd he had "a special guest with me today, uh, via satellite downlink" — and Bill Gates's face, magnified many times larger than life, filled the screen behind him. The audience's reaction was instant: laughter, scattered applause, and, rising above both, a wave of boos loud enough that Jobs had to work to keep the room with him. It is one of the few moments in Apple's history captured on video where Jobs looks genuinely uncomfortable in front of his own crowd, visibly working to sell a decision he knew, in the moment, his most devoted fans did not want to hear. He did not back down from it, and he did not pretend the discomfort wasn't there; he simply kept explaining, patiently, why the deal was necessary, which is part of why the moment has endured as a case study in leading an audience somewhere it does not want to go.

The terms of the settlement, laid out that day, went well beyond the headline investment. Microsoft agreed to buy one hundred fifty million dollars of Apple stock at market price — non-voting shares, with an agreement not to sell for at least three years, a structure designed to signal confidence without handing Microsoft any influence over Apple's board. Microsoft also committed to producing Microsoft Office for the Macintosh for a period of years, the two companies settled a tangle of patent lawsuits through cross-licensing, and Apple agreed to make Internet Explorer the default browser on the Mac. None of this was charity, and Jobs never pretended it was; it was a negotiated exchange of things each company needed from the other, struck at the exact moment Apple's negotiating position was weakest.

A common retelling of this moment casts it as Microsoft magnanimously "saving" a helpless Apple out of goodwill, but that framing gives Redmond too much credit and Jobs too little. Microsoft had its own reasons to want Apple alive: an antitrust-wary Microsoft, then under increasing scrutiny from federal regulators for monopolistic behavior in the PC operating-system market, benefited from being able to point to a surviving, independent competitor, however small, as evidence that the market was not entirely its own. Jobs understood this leverage and used it, extracting a package of commitments — the Office pledge above all — that mattered far more to Apple's survival than the cash did. The truce was less a rescue extended out of Gates's generosity than a trade struck between two parties who each had something the other badly wanted, negotiated by a returning executive shrewd enough to see that the appearance of surrender could conceal the reality of a very good deal.

The patent settlement folded into the truce was not a minor housekeeping item, and its backstory gives Jobs's negotiating position a harder edge than the headline of "a hundred fifty million dollar investment" suggests. Years before the Boston stage, Apple had sued Microsoft and Intel, alleging that a small contractor called San Francisco Canyon Company had been used as a conduit to smuggle several thousand lines of Apple's own QuickTime video code into Microsoft's competing Video for Windows software — a case Apple had pursued patiently through years of discovery, and one in which, by the time the two companies sat down in 1997 to negotiate a broader peace, Apple's lawyers believed they were holding genuinely damaging documentary evidence. That leverage, invisible to the audience booing Bill Gates's face on the screen above Jobs, was very much present in the room where the actual terms were hashed out, and it helps explain why a company as dominant and as litigious as Microsoft was willing to write Apple a check and commit to years of continued Office development rather than simply let Apple's software business wither on its own. The publicly announced hundred fifty million dollars in stock was, by later industry estimates, dwarfed by what Microsoft ultimately paid out to Apple over the following years in licensing fees tied to the settlement — sums that some reports placed in the hundreds of millions and, cumulatively, well beyond a billion dollars — money that had far more to do with a patent dispute over stolen video code than with any goodwill gesture toward a fallen rival.

Seen in that light, the moment on the Macworld stage looks less like an act of grace extended by a triumphant Microsoft to a defeated one and more like the public unveiling of a settlement whose real terms had been fought over, line by line, in a lawsuit that predated the stage show by years. Jobs understood, as his booing audience did not, that Apple was not merely accepting Microsoft's charity but collecting on a genuine legal claim while simultaneously securing the platform commitment — continued

Office development — that Apple's survival actually required. It is a detail that rarely survives in the popular retelling of the booing crowd, in which Microsoft is cast simply as a merciful conqueror and Apple as a supplicant — a version of the story that flatters Redmond's generosity while erasing the legal spadework that made the generosity considerably less voluntary than it appeared.

The line Jobs used to calm the booing crowd that day has outlived the specific dispute it addressed and become one of the most quoted sentences in Apple's history: "We have to let go of this notion that for Apple to win, Microsoft has to lose," he told them, adding that "for Apple to win, Apple has to do a really good job" on its own merits, and that if competitors chose to help along the way, "that's great, 'cause we need all the help we can get." It is a sentiment that could just as easily describe Apple's later relationships with erstwhile rivals — the recording industry it once threatened, the carriers it later depended on, the app developers it both empowers and constrains — and it marks the moment Jobs stopped running Apple as a wounded insurgency and started running it as a company confident enough to coexist with competitors rather than define itself entirely in opposition to them.

There is an irony in the Microsoft truce that deepens with time, and it is worth naming. Bill Gates and Steve Jobs had one of the most consequential rivalries in the history of business — two men born in the same year, who had risen together, whose companies had shaped the personal-computer era in opposition to each other, and whose philosophies could hardly have been more different. Gates believed in software that ran on anyone's hardware, in licensing widely, in the open, messy, dominant model that had made Microsoft the most powerful company in technology; Jobs believed in controlling the whole widget, hardware and software together, in the closed, integrated, beautiful model that had made Apple distinctive and, for years, marginal. In 1997, Gates's model had won decisively; Windows ran the world, and Apple was a struggling niche player kept alive partly by Microsoft's charity. And yet within fifteen years the positions would reverse in the most dramatic way imaginable: Apple, following Jobs's integrated model, would become the most valuable company in the world, worth many times what Microsoft was worth at the peak of the disparity, while the personal computer that Microsoft dominated would be eclipsed by the mobile devices that Apple defined. The booing crowd in Boston could not have imagined it. Neither, perhaps, could Jobs. But the deal he made that day, humiliating as it looked, kept Apple alive long enough to get to the products that would vindicate his whole philosophy — and the first of those products was only a year away, a translucent, curvaceous, candy-colored machine that would announce, to a skeptical world, that Apple was not only alive but interesting again, and that would introduce the world to the designer whose partnership with Jobs would define the golden age to come.

Chapter 29 — Think Different

In 1997, as Apple clawed its way back from the edge, it launched an advertising campaign that did something advertising almost never does: it told the truth about the company's soul and, in doing so, helped the company remember what that soul was. The campaign was called "Think Different," and it consisted, in its purest form, of black-and-white photographs of great creative and intellectual rebels of the twentieth century — Albert Einstein, Bob Dylan, Martin Luther King Jr., Mahatma Gandhi, Picasso, Amelia Earhart, John Lennon, and many others — accompanied by the words "Think Different" and, in its fullest expression, a piece of prose-poetry that has become one of the most quoted texts in the history of marketing.

"Here's to the crazy ones," the text began. "The misfits. The rebels. The troublemakers. The round pegs in the square holes. The ones who see things differently. They're not fond of rules, and they have no respect for the status quo... While some may see them as the crazy ones, we see genius. Because the people who are crazy enough to think they can change the world are the ones who do." Steve Jobs was deeply involved in the creation of the campaign, and he is said to have wept when he first saw the finished piece, and it is easy to understand why, because the text is, transparently, about him and about the company he had co-founded and been thrown out of and come back to save. Apple was casting itself, and its customers, as the crazy ones, the misfits, the rebels who saw things differently and changed the world — and it was doing so at the moment of its greatest vulnerability, when it was closest to death, as a defiant assertion of identity in the face of near-extinction.

The genius of "Think Different" was that it did not talk about products at all. It did not mention a single computer, list a single specification, make a single claim about speed or price or features. It was pure brand, pure identity, an argument not about what Apple made but about what Apple was and, by extension, about who its customers were. To buy an Apple product, the campaign implied, was not merely to purchase a tool; it was to align yourself with a tradition of creative rebellion, to declare yourself one of the people who thought different, who saw things others could not, who might be crazy enough to change the world. This was the "1984" mythology, restated for a new era and a new crisis — Apple as the rebel, the individual, the creative outsider against the gray conformity of the mainstream — and it worked because it tapped into something people genuinely wanted to feel about themselves. The campaign restored Apple's sense of purpose internally, reminding a demoralized company of what it stood for; it reminded loyal customers why they had loved the brand; and it announced to the wider world that Apple was back, and that it was still, defiantly, itself.

It is worth pausing to reckon honestly with the "Think Different" campaign, because it sits at the exact intersection of Apple's genuine idealism and Apple's brilliant salesmanship, and the two are genuinely difficult to separate. On one reading, the campaign is inspiring and true: Apple really did attract creative people, really did make tools that empowered artists and designers and writers and thinkers, really was founded by rebels who thought different and changed the world. On another reading, it is one of the most sophisticated pieces of manipulation in the history of commerce: a corporation appropriating the images of Gandhi and King and Einstein — people who had nothing to do with Apple, some of whom stood for values quite at odds with mass consumer capitalism — to sell computers, flattering customers into believing that a purchasing decision was an act of rebellion and self-expression. Both readings are correct, and the discomfort of holding them together is the discomfort of understanding Apple. The company genuinely made empowering creative tools and genuinely attracted brilliant, unconventional people, and it also genuinely used the mythology of rebellion and individuality as one of the most effective marketing weapons ever devised, selling conformity of a kind — the conformity of everyone buying the same beautiful products — under the banner of nonconformity. Apple's rebellion was real and Apple's rebellion was a brand, and the brilliance and the unease of the company both live in the fact that it was never quite possible to tell where one ended and the other began.

The campaign's creation was messier than its polished final form suggests, and the messiness complicates a common myth about its origin — that it sprang, fully formed, from Jobs's own poetic sensibility. The words were written at Apple's longtime advertising agency, TBWA\Chiat\Day, where the "Crazy Ones" script is credited to the copywriters Rob Siltanen and Ken Segall, and the "Think Different" line itself is attributed to another member of the agency team, Craig Tanimoto, who also proposed pairing the slogan with portraits of twentieth-century iconoclasts. Jobs's role was that of an unsparing editor and final arbiter rather than sole author: by the account of people who worked on it, his first reaction to an early cut of the commercial was blunt and unflattering — he is reported to have said it was advertising agency nonsense and that he had wanted something closer in spirit to a work of real cinema. Only after revisions did he come around to the version that finally aired. The finished commercial, narrated by Richard Dreyfuss over black-and-white footage of Einstein, Gandhi, Dylan, Lennon, Picasso, Amelia Earhart, and more than a dozen other figures, debuted on September 28, 1997, and went on to win an Emmy Award for outstanding commercial the following year.

This corrects a persistent flattening of the story into a solo act of Jobsian genius. What actually happened is closer to Apple's usual pattern of collaborative craftsmanship pushed relentlessly by an executive with near-absolute veto power and impossibly high standards: a team of skilled writers and art directors generated the raw material, and Jobs's contribution was to reject draft after draft until the surviving version met a bar that satisfied him, a process that by several accounts left agency staff exhausted and occasionally furious, and that nonetheless produced work considerably sharper than what would have emerged from either party working alone. The myth of the lone visionary obscures how much of Apple's best work — the campaign, and later the products themselves — was actually the product of exactly this friction: talented outside collaborators pushed past their own first instincts by a client who refused to settle.

One detail of the commercial's production that rarely makes it into the campaign's now-standard telling concerns the narration itself, and it says something about how carefully even Jobs's own voice was weighed as a creative choice rather than assumed as the obvious one. Apple's longtime creative director at the agency, Lee Clow, argued at one point that Jobs himself should read the words on camera — or at least in voiceover — reasoning that having the newly returned, once-exiled co-founder speak the lines about crazy ones and misfits and rebels would carry an extra layer of meaning, a living embodiment of the very idea the commercial was selling. A version was in fact recorded with Jobs's own voice reading the script, and by several later accounts it existed as a genuine alternative all the way through the production process. In the end, the version that aired nationally used Richard Dreyfuss's practiced, resonant delivery instead, a choice that let the words function as pure myth-making rather than as a specific man's self-description — the difference between a company describing an ideal and its own chief executive appearing to describe himself in the same breath, a distinction subtle enough that reasonable people on the creative team disagreed about which version worked better.

The print campaign that ran alongside the television commercial extended the same roster of faces into magazines and billboards, using large-format black-and-white portraits with only the Apple logo and the words "Think Different" in the corner, no product, no price, no specification anywhere on the page. Among the figures who appeared across the television spot and the print advertising were the puppeteer Jim Henson, pictured with Kermit the Frog in a rare combination of a real person and his most famous creation in the same frame, and the opera soprano Maria Callas, chosen alongside scientists, artists, and political figures as further proof that the campaign's definition of genius deliberately reached across fields that had nothing to do with computers or even with each other. The breadth of the roster — spanning music, science, civil rights, aviation, film, and dance — was itself part of the argument the campaign was making: that the impulse to think differently was not a trait confined to inventors or engineers, and that Apple, by extension, belonged in the company of people whose achievements had nothing to do with technology at all. It was an audacious claim for a computer company teetering on the edge of bankruptcy to make about itself, and the fact that audiences broadly accepted the claim, rather than scoffing at the presumption of it, is itself a measure of how skillfully the whole campaign was constructed.

It is also worth noting what the campaign conspicuously never claimed, because the omission was as calculated as anything it included. None of the historical figures used in the commercial had endorsed Apple, used a Macintosh, or had any commercial relationship with the company; several, including Gandhi and King, held views about consumerism and material acquisition that sat awkwardly beside their use to sell computers, a tension media critics raised at the time and that Apple never really answered, because there was no answer that did not undercut the campaign's own premise. Apple's response, in effect, was simply to let the images do the persuading and to let viewers resolve the tension themselves, which most of them did by finding the campaign moving rather than troubling — a testament to how effectively the juxtaposition of image, music, and Dreyfuss's measured, sincere narration overrode the interpretive objections a more skeptical audience might have raised on paper.

Two and a half decades later, "Think Different" remains a fixture of advertising-school curricula and of Apple's own self-mythology, still referenced by name whenever the company wants to signal continuity with its founding spirit — a sign that the myth-making the campaign performed for Apple in 1997 was durable enough to outlive the specific products, and even the specific chief executive, it was created to rescue.

"Think Different" also marked the reemergence of Steve Jobs as the master of Apple's public identity, and it established the tone of the whole second act. Everything Apple would do over the following fifteen years — the product launches, the retail stores, the packaging, the advertising, the relentless cultivation of an image of taste and creativity and human-centered design — would flow from the sensibility that "Think Different" crystallized. The campaign was, in a sense, a statement of the strategy Jobs had brought back to Apple: that the company would not compete on price or specifications, would not try to be the cheapest or the most powerful, but would win by being the most desirable, by making products that people did not merely use but loved, by selling an identity and an experience rather than a commodity. It was a bet that in a world of increasingly interchangeable technology, the differentiator would be design, brand, and feeling — that people would pay more, and stay loyal, for products that made them feel a certain way about themselves. That bet would prove, over the next decade and a half, to be one of the most lucrative in the history of business. But a brand campaign, however brilliant, is only a promise, and a promise has to be kept by actual products. Apple's "Think Different" advertising told the world that Apple was the company for the creative rebels. Now Apple had to make something that lived up to it — a real product, a computer, that would be as distinctive and desirable as the campaign claimed the company to be. That product arrived in 1998, and it was unlike any computer the world had seen: a friendly, translucent, teardrop-shaped machine in a startling shade of blue-green, designed by a soft-spoken Englishman whom Jobs was about to make the most important designer in the world.

Chapter 30 — The iMac

In May 1998, Steve Jobs unveiled the iMac, and it did not look like a computer. Every personal computer of the era was a beige box, a rectilinear tower or a flat pizza-box case in the same dull off-white plastic, sitting inertly on or under a desk, radiating the message that it was a serious, boring, corporate machine. The iMac was a curvaceous, translucent teardrop in a shade Apple called Bondi blue, a blue-green like tropical seawater, through which you could see the ghostly shapes of the electronics inside. It was an all-in-one, with the monitor and computer fused into a single rounded body, a handle molded into the top as if inviting you to pick it up and carry it. It was friendly, playful, almost edible, and it looked like it had arrived from a future that was more fun than the present. It announced, more loudly than any advertising could, that Apple was alive, that it was different, and that it intended to make computers beautiful.

The iMac was the first major product of the partnership that would define Apple's golden age: the collaboration between Steve Jobs and a British industrial designer named Jonathan Ive, known as Jony. Ive had actually been at Apple for years before Jobs returned, laboring in a design studio whose work the failing company had largely ignored, frustrated and on the verge of leaving. When Jobs came back, he discovered Ive and recognized in him a kindred spirit and a rare talent — a designer who cared about objects with the same near-religious intensity Jobs did, who believed in simplicity and craft and the emotional power of physical form, and who was capable of translating Jobs's taste and vision into manufacturable reality. Jobs elevated Ive, gave him unprecedented power and resources, and made him one of the most important people in the company; and the partnership between Jobs's vision and product judgment and Ive's design genius would produce, over the following thirteen years, the most influential run of consumer-product design in modern history. The iMac was its opening statement, and it bore Ive's fingerprints in every curve.

The iMac made a series of bold, controversial choices that captured the returning Apple's philosophy, and the most consequential of them was about the future rather than the present. The machine had no floppy disk drive — the removable magnetic disks that had been the standard way of moving files and installing software for two decades, and that every other computer still included. Apple simply left it out, a decision that struck many observers as reckless and arrogant, because customers relied on floppy disks and there was no obvious replacement. But Jobs and Ive were betting on the future: they believed the floppy disk was obsolete, that the internet and new technologies would make it unnecessary, and that a truly forward-looking computer should shed the dead weight of the past even before the world was quite ready. In its place, the iMac embraced a new connection standard called USB, then barely used, and by building a popular computer around USB, Apple helped make it the universal standard it remains today. This pattern — Apple removing a beloved, familiar technology before the market was ready, betting on the future, absorbing the criticism, and being proven right — would recur again and again over the following decades, from the floppy drive to the optical disc to the headphone jack, and it began with the iMac. The willingness to amputate the past, to force the future by refusing to accommodate obsolescence, became one of Apple's signature and most divisive habits.

Commercially, the iMac was exactly the hit Apple desperately needed, and its success did something as important as the revenue it generated: it proved that the turnaround was real and that Jobs's philosophy worked. The machine sold in large numbers, bringing new customers to Apple — including many who had never owned an Apple product, drawn in by the design and the friendliness and the sheer desirability of the thing — and demonstrating that people would pay a premium for a computer that was beautiful and easy to use, that design was not a frivolous luxury but a decisive competitive advantage. Apple soon released the iMac in a rainbow of additional colors, and the sight of these candy-colored machines in homes and offices and on television and in films made Apple, for the first time in years, feel current and desirable rather than embattled and obsolete. The iMac's success validated the entire strategy Jobs had brought back to Apple: focus on a few great products, control the whole widget, compete on design and experience rather than price and specifications, and make objects that people love rather than merely tolerate. It was the proof of concept for everything that followed.

The precise numbers behind that success are worth setting down, because they show just how fast the reversal happened. The iMac went on sale August 15, 1998, at $1,299, a price that undercut the beige-box competition while still carrying a premium over the cheapest Windows machines, and it sold 278,000 units in its first six weeks on shelves and roughly 800,000 within its first twenty weeks — extraordinary velocity for a company that, a year earlier, had been widely written off as terminal. It was the best-selling desktop computer in the United States for the several months following its launch, and a meaningful share of its buyers, by Apple's own later estimates, were purchasing their first computer of any kind or switching over from Windows, meaning the iMac was not merely retaining Apple's shrinking base of loyalists but actively pulling in customers the company had never reached before.

Before it was the iMac, the machine went by a code name that gives away nothing about the personality it would eventually radiate: inside Apple, during development, it was known simply as C1, the "C" standing for "consumer," a placeholder as flavorless as the beige boxes it was designed to replace. The name that very nearly stuck instead was not much livelier. Jobs's own preference, floated to Apple's advertising team at TBWA\Chiat\Day, was "MacMan" — a name suggested by marketing executive Phil Schiller, who by his own account had been trying to capture something of the appeal of Sony's Walkman, a product whose brand had become a synonym for an entire category. Ken Segall, the agency's creative director, thought the name was a mistake, evoking a cheap knockoff or a video-game character rather than a beautifully designed machine, and he spent a week with his team generating alternatives before landing on "iMac" — short, unmistakably a Macintosh, and carrying, in that single lowercase "i," an implicit promise of the internet that the machine was designed to make painlessly accessible. Jobs was not immediately won over. At the presentation where Segall pitched it, Jobs said he no longer hated the name but still preferred his own; Segall left the meeting believing he had failed to make the sale. It was only the next day that word came back that Jobs had floated "iMac" to other Apple executives and found the response encouraging enough to let it stand — a small, almost anticlimactic resolution to a naming argument that produced what would become one of the most recognizable product-name prefixes in the history of consumer technology, stamped in the years that followed onto the iPod, the iPhone, and the iPad.

That the machine ultimately named for its connection to the internet came dressed in a color drawn from an ocean beach on the other side of the world is one of the small ironies buried in the iMac's creation, and it deserves setting down alongside the naming story rather than apart from it, because both reveal the same instinct at work: an insistence on choosing words and colors for their feeling rather than their function, in a product category that had, until that moment, treated both as afterthoughts. A machine that might have shipped as the "C1 MacMan," a beige-adjacent placeholder wearing a derivative brand name, instead emerged as the iMac in Bondi Blue — a pairing of name and color that, taken together, told customers everything about what kind of computer this was supposed to be before they had even seen it turned on.

The color itself has a small, charming, verifiable origin story. Jobs and Ive settled on the name "Bondi Blue" for the machine's translucent shell after Bondi Beach in Sydney, Australia, reportedly because the hue reminded Jobs of the blue-green of the water and the worn sea glass found along that shoreline — a strange, almost whimsical detail to attach to a piece of consumer electronics, but entirely consistent with the obsessive, sensory specificity that Jobs and Ive brought to even the smallest decisions. Within a year, Apple would broaden the palette into a string of candy-like colors — tangerine, lime, grape, blueberry, strawberry — reinforcing an idea that seems obvious now but was nearly unthinkable in the beige-and-black computer market of 1998: that the color of a machine could be a legitimate, marketable feature in its own right, not an afterthought bolted on at the factory.

A misconception worth correcting concerns the iMac's supposed instant, universal acclaim. In fact the machine drew real skepticism from parts of the trade press and from longtime Mac users at the moment of its unveiling, precisely because of the decisions the chapter has already described — the missing floppy drive chief among them, but also its single USB-based approach to peripherals, which orphaned an entire installed base of printers, scanners, and other add-ons that had relied on the older serial and SCSI connectors Apple was discarding. Reviewers at the time debated in print whether Apple, so recently rescued from the edge of bankruptcy, could really afford to alienate its own existing customers by forcing them to replace their peripherals along with their computer. The iMac's commercial triumph did not settle that argument so much as overwhelm it: the sales numbers made the objections look, in retrospect, like caution that history did not reward, but at the time the confidence Jobs projected on stage was not universally shared even inside the Apple faithful, and the company was, in a very real sense, betting the turnaround on being right.

The iMac's deepest significance, though, is that it established the template — aesthetic, strategic, and philosophical — for the entire second act of Apple, the era that would produce the iPod and the iPhone and the iPad and make Apple the most valuable company on earth. Everything that would come was prefigured in that translucent blue teardrop: the obsession with design and physical beauty; the partnership of Jobs and Ive; the willingness to make bold, controversial choices and to bet on the future against the present; the strategy of premium pricing for desirable, human-centered products; the treatment of a computer not as a tool but as an object of delight. The iMac announced that the company that had nearly died was not merely going to survive but was going to lead, and lead by making technology beautiful and human in a way no one else could match. Apple had its identity back, its designer, its philosophy, and its confidence. What it did not yet have — what no one, including Jobs, could yet see — was that the computer itself, the thing Apple had been founded to make, was about to become the least important product in the company's future. The revival that began with the iMac would carry Apple, over the next few years, entirely out of the computer business as its center of gravity, into music, and then into phones, and then into a position of dominance over the whole of digital life. The bridge to that future was an idea Jobs began to articulate at the turn of the millennium: that the personal computer would become the digital hub of a person's whole life, the center around which a constellation of new devices would orbit. The first of those devices would fit in a pocket and hold a thousand songs.

Chapter 30½ — Jobs and Gates

No account of Steve Jobs is complete without his opposite, and his opposite was Bill Gates, and the rivalry between them is one of the great dualities in the history of business — two men born in the same year, 1955, who came of age together at the dawn of the personal computer, who built the two companies that defined the era, whose philosophies were nearly perfect inversions of each other, and whose long, tangled, competitive, and finally almost affectionate relationship illuminates both of them. To understand Jobs, it helps enormously to understand how he differed from Gates, because the contrast throws each man's essential nature into relief.

They were, temperamentally and intellectually, profoundly different. Gates was, at bottom, an engineer and a businessman of extraordinary analytical power — a brilliant programmer in his youth, a ferociously logical strategic thinker, a man who understood software and markets and competition with a cold clarity, and who built Microsoft into the dominant force in computing through shrewd business maneuvering as much as through technology. Jobs was, at bottom, an artist and an impresario — not a programmer or an engineer, but a person of taste and vision and showmanship, who cared about beauty and experience and feeling, who built Apple through design and marketing and the force of his personality. Gates cared about the software and the business; Jobs cared about the product and the experience. Gates was rumpled, analytical, and indifferent to aesthetics; Jobs was intense, aesthetic, and theatrical. Gates wanted his software on every computer in the world; Jobs wanted to make a few perfect objects. They represented two fundamentally different theories of what mattered in technology — Gates's that it was about capability and ubiquity and business, Jobs's that it was about design and integration and human experience — and for most of their careers, Gates's theory won.

The competitive history between them was long and often bitter, and Jobs's resentment of Gates ran deep. The original wound was the graphical interface: Microsoft, which developed software for the Macintosh, had access to the Mac's graphical interface, and then developed Windows, which brought a graphical interface to the IBM-compatible world — and Jobs regarded this as theft, as Gates stealing Apple's ideas just as, the more honest observers noted, Apple had adapted ideas from Xerox. The famous exchange, whether or not it happened in exactly the quoted form, captures the dynamic: when Jobs accused Gates of stealing from Apple, Gates is said to have replied that it was more as if they both had a rich neighbor named Xerox, and Jobs had broken in to steal the television only to find that Gates had already taken it. The point was fair and it stung: Apple's outrage at Microsoft's borrowing was hard to sustain given Apple's own borrowing from PARC. And Windows, cruder than the Mac but running on cheap hardware everywhere, went on to conquer the world, relegating Apple to a niche and making Microsoft the most powerful and valuable company in technology while Apple nearly died. For most of the 1980s and 1990s, Gates won, comprehensively, and Jobs had to watch the man he considered a tasteless copyist build a dominant empire on ideas Jobs believed Apple had pioneered.

The exchange about Xerox is worth quoting in its most precise, documented form, because the paraphrase that circulates in popular retellings sharpens it into something a little too clean. In the 1996 PBS documentary "Triumph of the Nerds," Gates, asked about Apple's charge that Microsoft had stolen the Macintosh interface, responded: "Well, Steve, I think it's more like we both had this rich neighbor named Xerox, and I broke into his house to steal the TV set, and found out that you had already stolen it." The line works because it is not really a denial — Gates concedes the theft outright — it is a redirection, an insistence that Apple's outrage rested on a double standard, since Apple's own interface had been built on ideas its engineers had toured and studied at Xerox's Palo Alto Research Center years before Windows existed. Both companies, in other words, built their signature products by commercializing research that a third company had developed and then largely failed to bring to market itself, and the rivalry between Jobs and Gates was, from its earliest days, partly a dispute over which of two beneficiaries of the same windfall had the better claim to originality.

The correction worth making here is to a popular version of the Jobs–Gates story that casts Jobs as the wronged originator and Gates as the pure imitator, full stop. The historical record is less flattering to Apple than that telling allows. Apple licensed early versions of its interface concepts to Microsoft for use in early Windows and Word products in the mid-1980s, and when Microsoft's later versions of Windows went further than Apple believed the license permitted, Apple sued — and lost, decisively, in a long federal case that a court substantially resolved in Microsoft's favor by the early 1990s, on the grounds that copyright law did not give Apple the sweeping protection over a graphical "look and feel" that its lawyers had argued for. Jobs's grievance was genuine and his sense of betrayal was sincerely felt, but the notion that Microsoft's rise rested on simple, provable theft that the legal system somehow failed to punish is a simplification; the courts examined the claim directly and did not agree with Apple's account of it.

Gates's own reflections on Jobs, offered across several decades of interviews, add a dimension the rivalry narrative tends to flatten: a real, if grudging, professional respect that long predates their late-life reconciliation. Gates repeatedly described Jobs, even during their most competitive years, as possessing a design and product sense that Gates knew he himself lacked, and the admiration ran alongside the competition rather than replacing it. That respect became explicit and public the day Jobs died. Gates's statement, released within hours on October 5, 2011, read in part: "Steve and I first met nearly 30 years ago, and have been colleagues, competitors and friends over the course of more than half our lives. The world rarely sees someone who has had the profound impact Steve has had, the effects of which will be felt for many generations to come. For those of us lucky enough to get to work with him, it's been an insanely great honor." The phrase "insanely great" was itself an echo, deliberate or not, of Jobs's own favorite piece of Apple slang, a small linguistic bow from one rival to another at the close of a rivalry that had run the length of both their careers.

Long before the rivalry hardened into litigation and resentment, the two men had appeared together in a much friendlier register, in a 1983 internal Apple promotional video made to introduce the still-unreleased Macintosh to company employees and business partners. Gates, then still primarily a software supplier to Apple rather than a rival platform-maker, appeared on camera praising the new machine in terms that read, in hindsight, almost startlingly warm: he called the Macintosh, of all the computers he had ever seen, the only one that met the standard he believed a truly great machine should meet. It is a strange artifact to set beside the decades of bitterness that followed — the lawsuits, the Xerox recriminations, the years in which Jobs treated Gates's success as a standing insult to Apple's originality — because it captures a moment, brief and soon overtaken by events, when the two men's interests were genuinely aligned rather than opposed, Microsoft as an eager developer for a machine it had not yet learned to compete against.

That alignment did not last long, and one of the more revealing episodes from the years when it began to fray involved Jobs traveling to Seattle, well before the Macintosh shipped, to describe the machine in person to Gates and try to enlist Microsoft's continued enthusiasm for it — a visit later described, by people who observed the two men's evolving relationship over the following decades, as having the tone of an elaborate courtship, Jobs working to charm and persuade a software partner whose cooperation Apple needed and whose own ambitions in operating systems were not yet fully apparent to the man doing the courting. Jobs came away from these early years believing he had shown Gates the future and gotten a partner in return; what he had actually done, as Windows would eventually prove, was hand Microsoft a detailed preview of exactly the kind of interface it would need to build to compete, delivered by the one person in the industry most invested in explaining, patiently and at length, exactly why it mattered. The friendliness of the early promotional video and the warmth of those early visits make the bitterness of the following decade land harder in retrospect, because they establish that the enmity was not present from the start — it was manufactured, over years, by a competitive dynamic that turned an eager software partner into the single rival Jobs resented more than any other, before decades later turning them, at the very end, back into something closer to what they had briefly been at the beginning.

And then, in the twenty-first century, the story reversed with a completeness that neither man could have predicted, and the reversal is one of the great vindications and ironies in business history. Jobs's Apple, following his integrated, design-obsessed, whole-widget philosophy, produced the iPod and the iPhone and the iPad and became, within a few years, the most valuable company in the world, worth many times what Microsoft was worth at the peak of their disparity. Gates's model, which had won the PC era so decisively, proved less suited to the mobile era that Apple defined; Microsoft, dominant in the world of the personal computer, largely missed the smartphone revolution, and its relative importance declined as Apple's soared. The man who had lost the first round won the second so decisively that it reframed the whole rivalry: Jobs's theory, that design and integration and experience were what ultimately mattered, was vindicated on the largest possible stage, in the era that came after the one Gates had ruled. It was not that Gates had been wrong about the PC; it was that the world had moved to a new kind of device, and on that new terrain, Jobs's philosophy won.

The human coda to the rivalry is unexpectedly moving, and it complicates the simple story of enmity. For all their competition and Jobs's resentment, the two men shared something that no one else on earth quite shared — the experience of having been present at the creation, of having built the two companies that made the personal-computer age, of having been rivals and reference points for each other across their entire adult lives. Near the end of Jobs's life, as he was dying, Gates visited him, and the two spent hours together, talking about their shared history, their companies, their families, the strange parallel arc of their lives. Whatever their differences and their battles, there was, at the end, a mutual respect and even affection between them, a recognition of what they had shared and what each had accomplished. When Jobs died, Gates's tribute was heartfelt, speaking of the privilege of having known and worked alongside and competed with him for so long. The two theories of technology that they embodied would go on contending after both men were gone — the open versus the closed, the ubiquitous versus the integrated, capability versus experience — because the tension between them is permanent, built into the nature of the thing. But the two men who had embodied that tension most vividly, born in the same year at the dawn of the same revolution, ended not as enemies but as the last two witnesses to a world they had made together.

Chapter 31 — Mac OS X

In March 2001, Apple released Mac OS X, the modern operating system it had spent a decade failing to build and had finally acquired by buying NeXT — and with it, the software foundation of every Apple product of the twenty-first century was laid. The new operating system was, at its core, NeXTSTEP, the software Steve Jobs had built in exile, adapted and extended and given a beautiful new face; and its arrival marked the moment when the long, strange loop of Jobs's career closed, when the work of the wilderness years became the bedrock of the empire to come. It is one of the least glamorous chapters in the Apple story — an operating system is invisible plumbing, not a shiny object to hold — and it is one of the most important, because everything Apple would build for the next quarter-century would stand on it.

The technical achievement of Mac OS X was to give the Macintosh, at last, a modern foundation. Where the old Mac OS had been fragile — unable to run multiple programs robustly, prone to total crashes when a single program misbehaved, primitive in its handling of memory — Mac OS X was built on the solid, industrial-strength core that NeXTSTEP had inherited from Unix, the operating system that ran much of the internet and the serious computing world. This gave the Mac stability, security, and power it had never had: programs that crashed no longer took down the whole machine; the system could run many things at once without falling over; it had the robust underpinnings that modern software demanded. At the same time, Apple wrapped this powerful core in an interface of striking beauty, a design called Aqua, full of translucent, glossy, water-like elements — buttons that looked like drops of liquid, a dock of icons that magnified as your pointer swept across them, animations and visual flourishes that made the machine feel alive and luxurious. The combination — a serious, powerful, Unix foundation married to a beautiful, friendly, human interface — was quintessentially Apple, and quintessentially the fusion of NeXT's engineering with the Macintosh's design soul. It was the two halves of Jobs's career, the exile's operating system and the founder's aesthetic, joined at last.

The transition to Mac OS X was not painless, and the way Apple managed it revealed a discipline that would characterize the whole second act. Moving from the old Mac OS to the new one meant abandoning, eventually, all the software written for the old system, forcing developers to rewrite their programs and users to replace their applications — a wrenching change that companies often botch and that can destroy a platform if handled badly. Apple managed it with a combination of patience and firmness: it built a compatibility technology that let old programs keep running for years while the transition proceeded, giving developers and users time to adapt; it invested heavily in the tools that made writing new software for Mac OS X attractive; and it moved the whole ecosystem forward with a steady hand, absorbing the short-term pain for the long-term gain of a modern foundation. This willingness to endure a difficult transition in service of a better future would become an Apple signature, repeated when the company moved its Macs from one kind of processor to another, and again when it built entirely new software ecosystems for the iPhone. Apple learned, in the Mac OS X transition, how to move a whole platform and its community from an old world to a new one without losing them — a capability most companies never develop, and one that would prove essential again and again.

The road to that final release was longer and more tangled than the finished product lets on, and the tangle is itself a small history of Apple relearning how to ship software. Apple's first announced plan, code-named Rhapsody, proposed grafting the NeXTSTEP core onto the Mac with only a thin, and by most developer accounts unconvincing, layer of backward compatibility for existing Mac software — a plan that alarmed the very developer community Apple needed to bring along, since it would have forced a wholesale, immediate rewrite of every Macintosh application in existence. Apple listened to the backlash, reworked the strategy, and by 1998 had rebranded the effort Mac OS X, with a much deeper compatibility layer that let classic Mac software run inside the new system while developers migrated at their own pace. The interface that would eventually clothe this new foundation, called Aqua, was not unveiled until Macworld Expo in January 2000, more than three years after the NeXT acquisition, and the finished Mac OS X 10.0 did not reach ordinary customers until March 2001 — a gap that gives some sense of just how much engineering work stood between owning a good operating system and actually shipping one.

Jobs's own description of the Aqua interface, delivered at that January 2000 unveiling, has become one of his most quoted lines about design, and it survives in something close to its original form: he told the audience that the interface used so much saturated color and gloss and translucency that "when you saw it you wanted to lick it." Commentators seized on the remark, and one well-known technology writer, David Pogue, later described the effect as resembling "lickable globs of Crest Berrylicious Toothpaste Gel" — an unglamorous comparison that nonetheless captured something real about Aqua's design language, its buttons rendered as glassy, dimensional objects rather than the flat gray rectangles that had defined computer interfaces for the previous fifteen years. It is worth noting, as a small correction to the record, that this "lickable" interface debuted at Macworld in January 2000, a full year before Mac OS X itself actually shipped to the public in March 2001 — the polished face of the new operating system arrived well ahead of the operating system it belonged to, generating excitement Apple then had to sustain through more than a year of further engineering before customers could buy the finished product.

Beneath Aqua's glossy surface, Apple also made an unusual and, for a company as famously secretive as Apple, almost countercultural decision: it released the core of Mac OS X's underlying software as open source, under a project it named Darwin, making the operating system's foundational code freely available for outside programmers to inspect, modify, and build upon even as Apple sold the finished, polished product for a price. Jobs, presenting the decision, explained the name with characteristic bluntness, telling an audience that the operating system was being open-sourced "because it's about evolution" — a small pun on the naturalist's name that also captured something true about the strategy, since Apple was betting that exposing its Unix-based core to outside scrutiny and contribution would make the foundation stronger and more trustworthy even as the company kept its interface, its applications, and its overall product experience tightly closed. It was a hybrid model that few other consumer-technology companies of the era were attempting, open at the plumbing and closed at the fixtures, and it reflected a pragmatism about software engineering that sat somewhat at odds with Apple's public reputation for controlling every aspect of its products down to the smallest detail.

The finished 10.0 release, whatever its long-term significance, was by no means an unqualified triumph the moment it reached customers in March 2001, and it is worth being honest about the gap between the operating system's historic importance and its immediate, lived experience on ordinary Macintosh hardware. Reviewers and everyday users alike found the new system markedly slower than the Mac OS it was replacing, even when running on the exact same computer — boot times routinely stretched past two minutes, common tasks lagged and stuttered, and the striking, glass-like Aqua interface that had generated so much excitement at its unveiling turned out to demand more graphics processing than the hardware of the day, and Apple's own initial software, could comfortably deliver. Bertrand Serlet, the engineering executive who had overseen much of Mac OS X's development, later acknowledged plainly that the first release was genuinely slow and expensive enough, in practical terms, that plenty of customers who tried it went away disappointed rather than delighted — a candid admission that cuts against the tidier story in which Mac OS X arrived fully formed and universally admired. Apple's response was to keep iterating with unusual speed: a follow-up release less than a year later addressed much of the sluggishness, and the operating system that would eventually be remembered as the stable, elegant foundation of Apple's next quarter-century took several further versions to actually earn that reputation. The DNA was right from the start, in other words, but the execution needed real time to catch up to the ambition — a pattern that would recur, in smaller ways, throughout Apple's history of shipping bold ideas slightly ahead of the hardware and software polish required to make them shine on arrival.

The strategic importance of Mac OS X extends far beyond the Macintosh, and this is the point that is easy to miss because the operating system is invisible. The same software foundation that Apple built for the Mac would become, in adapted form, the basis of the operating systems for every product Apple would create. When Apple built the iPhone, its operating system — later called iOS — was a version of Mac OS X, shrunk and reshaped for a touchscreen phone but built on the same core. The iPad, the Apple Watch, the Apple TV, and eventually the Vision Pro would all run operating systems descended from the same source. This meant that Apple had, in Mac OS X, not just a good operating system for its computers but a single, unified software foundation on which it could build an entire family of devices — a technological common ground that let the company create a seamless ecosystem in which its products worked together, shared code and concepts, and presented a consistent experience. The decision to buy NeXT in 1996, made by a desperate Apple looking for any modern operating system to save the Mac, turned out to have bought the company far more than a Mac OS: it had bought the software DNA of a whole generation of products, the common ancestor of everything Apple would become. NeXTSTEP, the commercial failure of the wilderness years, became the most valuable software Apple ever acquired.

Mac OS X also, more subtly, completed Steve Jobs's return in a way that went beyond the corporate. When the operating system he had built at NeXT became the foundation of Apple's future, the exile was not just ended but redeemed — the years everyone had counted as failure were revealed as the years in which he had built the thing that would matter most. And with a modern, stable, beautiful operating system finally in place, Apple had the platform it needed to build outward, to make the Macintosh not just a computer but the center of a new kind of digital life. Jobs had a vision for what came next, and he began articulating it at the turn of the millennium in a phrase that would organize Apple's strategy for years: the digital hub. The personal computer, he argued, was becoming the hub of a person's digital life, the center around which a growing constellation of digital devices — cameras, music players, camcorders, phones — would revolve, with the computer as the place where all the digital content of a life was stored, organized, and given meaning.

Apple's opportunity, Jobs saw, was to make the Mac the best possible hub and to build the devices that would orbit it. The first of those devices, and the one that would begin Apple's transformation from a computer company into something far larger, was a small white rectangle that played music, and it would change not just Apple but the entire music industry, and the way human beings carried sound with them through the world.

Chapter 32 — The Apple Store

In 2001, Apple did something that nearly every retail expert and business commentator considered a foolish and probably doomed idea: it opened its own chain of retail stores. The conventional wisdom was overwhelming and confident. Computer companies did not run their own stores; they sold through resellers, big-box electronics retailers, and mail order. Gateway, another computer maker, had tried company-owned stores and was failing at it. Retail was a brutal, low-margin business with high fixed costs and a graveyard of failures; the last thing a company recently returned from the edge of bankruptcy should do was sink capital into expensive real estate to sell products people could already buy elsewhere. Business analysts predicted the Apple stores would be an embarrassing and costly mistake. They could not have been more wrong. The Apple Store would become, by many measures, the most successful retail operation in the world, generating more sales per square foot than any other retailer, and it would transform not just how Apple sold its products but how the entire industry thought about retail.

Steve Jobs's reasoning for the stores flowed directly from the philosophy that governed everything he did, and it was, characteristically, about control of the experience. Jobs was tormented by the fact that Apple's beautiful, carefully designed products were being sold in the fluorescent-lit aisles of big-box stores, sandwiched between cheaper Windows machines, demonstrated on dirty display models by salespeople who neither understood nor cared about them, in an environment that communicated nothing of what made Apple special. The purchase of an Apple product — which Jobs believed should be a moment of delight, the beginning of a relationship, an experience worthy of the object being bought — was instead a dispiriting slog through a warehouse. If Apple made the whole product, controlled the hardware and the software to deliver a seamless experience, then why should it surrender the crucial final step, the actual buying, to third parties who would degrade it? The store was the logical extension of the whole-widget philosophy: Apple would control not just the product but the place and the manner in which it was sold, the last mile of the experience, so that everything from the first sight of the product to the moment of purchase and beyond would be exactly as Apple intended.

To design the stores, Jobs recruited a retail executive named Ron Johnson, and together they rethought what a store could be from first principles, with the same obsessive attention Apple brought to its products. The stores were spare, bright, and minimalist — open spaces of wood, glass, and stone, with products laid out on clean tables for people to touch and use freely rather than locked behind glass or chained to displays. The famous glass staircases, the enormous glass storefronts (one flagship store in New York would be marked by nothing but a giant glass cube on Fifth Avenue, an object so striking it became a tourist attraction and, eventually, one of the most photographed structures in the city), the careful lighting, the uncluttered displays — every element was designed to make the store feel less like a shop and more like a gallery or a public space, a place you would want to spend time even if you were not buying anything. And at the back of each store, Johnson and Jobs placed an idea that would become one of the stores' most beloved and imitated features: the Genius Bar, a counter staffed by knowledgeable employees who would help customers with their problems, answer their questions, and repair their devices, free of the pressure to sell. The Genius Bar transformed the relationship between the company and its customers, turning the store into a place of ongoing support and community rather than a one-time point of sale, and it built a loyalty that no advertising could buy.

The two men behind the stores made an improbable pair. Ron Johnson, whom Jobs recruited to design and run the retail effort, had spent more than a decade at Target, where he had helped that chain build its reputation for stylish, design-forward merchandising within the unglamorous category of discount retail — an unusual pedigree for a company as fanatical about premium experience as Apple, but exactly the combination Jobs wanted: someone who understood mass retail operationally but who also believed, as Target had shown, that ordinary consumers would respond to good design in a big-box setting. Before committing to the public rollout, Jobs and Johnson are said to have built a full mock-up store near Apple's Cupertino headquarters and quietly revised the entire layout at the last minute when Jobs decided the space was organized around Apple's product categories rather than around what customers actually wanted to do — an expensive, deadline-threatening reversal that Jobs insisted on anyway, in keeping with his pattern of delaying a launch rather than shipping something he considered wrong.

The first two stores opened on the same day, May 19, 2001, one in Tysons Corner, Virginia, and the other in the Glendale Galleria in Glendale, California — a deliberate pairing of an East Coast and a West Coast location rather than a single flagship debut. Together the two stores drew roughly 7,700 visitors and rang up about $599,000 in combined sales over their opening weekend, respectable but hardly overwhelming figures for what was, at the time, still widely regarded by retail analysts as a vanity project doomed to the same fate as Gateway's failed company-owned stores. Roughly thirty more Apple Stores opened within the following year, and it would take longer than the opening weekend's numbers suggested before the format's extraordinary per-square-foot productivity — the metric by which the stores would eventually be judged the most successful retail operation in the world — became fully apparent.

It is worth correcting the tidy version of this story in which industry skepticism evaporated the moment the doors opened. In the months immediately following the May 2001 launch, several prominent business publications continued to publish skeptical assessments of the stores' prospects, pointing to Apple's tiny share of the personal-computer market as evidence that a national retail footprint made little economic sense for a company selling to such a narrow customer base. That skepticism was not unreasonable given the information available at the time; it simply turned out to be wrong, and it took a few years of accumulating sales data — rather than the opening weekend alone — for the doubters to be proven so.

The stores succeeded beyond anyone's expectation, including Apple's own, and their success rested on the same insight that drove the whole company: that people would respond powerfully to a well-designed experience, that the environment and the manner of a purchase mattered as much as the product itself, and that treating customers with respect and delight would build a loyalty worth more than any discount. The Apple stores became gathering places, destinations, community centers for the Apple faithful and recruiting grounds for the curious; they made buying and owning an Apple product feel like joining something; they generated staggering revenue while doubling as the most effective marketing Apple had, giving millions of people their first hands-on encounter with products they might otherwise never have tried. The stores that experts had predicted would fail became a profit engine and a brand cathedral, and their design was so influential that retailers across every industry — phone carriers, car companies, clothing brands — copied the open layouts, the clean tables, the helpful staff, the whole vocabulary of the Apple Store, until it became the default template for premium retail everywhere.

Even Steve Jobs's own instincts, so often vindicated by history, worked against one of the store's most beloved features before they came around to it. Ron Johnson later recalled that when he first pitched the idea of a support counter staffed by walk-up technicians, Jobs's initial reaction was blunt dismissal: he thought the idea was, in Johnson's word, "idiotic," certain that ordinary retail employees could never combine deep technical competence with genuine warmth, and skeptical that customers would trust a stranger behind a counter with something as personal as a malfunctioning computer. Johnson persisted, arguing that the best service experiences he could think of — the concierge desk at a fine hotel, the bar at a good restaurant, where a customer could sit, ask, and be helped without being rushed — offered the right model, and the name Genius Bar followed directly from that comparison. Jobs, persuaded, let the idea proceed, and it went on to become the single feature customers cite most often as the reason for their loyalty to the stores, a piece of retail history that came within a conversation of never existing at all because the man whose name is now inseparable from it did not, at first, believe in it.

The store's physical vocabulary, too, was patented rather than merely designed, a detail that captures how literally Jobs took the idea that a retail experience could be intellectual property. In 2003, the U.S. Patent and Trademark Office granted a design patent, number D478,999, covering the ornamental appearance of a floating glass staircase — the kind that would become a signature of Apple's flagship locations — and Steve Jobs himself was listed among its named inventors, alongside several of Apple's in-house architects and engineers. It was an unusual thing for a chief executive to have his name attached to, a staircase rather than a circuit board or an operating system, but it reflected Jobs's conviction, expressed no differently here than in a keynote or a product review, that even the mundane architecture separating one floor of a store from another deserved the same obsessive originality Apple brought to everything else, and that originality, once achieved, deserved the same legal protection a chip design or a piece of software would receive. Apple would go on, in the years that followed, to secure design patents covering other elements of its stores as well, an approach to retail architecture that no competitor had previously thought to attempt, treating the store itself, and not merely the products sold inside it, as an invention worth defending. That single patent was only one piece of a broader portfolio Apple built around the store as an object rather than a mere location — filings covering everything from table designs to signage to the layout of an entryway — reflecting an approach to retail architecture that few other companies had ever thought to treat as intellectual property worth defending in court, let alone worth attaching a chief executive's own name to as an inventor.

The Apple Store is, in the end, another expression of the theme that runs through this entire book: Steve Jobs's conviction that the experience is the product, that people respond to how a thing makes them feel, and that a company willing to control and perfect every element of that experience — the hardware, the software, the packaging, the advertising, and now the store — could create a bond with customers that transcended the ordinary relationship between a business and its buyers. It also demonstrated, once again, Jobs's willingness to ignore conventional wisdom and expert consensus, to bet on his own conviction against the confident predictions of the entire industry, and to be spectacularly vindicated. The stores opened in 2001, the same year as Mac OS X, and the same year as the product that would begin Apple's transformation into a consumer-electronics colossus. Because a few months after the first Apple Store opened its glass doors, Steve Jobs stood on a stage and pulled from his pocket a small white device, smaller than a deck of cards, and told the world that it held a thousand songs — and with it, Apple began to leave the computer business behind and become something the world had never seen: the company that would put all of music, and then all of communication, and then much of human life itself, into the palm of a hand.

Chapter 33 — A Thousand Songs in Your Pocket

On October 23, 2001, Steve Jobs introduced the iPod, and he described it with a phrase that captured everything: "a thousand songs in your pocket." The device was a small white rectangle, a little larger than a deck of cards, with a bright screen and a distinctive circular control — a scroll wheel that let you spin through your music library with your thumb — and it could hold a thousand songs, an entire music collection, in something that fit in a shirt pocket. It cost three hundred and ninety-nine dollars, which many observers thought was far too expensive for a music player, and it initially worked only with Macintosh computers, which limited its market to Apple's small user base. The reaction was skeptical. It was, after all, just an MP3 player, and MP3 players already existed; Apple had not invented the category, and the iPod's price and Mac-only limitation seemed like handicaps. But the skeptics, as they so often did with Apple, were measuring the wrong things, and within a few years the iPod would become a cultural phenomenon, the defining gadget of its era, the product that transformed Apple's business and prepared the way for everything that followed.

The context that made the iPod necessary — and that made it, for a time, controversial — was the upheaval that digital music had brought to the world. In the late 1990s, the MP3 file format had made it possible to compress a song into a small digital file that could be easily copied and shared, and a service called Napster had let millions of people share those files with one another over the internet, freely and, in the view of the record industry, illegally. Music was being ripped from CDs, downloaded, traded, and collected in vast digital libraries on people's computers, and the record labels were in a panic, watching their business model collapse as people stopped buying physical albums and started acquiring music, often without paying, as files. The technology had raced ahead of the industry, and there was chaos: enormous appetite for digital music, no good legal way to buy it, no good hardware to carry it, and a music industry that was fighting the future with lawsuits rather than adapting to it. Into this chaos Apple stepped, first with the hardware and then, more consequentially, with a legal way to buy the music — but the hardware came first, and the hardware was the iPod.

What made the iPod succeed where other MP3 players had failed was not any single breakthrough but the Apple synthesis: the integration of hardware, software, and design into a seamless whole that made the experience effortless. Other MP3 players existed, but they were, almost uniformly, terrible to use — clumsy to load with music, confusing to navigate, ugly, with small storage and worse software. The iPod was different in every dimension at once. Its storage was large, enough for a real music collection, made possible by a tiny hard drive Apple had spotted and secured. Its scroll wheel made navigating through hundreds of songs fast and intuitive and even pleasurable, a genuine interface innovation. And crucially, it worked in tight integration with software on the computer — iTunes, Apple's music-management program — so that loading music onto the device, organizing it, and syncing it was simple and automatic, where rivals made it a chore. The whole system — the device, the software, the way they worked together — was designed as a single experience, and that experience was so much better than anything else available that once people tried an iPod, they were converted. It was the whole-widget philosophy applied to music, and it produced a product that felt not like a gadget but like magic.

The engineering behind the first iPod came together with startling speed, and it is worth naming the people who built it, because the finished product is so associated with Jobs alone that the team behind it is easy to forget. Tony Fadell, a hardware engineer who had previously prototyped hard-drive-based music players at General Magic and Philips without finding a company willing to build one properly, brought his concept to Apple as a contractor in January 2001; working alongside Jon Rubinstein, who had come to Apple from NeXT and now ran hardware engineering, and with Phil Schiller credited with proposing the scroll wheel as the way to navigate long song lists, a team that numbered fewer than ten engineers took the device from concept to shipping product in well under a year. The crucial piece of hardware that made the whole thing possible was a then-new 1.8-inch hard drive from Toshiba, small enough to fit in a shirt pocket and yet large enough, at five gigabytes, to hold roughly a thousand songs — the very number Jobs would put in the product's name and its first advertising line. Apple secured a period of exclusive access to the drive, denying rivals the one component that made the iPod's combination of size and capacity possible at the time.

It is worth directly correcting one of the most common misconceptions about the iPod: that Apple invented the MP3 player. It did not. Dedicated digital music players had been sold since the late 1990s — South Korean and American companies had brought flash-memory players to market years before the iPod existed, and even hard-drive-based players preceded it. What Apple actually did, as the chapter's own account of the "Apple synthesis" makes clear, was take a product category that already existed and had already been tried, repeatedly, by other companies, and combine hardware, software, and design into something so much easier and more pleasant to use that it made its predecessors look like unfinished prototypes. The iPod's originality lay almost entirely in execution and integration rather than in the invention of the underlying idea, and that distinction — succeeding not by being first but by being dramatically better — would become one of the most consistent patterns across Apple's entire history, repeated a few years later with the smartphone and, later still, with the tablet.

The commercial ramp-up in the iPod's first year was gradual rather than explosive, a detail that complicates the myth of an instant, universal sensation. The device launched on November 10, 2001, priced at $399, working at first only with Macintosh computers via FireWire — a limitation that meant it was compatible with only a small fraction of American households, since Macs held a low single-digit share of the personal-computer market at the time. Apple sold around 125,000 units in the final quarter of calendar 2001, respectable for a brand-new accessory category but hardly the sales figures of a phenomenon; sales climbed only gradually through 2002, and the iPod did not become the mass-market, culture-defining object it is remembered as today until Apple released a Windows-compatible version and, even more importantly, opened the iTunes Store in 2003, giving owners of the device a legal, simple way to fill it with music. The device that transformed Apple's fortunes so completely spent its first eighteen months or so as a promising but modest niche product, its true commercial explosion inseparable from the software and legal breakthrough that followed it.

The iPod's earbuds deserve their own small note of correction, since popular memory sometimes assumes the white cord was simply Apple's habitual design choice. In fact the white color was a deliberate point of differentiation: at a moment when nearly every portable music player and headphone on the market used black cords and black earbuds, Apple's choice of white made an iPod owner visually identifiable at a glance, on a train platform or a city sidewalk, well before the product had any meaningful brand recognition of its own — a piece of guerrilla marketing built directly into the hardware, years before the famous silhouette advertisements made the white cords into a full-blown cultural icon.

The iPod's cultural impact, once it took off, was enormous and went far beyond Apple's balance sheet, though the balance sheet was transformed too. The white earbuds that came with the iPod became a visible sign, a status symbol and a tribe marker, so ubiquitous that Apple built an entire advertising campaign around them — silhouetted dancers against bright colored backgrounds, black figures with glowing white earbud cords, an image that became iconic and that sold the iPod as an object of cool rather than a mere utility. The device changed how people related to music, letting them carry their entire collection everywhere, listen on shuffle, soundtrack their lives continuously in a way that had never before been possible. It made Apple, for the first time, a mass-market consumer-electronics company rather than a maker of computers for a niche of enthusiasts; the iPod reached people who had never owned and would never own a Mac, putting Apple's design and Apple's brand into millions of hands and pockets and ears. And it drove Apple's finances to heights the computer business alone could never have reached, becoming, at its peak, a huge share of the company's revenue and profit, funding everything else and proving that Apple's future lay in consumer devices as much as, and eventually far more than, in computers.

The click wheel that made the iPod so pleasurable to navigate also entangled Apple in a legal fight that its own patent filings had not anticipated. Singapore-based Creative Technology, a longtime maker of sound cards and its own line of hard-drive music players, held a patent — granted in 2005 for an invention it had actually filed years earlier — covering a method for navigating a hierarchical menu system on a portable music player using a single control, the same basic scheme by which an iPod user scrolled through artists, then albums, then songs. Creative sued, and rather than fight the claim through years of litigation, Apple settled in August 2006, agreeing to pay Creative one hundred million dollars in a single lump sum for a paid-up license covering all of Apple's products, present and future. Creative, for its part, gained something beyond the cash: admission into Apple's "Made for iPod" accessory program, letting it sell iPod-compatible speakers and other add-ons under Apple's own licensing umbrella rather than remain locked out as a rival. It was a strikingly large sum for Apple to concede without a trial, and it was a quiet reminder that even the interface widely credited as one of the most original strokes of the entire iPod project rested on a foundation more legally contested, and more expensive to secure, than the tidy story of in-house genius usually allows. Apple's own attempt to patent a similar navigational scheme, filed only after Creative's original application had already been recorded, was in fact rejected outright by the patent office on the grounds that Creative's earlier filing already covered the same basic idea — a detail that undercuts, more directly than any settlement figure alone, the comfortable assumption that the iPod's interface sprang from ground no one else had already staked out.

The device's engineering also outran Apple's own turnaround-time expectations in ways that later, more comfortable retellings of the iPod's birth tend to compress. Tony Fadell's small team, drawing on the Toshiba drive and a compressed development schedule Jobs himself had set, took the iPod from an approved concept to a shipping product in roughly eight months — an astonishingly short cycle for a piece of consumer hardware built essentially from scratch, achieved only because the interface software, the mechanical design, and the industrial design were all developed in parallel rather than in the usual sequence, at a pace of overlapping deadlines that several of the engineers involved later described as the most demanding stretch of their careers. That speed came at a cost that the finished, gleaming white object gave no hint of: components were sourced under intense time pressure, some of the earliest software had to be simplified rather than perfected simply because there was no time left to do otherwise, and the finished device that Jobs unveiled in October 2001, hailed almost instantly as a paragon of unhurried, considered design, was in fact the product of one of the most compressed and improvisational engineering sprints in the company's history.

But the iPod, for all its success, was only half of a two-part revolution, and the second part mattered even more, because it solved the problem the hardware alone could not. A device that held a thousand songs was wonderful, but where were people supposed to get the songs? In 2001, the only ways to fill an iPod were to laboriously copy music from CDs you already owned, or to download files illegally from the chaotic, legally dubious world of file-sharing. There was no good, legal, easy way to simply buy digital music, one song at a time, and own it. The record industry, terrified of piracy and hostile to the digital future, had failed to provide one, clinging to the album and the CD and the lawsuit. Steve Jobs saw the opportunity and the necessity, and over the following two years he would do something that no one thought possible: he would persuade the entire, resistant, frightened music industry to let Apple sell their music digitally, song by song, at a price he set, through a store built into iTunes. In doing so he would rescue the music business from the chaos of piracy, establish Apple as the most powerful force in music, and demonstrate a pattern — Apple entering a troubled industry and reorganizing it around Apple's own platform and terms — that would define the company's future. The iTunes Store would change the music industry forever, and it is where we turn next.

Chapter 34 — iTunes

In April 2003, Apple opened the iTunes Music Store, and it changed the economics of an entire art form. The idea was simple to state and had proven, for years, impossible to achieve: a place where anyone could legally buy digital music, one song at a time, for a fixed low price — ninety-nine cents a track — download it instantly, own it, and play it on their computer and their iPod. Within its first week the store sold a million songs; within a few years it would sell billions, become the largest music retailer in the world, and establish digital downloads as the dominant way people bought music. That it happened at all was a testament to Steve Jobs's extraordinary powers of persuasion, because the hard part of the iTunes Store was never the technology. The hard part was the record labels, and getting them to agree was one of the most consequential negotiations of Jobs's career.

The record industry in 2003 was a frightened, angry, and deeply conservative business. It had watched digital piracy — Napster and its successors — erode its sales and it blamed technology for its troubles, and its instinct was to resist the digital future with every weapon it had: lawsuits against file-sharing services, lawsuits against individual downloaders, digital-rights-management schemes to lock down music, and a stubborn insistence on the album as the unit of sale, because albums, with their filler tracks bundled around a hit or two, were far more profitable than selling singles. The labels were terrified that selling music as individual downloadable songs would destroy the album and cannibalize their business, and terrified that letting a technology company control the digital distribution of their music would hand away their power. Convincing them to license their entire catalogs to Apple, to sell individual songs at a price Apple set, through a store Apple controlled, required overcoming all of that fear and conservatism, and it required a salesman of genius.

Jobs was that salesman, and he brought several advantages to the negotiation. He had, in the iPod and the Macintosh, a platform; he could argue, truthfully at first, that because iTunes initially ran only on the Mac with its small market share, the labels could experiment with digital sales at low risk, and this framing helped get the first agreements. He had personal credibility and charisma, and he used them relentlessly, meeting with label executives, dazzling them, cajoling them, wearing down their resistance one by one. He had, crucially, a solution to the piracy that terrified them: a legal, convenient, well-designed store might, he argued, actually reduce piracy by giving people an easy, affordable, honest alternative to stealing — the theory that most people would rather pay a fair price for a good experience than steal if stealing was the only convenient option, a theory the store would substantially vindicate. And he had the discipline to insist on the things that made the store work for customers even when the labels resisted: the ninety-nine-cent price, low enough to make buying an impulse; the ability to buy individual songs, breaking the album's tyranny; and a design so simple that purchasing a song took a single click. Song by song, label by label, Jobs assembled the agreements, and the iTunes Store launched with the catalogs of the major labels behind it, the first time the whole industry had sanctioned a digital music store.

The iTunes Store's success reshaped the music industry in

ways both liberating and destructive, and an honest history has to hold both. On one hand, it rescued the industry from the chaos of unchecked piracy, established a viable business model for digital music, gave consumers a convenient and affordable way to buy music legally, and reasserted the principle that music was worth paying for. On the other hand, it accelerated the destruction of the album as an art form and an economic unit, as people increasingly bought only the individual songs they wanted rather than whole albums, hollowing out a business model musicians had relied on for decades. And it transferred enormous power from the record labels to Apple, which now controlled the dominant channel through which digital music was sold and could dictate terms to an industry that had once been the master of its own domain. The labels had let Apple into their business to solve the piracy crisis, and they discovered, too late, that they had handed Apple the keys — that Apple now stood between them and their customers, set the prices, owned the relationship, and held the power. It was the same pattern that VisiCalc had shown decades earlier, that the App Store would show a few years later: whoever controls the platform through which people acquire what they want controls the industry, and the makers of the content become, over time, subordinate to the owner of the store. Apple had done to the music industry what it would do, again and again, to whatever industry it entered — reorganized it around an Apple-controlled platform, on Apple's terms.

The numbers behind that first week are worth setting down precisely, because they still startle decades later. The store opened with a catalog of roughly two hundred thousand songs — modest by the standards of any later era, but apparently enough, since Apple would later report that more than half of them had been bought at least once within days of launch. Within a year the store had sold more than seventy million songs, a pace that made a mockery of the caution the labels themselves had brought to the deal. And the reaction inside Apple's fiercest rival captures, better than any retrospective account could, how completely the industry had been blindsided. Two days after the store opened, Bill Gates sent an email to Microsoft's senior leadership — later made public — with the subject line "Apple's Jobs again... and time to have a great Windows download service." In it, Gates wrote, with evident and grudging admiration, that "Steve Jobs['s] ability to focus in on a few things that count, get people who get user interface right and market things as revolutionary are amazing things." What troubled Gates far more than the interface, though, was the deal itself: the labels' own services, Pressplay and MusicNet, were by every account clumsy and user-hostile, hobbled by restrictive copy protection and thin catalogs, and yet those same labels had handed Apple — a company with a single-digit share of the personal-computer market — terms good enough to build something people actually wanted to use. "This is very strange to me," Gates wrote, and it was a fair question, because he had run headlong into the same conservative, frightened industry and gotten nowhere.

The Pressplay and MusicNet failures point to a misconception worth correcting directly, because the standard telling of the iTunes story often implies that Apple invented the very idea of legal digital music and simply willed it into being. In truth, the record labels themselves had tried first, launching Pressplay and MusicNet years before the iTunes Music Store existed, each backed by a consortium of major labels determined to control digital distribution on their own terms. Both were widely regarded as nearly unusable — bundled with confusing subscription rules, restrictive digital locks that limited how many computers a song could play on or whether it could be burned to a disc at all, and catalogs deliberately incomplete because each label held back its best-selling artists from services co-owned by its competitors. Apple did not invent the idea of paying for digital music; it succeeded where the labels' own attempts had already failed, by insisting on the two things the labels' own services had refused to offer — a simple flat price and a catalog broad enough to be worth using — and by being an outsider with no rival label relationships to protect, which made Apple, paradoxically, more trustworthy to the labels collectively than any of their own joint ventures had been to each other.

None of this software engineering happened without human cost to the deal-making itself, and the record of Jobs's actual negotiating style, preserved in the recollections of executives who sat across the table from him, shows a man who mixed flattery, technical demonstration, and blunt intimidation in whatever proportion the moment required. He would fly to New York and sit for hours with label chiefs, walking them personally through mockups of the store, and then warn them, just as bluntly, that piracy would hollow out their business entirely if they refused to act — a warning made credible by the demonstrable, measurable collapse in CD sales that piracy was already causing. It took this combination, sustained over months and applied one label at a time, to produce something the labels, left to their own devices and their own joint ventures, had already proven three separate times they could not build for themselves.

The iTunes Music Store did not last forever in the form it launched in, and its eventual fate is itself instructive about how completely it succeeded. By 2019, the "iTunes" application that generations of Mac and Windows users had opened to buy songs, sync iPods, and manage libraries had grown so bloated with unrelated functions — music, movies, television, podcasts, audiobooks, device backups — that Apple retired it altogether, splitting its duties among separate Music, TV, and Podcasts apps on the Mac, mirroring the separate apps the iPhone had used for years. The iTunes Store as a brand largely disappeared from the interface a customer sees, folded into the Music and TV apps that replaced it, even as the underlying purchasing infrastructure Jobs had built in 2003 — the accounts, the payment system, the one-click purchase flow, the relationship with rights holders — quietly kept functioning underneath the streaming era that came to dominate music consumption. Anyone today who buys a song or a movie through an Apple device, rather than merely streaming it, is still, whether they know the name or not, using the store Jobs built by force of will in 2003, even though the word "iTunes" itself has all but vanished from the products people actually touch.

Extending the store beyond the Macintosh required a reversal from Jobs every bit as personal as the concessions he extracted from the record labels, and the process is remembered, inside Apple, by the phrase that became the campaign's own advertising line. Through 2002 and into 2003, Jon Rubinstein and Phil Schiller pressed Jobs to bring iTunes to Windows, arguing that restricting the software to the Mac's small installed base was strangling the very store Jobs had just spent a year building, since the overwhelming majority of iPod buyers used a Windows machine at home and could not, at first, use the device without a Macintosh nearby. Jobs resisted for months, reluctant to hand any part of the Macintosh's software advantage to the platform he considered inferior, until Rubinstein finally told him the debate was over and he and Schiller were doing it regardless of what Jobs decided. According to Rubinstein's own later account, Jobs's response was characteristically blunt — "Fuck you guys, do whatever you want, you're responsible for it" — and then he walked out of the room, only to reappear weeks later, once the Windows version worked, embracing the decision so completely that he chose the launch's own tagline. When iTunes for Windows shipped on October 16, 2003, Apple's own marketing declared, on posters and in advertisements, "Hell froze over," a line Jobs delivered from the keynote stage with evident delight at his own reversal, turning what had been forced upon him into one of the most quoted lines of his career. Within days of the Windows launch, downloads of iTunes and purchases through the store surged past anything the Mac-only version had produced, vindicating exactly the argument Rubinstein and Schiller had made and Jobs had spent months refusing to hear.

The episode is worth dwelling on because it complicates the image of Jobs as a leader whose product instincts were simply always correct from the outset. He had been wrong, for the better part of a year, about a decision that turned out to be foundational to the iPod's eventual dominance — the Windows version of iTunes, more than any single feature of the hardware itself, was what turned the iPod from a niche accessory for Macintosh owners into a mass-market phenomenon capable of reaching the ninety-some percent of computer users who had never owned an Apple product. What redeemed the delay was not Jobs's initial judgment but his willingness, once outvoted by his own lieutenants and confronted with the commercial logic, to abandon a position he had defended stubbornly and to do so without pretending he had held it all along; the joke embedded in "Hell froze over" was, pointedly, a joke Jobs told on himself.

The music revolution of the iPod and the iTunes Store did something else, less obvious but ultimately more important than any of its immediate effects: it transformed Apple's identity and set the stage for the product that would make everything before it look small. Apple was no longer a computer company that also made a music player; it was becoming a consumer-electronics and digital-services company, a company that made devices ordinary people carried everywhere and a company that ran a store selling digital goods to hundreds of millions of customers. It had learned to make small, beautiful, mass-market devices; it had learned to run a massive digital storefront and to negotiate with entire industries; it had built relationships with a customer base far larger than the Macintosh had ever reached; and it had, in the iPod's tight integration of hardware, software, and an online store, prototyped the whole system that its next and greatest product would perfect.

For the iPod, brilliant as it was, did just one thing — it played music — and the world was full of other single-purpose devices that people also carried: cameras, and above all, mobile phones. Steve Jobs looked at the phone, the device that everyone already carried and that everyone hated, clumsy and ugly and hard to use, and he saw both a threat and an opportunity. A phone that could also play music could kill the iPod. But a phone reimagined the way Apple reimagined things — a phone that was also an iPod, and also an internet device, and also a small computer, all controlled not by tiny plastic buttons but by the touch of a finger on glass — could be the most important product Apple ever made. He set his best people to build it, in total secrecy, and it nearly broke them.

Chapter 35 — The Digital Lifestyle

Before we follow Apple into the phone that changed everything, it is worth pausing to take stock of what the company had become by the middle of the 2000s, because the transformation was profound and it is easy to lose in the rush toward the iPhone. In less than a decade, Steve Jobs had taken a company ninety days from bankruptcy and turned it into one of the most admired and profitable consumer brands in the world — and, more importantly for what came next, he had changed what kind of company it was. The Apple of 1997 had been a struggling computer maker. The Apple of 2006 was a consumer-electronics and digital-media powerhouse whose most important product was not a computer at all, whose brand meant beauty and simplicity and cool to a mass audience of hundreds of millions, and which had demonstrated a repeatable capacity to enter an industry, reorganize it around its own platform, and dominate it. The pieces were all in place for something larger, and the vision that organized them had a name Jobs used constantly in these years: the digital hub, and its human face, the digital lifestyle.

The digital-hub strategy, which Jobs first articulated clearly around 2001, was the conceptual framework for everything Apple did in this period, and understanding it clarifies why the seemingly disparate products fit together. Jobs observed that people's lives were filling up with digital devices — digital cameras, camcorders, music players, phones, handheld organizers — each of which produced or consumed digital content, and each of which, on its own, was an island. His insight was that the personal computer, with its large storage, big screen, and processing power, was ideally positioned to become the hub that connected all these devices, the central place where a person's digital content — their photos, their music, their videos, their information — would be stored, organized, edited, and given meaning, with the other devices as spokes radiating out from it. Apple's opportunity was to make the Mac the best possible hub and to build the software and the devices that would make the whole digital life seamless. This strategy produced a suite of Apple software — iTunes for music, iPhoto for photographs, iMovie for home video, and others, collectively branded with the lowercase "i" that had begun with the iMac and become Apple's signature — designed to make managing the content of a digital life effortless and even pleasurable. And it produced the iPod, the first great spoke, the device that proved the hub could sell hardware and win a mass market.

What made the digital-hub strategy so powerful was that it turned Apple's greatest structural weakness into a strength. Apple's whole-widget philosophy — its insistence on controlling both hardware and software, its refusal to license its software to run on other companies' hardware — had been, in the personal-computer wars, a weakness, the reason Windows on cheap commodity hardware had conquered the market while Apple remained a niche. But in the world of the digital hub and its constellation of devices, the whole-widget approach became decisive, because the value was in the seamless integration of all the pieces — the way the iPod worked flawlessly with iTunes on the Mac, the way everything synced and connected without the user having to think about it. In a world of many devices that had to work together, the company that made all the pieces and controlled how they fit could deliver an experience that no assemblage of components from different makers could match. The integration that had been a liability in the era of the standalone computer became, in the era of many connected devices, Apple's central advantage. Jobs's lifelong conviction that Apple must control the whole widget, which had nearly killed the company in the 1980s and 1990s, was about to make it the most valuable company on earth, because the future was not the standalone computer but the ecosystem of connected devices, and the ecosystem rewarded exactly the integration Apple had always insisted on.

The "digital lifestyle" was the consumer-facing expression of all this, and it was as much a marketing vision as a technical one — the promise that Apple's products would let ordinary people do wonderful things with the digital content of their lives, easily and beautifully. In Apple's telling and in its software, a family's photographs became slideshows and books; a child's soccer game became an edited home movie; a music collection became a personal soundtrack carried everywhere; and all of it was easy, all of it just worked, all of it was beautiful, in a way that the complicated, ugly, frustrating technology of the PC world was not. This was, again, the Apple synthesis — the marriage of powerful technology with human-centered design and a compelling story about how the products would improve your life — and it was aimed squarely at ordinary people rather than at technology enthusiasts, at the vast market of humans who wanted the benefits of digital technology without its complexity. The digital lifestyle was Apple's argument that it, uniquely, could deliver those benefits, and by the mid-2000s a growing mass of consumers believed it.

Jobs unveiled this whole framework in a single keynote, on January 9, 2001, and his own words to the Macworld audience that day are worth recovering, because they show how deliberately he had thought the strategy through rather than stumbling into it product by product. He told the crowd that the personal computer had already lived through two "golden ages" — the productivity age of the early 1980s and the internet age of the mid-to-late 1990s — and that both were now, in his telling, essentially played out. "We think the PC is on the threshold of entering its third great age," he said, "and that age is the age of digital lifestyle — and that's being driven by an explosion of new digital devices." The Mac's role in that third age, he argued, was not to be one device among many but the organizing one: "the Mac can become the digital hub of our new emerging digital lifestyle, with the ability to add tremendous value to these other digital devices." At that same event he introduced iDVD, for burning home movies onto disc, alongside iTunes, having already shipped iMovie two years earlier for editing home video; iPhoto, the piece that would let people organize and print their photographs, followed about a year later, completing the suite of "i" applications that gave the strategy its consumer face.

The lowercase "i" that adorned all of these products and that would eventually christen the iPod, the iPhone, and the iPad had an origin story that undercuts a common assumption about it — the assumption that it was always understood, precisely and officially, to stand for "internet." It began with the iMac in 1998, named by the advertising executive Ken Segall, who had pitched "i" as shorthand for internet, since easy internet access was the machine's signature feature. But when Jobs unveiled the name to the world, he put up a slide listing not one meaning but five — internet, individual, instruct, inform, and imagination — and said outright that the letter did not have a single official meaning at all. That ambiguity was not an oversight; it was the point. A single fixed meaning would have tied the prefix to one feature that would eventually date the product, whereas a deliberately vague, suggestive letter could be stretched to cover a music player, a phone, and a tablet a decade later without ever being wrong. The "i" survived because Jobs refused to define it too precisely, which is a small but telling example of a pattern that runs through Apple's whole history: the company's most durable ideas were often the ones left just imprecise enough to grow into whatever came next.

It is worth pausing, too, on how contested this hub strategy looked at the moment Jobs announced it, because in hindsight the digital hub can seem like an obviously correct prediction rather than the bet it actually was. In January 2001 the dot-com crash was well underway, technology stocks were collapsing, and much of the press treated Apple's proposed future — an operating system, a suite of unglamorous consumer applications, and a bet that ordinary families wanted to edit home movies and burn their own DVDs — as a modest, even underwhelming, answer to a company that desperately needed a hit. Nobody watching that keynote could have known that the strategy's true payoff was still years away, arriving first through a five-gigabyte music player and only much later through a phone; the digital hub looked, to contemporary observers, like housekeeping rather than the opening move in the most valuable product cycle in the company's history.

The digital hub's deeper legacy is visible today in a form Jobs himself did not live to see fully realized, and it is worth naming because it shows the idea did not simply vanish with the rise of the smartphone — it relocated. The Mac that Jobs described in 2001 as the fixed center of a person's digital life, the place all the spokes connected to, has itself been displaced from that role; for most people today the actual hub of their digital lifestyle is not a desktop computer at all but an iPhone paired with an iCloud account, with photos, messages, purchases, and settings synchronized invisibly across every device a person owns rather than physically tethered to any single machine sitting on a desk. The specific device changed, and the tether loosened from a cable to a wireless connection to an ambient background process nobody thinks about, but the underlying architecture Jobs sketched in that 2001 keynote — one company's ecosystem serving as the seamless connective tissue between a growing constellation of personal devices — is precisely the architecture that still defines how hundreds of millions of people experience their own digital lives today.

The digital-hub strategy did not unfold without friction, and the clearest evidence of how threatening Apple's vision looked to outsiders at the time came from the marketing campaign built around one of the hub's earliest and most ordinary features: the ability to copy music from a CD onto a computer and burn a new CD of your own choosing. In 2001, to promote the new iMacs equipped with Apple's SuperDrive, capable of both reading and writing CDs, Apple ran an advertising campaign built around three blunt verbs — "Rip. Mix. Burn." — over the tagline "It's your music; burn it on a Mac." The phrase was accurate enough as a plain description of what the hardware did, letting a person rip songs from a CD they owned, arrange them into a mix, and burn the result onto a blank disc for personal use, an activity that both the recording industry and civil-liberties groups agreed was lawful when done with music a person had legitimately purchased. But the record industry, already reeling from Napster and in no mood to see a computer company advertise the very behavior it associated with piracy, treated the campaign as an open provocation. Michael Eisner, then the chief executive of Disney, told a congressional committee in 2002 that campaigns like "Rip. Mix. Burn." amounted to telling ordinary consumers "that they can create a theft if they buy this computer," an accusation that placed Apple, still years away from opening its own legitimate music store, on the wrong side of Washington's growing anxiety about digital copying.

The controversy is worth recovering because it shows how contested the digital hub looked from the outside even as

Jobs was building the very system — the iTunes Store, licensed and paid for, song by song — that would answer Eisner's charge more effectively than any legal argument could. "Rip. Mix. Burn." was, in retrospect, Apple advertising a genuine and lawful capability of the personal computer using language deliberately chosen to sound daring rather than technical, and the entertainment industry's furious reaction to three ordinary verbs is a reminder of how raw the wound of Napster still was in 2001 and 2002, and how easily any suggestion of copying, however legal, could be read by an anxious industry as an endorsement of theft. Apple did not back down from the campaign, and within two years it would offer the industry a settlement more valuable than any apology: a store that made buying music, rather than merely copying it, into the easiest and most natural choice a person could make. The controversy grew pointed enough that a rival tried to capitalize on it directly: Gateway, one of Apple's competitors in the personal-computer business, later ran its own advertising built around the slogan "Rip. Burn. Respect.", explicitly positioning its own CD-burning machines as the responsible alternative to what Apple was selling — a small, telling sign of how central the argument over what counted as legitimate copying had become to an industry racing to sell the very hardware that made copying possible.

All of this — the transformation from computer company to consumer-electronics power, the digital-hub strategy, the whole-widget integration turned from weakness to strength, the mass-market brand, the demonstrated ability to enter and reorganize industries, the base of hundreds of millions of customers — was the foundation on which the iPhone would be built, and it is why the iPhone, when it came, was not a bolt from the blue but the culmination of everything Apple had been becoming. The company had learned to make small beautiful devices, to run massive digital stores, to integrate hardware and software and services into seamless experiences, to sell to the whole world rather than a niche, and to reimagine entire product categories. It had, in the iPod and iTunes, essentially built a prototype of the iPhone's whole model — a beautiful handheld device, tightly integrated with software and an online store, sold to a mass market. What remained was to take everything Apple had learned and pour it into a single device that would combine the phone everyone already carried with the music player, the internet, and a small computer, all controlled by touch — and in doing so to create not just a product but a platform that would become the most successful and lucrative in the history of technology. Steve Jobs began the secret project to build it in the mid-2000s, and it consumed the company. He called the effort, internally, Project Purple.

Chapter 36 — Project Purple

The iPhone was born, in part, out of fear. By the mid-2000s the iPod was Apple's golden product, generating a huge share of the company's revenue and profit, and Steve Jobs could see a threat on the horizon that kept him awake: the mobile phone. Phones were beginning to add music-playing capability, and Jobs understood that the device people carried everywhere and would never leave home without was the phone, not a separate music player. If phones became good enough at playing music, no one would buy a standalone iPod; the phone would simply absorb the iPod's function, as it would eventually absorb the functions of the camera, the calculator, the watch, the map, and a dozen other devices. Apple's most important product was vulnerable to being eaten by a device Apple did not make. Jobs's conclusion was characteristically aggressive: rather than wait for someone else's phone to kill the iPod, Apple should build the phone that would kill the iPod itself — should cannibalize its own best product before a competitor could, and in doing so seize the far larger prize of the phone market. "If we don't do it," he reportedly said, "somebody else will." The willingness to destroy your own successful product to get to a bigger opportunity is rare and difficult, and it was one of the strategic insights that made the iPhone possible.

There was also opportunity, and it came from Jobs's contempt for the phones that existed. The mobile phones of the mid-2000s were, in Jobs's view and in the view of most people who paid attention, terrible — clumsy, ugly, and frustrating. They were controlled by tiny physical buttons and by baffling, poorly designed software; their web browsers were pathetic, showing stripped-down, broken versions of the internet; they were, in the language of the industry, "smart" only in the sense that they crammed in features nobody could figure out how to use. Worst of all, from Apple's perspective, they were controlled not by the companies that made them but by the wireless carriers — the phone networks — which dictated what features phones could have, loaded them with their own inferior software, and treated the handset makers as subordinate suppliers. The whole industry was a mess of bad hardware, worse software, and carrier domination, and Jobs saw in that mess exactly the kind of opportunity Apple had exploited before: a large, important product category that everyone used and everyone hated, ripe for reinvention by a company that would rethink it from first principles and control the whole widget. If Apple could build a phone that was actually good — beautiful, easy to use, with real internet and real software — it could do to the phone what the iPod had done to the music player, and the phone market was vastly larger than the music-player market.

The technical origin of the iPhone lay in an unexpected place: a research project on touchscreens that Apple had been pursuing with the idea of building a tablet computer. Apple's engineers had developed a sophisticated multi-touch technology — a screen that could sense multiple finger touches at once and respond to gestures like pinching, swiping, and tapping — and Jobs, seeing a demonstration of it, had an insight that redirected the whole effort. He realized that this touch technology, meant for a tablet, was the answer to the phone: a phone controlled not by physical buttons but entirely by a large touchscreen, with the interface rendered in software that could change to suit whatever you were doing, so that the same device could be a phone, a music player, a web browser, and anything else, each with its own perfect interface summoned onto the glass. The physical keyboard and buttons that cluttered every other phone could be eliminated entirely, replaced by a screen that became a keyboard when you needed to type and a photograph when you wanted to look at pictures and a map when you needed directions. It was a radical idea — a phone that was almost all screen, controlled by touch — and it was risky, because no one knew if people would accept typing on glass instead of physical keys, or whether the technology could be made to work reliably in a pocket-sized device. Jobs bet the company on it. He shelved the tablet, redirected the touchscreen work toward the phone, and set Apple's best people to building it under conditions of extreme secrecy.

The project, code-named Purple, was one of the most intense and grueling efforts in Apple's history, and the accounts of those who lived through it describe a period of near-total consumption. The engineers and designers worked punishing hours for years, sworn to absolute secrecy, forbidden to tell even their families what they were working on, laboring in a locked-down building. The problems were enormous and everything had to be invented at once: how to make a touchscreen respond precisely and pleasurably to fingers; how to build a software keyboard that people could actually type on, complete with the predictive auto-correction that made typing on glass feasible; how to design an entire operating system and interface for a device with no buttons; how to make a web browser that showed the real internet on a tiny screen, with the now-familiar ability to pinch and zoom into a page; how to fit all of this into a pocket-sized device with acceptable battery life. There were bitter internal rivalries — famously, two groups within Apple competed over whether the iPhone should be built by shrinking the Mac's operating system or by extending the iPod's, a competition Jobs allowed to run and that the Mac-based approach won, giving the iPhone a real, powerful operating system descended from NeXTSTEP. There were moments when the whole thing seemed impossible, when the technology would not cooperate, when the schedule was insane. The reality distortion field was working overtime, and it was burning people out. The multi-touch technology at the center of the phone did not spring fully formed from Apple's own laboratories, whatever the tidy legend of Jobs's singular genius might suggest, and correcting that impression matters because it shows how the iPhone was assembled as much as invented. In 2005, quietly and with no public announcement, Apple acquired a small company called FingerWorks, founded by Wayne Westerman and John Elias, two researchers connected to the University of Delaware who had spent years developing gesture-based, multi-finger touch surfaces originally intended to help people with repetitive-strain injuries type without physical keys. Apple brought Westerman and Elias in-house along with their patents, and their work on recognizing pinches, swipes, and multi-finger gestures became the technical foundation beneath the interface Jobs would later present as though it had emerged whole from Apple's own design studio. The company's real genius lay not in inventing multi-touch from nothing but in recognizing which outside idea, quietly acquired and then integrated with Apple's design sensibility and its own operating-system expertise, could be turned into the single defining gesture of a new kind of computer.

Even within Apple, the path to that interface was not a straight line handed down from Jobs but the product of an internal contest that the historical record has only recently made vivid. Jobs set two separate teams against each other, each building a competing prototype phone under the Project Purple umbrella: one, code-named P1 and led by Tony Fadell, the executive who had built the iPod, extended the iPod's familiar click-wheel into a phone, its menus scrolled by a rotating digital wheel rendered on screen; the other, code-named P2 and led by Scott Forstall, abandoned the wheel entirely for a direct multi-touch interface of icons a finger could tap, drag, and pinch. Both teams worked on the same underlying hardware and software platform, each straining to impress Jobs and to be the version that shipped, and the rivalry between them was real and, by every account, fierce. Jobs chose Forstall's touch-based P2, a decision that determined the entire subsequent history of the smartphone, and Forstall went on to lead the development of the iPhone's operating system for years afterward, while Fadell's click-wheel phone was set aside — a reminder that even inside the company that built the iPhone, its most consequential design decision was genuinely contested, not obvious in advance even to the people closest to it.

The screen itself very nearly shipped as plastic rather than the glass everyone now takes for granted, and the story of how it changed captures Jobs's method at its most characteristic. Early prototypes used a plastic cover over the display, but after carrying one in his pocket for weeks, alongside his keys, Jobs grew alarmed that the surface would scratch, and he decided the iPhone needed real, scratch-resistant glass instead — with the launch only months away. He summoned Wendell Weeks, the chief executive of Corning, the glass manufacturer, and pressed him about a scratch-resistant material called Gorilla Glass that Corning had developed decades earlier but never put into mass production. Weeks warned that his own board doubted Corning had the manufacturing capacity to deliver glass at the scale and speed Apple needed, and suggested Apple find a second supplier as a hedge. Jobs refused the hedge outright, telling Weeks, by his own later account, "No, you're going to do all of it," and when Weeks pushed back on the sheer difficulty of the engineering involved, Jobs told him simply, "Don't be afraid. You can do this." Corning converted a Kentucky factory built decades earlier for Cold War-era optical products into a Gorilla Glass production line and delivered the material within six months — the same glass, in updated formulations, that still covers the overwhelming majority of the world's smartphones today, iPhones and their imitators alike, a material that exists in mass production because one company's chief executive was bullied and cajoled into an act of manufacturing courage he had not planned to attempt.

Before Apple built its own phone in total secrecy, Jobs had already tried, briefly and in public, to get into the phone business by other means, and the failure of that earlier attempt is what convinced him a partnership would never work. In 2005, Apple collaborated with Motorola on a handset called the ROKR E1, marketed explicitly as the first "iTunes phone," a conventional candy-bar-style mobile phone, built and manufactured entirely by Motorola and sold through Cingular, that came loaded with a stripped-down version of iTunes for loading and playing music. Jobs unveiled it himself, sharing a stage with Motorola's chief executive at a September 2005 event, but his own enthusiasm on stage was visibly restrained; he described the device, with a candor rare for a product he was personally introducing, as essentially "an iPod shuffle on a cell phone," a description that damned the product with the faintest of praise even as he introduced it to the world. The ROKR deserved the tepid billing. Limited by its carrier and its manufacturer to holding no more than one hundred songs regardless of its actual storage capacity, saddled with a clumsy interface for transferring music that bore little resemblance to the effortless syncing iTunes offered on a real iPod, encased in cheap-feeling plastic, and incapable of downloading music wirelessly at all, it fell so far short of what Jobs and his engineers knew a phone built entirely by Apple could do that its main effect inside the company was to harden Jobs's conviction that Apple would never again build a product by asking another company to manufacture Apple's software into someone else's hardware. Motorola quietly discontinued the ROKR within about a year of its release, and less than eighteen months after that underwhelming Cingular event, Jobs stood on a different stage and introduced a phone Apple had built entirely on its own terms.

The ROKR's failure sharpened, rather than dampened, Jobs's appetite for the category, and its lesson ran through every subsequent decision Project Purple's engineers made. Where the ROKR had been hobbled by a carrier partner's restrictions and a hardware partner's compromises, the iPhone would be designed and manufactured entirely under Apple's own control, with AT&T brought in only as a distribution partner rather than as a co-designer with veto power over the software. Where the ROKR's interface for managing music had been an afterthought bolted onto an existing Motorola phone, the iPhone's software would be built from its very foundation around the same principles that had made the iPod's interface a pleasure to use. The humiliation, mild but public, of standing on a stage introducing a product he could not fully vouch for taught Jobs a lesson that Project Purple's total secrecy and its total, obsessive control over every component were built specifically to avoid repeating.

But it worked, and the culmination came in January 2007, when Steve Jobs walked onto a stage in San Francisco to reveal what Apple had built — and delivered what many consider the single greatest product introduction in the history of business.

Chapter 37 — Three Revolutionary Products

The keynote Steve Jobs delivered on January 9, 2007, at the Macworld conference in San Francisco, is studied and re-watched two decades later as a masterpiece of the form, and its central rhetorical device has become legendary. Jobs told the audience that Apple was going to introduce three revolutionary products. The first, he said, was a widescreen iPod with touch controls. The second was a revolutionary mobile phone. The third was a breakthrough internet communications device. He repeated the three — an iPod, a phone, an internet communicator — and then said them again, and again, faster each time, letting the rhythm build, letting the audience begin to realize what was happening. "Are you getting it?" he asked. "These are not three separate devices. This is one device. And we are calling it iPhone." The hall erupted. It was theater of the highest order, the culmination of the keynote form Jobs had been perfecting since the Macintosh launch in 1984, and it framed the iPhone exactly as Jobs wanted it framed: not as a phone with extra features, but as a convergence, a single device that swallowed the whole constellation of things people carried.

The demonstration that followed delivered on the promise, and it is worth dwelling on how strange and new the iPhone actually looked in 2007, because familiarity has erased our ability to see it. Every other phone had a physical keyboard or keypad taking up half its face; the iPhone was almost entirely a single sheet of glass, with just one button below the screen. To use it, you touched the screen directly with your fingers — you scrolled through lists by flicking, and the list slid and slowed as if it had real physical momentum; you zoomed into a photograph or a web page by pinching two fingers apart; you tapped icons to launch programs. Jobs demonstrated the web browser showing real web pages — not the stripped-down, broken mobile versions other phones displayed, but the actual internet, which you could pinch and zoom to read — and the audience gasped, because no phone had ever shown the genuine web before. He showed the iPhone playing music and video with the iPod's elegance, showed it handling email, showed it displaying maps, showed the way you could turn the device sideways and the screen would rotate to match. Every interaction was fluid, responsive, and obvious in a way that no phone had ever been, and the cumulative effect was of watching a device from the future being handled casually on a stage in the present. The gap between the iPhone and every other phone on the market was so vast that it did not look like a better phone; it looked like a different kind of object entirely.

The response, both immediate and over the following months, was extraordinary and not universal, and the skeptics are worth remembering, because they illustrate how even brilliant industry insiders can fail to see a revolution. Many established players in the phone industry were dismissive. The chief executive of one of the dominant phone makers reportedly scoffed at the iPhone's lack of a physical keyboard and its high price, confident that serious users would never abandon real keys for typing on glass. Commentators pointed out that the iPhone was expensive — five hundred dollars or more, a stunning price for a phone at the time — that it was initially tied to a single carrier, that its first version lacked features other phones had, that typing on glass was unproven. There was genuine uncertainty about whether people would accept a touchscreen phone, whether the onscreen keyboard would work well enough, whether the market wanted what Apple was offering. And it is true that the first iPhone had real limitations: it was slow to connect to the internet on the cellular networks of the day, it could not run third-party applications at all in its first year (a limitation Jobs initially defended and would soon reverse), and it was, by later standards, primitive. But the fundamental thing — the touchscreen, the real internet, the fluid interface, the convergence of devices — was so obviously right that it swept away the objections. People who held an iPhone wanted one, and the demand built into a phenomenon, and the phone industry that had scoffed found itself, within a few years, scrambling to copy an approach it had declared a mistake.

The flawless-looking demonstration that so impressed the audience was, in reality, one of the most precarious performances in the history of product launches, and knowing how precarious it was changes how one should read Jobs's composure on that stage. The device he held had been finished only weeks earlier and remained riddled with bugs; in rehearsals it would play a song, or send an email, or load a map, but doing those things in a different order than the one the engineers had tested could crash it outright. The team's solution was what its engineers, including Andy Grignon, who helped build the demo, privately called "the golden path" — a rigidly scripted sequence of taps and swipes, rehearsed by Jobs for days beforehand, that avoided every combination of actions known to make the software fail. The signal-strength bars on the display were hard-coded to show a full five bars regardless of the iPhone's actual reception, AT&T quietly parked a portable cell tower near the venue to guarantee a strong connection for Jobs's live call, and the device's Wi-Fi was deliberately shielded so that the thousands of journalists and enthusiasts in the audience, phones in hand, could not accidentally flood the same wireless channel Jobs depended on. Because the prototype's limited memory could not reliably run the whole sequence of demonstrations back to back, multiple iPhones were kept ready backstage, and Jobs, apparently seamlessly, switched between them as he moved from one feature to the next. None of this diminished what the audience saw — the interactions themselves were genuine, not simulated — but the seeming effortlessness of the hour was itself an engineering triumph layered on top of the hardware, achieved only because Jobs and his team had mapped, with obsessive precision, exactly which paths through the software were safe to walk.

It is worth naming directly the misconception that this history corrects, because the myth of a Steve Jobs keynote as pure, spontaneous mastery is one of the most durable stories told about him, and it is not quite true. Jobs's command of the stage was real and it was the product of genuine skill, but the confidence audiences read as effortless spontaneity was manufactured by a team of engineers working through the night to constrain every variable that could embarrass him, and by Jobs's own willingness to rehearse a single ninety-minute performance for the better part of a week until each gesture was reflexive. The takeaway is not that the achievement was fraudulent — the iPhone was real, and it worked, if imperfectly, exactly as shown — but that the seamlessness Apple came to be famous for, on stage as much as in its products, was never accidental. It was manufactured, deliberately and at real cost, by people willing to solder an antenna wire to a prototype and run it offstage rather than trust an unproven radio to behave in front of the world's press.

The name Jobs gave the device at the climax of his three-products routine was not the only naming decision unveiled that morning, and the other change, easy to overlook next to the thunderclap of "iPhone," was in its own way just as significant. Partway through the same keynote, Jobs told the audience that the company would be dropping the word "Computer" from its legal name, becoming simply Apple Inc. rather than Apple Computer, Inc., a change the company made official that same week. His explanation was understated compared to the theatrics of the iPhone reveal: with the iPod, and now the iPhone, and the Apple TV device also introduced that day, only one of the company's four principal product lines, the Macintosh, was still recognizably a computer in the traditional sense, and the old name, Jobs said, no longer described what Apple had become. It was a modest administrative announcement wedged into the same ninety minutes that produced the most celebrated product reveal of Jobs's career, and it received, understandably, a small fraction of the attention paid to the phone. But the two announcements were, in truth, a single argument made twice, once in the language of hardware and once in the language of corporate identity: that the company founded in a garage to sell a hobbyist's computer kit had, three decades later, outgrown the very category of its own founding, and that the device about to be unveiled was not a new product from a computer company but the flagship of something larger that no longer had a settled name for what it made.

The renaming carried a symbolic weight that the keynote's rush of demonstrations left little time to dwell on, but that later retellings of Apple's history have come to treat as a hinge point in its own right. Apple Computer had been the company's name since its incorporation in 1977, through the Apple II, the Macintosh, the wilderness years of the 1990s, and the iMac-led recovery that followed Jobs's return — three decades in which, whatever else Apple built, a computer of some description had always been the thing that ultimately defined the company in the public's mind. Dropping "Computer" in January 2007 was Apple's own quiet acknowledgment, made in a single sentence between demonstrations of a touchscreen phone, that the center of gravity had shifted permanently toward consumer devices the company had once treated as accessories to the Macintosh, and that the phone Jobs was about to unveil, rather than the computer that had given the company its name, was now the more accurate symbol of what Apple Inc. intended to become.

That same discipline — script the path, hide the seams, rehearse until the risk disappears — became the template for every major Apple product unveiling that followed, and it is visible still in the corporate keynotes that companies across the technology industry stage today, each one drilled, storyboarded, and pre-tested against failure long before an audience or a camera ever sees it. The golden path Jobs's engineers built in the small hours before January 9, 2007, was not merely a solution to one night's technical panic; it became, in effect, the operating procedure for how Apple would introduce nearly everything that mattered for the following two decades; and it is a small irony of the iPhone's history that the moment most often cited as proof of Jobs's untouchable stagecraft was also the moment he came closest to disaster, saved only by engineers willing to cheat, in the narrowest and most literal sense, on his behalf.

The iPhone's introduction also marked the culmination of Steve Jobs's development as a communicator and showman, and it is worth naming the skill directly because it was a genuine competitive weapon, not mere showmanship. Jobs had spent thirty years learning how to unveil a product — how to build suspense, how to control the pace, how to reduce a complex thing to a simple story, how to make an audience feel they were witnessing history and want desperately to be part of it. The 2007 keynote was the perfect expression of that craft: meticulously rehearsed (Jobs rehearsed obsessively, for days, refining every word and every demonstration), perfectly paced, emotionally engineered. It generated an avalanche of free media coverage worth far more than any advertising, put the iPhone on the cover of magazines and at the top of newscasts, and created a wave of desire that carried the product to market on a tide of anticipation. This ability to make a product launch into a global cultural event was something no competitor could match, and it was as much a part of Apple's advantage as the engineering. The iPhone would have been a great product regardless, but Jobs's presentation made it a phenomenon, and the phenomenon translated into sales, into brand, into the sense that Apple was not merely a company but the source of the future. Between the unveiling in January and the release in June 2007, the anticipation built to a fever, and when the iPhone finally went on sale, people lined up around blocks and camped overnight outside Apple stores to be among the first to hold it. What they were lining up for was not just a phone. It was the beginning of a change in human life as profound as any technology has ever wrought — though no one, standing in those lines, could have known how far it would go.

Chapter 38 — June 29, 2007

The iPhone went on sale on June 29, 2007, and the scenes outside Apple stores — lines stretching around city blocks, people who had camped overnight, the atmosphere of a product launch that felt more like a cultural event or a religious observance — announced that something unusual was happening. People do not, as a rule, sleep on sidewalks to buy a telephone. The iPhone's launch had the quality of a happening, a moment people wanted to be part of, and it established a ritual — the launch-day line outside the Apple Store — that would recur with every major new iPhone for years, becoming a fixture of modern consumer culture. What those first buyers were acquiring, though they could not have fully known it, was not merely a well-made gadget but the first version of the device that would, over the following decade, become the single most important and ubiquitous piece of technology on earth, more widespread than the personal computer had ever been, carried by billions of people, integrated into nearly every aspect of human life.

It is worth being precise about what the iPhone did and did not do at launch, because the honest history is more interesting than the myth of instant perfection. The first iPhone was, in important ways, incomplete. It ran only on the slower cellular networks of the day, making internet access frustratingly sluggish. It had a decent but not remarkable camera. And, most significantly, it could not run any software beyond the applications Apple itself provided — there was no way for outside developers to create programs for it, no App Store, none of the vast universe of third-party apps that would later define the device. Jobs had initially resisted the idea of letting outsiders write software for the iPhone, worried that third-party apps would compromise the device's reliability, security, and the seamless experience he was obsessed with controlling; his initial answer to developers who wanted to build for the iPhone was that they could make web applications that ran in the browser, a solution that satisfied almost no one. The iPhone at launch was, in this sense, a closed and limited device, a beautiful phone that did a fixed set of things very well and could not be extended. That it became the foundation of the largest software platform in history required a reversal that Jobs would make within a year — one of the most consequential decisions in the company's history, and one he came to only after resistance.

But even in its limited first version, the iPhone was transformative, because it got the fundamental thing right, and the fundamental thing was the interface. The direct-manipulation touchscreen — the ability to touch and move things on the screen directly with your fingers, with the interface responding fluidly and intuitively, objects sliding with physical momentum, pages zooming under a pinch — was a genuine revolution in how humans interact with computers, as significant in its way as the mouse and the graphical interface had been a generation earlier. It made the device usable by anyone, immediately, without instruction; a small child or an elderly person who had never touched a computer could pick up an iPhone and start using it, because touching things directly is the most natural interaction there is. This immediacy, this collapse of the distance between the person and the machine, was what made the iPhone not just a better phone but a new kind of device, and it was what let the smartphone become universal in a way earlier "smart" phones, with their tiny keyboards and baffling menus, never could. The iPhone made the internet, and computing itself, available to billions of people who would never have mastered a traditional computer, and in doing so it changed the world more broadly and more deeply than the personal computer ever had.

The competitive impact was swift and brutal, and it reshaped an entire industry within a few years. The dominant phone makers of 2007 — the companies that had ruled the mobile-phone business, that had scoffed at the iPhone's keyboard-less design and its price — were, within a few years, devastated. One by one, the giants of the pre-iPhone era collapsed or were reduced to shadows, unable to match the iPhone's interface, software, and ecosystem, having failed to see that the touchscreen smartphone was the future until it was too late to catch up. The one competitor that adapted successfully was Google, which had been developing a mobile operating system called Android and which, after the iPhone's unveiling, reshaped Android around the same touchscreen, full-screen model that Apple had pioneered. Android, given away free to phone makers and running on hardware from many manufacturers, would go on to power the majority of the world's smartphones — the Windows-versus-Mac dynamic replaying itself, with Google's open, widely licensed software reaching more devices while Apple's integrated, premium approach captured the most valuable customers and the great majority of the industry's profits. But whether running iOS or Android, essentially every smartphone made after 2007 was, in its fundamental design, a descendant of the iPhone: a slab of glass controlled by touch, an object Apple had defined and that the whole world then adopted. Apple had not merely made a successful product; it had created the template for the defining device of the age, and every phone that followed, from every maker, was working within the paradigm the iPhone established.

The actual numbers from that first weekend are worth setting against the legend, because they complicate the tidy story of instant, overwhelming triumph. All 164 Apple retail stores in the United States stayed open until midnight on the evening of June 29, and customers were limited to two iPhones each as employees tried to manage the crush at the doors. Analysts, working from foot traffic and guesswork, floated first-weekend estimates ranging anywhere from a quarter-million to seven hundred thousand units sold. The one hard number that actually surfaced came from AT&T, the exclusive carrier, which confirmed roughly one hundred and forty-six thousand activations over the opening weekend — a real and gratifying result for a five-hundred-dollar phone tied to a single carrier, but a fraction of the multi-million-unit opening weekends that later iPhone generations would routinely produce. The frenzy outside the stores was genuine, but the frenzy and the sales volume were not the same thing, and it is worth remembering that the iPhone's initial commercial performance, however satisfying to Apple, was modest by the standard the device itself would soon establish.

Among the people waiting in those lines was a man named Greg Packer, and his presence complicates the sentimental image of devoted early adopters camping out purely for love of the product. Packer, a retired highway worker from Long Island, arrived outside the Fifth Avenue Apple Store in New York days before the launch and held his spot for nearly a week, becoming, by wide consensus, the very first person on earth to purchase an iPhone. He was not, however, a typical fan; Packer had built something of a career out of being first in line and first on camera for any newsworthy event, and reporters who recognized him from previous stakeouts dubbed him, only half-jokingly, "iLoser" in the press coverage that followed his moment of iPhone fame. The most photographed image of Apple's most mythologized launch day, in other words, belonged not to an ordinary customer whose life the device was about to transform, but to a professional line-sitter chasing a headline — a detail that undercuts, gently, the tendency to read every detail of that day as evidence of some pure, spontaneous public passion for what Apple had built.

The truth those numbers and that anecdote point toward is that June 29, 2007, mattered less for what it proved in the moment than for what it set in motion. The iPhone did not conquer the phone market in a single weekend; it entered, in its first version, a fairly narrow slice of it, tied to one carrier, priced beyond most people's casual budget, missing the third-party software that would define it within a year. The device's real triumph was cumulative rather than instantaneous — each successive model selling faster and wider than the one before, the volumes climbing from the hundreds of thousands of that first weekend into the tens of millions within a few years and, eventually, into launch weekends measured in the tens of millions of units sold within days, a scale of consumer demand that dwarfs anything the phone industry had produced before it or has produced since. The line outside the Fifth Avenue store in 2007, camped by curiosity-seekers and one professional line-sitter, was the small, almost quaint beginning of a ritual that would eventually be reenacted, at vastly greater scale, on nearly every continent on Earth.

That ritual persists today in recognizable form even as the mechanics of buying an iPhone have been almost entirely redesigned to avoid the exact chaos of 2007; online reservations, timed pickup windows, and staggered regional releases now channel the demand that once expressed itself only as a line stretching around a city block. But the line itself never disappeared — outside flagship stores in cities like New York, London, Tokyo, and Sydney, some number of customers still choose to camp overnight for each new iPhone, less out of necessity than out of a willingness to participate in something that has become, itself, a piece of consumer folklore Apple did not invent but has never discouraged. The company that once measured its opening weekend in the low hundreds of thousands now treats an iPhone launch as a matter of routine global logistics, moving tens of millions of units within days — proof that the frenzy of that first Friday night, modest as its actual sales figures were, correctly previewed an appetite that had nowhere to go but up.

The goodwill generated by that launch-weekend frenzy was tested only ten weeks later, in a way that the legend of the iPhone's triumphant debut tends to omit entirely. On September 5, 2007, Apple cut the price of the eight-gigabyte iPhone by two hundred dollars, from five hundred and ninety-nine dollars to three hundred and ninety-nine, a reduction so steep, so soon after the device's release, that it provoked a genuine consumer backlash among the very customers who had queued around the block to buy it at full price only weeks before. Early adopters flooded Apple's feedback channels and the press with complaints that they had paid a premium to be first, only to watch the company slash the price before the device had even been on sale for a full quarter; Jobs himself later said the volume of angry correspondence he personally received was substantial enough that he felt compelled to respond publicly rather than let the complaints simply pass. On September 6, Apple posted an open letter from Jobs on its website acknowledging the anger directly. "We apologize for disappointing some of you," he wrote, and announced that Apple would issue a one-hundred-dollar store credit, redeemable at Apple's retail and online stores, to every customer who had bought a first-generation iPhone at the original price. It was a costly concession for a company that rarely conceded anything in public, and it stood out precisely because Apple's culture, cultivated so carefully by Jobs himself, treated public apology as almost a foreign language.

The episode is a useful corrective to the tendency, encouraged by the mythology of June 29, to remember the iPhone's first months as an uninterrupted triumphal march. The same device that had drawn campers and lines around city blocks generated, ten weeks later, enough genuine customer anger over a pricing decision that Jobs judged a public apology and a real financial concession the only adequate response — a reminder that even Apple's most celebrated launch produced ordinary business friction of the kind that accompanies any new consumer product, and that the company's early reputation for treating its most devoted customers well was earned, in this instance, not by avoiding a costly misstep but by owning one publicly and paying to make it right. The price cut itself was not made lightly on Apple's side either: accounts of the decision describe it as driven by the need to broaden the iPhone's reach beyond its earliest and wealthiest adopters just as the critical holiday shopping season approached, trading a slower, more exclusive rollout for the higher volumes the device would need to build the ecosystem Apple was counting on. Whether the trade was made cynically or not, the compensation Apple extended came only as store credit, redeemable solely at Apple's own retail and online channels, rather than as cash — a detail that meant the company's public contrition doubled, in its execution, as a mechanism for pulling angry early buyers back into Apple's stores to spend their refund on something else Apple sold.

The iPhone's success also transformed Apple's own scale and nature beyond anything the iPod had achieved, and it set the company on the path to becoming the most valuable enterprise in history. The phone market was enormous — everyone on earth wanted a phone, in a way that not everyone wanted a music player or a computer — and Apple, selling a premium phone at a premium price to hundreds of millions of the world's customers, generated profits on a scale that dwarfed everything in its past. The iPhone would become, and would remain for years, the most profitable product in the history of consumer electronics, the engine that drove Apple to a trillion dollars and beyond. But the iPhone's full potential, and its full impact on the world, would not be unleashed until Steve Jobs reversed his initial position and did the thing he had resisted: opened the device to outside developers, and let anyone build software for it, distributed through a store Apple controlled. That decision, made in 2008, created the App Store, and the App Store turned the iPhone from a great device into a platform — an entire economy, a new medium, a foundation on which millions of developers would build businesses and on which whole new industries would arise. It is impossible to overstate how much the App Store changed, and it is where the iPhone's story truly opens out into the world.

Chapter 39 — The App Store

In July 2008, a little over a year after the iPhone went on sale, Apple opened the App Store, and it is not an exaggeration to say that this single decision created a new global economy and changed the shape of the technology industry more than the iPhone hardware itself. The App Store was a place, built into the iPhone, where users could browse, buy, and instantly download software applications — "apps" — written not by Apple but by anyone, from a lone teenager in a bedroom to a giant corporation, and where those developers could reach hundreds of millions of iPhone users and get paid, with Apple handling the payment, the distribution, and taking a cut of every sale. It transformed the iPhone from a device that did what Apple decided it should do into a platform that could do almost anything anyone could imagine and build, and it unleashed a wave of creativity and enterprise that would produce entire industries — mobile gaming, ride-hailing, social media as we know it, mobile photography and messaging and shopping and dating and banking — that could not have existed before.

The decision to create the App Store required Steve Jobs to reverse himself, and the reversal is instructive because it shows that even Jobs's famous stubbornness could bend to a good enough argument. As we have seen, Jobs had initially opposed letting outside developers write native software for the iPhone, out of his deep instinct for control — his fear that third-party apps would introduce instability, security holes, malware, and clutter, degrading the pristine experience he had labored to create. He wanted the iPhone to be a sealed, perfect appliance, not an open platform where anyone's possibly-shoddy software could run. But he was persuaded — by colleagues, by the obvious hunger of developers to build for the device, by the demonstrated demand — that the potential of an open platform was too enormous to forgo, and, crucially, that Apple could capture the benefits of openness while controlling the risks through a specific mechanism: curation. The App Store would be open to any developer, but every app would have to be submitted to Apple for review and approval before it could be sold, and all apps would be distributed only through Apple's store, running in a restricted "sandbox" that limited what they could do to the device. This was the compromise that resolved Jobs's dilemma: the iPhone would become a platform, open to the creativity of the whole world, but Apple would stand as the gatekeeper, reviewing every app, controlling distribution, enforcing rules, and taking a cut — typically thirty percent — of every transaction. Openness with a toll booth. Freedom within a walled garden.

The results exceeded every expectation and reshaped the digital world. Developers flooded to the platform, and the number of apps exploded from thousands to hundreds of thousands to, eventually, millions. The phrase "there's an app for that" entered the language, capturing the sense that the iPhone, through its apps, could do virtually anything. Whole categories of company were born that existed only because the App Store and the smartphone existed: services that let you summon a car with a tap, that let you rent a stranger's home for the night, that turned photo-sharing and messaging into the dominant forms of social life, that put games of astonishing sophistication into everyone's pocket. Small developers became wealthy; a well-made app could reach a global market of hundreds of millions overnight, and a handful of individuals could build businesses that would once have required factories and distribution networks. The App Store generated staggering revenue — tens of billions of dollars a year flowing to developers, and a large share flowing to Apple through its cut — and it became a central pillar of Apple's business, the heart of a services empire that would grow, over the following years, into one of the company's most important sources of profit. More than that, it locked customers into Apple's ecosystem more powerfully than any hardware feature could: once you had bought apps, built your digital life around them, learned their conventions, the cost of switching to a different kind of phone became a genuine barrier, and the App Store became a moat around Apple's business.

It is worth correcting a natural assumption about this whole sequence — the assumption that Apple always intended the App Store, that native third-party software was simply waiting in the wings until Apple found time to ship it. In fact, at the developer conference that immediately preceded the iPhone's release in the summer of 2007, Jobs stood on stage and offered developers what Apple itself called a "sweet solution" to the demand for third-party software: not native applications at all, but web applications, built with the same web technologies used to build ordinary websites, running inside the iPhone's browser rather than on the device itself. The reception in the room was telling — when an Apple executive demonstrated the web-app approach, the audience offered only the faint, polite applause of people being handed less than they had hoped for. Developers wanted to write real software that lived on the device, took advantage of its hardware, and could be discovered and sold like a product, and a browser-based workaround satisfied almost none of that appetite. It took roughly a year of mounting developer frustration, a reversal of position by Jobs, and the announcement of a genuine software development kit — released in March 2008, four months before the App Store itself opened — before Apple arrived at the model that stuck. The "sweet solution" of 2007 is a useful corrective to any tidy narrative of Apple's foresight: for a full year, the company's official answer to the question of third-party software was a proposal so unsatisfying that its own audience could barely bring itself to clap.

The App Store that finally opened on July 10, 2008, did so modestly by later standards, and the figures are worth setting down because they show how quickly the platform's own momentum outran anyone's initial expectations. It launched with roughly five hundred applications available for download, about a quarter of them free, a catalog that looks vanishingly small next to the millions of apps the store would eventually hold. Yet even that small catalog produced ten million downloads in its first weekend alone, an appetite that told Apple, within days, that it had built something far larger than a modest add-on feature for the iPhone. The gap between those two numbers — five hundred apps, ten million downloads — is itself the clearest evidence of how much pent-up developer and consumer demand Jobs's year of resistance had been holding back, and of how badly the "sweet solution" had underestimated what people actually wanted from their phones.

The review process Apple built to police that flood of new software could be arbitrary in ways that became, almost immediately, a source of both amusement and irritation, and one submission from the App Store's earliest weeks captures the absurdity better than any policy debate could. In August 2008, barely a month after the store opened, a German developer named Armin Heinrich submitted an application called I Am Rich, priced at the store's maximum allowed amount of nine hundred and ninety-nine dollars and ninety-nine cents, whose entire function was to display a glowing red gem on the screen along with a short affirming message — nothing else, no calculator, no utility of any kind, an app whose only purpose was to prove, to anyone glancing at a stranger's phone, that its owner had been willing to spend a thousand dollars on nothing at all. Heinrich later said he had built it as a kind of art piece, a joke aimed at iPhone owners who complained that ninety-nine-cent apps felt too cheap to be worth their time, and he said plainly that he had not expected anyone to actually buy it. Eight people did, before Apple, facing a wave of press coverage mocking both the app and the review process that had approved it, pulled it from the store within about a day.

The episode became an early and durable joke about the App Store's review process precisely because it was so difficult to explain: a submission with no function beyond ostentatious self-display, priced at the maximum the store's own rules allowed, had passed whatever scrutiny Apple's reviewers applied before removal, undercutting, in one small and almost comic case, the story Apple told about curation as a serious safeguard against low-quality or bad-faith software. It was a minor embarrassment rather than a genuine scandal, and Apple's review standards tightened considerably in the years that followed as the store scaled from hundreds of apps to millions of submissions a year, each one still, in principle, subject to the same human review that had waved a thousand-dollar gem emoji through in the store's very first weeks. But I Am Rich has endured in the App Store's own folklore, cited for years afterward whenever critics wanted a shorthand example of how a review process built to protect users from exactly this kind of nonsense could, in its first weeks of operation, wave it straight through. The pulled listing did not disappear from public memory the way most rejected apps do; screenshots of its glowing red gem continued circulating on technology blogs for years afterward, less because the app itself mattered than because it so neatly punctured the premise, central to Apple's whole pitch for the curated model, that human review guaranteed some baseline of genuine usefulness before a piece of software ever reached a paying customer's screen.

The tension the App Store created between Apple and the developers who depended on it, gestured at in general terms above, eventually produced a legal reckoning specific enough to name here. In August 2020, Epic Games, the maker of the enormously popular game Fortnite, deliberately built a direct payment system into its iOS app to bypass Apple's mandatory in-app purchase system and its accompanying thirty-percent commission; Apple responded by removing Fortnite from the App Store entirely, and Epic, which had engineered the confrontation on purpose, filed suit accusing Apple of running an illegal monopoly over how software reached iPhone users. The case went to trial in 2021, and the judge's ruling split the difference in a way that satisfied neither side completely: she found that Apple was not, in the strict legal sense, an illegal monopolist, but she also ordered the company to stop forbidding developers from telling their own customers, inside their own apps, about cheaper ways to pay outside Apple's system — a real crack in the walled garden's outer wall, even if the wall itself remained standing. The fight continued in the courts for years afterward, with further rulings finding Apple in violation of the original order, evidence that the argument the App Store started in 2008 was, decades later, still unresolved.

But the App Store also planted the seeds of the fiercest controversies of Apple's later years, and an honest history has to name them here even though their full flowering came a decade later. The same gatekeeping power that made the App Store safe and profitable — Apple's absolute control over what software could run on the iPhone, its power to approve or reject any app, its mandatory thirty-percent cut of transactions, its prohibition on any competing way to install software — would come to be seen by many as a monopolistic abuse, a stranglehold that Apple used to tax and control an entire economy that had grown up on its platform. Developers who had once been grateful for access to Apple's customers came to resent the toll they paid and the rules they had to obey; some, like the maker of a hugely popular game, would eventually sue Apple, arguing that its control of the App Store was an illegal monopoly. Governments and regulators around the world would investigate and, in time, act against Apple's control of the store, forcing changes to the closed model Jobs had built. The App Store thus embodies, more clearly than any other Apple product, the central tension and irony of the company's whole history: the walled garden that made Apple's products so good — so seamless, so secure, so profitable — was also a mechanism of control that Apple used to dominate an entire economy, and the company that had been founded by two rebels selling blue boxes to defy a monopoly had become, itself, one of the most powerful and criticized gatekeepers on earth. That reckoning was years away in 2008. For now, the App Store was a triumph, the master stroke that turned the iPhone into the most important platform in the world and set Apple on the path to becoming the most valuable company in history. It was the fullest vindication of a philosophy Jobs had held since the beginning, and it deserves a chapter of its own to understand why the whole widget, in the end, won.

Chapter 40 — The Whole Widget Wins

The triumph of the iPhone and the App Store settled, at least for a generation, an argument that had run through the entire history of the personal computer and through this entire book: the argument between the open model and the closed model, between Bill Gates's philosophy and Steve Jobs's, between software that runs on anyone's hardware and a whole widget controlled end to end by a single company. In the era of the personal computer, the open model had won decisively; Microsoft's Windows, licensed to any hardware maker, running on cheap commodity machines, had conquered the market, and Apple's insistence on making the whole widget had nearly killed it. In the era of the smartphone, the closed, integrated model — the whole widget — triumphed, and understanding why is essential to understanding both Apple's success and the deeper logic of the technology industry.

Jobs's whole-widget philosophy held that a company should control both the hardware and the software of its products, designing them together as an integrated whole rather than making one and licensing it to run on the other's products. His argument for this had always been about the quality of the experience: only by controlling every layer, he believed, could a company make the pieces fit together seamlessly, eliminate the compromises and incompatibilities that plague products assembled from parts made by different companies with different priorities, and deliver something that simply worked, beautifully, without the friction and frustration that came from the open model's necessary compromises. The cost of this philosophy was reach: because Apple would not license its software to other hardware makers, its products would always be made only by Apple, would always be more expensive than commodity alternatives, and would always, therefore, reach fewer people than an open platform that ran on everyone's cheap hardware. In the PC wars, this cost had been fatal; the market had chosen cheap and open and good-enough over expensive and integrated and excellent, and Apple had been marginalized.

Why did the same philosophy that lost the PC war win the smartphone war? Several reasons converged. The first is that in a mobile device — a small, battery-powered, always-carried computer — the benefits of tight hardware-software integration were far greater and the penalties for the open model's compromises far more severe. Making a phone that was fast, reliable, and long-lasting on a battery, with a fluid touch interface, demanded a degree of coordination between hardware and software that the open model struggled to achieve; the phones built from standardized parts and licensed software were, for years, noticeably worse — buggier, slower, clumsier — than the integrated iPhone. The second reason is that Apple had learned from the PC defeat and had built, in the App Store, an answer to the open model's greatest advantage. The reason open platforms win is usually software: more hardware means more users means more developers means more software means more users, the virtuous cycle that had made Windows unbeatable. But the App Store gave Apple that same cycle within its own closed world; because the iPhone sold in the hundreds of millions, it was a large enough market to attract essentially all the world's developers, so Apple got the abundance of software that openness usually provides without having to open its hardware. The closed platform was big enough to have the software advantages of an open one. And the third reason is that Apple's premium, integrated approach captured the most valuable customers and, therefore, the overwhelming majority of the industry's profits, even as Android captured the majority of the units; Apple did not need to sell the most phones, only to sell the most profitable ones, and its whole-widget model was ideally suited to that.

The vindication was, for Steve Jobs, deeply personal, because it validated a conviction he had held and been punished for since the beginning. He had believed, against the entire trend of the industry, against the lesson of the PC wars, against the conventional wisdom that open always beats closed, that controlling the whole widget was the path to greatness — and the iPhone proved him right on the largest possible stage, making Apple, within a few years of the iPhone's launch, not the marginal niche player it had been for two decades but the most valuable and profitable company in the world. The man whose insistence on integration had nearly bankrupted Apple in the 1980s and 1990s was, in the 2000s and beyond, vindicated by that same insistence, as the world moved from the standalone computer, where openness won, to the ecosystem of connected mobile devices, where integration won. It was one of the great reversals in business history, and it rested on Jobs's refusal, through decades of being told he was wrong, to abandon his belief in the whole widget.

The numbers behind that vindication are worth setting down in full, because they show a more complicated victory than the phrase "the whole widget won" can capture on its own. By late 2011, Google's Android, running on hardware from dozens of manufacturers, had already overtaken the iPhone in raw market share, holding roughly fifty-three percent of the smartphone market to the iPhone's twenty-nine percent — precisely the open-versus-closed dynamic that had crushed Apple in the personal-computer era, replaying itself on schedule. And yet, measured by profit rather than units, the story inverted entirely: in 2012, Apple captured sixty-nine percent of the entire handset industry's operating profits, more than double the next-largest share, and by the fourth quarter of that year, when the iPhone 5 was on sale, Apple's share of industry profits reached seventy-two percent while Samsung, the largest Android manufacturer, took a comparatively distant twenty-nine percent. Apple had, in other words, lost the unit war precisely as it had in the 1980s and had not really needed to fight it; it had built a smaller, far more profitable kingdom sitting on top of a market that Android, in sheer volume, actually ruled — the whole widget had not conquered the industry so much as claimed the most valuable room in it.

Jobs's fury at watching Android succeed at all, even from that smaller and more profitable room, was not academic, and the rawness of his reaction, preserved in his own words to his biographer Walter Isaacson, shows how personally he took what he regarded as theft rather than mere competition. Convinced that Google, led by a company whose own chief executive had once sat on Apple's board, had lifted the touchscreen interface his teams had built at such cost, Jobs told Isaacson, in language his biographer published without softening it, "I will spend my last dying breath if I need to, and I will spend every penny of Apple's forty billion dollars in the bank, to right this wrong." He went further still, calling Android "a stolen product" and declaring, "I'm going to destroy Android, because it's a stolen product. I'm willing to go thermonuclear war on this." He did not, in the end, destroy Android, which today runs on the majority of the world's smartphones and remains, by unit count, the dominant mobile operating system on Earth — a fact that sits uncomfortably next to the triumphant framing of "the whole widget wins," and a reminder that Apple's victory was real, immense, and permanent in the terms that mattered most to its bank account, but never total in the terms Jobs himself, in his angrier moments, seemed to want.

What the whole-widget model did deliver, unambiguously, was a scale of financial success with no real precedent in corporate history, and the milestone that best captures it arrived on August 2, 2018, when Apple's shares closed high enough to push its market valuation past one trillion dollars, making it the first publicly traded American company ever to cross that threshold — a company that, barely two decades earlier, under a different, defeated version of itself, had been ninety days from running out of cash. The path from that 1997 brink to the trillion-dollar close of 2018 ran directly through the sequence this book has traced: the iMac's rescue, the iPod's reinvention of an industry, the iTunes Store's re-founding of the music business, and finally the iPhone and the App Store, whose profits, concentrated and compounding for a decade, built the balance sheet that made the trillion-dollar figure possible. Apple would go on, in the years after Jobs's death, to blow past that figure entirely, but the crossing itself, in the summer of 2018, stands as the clearest possible number attached to the argument this chapter has made: that in the world of connected mobile devices, unlike the world of the standalone PC, owning the whole widget and selling it at a premium to the customers who could afford it was worth more, in the end, than owning the largest share of the market itself.

Jobs's vow to go "thermonuclear" on what he considered a stolen product was not merely rhetoric; it produced, within Apple's legal department, one of the largest and most consequential patent wars in the history of the technology industry, and its most decisive verdict arrived less than a year after Jobs's death, as if to deliver, posthumously, part of the vindication he had sworn to pursue. Apple sued Samsung Electronics, the largest maker of Android phones and tablets, accusing it of copying the design and the software of the iPhone and the iPad down to details as specific as the rounded rectangle of the device's shape, the grid of icons on its home screen, and the pinch-to-zoom gesture itself. On August 24, 2012, a nine-person jury in a federal court in San Jose returned its verdict after less than three days of deliberation: Samsung had willfully infringed multiple Apple patents across two dozen of its own products, and the jury awarded Apple damages of just over one billion dollars, a sum that made headlines around the world as one of the largest patent-infringement verdicts in American legal history. The jury rejected every one of Samsung's countersuing claims against Apple in the same verdict, a result so lopsided that commentators at the time described it as close to a clean sweep for Apple's legal team.

The verdict was later reduced and revised through years of appeals, retrials on damages, and further litigation that dragged the case's final numbers well below the jury's initial billion-dollar figure, and Samsung continued selling Android phones by the hundreds of millions throughout the entire fight, undercutting any suggestion that the courtroom victory had actually slowed Android's advance in the marketplace the way Jobs's fiercest words had promised. But the verdict mattered for reasons beyond the dollar figure attached to it, because a jury had now found, as a matter of law rather than mere marketing rhetoric, that the phone which had come to dominate the world's smartphone market by unit volume had done so, in significant part, by copying specific and patentable design choices Apple's own engineers had made first. It was as close as the legal system ever came to ruling on the argument Jobs had made to Isaacson in his angriest moments — that the touchscreen world Android now ruled by volume had been built, in no small part, on ideas that were never Google's or Samsung's to take. Among the Samsung products the jury found to infringe were several models in the Galaxy S and Galaxy Tab lines, devices that had, in the two years before the verdict, become Samsung's own most commercially important answer to the iPhone and the iPad — meaning the ruling struck directly at the products Samsung was relying on to compete in the present, rather than at some peripheral or already-discontinued line the company could shrug off and abandon.

There is a deeper lesson in the whole-widget triumph, and it connects to the largest theme of this book: the tension between the excellence that control makes possible and the power that control confers. The whole widget won because control produces quality — because a company that owns every layer can make something better than a coalition of companies that each own one layer. But the same control that produces quality also produces power, and dominance, and the ability to extract tolls and dictate terms and stand as the gatekeeper of an entire economy. The integrated iPhone was a better product because Apple controlled everything about it; and Apple's control of everything about it gave the company a power over developers, customers, and whole industries that would, in time, provoke lawsuits, regulation, and a global argument about whether such control had become abusive. The whole widget won, and its victory made Apple both the maker of the best products in the world and one of the most powerful gatekeepers in the history of commerce, and those two things are not separable — they are the same fact seen from two sides. That doubleness, the excellence and the power growing from the same root, is the essence of what Apple became, and it is the theme we will follow into the company's later years, its controversies, and its reckonings. But before Apple reached those reckonings, it reached the summit — and at the summit, at the very peak of his powers and his company's triumph, Steve Jobs was already dying. The iPhone that made Apple the most valuable company in the world was launched by a man who had been fighting cancer for years, and whose time was running out.

Chapter 41 — The Diagnosis

In October 2003, during a routine medical scan for an unrelated issue, doctors found a tumor on Steve Jobs's pancreas. The news was, on its face, a near-certain death sentence, because pancreatic cancer is one of the deadliest of all cancers, usually detected too late and almost always fatal within a short time. But Jobs's doctors quickly determined that he had an unusual and far more hopeful form of the disease: a pancreatic neuroendocrine tumor, a rare, slow-growing type that, unlike the common and lethal form of pancreatic cancer, was potentially treatable and even curable if caught early and removed surgically. This was, in the cruel lottery of cancer, extraordinarily good fortune — Jobs had been handed one of the rare pancreatic tumors that a person could actually survive, if he acted. And then Steve Jobs, one of the most brilliant decision-makers of his age, made a decision that his own doctors and friends begged him not to make, and that may have cost him his life: he refused, for nine months, to have the surgery.

Instead of the operation his physicians urged, Jobs turned to alternative medicine. For roughly nine months after his diagnosis, he attempted to treat his cancer with a regimen of his own devising and choosing: a strict vegan diet, juices, herbal remedies, acupuncture, and various other unconventional and unproven approaches, along with the counsel of practitioners outside mainstream medicine. He was, those close to him said, resistant to the idea of his body being opened, drawn to the notion that he could cure himself through diet and natural means, influenced by the same lifelong convictions — about purity of the body, about the power of the mind and of natural approaches, about his own specialness and exemption from ordinary rules — that had shaped his diets and his outlook since his youth. His wife, his friends, and his doctors pleaded with him to have the surgery, growing frantic as the months passed, and he resisted them, treating the decision as his own to make and trusting his own judgment over the unanimous urging of the medical experts. Only after nine months, when scans showed the tumor had grown and possibly spread, did he finally consent to the operation. By then, it is at least possible — his doctors could never say for certain, and the question is genuinely unresolvable — that the window in which surgery might have cured him had begun to close.

It is difficult, and important, to write about this decision honestly, because it is the point at which the qualities that made Steve Jobs extraordinary became, in a different context, catastrophic. The reality distortion field — the refusal to accept limits, the conviction that reality would bend to his will, the trust in his own judgment over the consensus of experts — had served him brilliantly in business, where it let him will impossible products into existence and defy the conventional wisdom that would have kept Apple small and safe. Applied to a tumor, the same qualities were lethal. Cancer does not respond to charisma; a tumor cannot be talked out of growing; the reality distortion field, which had reshaped so much of the world to Jobs's vision, met in his own pancreas a piece of reality that would not distort. The very refusal to accept constraints that had built Apple led him, faced with a treatable cancer, to reject the treatment in favor of an approach that had no chance of working, and to lose months that he might not have had to lose. Jobs himself, later, is said to have regretted the delay, to have understood that he had made a terrible mistake. It is one of the most human and tragic aspects of his story: that the same mind that could see further than anyone in matters of technology could not see, in the one matter that most concerned his own survival, the simple truth his doctors were begging him to accept.

Jobs's own explanation for his resistance, given years later to Walter Isaacson, the biographer he chose and cooperated with extensively in the final years of his life, is worth quoting directly, because it reveals something more specific than generalized denial. Asked why he had refused the operation his doctors were begging him to have, Jobs said simply, "I didn't want my body to be opened... I didn't want to be violated in that way." It is a strikingly intimate admission, less about alternative medicine as a positive belief system than about a visceral horror of surgery itself, one that his interest in diet and purification gave him a language and a set of rituals to justify. Isaacson, reflecting afterward on the many hours the two of them spent discussing this period, said plainly: "We talked about this a lot. He wanted to talk about it, how he regretted it... I think he felt he should have been operated on sooner." That regret, offered by the person closest to Jobs's own reckoning with the decision, is as close as the record comes to a verdict from Jobs himself on the nine months he had refused to operate.

It would be a distortion of its own, though, to conclude that Jobs rejected mainstream medicine entirely, at every stage, until his death — a version of the story that flattens nine months of documented resistance in 2003 and 2004 into the whole of his medical history. After the delayed surgery, Jobs was, in fact, treated repeatedly and extensively within conventional medicine for years afterward, submitting to chemotherapy, targeted radiological treatments, and a battery of scans and interventions as the disease progressed and eventually spread to his liver. The clearest evidence of this is the most dramatic medical episode of his final years: in the spring of 2009, gravely ill with liver failure, Jobs traveled quietly to Memphis, Tennessee, and underwent a liver transplant at Methodist University Hospital, performed by the surgeon Dr. James Eason, using an organ that became available after a young man died in a car accident on March 21 of that year. The secrecy of the trip — conducted with so little public disclosure that the hospital itself initially denied to reporters that Jobs had ever been a patient there — fed a wave of speculation that a billionaire had used money and connections to jump the transplant queue ahead of patients who needed the organ more urgently. Dr. Eason later addressed the accusation directly, explaining that Jobs had received the liver because his MELD score — the standard medical measure of how sick a liver-failure patient is — made him the most critical patient of his blood type on the regional waiting list at the moment a matching organ appeared, not because of any special favor. The myth of a bought transplant obscures a more mundane and, in its way, more sobering truth: by 2009 Jobs was simply among the sickest patients in the system, treated according to the same medical criteria applied to everyone else on the list.

The liver transplant bought Jobs perhaps two more years, and it is worth remembering, alongside the famous Stanford address already quoted here, one further line from that same speech that Jobs delivered while believing, wrongly, that he had already beaten his cancer — a line that reads differently once the reader knows how the story actually ended. "Death is very likely the single best invention of Life," he told the graduating class in 2005. "It is Life's change agent. It clears out the old to make way for the new." He meant it, in that moment, as a philosophical reflection offered from a position of apparent safety, a man who had stared at death and walked away. Heard again from the vantage of 2011, after the liver transplant, after the visible wasting of his final public appearances, the same words sound less like philosophy and more like a rehearsal — a man talking himself toward an idea he would need, sooner than he then believed, to actually live by.

The illness that Jobs had first tried to out-stubborn in 2003 finally forced from him, in August 2011, an admission he had spent his whole adult life structuring his company to avoid ever having to make: that he could no longer do the job. On August 24, 2011, Apple's board of directors received a short letter, later released publicly, in which Jobs resigned as chief executive of the company he had built twice. "I have always said if there ever came a day when I could no longer meet my duties and expectations as Apple's CEO, I would be the first to let you know," he wrote. "Unfortunately, that day has come." He asked to remain, if the board wished it, as chairman, and he recommended, in the same letter, that Tim Cook — who had already run the company's day-to-day operations during each of Jobs's earlier medical leaves — be named his successor as chief executive. The letter closed not with a statement about products or strategy but with something closer to gratitude: "I have made some of the best friends of my life at Apple, and I thank you all for the many years of being able to work alongside you." Six weeks later, on October 5, 2011, he was dead.

The letter's brevity, and its refusal to dwell on the illness that had produced it, was itself characteristic of a man who had spent eight years since his diagnosis disclosing as little as possible about his own body to a public and a shareholder base that had, at several points, demanded to know more. Even in resigning, Jobs offered no diagnosis, no prognosis, no accounting of the disease that both his closest colleagues and much of the outside world already understood to be in its final stages; he offered a plan for succession and a note of thanks, and left the rest unsaid, exactly as he had managed every previous disclosure of his illness since the tumor was first found on a routine scan eight years earlier. It was the last, and in some ways the most complete, expression of the same instinct that had led him, in 2003, to treat his own cancer as a private matter to be handled entirely on his own terms — an instinct that had cost him, quite possibly, months he could not afford to lose at the very beginning of his illness, and that now, at its end, gave him at least the small mercy of leaving on the terms he chose, in a letter of his own composition, rather than in a manner the disease dictated to him.

After the surgery in 2004, Jobs appeared, for a time, to have beaten the disease, and he returned to a period of astonishing productivity — the years in which the iPhone and the App Store and the iPad were conceived and launched, the greatest run of his career, all accomplished by a man who had been told he had cancer and who was, though the public did not know it, living under its shadow. He kept his illness private, disclosing almost nothing, both out of a fierce sense of privacy and out of concern for Apple's stock and public confidence — a secrecy that would later draw criticism, as the leader of a public company concealing a serious illness from the shareholders who had a stake in his health. He gave, in 2005, the commencement address at Stanford University that would become the most famous speech of his life, in which he spoke openly, for once, about death — telling the graduates that remembering he would die was the most important tool he had ever encountered to help him make the big choices in life, that almost everything falls away in the face of death, leaving only what is truly important. "Your time is limited," he told them, "so don't waste it living someone else's life." He was speaking, though few in the audience knew it, as a man who had recently confronted his own mortality and believed, at that moment, that he had survived it. He had not. Over the following years the cancer returned, or had never fully left, and it spread, and by 2008 and 2009 Jobs was visibly, alarmingly ill — gaunt, hollowed out, his weight dropping, the vigorous figure of the keynotes replaced by a shrinking man whose appearance frightened those who saw him. The disease that he had first tried to wish away was, slowly and then quickly, killing him, even as the company he led reached heights no company had ever reached. And in the middle of it, dying, he launched one more revolutionary product.

Chapter 42 — The iPad

In January 2010, Steve Jobs walked onto a stage — thinner than he had been, though he summoned the old energy — and introduced the iPad, a device whose idea had actually preceded the iPhone and whose realization completed the vision Apple had been building toward for a decade. The iPad was, in the simplest description, a large iPhone without the phone — a flat slab of glass, about the size of a small book, entirely touchscreen, that you held in your hands to browse the web, read books and magazines, watch video, play games, and run apps. Jobs had long dreamed of a tablet computer; the touchscreen research that had produced the iPhone had originally been aimed at a tablet, and Jobs had shelved the tablet to build the phone first, judging correctly that the phone was the more urgent and larger opportunity. Now, with the iPhone established and the touch interface proven and the App Store thriving, he returned to the tablet, and the iPad became the third pillar of Apple's mobile empire.

The iPad's reception, like the iPhone's, was initially divided, and the skeptics again had a plausible-sounding case that history would demolish. Critics asked what the iPad was for — it seemed to be neither a phone nor a real computer, a device that occupied an awkward middle ground, too big to carry in a pocket and too limited to replace a laptop. Some derided it as merely a large iPhone, an unnecessary third device, a solution in search of a problem; the name itself drew mockery. But once again the skeptics were measuring the wrong things, and once again the market answered them decisively. The iPad sold faster than any Apple product before it, faster even than the iPhone, becoming one of the most rapidly adopted consumer products in history. It turned out that there was an enormous appetite for exactly the thing the iPad was: a simple, intuitive, instant-on device for consuming digital content and doing lightweight computing, a device that ordinary people — including the very young and the very old, the people most intimidated by traditional computers — found natural and delightful in a way that laptops never were. Toddlers who could not yet read learned to navigate an iPad; elderly people who had never been able to use a computer took to the iPad easily; and for a vast range of everyday tasks — reading, browsing, watching, playing, communicating — the iPad was simpler and more pleasant than a full computer. It defined the modern tablet category as completely as the iPhone had defined the modern smartphone, and competitors again scrambled to copy it.

The iPad's deeper significance was that it, along with the iPhone, marked the arrival of what Jobs called the "post-PC" era, and this framing captures the magnitude of what Apple had accomplished. For more than three decades, the personal computer — the machine Apple itself had helped invent — had been the central device of digital life, the thing through which people did their computing. Now Jobs argued, and the market was proving, that a new class of devices — the smartphone and the tablet, simpler, more mobile, more human, controlled by touch — was displacing the PC as the primary way most people interacted with technology. For the majority of people and the majority of tasks, Jobs contended, these post-PC devices were not just alternatives to the computer but replacements for it; most people did not need the complexity and power of a full PC, and would increasingly do their computing on phones and tablets, leaving the traditional computer to the professionals and enthusiasts who truly needed it. This was a claim about the future that has been substantially borne out: for billions of people, especially those coming online for the first time in the developing world, the smartphone is the only computer they will ever own or need, and the PC has become, for the general public, a secondary or specialized device. Apple, which had helped create the PC era, had now led the world out of it and into the post-PC era, and it had done so with devices it defined and dominated.

The name itself, unveiled at that January 2010 event, produced an immediate wave of public mockery that is easy to forget once a product has become as familiar as the iPad did, and remembering it corrects any impression that Apple's announcements were, by this point in Jobs's career, greeted with automatic reverence. Within moments of the name's announcement, jokes comparing "iPad" to a feminine hygiene product spread across blogs and the still-young platform of Twitter, with "iTampon" briefly trending, and outlets ran roundups of the best period-related jokes at Apple's expense — an unglamorous but well-documented reminder that even a company at the peak of its cultural authority could stumble into a punchline. Apple also had to contend with a less comedic complication: the Japanese electronics maker Fujitsu had already been selling a handheld retail device called the iPad since 2002 and held a pending trademark application for the name, and Apple ended up paying an estimated four million dollars in March 2010, weeks before its own iPad shipped, simply to acquire the naming rights it needed to use the word at all. The tidy story of an obviously perfect, instantly beloved name obscures a messier reality: Apple's own christening of its most important new product category in years arrived amid public snickering and had to be purchased, in part, from a company most of its customers had never heard of.

The commercial numbers that followed the ridicule are what actually mattered, and they are worth setting beside the mockery for contrast. On its first day of sales, April 3, 2010, Apple sold more than three hundred thousand iPads in the United States alone, and buyers downloaded roughly a million apps and books for the device on that same first day. The pace of adoption from there was, by Jobs's own account, unlike anything Apple had produced before: the iPad reached its first million units sold in twenty-eight days, and Jobs pointed out, when Apple announced the milestone, that this was "less than half of the 74 days it took to achieve this milestone with iPhone" — a direct, verifiable comparison between Apple's two most important product launches, offered by Jobs himself as proof that the skeptics who had mocked the name and questioned the category were, once again, simply wrong about what people wanted. The device that had drawn jokes about feminine hygiene products in January was, by early May, selling faster than any gadget in Apple's history.

The category the iPad opened has endured far longer than early critics, distracted by a funny name, expected, and its persistence into the present is itself a kind of vindication. More than a decade and a half after that first model went on sale, Apple remains comfortably the largest tablet maker in the world, holding roughly two-fifths of a global tablet market that itself still ships well over a hundred million units a year, evidence that the category Jobs described in 2010 as a new, third kind of device between the phone and the laptop was not a passing fad but a genuine and lasting addition to how people compute. The iPad has since become a fixture of classrooms, hospitals, airplane cockpits, and restaurant kitchens in ways no one at that first unveiling anticipated, doing the unglamorous daily work of checklists, charts, and menus as often as the more glamorous work of browsing and video Jobs demonstrated on stage — a far cry from the "solution in search of a problem" its earliest detractors were certain they were watching fail in real time.

The clearest single measure of what the iPad had come to mean to Jobs personally arrived a year after its debut, at the unveiling of its successor, and it says something about the man that he could not stay away from it even when every medical circumstance argued that he should. By March 2011, Jobs was several weeks into his third medical leave from Apple, gravely ill, rarely seen in public, and the iPad 2 event scheduled for March 2, 2011, in San Francisco was expected, reasonably, to be handled by his executive team without him. Instead, Jobs walked out onto the stage himself, visibly thinner than the man who had introduced the first iPad barely a year before, to a standing ovation from an audience that had not expected to see him at all. He offered the crowd no elaborate explanation for his presence, only a single, understated sentence: "We've been working on this product for a while, and I just didn't want to miss today." He then sat through the presentation, occasionally rejoining the discussion of the device himself, before leaving the stage to his team and disappearing again from public view for weeks afterward.

The appearance told its own story about what the iPad had become to Jobs, a product he was willing to interrupt his own medical leave to introduce in person even as he declined to make similar appearances for other announcements during the same period of his illness. It was one of his last substantial public appearances, and among the last times the wider public would see him look, however briefly, like himself — animated, engaged, standing at the center of an audience's attention doing the thing he had done better than anyone else in the industry for three decades. Within the year he would resign the chief executive's role entirely, and within nineteen months of that single sentence about not wanting to miss the day, he would be dead; the iPad 2 event stands, in retrospect, as one of the clearest pieces of evidence for how much the products themselves, rather than the company's stock price or its public reputation, mattered to him personally in the time he had left. The event proceeded almost as though nothing were unusual once Jobs ceded the stage to Tim Cook and the rest of the executive team, who handled the bulk of the iPad 2's technical demonstrations while Jobs looked on from a seat near the front — a division of labor that, in hindsight, previewed the succession already quietly underway inside the company months before Jobs made it official in his resignation letter that August.

There is a poignancy to the iPad that comes from its timing in Steve Jobs's life, and it is impossible to separate the product from the dying man who introduced it. When Jobs unveiled the iPad in early 2010, he was seriously ill — he had undergone a liver transplant the previous year, a sign of how far his cancer had progressed, and though he rallied to deliver the launch with the old showmanship, the disease was advancing. The iPad was, in a sense, his last great product introduction, the final major new device he would personally bring into the world, the last of the revolutionary products he had promised throughout his career. He was intensely proud of it; he saw it as the fullest realization of his vision of a truly personal, truly human computer, the machine that finally dissolved the barrier between the person and the technology, that anyone could use, that just worked. He is said to have wanted, at the end of his life, to be remembered for having made tools that empowered ordinary people and enriched their lives, and the iPad — simple, beautiful, usable by a child or a grandparent — was perhaps the purest expression of that ambition. He launched it knowing, though the public did not, that his time was short, and it stands as a kind of testament, the final gift of a man who had spent his life trying to put the power of computing into human hands in a form so natural that the technology disappeared and only the experience remained. Within two years he would be dead. But in those last years, at the very summit, he had one more transformation to preside over — not a product this time, but the recognition, by the whole world, that the company he had twice built had become the most valuable enterprise on the face of the earth.

Chapter 43 — Post-PC

By 2010 and into 2011, Apple had become, by the ordinary measures of business, the most successful company in the world, and the numbers had grown so large that they had lost the power to shock and become simply abstract. The company that had been ninety days from bankruptcy in 1997 was now, a little over a decade later, the most valuable corporation on the planet — its stock-market value surpassing that of the great oil companies, the banks, the industrial giants, and, in a milestone rich with history, its old rival Microsoft, which Apple's market value overtook in 2010, an event that would have seemed like fantasy during the years Microsoft dominated and Apple begged for its charity. Apple was generating profits of a scale almost without precedent, accumulating a cash reserve so vast — eventually well over a hundred billion, then hundreds of billions of dollars — that commentators struggled to describe it, noting that Apple held more cash than many countries and could have bought entire industries outright. The transformation, from near-death to the summit of global capitalism in fourteen years, is one of the most remarkable corporate stories ever recorded, and it was, by common consent, overwhelmingly the achievement of one man's second act.

It is worth pausing to understand the source of this extraordinary wealth, because it was not simply that Apple sold a lot of products; it was the particular economics of what Apple sold. The iPhone was the greatest profit engine in the history of consumer products, and its profitability came from Apple's whole-widget, premium strategy: Apple sold a phone that people wanted so badly they would pay a premium for it, at prices far above what commodity phones commanded, while its scale and its mastery of manufacturing and supply chains kept its costs controlled. The gap between what it cost Apple to make an iPhone and what customers happily paid for one was enormous, and multiplied across hundreds of millions of units a year, it generated profits that no company had ever seen. Around the iPhone, Apple had built an ecosystem — the App Store, iTunes, iCloud, the accessories, the services — that generated additional revenue and, more importantly, locked customers in, so that once a person was in Apple's world, with their apps and their music and their photos and their habits all bound up in it, leaving became difficult and unlikely. Apple did not just sell products; it sold entry into an ecosystem that kept customers loyal and paying for years. This combination — premium products people loved, sold at high margins, wrapped in a sticky ecosystem — was the machine that made Apple the most profitable company in the world, and it was the direct fruit of the philosophy Jobs had insisted on since the beginning.

The post-PC era that Jobs had proclaimed was, by these years, visibly arriving, and its arrival meant that Apple's dominance rested on the devices of the future rather than the devices of the past. Sales of traditional personal computers were plateauing and beginning their long decline, while sales of smartphones and tablets exploded, and Apple sat at the profitable center of the new order it had created. The company that had helped invent the personal computer had successfully led the transition beyond it, positioning itself at the heart of the mobile, touch-based, app-driven world that was replacing the PC as the center of digital life. This was a feat that few companies in any industry ever manage: to lead one technological era and then, rather than being destroyed by the next one as incumbents usually are, to lead the transition to it and dominate the new era too. The history of technology is littered with companies that ruled one age and were annihilated by the next because they could not or would not cannibalize their own success. Apple, under Jobs, had done the opposite — had deliberately built the iPhone to kill its own iPod, had led the world from the PC it had helped create to the post-PC devices that displaced it — and in doing so had escaped the fate of the incumbent and secured its place at the top of the new order.

The scale of it can be dated with some precision. In May 2010 Apple's market capitalization passed Microsoft's for the first time in more than a decade, a passage of the torch that made headlines everywhere, with Apple's value that day standing near two hundred and twenty-two billion dollars; and on August 9, 2011, in the very weeks before Jobs's resignation, Apple went further still, its market value reaching roughly three hundred thirty-seven billion dollars against ExxonMobil's three hundred thirty-four billion, making Apple, for the first time in its history, the single most valuable publicly traded company on Earth. Exxon reclaimed the crown for a few months afterward — oil was not yet ready to yield to silicon — but by January 2012 Apple had overtaken it again, and never again would an oil company or a bank sit above Apple in the rankings of corporate value. It was a strange kind of victory for a company that, only fourteen years earlier, had needed a rescue investment from Microsoft merely to stay solvent, and it testified to how completely the iPhone had rewritten the economics of what a technology company could be worth.

Jobs himself had given the clearest account of what he meant by the "post-PC era" a year earlier, at the D8 technology conference in the early summer of 2010, only months after the iPad's debut. Pressed on what would become of the personal computer in the new order he was describing, he reached for an analogy drawn from his own boyhood in agricultural California. "When we were an agrarian nation, all cars were trucks, because that's what you needed on the farms," he said. "PCs are going to be like trucks. They're still going to be around, they're still going to have a lot of value, but they're going to be used by one out of X people." The remark was widely flattened in the press into a blunt prophecy that the personal computer was dying, a claim commentators delighted in mocking whenever PC sales ticked upward in some quarter or another. That was a misreading of what Jobs had actually said. He was not predicting the extinction of the PC but its demotion — from the default tool of computing to a specialized instrument used by a shrinking minority, a truck still essential to certain kinds of work even as the phone and the tablet became the vehicle nearly everyone actually drove.

The commentary about Apple's cash pile during these years produced its own mythology, most famously the recurring claim, repeated so often that it hardened into folk wisdom, that Apple at one point held more cash on hand than the United States government itself. The comparison made for an irresistible headline in the summer of 2011, when reports circulated that Apple's roughly seventy-six billion dollars in cash and marketable securities exceeded the Treasury's operating cash balance at a particular moment during that summer's debt-ceiling standoff. The comparison was true only in the narrowest and most misleading sense — it measured Apple's total reserves against the government's day-to-day operating account rather than its actual resources or borrowing capacity, and the Treasury was in no danger of the kind of insolvency the comparison implied. But the fact that the comparison seemed plausible at all, that a company built around consumer gadgets could be spoken of in the same breath as the finances of the world's largest government, told its own story about the strange new scale Apple's profits had reached, a scale that would only grow as the cash pile climbed past one hundred billion and then, within the decade, past two hundred billion dollars.

The scale of what the post-PC strategy ultimately built is almost impossible to hold in the mind even now. On August 2, 2018, Apple became the first publicly traded American company in history to close a trading day worth one trillion dollars, its shares touching just over two hundred dollars to push the company's total value past that threshold for the first time. Two years later, in August 2020, it reached two trillion; within a few more years it passed three. Practically no company in the post-PC world Jobs had described reached that scale so quickly, and none of them owed its ascent so directly to a single redefinition of what a personal computer even was. Every time a customer today unlocks a phone with a glance instead of a click, or hears a company's quarterly earnings reported in the hundreds of billions rather than the millions, they are living inside the order that Jobs, ill and running out of time, had already begun to describe in that conversation about trucks and cars.

The transition also produced spectacular wreckage among the rivals who misjudged it, and no single episode illustrates the brutality of the post-PC transition better than what happened to Hewlett-Packard in the very same weeks that Jobs was writing his resignation letter. HP had spent hundreds of millions of dollars and years of engineering effort on its own answer to the iPad, the TouchPad, a tablet built around the webOS software it had acquired along with Palm, and it had launched the device across the United States on July 1, 2011, with the kind of confident marketing push a company the size of HP could muster. Forty-nine days later, on August 18, 2011, HP announced it was discontinuing the TouchPad altogether, along with its entire line of webOS hardware, writing off the investment as a failure so complete that the company chose to exit the tablet and smartphone hardware business rather than continue competing. The fire sale that followed was almost comic in its scale: retailers slashed the TouchPad's price to ninety-nine dollars for the entry model, and shoppers who had shown no interest at the original price of five hundred dollars lined up outside Best Buy and Walmart stores, cleared out entire pallets of inventory within hours, and turned a device HP could not give away at full price into the most sought-after tablet in the country for one frantic weekend in August. By the accounting of some analysts, the panic-priced clearance actually made the TouchPad the best-selling non-Apple tablet of the year, an achievement that testified less to any merit in the product than to the fact that hundreds of thousands of units had to be dumped at a loss just to move them off shelves. It was, in miniature, exactly the transition Jobs had been describing since D8: an enormous, well-resourced incumbent, expert at the PC era, had poured its engineering and marketing muscle into the new category and been annihilated within seven weeks, while Apple, alone among the major computing companies, had both invented the transition and profited immensely from it.

The iPad's own numbers in that same year make the contrast complete. Apple sold roughly fifteen million iPads in 2011 alone, on top of the millions sold since the device's introduction the year before, and by the most widely cited market research of the period Apple controlled somewhere in the neighborhood of ninety percent of the entire global tablet market — a share so dominant that it left every other manufacturer, HP included, fighting over the remaining sliver. Dell, Hewlett-Packard's old rival and Apple's own antagonist from the years when Michael Dell had publicly suggested that Apple should simply be shut down and its cash returned to shareholders, watched its personal-computer business shrink as the industry it had once dominated contracted around it. The truck-and-car metaphor Jobs had used at D8 was no longer merely a prediction; by the second half of 2011 it was a description of what was actually happening to the industry, one failed product launch and one fire sale at a time.

For all the triumph, these years carried a shadow that the public only partially perceived, and the contrast between Apple's ascent and its leader's decline gives the period its tragic shape. As Apple climbed to the summit of global business, Steve Jobs was visibly failing. His illness, kept private but impossible to fully hide, was advancing; his appearances grew less frequent and more alarming, the gaunt figure on the stage a shadow of the vigorous man of a few years before. He took medical leaves of absence, handing day-to-day control to his trusted operations chief, Tim Cook, who ran the company capably in his absence and was, everyone understood, being groomed as the successor. The world watched, in a kind of morbid suspense, as the most celebrated business leader of his generation, at the very peak of his and his company's success, wasted away from a disease he could not defeat. There was something almost unbearably poignant in the juxtaposition: Apple more powerful and valuable than any company had ever been, and the man who had made it so, dying, unable to enjoy the summit he had reached, his time measured now in months. The company was immortal, or seemed so; the man was not. And Jobs, who had spoken at Stanford of death as life's great clarifier, who had confronted his mortality years earlier and won a reprieve he had now used up, was preparing, with characteristic control, for the end — arranging his succession, protecting his company, and, in his final months, cooperating with a biographer so that his story, at least, would outlast him. In the summer of 2011, too weak to continue, he did the thing he had once been forced to do against his will and now did on his own terms: he stepped down from the leadership of Apple. This time, no one pushed him. This time, he let go.

Chapter 43½ — Stay Hungry, Stay Foolish

On June 12, 2005, Steve Jobs stood before the graduating class of Stanford University and delivered a commencement address that would become the most famous speech of his life and one of the most watched and quoted graduation speeches ever given. He was, though the graduates did not know it, a man living under the shadow of cancer, roughly a year and a half past his diagnosis and surgery, believing at that moment that he had survived. The speech he gave was short, personal, and unadorned — no grand policy pronouncements, no lists of advice, just three stories from his own life and a closing benediction — and its power came precisely from its simplicity and its honesty, from a man who had been to the edge and back speaking plainly about what he had learned. It is worth pausing on, near the end of Jobs's story, because it is the closest thing he left to a summing-up of his own philosophy, delivered in his own voice.

The first story was about connecting the dots. Jobs told of dropping out of Reed College, of the calligraphy class he had wandered into with no practical purpose, of how that apparently useless knowledge had resurfaced ten years later in the Macintosh's typography. The lesson he drew was that you cannot connect the dots looking forward; you can only connect them looking backward, and so you have to trust that the dots will somehow connect in your future — trust in something, your gut, destiny, life, karma, whatever — because believing that the dots will connect down the road gives you the confidence to follow your heart even when it leads you off the well-worn path. It was a defense of curiosity and intuition over planning, of following what genuinely interests you even when its usefulness is not apparent, and it was drawn directly from his own improbable life, in which a series of apparently disconnected passions and detours had assembled, in retrospect, into a coherent whole.

The second story was about love and loss, and it was about getting fired from Apple. Jobs told the graduates, with striking candor, about being publicly dismissed at thirty from the company he had co-founded, about the devastation of that failure, and about how it had turned out to be the best thing that ever happened to him — how the heaviness of success had been replaced by the lightness of being a beginner again, freeing him to enter the most creative period of his life, the years of NeXT and Pixar that led back to Apple. The lesson was that sometimes life hits you in the head with a brick, but you must not lose faith; that the only way to do great work is to love what you do; and that if you have not found it yet, you should keep looking and not settle. This book has treated Jobs's claim that the firing was the best thing that ever happened to him with some skepticism, noting that it is a retrospective smoothing of a genuine catastrophe by a man who happened to survive it. But the underlying counsel — that failure need not be final, that love of the work is the engine of great achievement, that one should not settle — was earned by his own life and delivered with a conviction that has inspired millions.

The third story was about death, and it was the most powerful, because Jobs was speaking as a man who had just confronted his own mortality. He told the graduates that for the past thirty-three years he had looked in the mirror each morning and asked himself whether, if today were the last day of his life, he would want to do what he was about to do — and that whenever the answer was no for too many days in a row, he knew he needed to change something. Remembering that he would soon be dead, he said, was the most important tool he had ever encountered to help him make the big choices in life, because almost everything — external expectations, pride, fear of embarrassment or failure — falls away in the face of death, leaving only what is truly important. He told them about his cancer diagnosis, about being told he might have only months to live, about the reprieve he had received, and about what facing death had taught him. "Your time is limited," he said, "so don't waste it living someone else's life. Don't be trapped by dogma, which is living with the results of other people's thinking. Don't let the noise of others' opinions drown out your own inner voice. And most important, have the courage to follow your heart and intuition."

The speech itself was the product of unusual care, for a man who normally trusted his instincts to carry him through any presentation. Jobs had never delivered a commencement address before, and by his wife's account he spent roughly six months, on and off, working on it — sending himself notes and outlines, revising sections, working closely with Laurene as a sounding board and editor, because he wanted the speech to be personal rather than a compilation of career advice, and because an intensely private man was, for once, being asked to speak publicly about his own life rather than about a product. The strain showed on the morning of June 12, 2005: Laurene later said she had almost never seen him more nervous, that he woke with what she described as butterflies in his stomach — a description hard to reconcile with the image of the man who could unveil a new computer before thousands of people without a flicker of hesitation. Public confidence about Apple's products and private candor about his own life turned out to draw on two entirely different reserves of nerve, and on that particular morning the second reserve very nearly ran dry.

The nervousness did not show in the delivery, and the speech's afterlife has been extraordinary by any measure. It remains, by most tallies, the most watched commencement address ever recorded: Stanford's own upload of the video has drawn upward of forty million views on YouTube alone, and cumulative viewings across the platforms where it has been reposted and translated are commonly estimated to run past one hundred million, a reach no other graduation speech in history has approached. It is taught in business schools and read aloud in classrooms that have nothing to do with technology, quoted by other commencement speakers who borrow its structure of three simple stories, and it has probably done more than any other single document to fix in the public mind the image of Jobs as a reflective sage rather than the difficult, demanding executive described elsewhere in this book.

One detail of the first story is worth correcting, because it is often garbled in the retelling. Jobs did not simply audit a calligraphy course out of idle curiosity; Reed College at the time offered what was reputed to be some of the finest calligraphy instruction in the country, and the class he took was taught by Robert Palladino, a former Trappist monk who had left a monastery to teach lettering and type design to undergraduates. Jobs had already formally withdrawn from Reed by then, but he kept auditing classes that interested him for another eighteen months or so, freed from any obligation to sit through courses he found useless — a detail that matters, because it shows the calligraphy detour was not evidence of directionless drifting, as it is sometimes cast, but the deliberate exercise of a curiosity that a normal course of study would have suppressed. Dropping out was what made the calligraphy class, and the years of unstructured exploration that followed it, possible in the first place.

Today the speech occupies a curious dual position in Jobs's

legacy: it is at once the most humane, least mediated thing he ever said in public, and the single text most responsible for the sanded-down, inspirational-poster version of him that circulates on office walls and motivational calendars, largely emptied of the darker material this book has tried not to look away from. Search engines return it among the first results for almost any query about following one's passion; graduation speakers around the world still borrow its structure; and the Steve Jobs Archive, the foundation his family established after his death to preserve his own words, treats "Stay Hungry, Stay Foolish" as one of its central artifacts, the closest thing to a first-person account he left behind.

The speech so nearly took a completely different form that its final, spare simplicity looks, in hindsight, almost like an accident of failed collaboration. Early in his preparation, in February 2005, Jobs reached outside his own circle and approached Aaron Sorkin — already established as the screenwriter of *The West Wing* and a writer whose gift for the rhythms of persuasive speech Jobs evidently admired — and sent him notes and ideas for the address, apparently hoping Sorkin might help shape or even draft it. Sorkin did not respond for weeks; when Jobs followed up again in April, with the speech now only two months away, Sorkin's reply was brief and unhelpful, and nothing further came of the approach. Whatever a Sorkin-authored commencement address might have sounded like, it evidently was not what Jobs needed, and the silence forced him back onto his own resources and, above all, onto the patient editorial partnership of his wife, Laurene, whose involvement over the following months shaped the speech into the plain, unadorned, three-story structure that was eventually delivered. It is worth imagining the counterfactual only long enough to appreciate what was gained by its absence: a professionally polished, Sorkin-inflected address might have been wittier or more dramatically engineered, but it would not have been the artless, first-person account of dropping out, getting fired, and facing death that made "Stay Hungry, Stay Foolish" the document it became.

Stanford's own invitation had, by Laurene's account, been extended and gently renewed for several years before Jobs finally accepted it, and the reason he chose that particular platform, when he had declined every other university and organization that asked him to speak, had almost nothing to do with the commencement circuit as such. Stanford's president at the time, John Hennessy, had cultivated a genuine friendship with Jobs, and the university held a unique place in Jobs's own geography and mythology: it sat only a few minutes from the house in Palo Alto where he lived, its engineering culture was inseparable from the Silicon Valley Jobs had helped define, and, crucially, Stanford was one of the few major American universities that did not, as a matter of policy, award honorary degrees. Jobs is said to have found this fact wryly appealing rather than discouraging — joking to those around him that giving the commencement address was as close as he would ever come to earning a degree from the university in a single afternoon, a dropout's private joke about finally collecting, in the most oblique way imaginable, the credential he had walked away from at Reed three decades earlier. That combination — geographic proximity, genuine institutional friendship, and the wry symmetry of receiving no actual degree from the one school prestigious enough to make the absence of one a kind of honor — was, by his wife's account, the reason Jobs told her that if he was ever going to give a single commencement speech in his life, it was going to be this one, at this school, and nowhere else.

He closed with the line that became the speech's benediction and, in a sense, his epitaph. He told the graduates about the *Whole Earth Catalog*, the countercultural bible of his youth, and about its final issue, on the back cover of which was a photograph of an early-morning country road, with the words: "Stay hungry. Stay foolish." It had been the farewell message of the catalog's creators, and Jobs had always wished it for himself, and now he wished it for the graduating class. Stay hungry — keep wanting, keep striving, never grow complacent or satisfied. Stay foolish — keep taking risks, keep believing in things others think impossible, never let the accumulated caution of age and success extinguish the reckless faith of the beginner. It was the distilled essence of everything Steve Jobs believed and everything he had lived, delivered by a dying man to the young, and it has outlasted him as perhaps the purest statement of his creed. There is an irony, of course, which this book is bound to note: the philosophy of following your heart and trusting your gut, which served Jobs so brilliantly in his work, was the same philosophy that led him to trust his gut over his doctors and delay the surgery that might have saved his life. The inner voice that built Apple also, in the one matter that most concerned his survival, led him astray. But that complication does not diminish the speech; it deepens it, reminding us that the same qualities that make a person extraordinary can also be their undoing, and that Steve Jobs, who told the young to remember death, would be dead within six years of speaking those words.

Chapter 44 — Stepping Down

On August 24, 2011, Steve Jobs sent a letter to Apple's board of directors and, through them, to the world. It was short, dignified, and unmistakably final. "I have always said," it began, "if there ever came a day when I could no longer meet my duties and expectations as Apple's CEO, I would be the first to let you know. Unfortunately, that day has come." He resigned as chief executive of Apple, recommended that Tim Cook succeed him, and asked to serve as chairman of the board — a role he would fill only briefly. He closed the letter with words that, read now, are almost unbearable in their restraint: "I believe Apple's brightest and most innovative days are ahead of it. And I look forward to watching and contributing to its success in a new role. I have made some of the best friends of my life at Apple, and I thank you all for the many years of being able to work alongside you." It was the resignation of a dying man, and everyone understood it as such, and it marked the end of one of the most remarkable careers in the history of business.

The contrast with his first departure from Apple could not have been more complete, and the two exits together frame the whole arc of his life. In 1985 he had been thrown out — stripped of power against his will, humiliated, exiled by a board that had lost faith in him. In 2011 he left on his own terms, at the summit of his and his company's success, having built Apple into the most valuable enterprise in the world, universally celebrated as one of the greatest business leaders who had ever lived, choosing his own successor and handing over the company he loved in a state of health and strength it had never known. The man who had been cast out as a failure returned as a savior and departed as a legend. Twenty-six years separated the two exits, and in the span between them Steve Jobs had lived one of the great second acts, had proven the company that fired him catastrophically wrong, had reinvented multiple industries, and had, in the end, achieved the thing that the young man thrown out in 1985 could scarcely have imagined: he left Apple not because anyone made him, but because his body would no longer let him stay.

The succession to Tim Cook was the fruit of years of deliberate preparation, and it deserves attention because it was, in its quiet way, one of Jobs's most important achievements — the thing that would let Apple survive him. Cook had joined Apple in 1998, recruited by Jobs to run the company's operations, and over the following thirteen years he had become the indispensable second, the master of manufacturing and supply chains and the disciplined day-to-day management that Jobs had neither the temperament nor the interest to provide. Cook was, in almost every way, Jobs's opposite: calm where Jobs was volatile, private and understated where Jobs was theatrical, an operations and logistics genius rather than a product visionary, a consensus-builder rather than a reality-distorter. During Jobs's medical leaves, Cook had run Apple, and had run it well, demonstrating that he could steady and manage the company; and Jobs had come to trust him completely, to see in him the person who could preserve what he had built. In naming Cook his successor, Jobs was making a bet that the company he had created could outlast its creator — that he had built not just products but an institution, a culture, a set of principles and people, robust enough to continue without the singular genius who had defined it. Whether that bet would pay off was, in 2011, the great open question hanging over Apple. Many doubted it; the conventional wisdom held that Apple was Steve Jobs, that without him the magic would fade, that no company so completely the expression of one man's vision could thrive once that man was gone.

The market's immediate reaction to the letter revealed how much investors still equated Apple's fortunes with Jobs's personal presence, whatever succession planning had gone on behind the scenes. Trading in Apple shares was briefly halted after the letter became public that afternoon, and when trading resumed after hours the stock fell roughly five to seven percent, erasing billions of dollars in paper value within minutes on the news that the company's co-founder was leaving its top job. The board met the same day and formally elected Jobs chairman and Tim Cook chief executive, ratifying in a matter of hours the succession that Jobs had recommended in his letter and that the company had, in truth, been quietly rehearsing for years.

Cook moved immediately to steady the company, and the email he sent to Apple's employees the following morning is worth quoting in full, because it reveals how consciously the new leadership understood the challenge in front of it. "I want you to be confident that Apple is not going to change," Cook wrote. "I cherish and celebrate Apple's unique principles and values. Steve built a company and culture that is unlike any other in the world and we are going to stay true to that — it is in our DNA. We are going to continue to make the best products in the world that delight our customers and make our employees incredibly proud of what they do." The message was aimed less at customers than at the tens of thousands of employees who had reason to wonder, in that moment, whether the company they worked for was about to lose its center of gravity, and it set the tone — reassurance through continuity rather than through any claim to replace Jobs's genius — that would define Cook's approach to the job for years afterward.

The public sometimes treated the August 2011 resignation as a sudden thunderclap, but it was in fact the last of a sequence of warnings stretching back years, and naming them shows how long the company had quietly been rehearsing this moment. Jobs had already taken three separate medical leaves of absence as chief executive: the first in 2004, after his initial cancer surgery; a second, far longer leave from January to June 2009, during which he received a liver transplant in Memphis, Tennessee, while Apple told the public only that he was being treated for a hormonal imbalance; and a third beginning in January 2011, from which he never fully returned to daily operations. Each leave had handed the company's daily management to Cook for months at a stretch, effectively auditioning him for the role years before he formally received it, so that by the time the resignation letter arrived, Apple's board, its executive team, and its investors had already lived through three dress rehearsals of a Jobs-less Apple, even if most of the public had not registered them as such.

A single private document from this period, made public only years later, captures something of the interior life running beneath the public drama of resignation and succession, and it deserves a place in the record because it complicates the portrait of Jobs as a man wholly defined by will, control, and combat. On September 2, 2010 — about a year before he wrote his resignation letter, and while he was still, publicly, Apple's chief executive — Jobs sat down and wrote an email addressed to no one but himself, a private note he apparently never intended anyone else to read, titled simply "I do not..." It was not a business memo, not a strategy note, not even, in any conventional sense, a reflection on Apple; it was a quiet meditation on dependence and gratitude, an inventory of everything in his life that he had not made or earned alone. "I grow little of the food I eat, and of the little I do grow I did not breed or perfect the seeds," he wrote. "I do not make any of my own clothing. I speak a language I did not invent or refine... I am moved by music I did not create myself." The note went on in this vein, cataloging the debts — to other people, past and present, to the accumulated inheritance of civilization — that even a man as singularly self-willed as Steve Jobs owed to a species he described himself as "totally dependent" upon for his own life and well-being.

The email surfaced publicly only in 2023, when the Steve Jobs Archive — the foundation established after his death by Laurene Powell Jobs, Tim Cook, and Jony Ive to preserve and share his own words rather than let his memory be defined entirely by others' accounts of him — chose to release it as one of the few genuinely private documents in its collection. Its existence sits oddly, and instructively, beside almost everything else this book has recorded about the man: the executive who took credit for other people's work, who could be casually cruel to the colleagues and family members closest to him, who staged his own reality distortion field to bend the world to his will, had also, in a note meant for no eyes but his own, described himself as dependent, humbled, and grateful, a single strand in a vast collaborative human inheritance rather than the self-made genius of his own public mythology. It is impossible to know how much weight to give a single private email against a lifetime of documented behavior, and this book has been reluctant throughout to let one flattering document erase a pattern of harder evidence. But the note is real, it was written in his own hand at a moment when he had every reason to believe his time was running out, and it belongs in the record precisely because it does not fit neatly with either the hagiography or the indictment — because it shows a man, in the last year of his life and away from any stage or audience, quietly counting what he owed rather than what he had built.

Jobs's final months, after the resignation, were spent at home, with his family, as the cancer took its course. He had married Laurene Powell in 1991 — a marriage officiated by his old Zen teacher — and they had three children together, and he had, late and imperfectly, reconciled with Lisa, the daughter he had denied for years, who was part of his life at the end. He worked, in these last months, with the writer Walter Isaacson, to whom he had granted extraordinary access for an authorized biography, cooperating with unusual candor because, it seems, he wanted his children to understand who he had been and wanted his story told, warts and all, in his own time. He continued, even as he weakened, to think about Apple, to weigh in on products, to care about the details, unable to fully let go of the thing that had been his life's work. And he prepared, in his fashion, for death — the death he had spoken of at Stanford as life's great clarifier, the awareness of which had, he said, guided his most important choices. He had spent his life as a Buddhist and a builder, a seeker of enlightenment and a maker of objects, and at the end the two strands of his life came together in a man facing his mortality with a mixture of acceptance and reluctance, of Zen calm and human grief at leaving a world he had done so much to shape. He had put his dent in the universe. The universe, indifferent as ever to charisma and will, was about to take him out of it. On October 5, 2011, at his home in Palo Alto, surrounded by his family, Steve Jobs died. He was fifty-six years old.

Chapter 45 — October 5, 2011

The death of Steve Jobs on October 5, 2011, produced a global outpouring of grief unlike anything ever seen for a business executive, and the scale and character of the mourning said something profound about what Jobs had become and what his products meant to people. Apple Stores around the world became spontaneous shrines, their glass walls covered with handwritten notes, flowers, candles, and — poignantly, fittingly — apples, some with a single bite taken out of them in imitation of the logo. People wept in the streets. Tributes poured in from presidents and prime ministers, from rivals and competitors, from artists and scientists and ordinary people who had never met him but felt, somehow, that they had lost someone who mattered to them personally. Bill Gates, his great rival of forty years, issued a heartfelt statement about their long, complicated relationship and the privilege of having worked alongside him. The mourning had the quality usually reserved for beloved public figures — musicians, actors, leaders — not for the chief executive of a technology company, and its intensity revealed how deeply Jobs and his products had woven themselves into people's emotional lives.

Why did the death of a corporate executive move so many

people so deeply? The answer lies in the nature of what Jobs made and how people experienced it. His products were not abstractions or infrastructure; they were intimate objects that people held in their hands, carried in their pockets, touched hundreds of times a day, used to connect with the people they loved, to capture the moments of their lives, to navigate the world. An iPhone was not like a piece of software people never saw or a component buried in a machine; it was a personal companion, a beautiful object of daily affection, something people genuinely loved in a way they rarely love the products of a corporation. And Jobs, through decades of storytelling and showmanship and the "Think Different" mythology, had made himself the human face of these beloved objects, had positioned himself as the artist who made the tools that empowered and delighted them, the rebel who cared about beauty and the individual in a world of soulless technology. When he died, people mourned not a distant billionaire but the maker of the things they loved, the man they associated with the objects that had become extensions of themselves. It was a testament to how completely he had achieved his ambition — to make technology personal, human, emotional — that his death felt, to millions, like a personal loss.

The tributes and the mourning also, inevitably, involved a degree of mythologizing that an honest history must note even while respecting the genuine grief. In death, Jobs was rapidly canonized, transformed into a secular saint of innovation, a genius whose flaws were forgotten or reframed as the necessary edge of greatness, a figure held up in a thousand eulogies and business books as the model of visionary leadership. The reality distortion field, in a sense, outlived him, as the culture wrapped his memory in a haze of reverence that smoothed away the cruelty, the abandoned daughter, the denied credit, the humiliated colleagues, the human wreckage that had always accompanied the genius. This book has tried, throughout, to resist that smoothing — to hold together the extraordinary achievement and the real damage, the visionary and the tyrant, the man who changed the world and the man who could be casually, gratuitously cruel to the people closest to him. The mourning was genuine and deserved; Jobs really had enriched billions of lives, really had made objects of beauty and utility that people loved, really had been one of the most consequential figures of his age. And the canonization was also a distortion, because the real Steve Jobs was more complicated, more flawed, and more human than the saint the eulogies created, and the truth of him is more valuable than the myth.

The family's own statement, released within hours of his death, was notable for its restraint amid the global outpouring it helped set in motion. "Steve died peacefully today surrounded by his family," it read. "In his public life, Steve was known as a visionary; in his private life, he cherished his family... We know many of you will mourn with us, and we ask that you respect our privacy during our time of grief." Apple's own board of directors, in a separate statement issued the same day, wrote that "Steve's brilliance, passion and energy were the source of countless innovations that enrich and improve all of our lives," and that "the world is immeasurably better because of Steve." The tributes that followed came from an unusually wide span of public life: President Obama called Jobs "among the greatest of American innovators — brave enough to think differently, bold enough to believe he could change the world, and talented enough to do it," while Bill Gates, whose rivalry with Jobs had defined an entire industry for three decades, said simply that "the world rarely sees someone who has had the profound impact Steve has had, the effects of which will be felt for many generations to come."

Two weeks after his death, on October 19, 2011, Apple closed its retail stores across the country for the length of a private memorial service held for employees at an outdoor amphitheater on the company's Cupertino campus. Tim

Cook and Jony Ive spoke, along with former Vice President Al Gore, who had served on Apple's board; the singer Norah Jones performed a cover of Bob Dylan's "Forever Young"; and the band Coldplay played "Yellow" and "Fix You" for an audience of employees, while stores that could not attend in person watched a company-wide broadcast. It was an unusual scene for a corporation — a rock concert as corporate eulogy — but it matched the register in which Jobs's death was being processed everywhere: not as the retirement of an executive but as the loss of a cultural figure whose passing called for the kind of public mourning normally reserved for musicians or heads of state.

One piece of writing about Jobs's death deserves specific correction, because it has circulated for over a decade and still resurfaces regularly. Beginning around 2015, four years after Jobs died, a lengthy essay attributed to him began spreading online, purporting to be a deathbed meditation on the emptiness of wealth and business success; it has been shared hundreds of thousands of times, and fact-checkers have traced its actual origin to an anonymous blog post with no connection to Jobs, his family, or anyone who knew him. No such document exists in any authentic account of his final days. What we do have, by contrast, is genuine and more affecting than the fabrication: his sister, the novelist Mona Simpson, delivered a eulogy at his memorial that was later published, in which she described being at his bedside as he died, and recounted that in his last hours he looked for a long time at his sister, his wife, and his children before his last words, spoken as he gazed past them, were, "Oh wow. Oh wow. Oh wow." The detail needs no embellishment, and the fact that a saccharine, fabricated speech had to be invented years later, when the real, spare, and mysterious truth was already on the record, says something about how badly the world wanted Jobs's death to deliver a moral it could package and share.

Where a visitor meets Jobs today is, fittingly, a building

rather than a statue. When Apple completed its circular Cupertino headquarters, it named the campus's product-launch auditorium the Steve Jobs Theater — an underground, thousand-seat hall entered through a glass cylinder more than a hundred feet across, roofed by a freestanding carbon-fiber canopy with no visible supports, an engineering feat as demanding in its own way as anything the design studio had produced in his lifetime. It is there, since 2017, that Apple has unveiled its new iPhones and watches each autumn, walking new products across a stage bearing his name — a literal architecture of continuity built to answer, one keynote at a time, the question this book must now turn to: whether the company Steve Jobs built could go on being Apple without him.

Apple's own digital response to the flood of grief took an unusually simple and, in retrospect, telling form. Within hours of announcing Jobs's death, the company replaced its ordinary corporate homepage with nothing more than a black-and-white photograph of Jobs and the years of his life, along with a single email address — rememberingsteve@apple.com — where anyone in the world could send a private message of condolence or gratitude. There was no product for sale on the page, no press release, no corporate messaging of any kind, an almost startling restraint for a company that had built its identity on the theater of the announcement. The response overwhelmed even Apple's own expectations: within two weeks the address had received more than a million messages, sent by strangers who had never met Jobs but felt compelled to write anyway, and Apple began publishing a rotating selection of them on a dedicated "Remembering Steve" page, a wall of anonymous, unpolished testimony from people describing what an iPod or a Mac or an iPhone had meant to them, alongside notes from people who said they had once met him briefly, or worked with him, or simply admired him from a distance for decades. The page remained live for years afterward, a strange kind of open-ended, crowd-authored eulogy running in parallel to the more formal tributes from presidents and rivals, and it captured, in its sheer volume and its ordinariness, the same phenomenon the more famous tributes were also describing from a different angle: that an extraordinary number of people who had never known Jobs personally experienced his death as something close to a personal loss.

The company's chosen restraint — a photograph, two dates, and an email address, nothing more — was itself a kind of design statement, of a piece with everything this book has described about Apple's aesthetic instincts. Where a lesser company might have filled its homepage with a lengthy statement, a slideshow of product highlights, or a corporate video tribute, Apple offered almost nothing, trusting the starkness of the image and the simplicity of the gesture to carry the appropriate weight, and betting, correctly, that the world did not need Apple to tell it how to feel about Steve Jobs's death. It was the same instinct for subtraction, for saying less in order to say more, that had governed the design of every product this book has described — applied, for once, not to a phone or a computer but to grief itself, and it worked, in the sense that the sparse page and the flood of a million private messages it invited said more about what Jobs had meant to people than any officially drafted statement could have managed on its own.

What Jobs left behind, beyond the grief and the mythology, was a genuine and enormous legacy, and the shape of it is the subject of the rest of this book. He left Apple, of course — the most valuable company in the world, a machine for producing beloved products, an institution he had built twice and hoped would outlast him. He left a set of products and a design philosophy that had reshaped multiple industries and changed how billions of people lived, worked, communicated, and experienced the world. He left a model of how to build a company and how to make products — the obsession with design, the whole-widget integration, the focus, the willingness to say no, the marriage of technology and the humanities — that would be studied and imitated for generations, sometimes wisely and often not. And he left an open question, the question that hung over Apple in the days after his death and that this book must ultimately try to answer: whether the company he built could survive without him, whether he had created something robust enough to continue, or whether Apple was so completely the expression of one singular man that it would, without him, slowly lose the magic that had made it extraordinary. The skeptics were legion, and their doubt was reasonable, because history offered few examples of founder-defined companies that thrived after the founder was gone. Tim Cook, the quiet operations genius, now had to answer that question — not with words but with years of results — and the answer he would give, over the decade and a half that followed, would be more surprising, and in some ways more impressive, than almost anyone expected. But before we follow Apple into its life after Steve Jobs, we should pause, as he himself might have wanted, to understand how Apple actually made the things it made — the design, the secrecy, the discipline, the strange and demanding culture that produced the products and that was, perhaps, his deepest and most lasting creation.

Chapter 46 — The Design Studio

At the heart of Apple, physically and philosophically, was the design studio — a locked, secretive space where a small team led by Jony Ive shaped the physical form of every product, and where the objects that would be held by billions of people took their shape through a process of obsessive refinement. To understand Apple is to understand what happened in that room, because the design studio was where the company's deepest values became physical, where the abstract philosophy of simplicity and craft and human-centeredness was translated into aluminum and glass, and where Steve Jobs spent, by his own account, some of the happiest and most engaged hours of his working life.

The design philosophy that governed the studio had deep roots, and naming them illuminates what Apple was really doing. Jony Ive was an admirer of the mid-twentieth-century German designer Dieter Rams, who had shaped the products of the Braun company according to a set of principles that became, in effect, Apple's own: that good design is as little design as possible, that it makes a product understandable, that it is honest and unobtrusive and long-lasting, that it concerns itself with every detail. Rams's dictum — "less, but better" — could have been Apple's motto. Behind Rams lay the Bauhaus and the whole modernist tradition of functional simplicity, the belief that beauty comes from the honest expression of function and the ruthless elimination of the unnecessary, that ornament is a kind of dishonesty and that the highest design achievement is to make something so simple, so reduced to its essence, that it seems inevitable. And behind Apple's version of this tradition lay also Steve Jobs's own aesthetic formation — the Zen simplicity absorbed in his youth, the calligraphic care for form, the machinist father's insistence on craftsmanship in the parts no one sees. Apple's design was the confluence of these streams: German modernist functionalism, Japanese Zen minimalism, and Californian countercultural idealism, fused into a philosophy that treated the reduction of complexity as a moral and aesthetic imperative.

The practice of design in the studio was famously, exhaustingly iterative, and it reveals how much labor lay behind the appearance of effortless simplicity. Apple did not arrive at its clean, simple forms by having a single flash of inspiration; it arrived at them through relentless iteration, making dozens or hundreds of physical models and prototypes of a product, refining each detail over and over, trying endless variations of a curve or a material or a proportion, subtracting and subtracting until nothing remained that could be removed. The simplicity that looked so effortless in the finished product was the hard-won result of enormous effort, because true simplicity — simplicity that works, that feels inevitable, that hides its complexity rather than merely lacking sophistication — is far harder to achieve than complexity. "Simple can be harder than complex," Jobs said. "You have to work hard to get your thinking clean to make it simple. But it's worth it in the end, because once you get there, you can move mountains." The studio was where that hard work of achieving simplicity happened, where teams labored for months over details most users would never consciously notice — the exact radius of a corner, the precise weight and balance of a device in the hand, the way a material felt against skin, the sound a button made — in the conviction that all these unnoticed details added up, subconsciously, to the difference between a product that felt magical and one that felt ordinary.

The obsession extended to manufacturing, and this is a crucial and underappreciated point: Apple's design was inseparable from its command of how things were made. Achieving the forms Ive and Jobs wanted often required inventing new manufacturing processes, because existing methods could not produce the seamless, precise, beautiful objects they demanded. Apple pioneered techniques for machining aluminum, for making glass strong and precise enough for its purposes, for achieving joints and finishes and tolerances that had not been possible before, and it invested billions in the specialized machinery and manufacturing partnerships required. The design, in other words, was not just drawn; it was made possible by a mastery of manufacturing that most companies could not match, and this integration of design and manufacturing — designing objects that could only be built by processes Apple itself developed or commissioned — was one of the sources of Apple's advantage, because competitors could copy the appearance of an Apple product but not easily reproduce the manufacturing sophistication that made it feel the way it felt. The care for the unseen that Paul Jobs had taught his son at the workbench had become an industrial philosophy: Apple built the inside of the box as beautifully as the outside, held the invisible parts to the same standards as the visible ones, and lavished on the process of manufacturing the same obsessive attention it gave to the form.

The connection to Dieter Rams was not merely a matter of shared taste; Ive spoke of it openly, and the parallels between Rams's work at Braun and Apple's own products are concrete enough to trace object by object. Rams spent roughly four decades as Braun's chief of design, overseeing some five hundred products built around his famous formulation that good design is "as little design as possible" — innovative, useful, honest, unobtrusive, long-lasting, thorough down to the last detail, and, in his own summary phrase, "less, but better." The debt shows up directly in Apple's own interfaces: the calculator application that shipped on iPhones for years was a close visual echo of Braun's 1987 ET66 calculator, a device Rams designed himself, and an early version of Apple's mobile world-clock face likewise borrowed its layout from a Braun clock design. Apple did not merely admire Rams from a distance; for years it carried his catalogue into some of its most-used everyday interfaces as a kind of quiet, ongoing tribute.

The physical studio itself was treated with a degree of security that startled outsiders whenever it was described in public. For a period, the design studio sat in a nondescript building separated from Apple's main campus so that Ive's team could work without the daily interruptions of the rest of the company, though it was later brought back inside the main campus so Jobs could visit more easily; wherever it sat, the room was shielded by tinted glass and a single heavy, badge-locked door, and access was restricted to designers and a small handful of senior executives — a restriction so tight that Tim Cook once joked to an interviewer that there was "probably more secrecy" inside the studio "than there is at the CIA." What is perhaps most striking, given how much of the world's technology aesthetic traces back to that room, is how small it actually was: through the years that it shaped the iMac, the iPod, the iPhone, and the iPad, Apple's core industrial design team numbered only around twenty people, small enough that Ive knew every one of their working habits intimately and could run the studio less like a corporate department than like a single, tight-knit workshop.

It is tempting, given how thoroughly Ive's own name became attached to Apple's design language, to imagine him as a solitary author, sketching forms alone and handing them down to be manufactured. The truth, by every account of people who worked alongside him, was more collaborative and more laborious than that image allows: the same core group of designers, several of whom stayed with Ive for fifteen or twenty years, worked communally around shared tables, passing physical models back and forth, arguing over fractions of a millimeter, building foam and aluminum mock-ups by the hundreds for a single product before anyone was satisfied. The myth of the lone genius designer obscures the reality of a durable, tightly bonded team whose continuity — the same hands shaping product after product across two decades — was itself one of the studio's least visible and most important assets, letting Apple's design language mature gradually across generations rather than being reinvented, and diluted, with every personnel change.

The design sensibility that Jony Ive brought to fruition in the 1990s and 2000s did not emerge from nothing, and the studio's own history reaches back further than Ive's arrival, to a formative partnership Jobs forged more than a decade earlier with a German industrial designer named Hartmut Esslinger. The two men met in January 1982, when Apple's product line — the beige, boxy Apple II family — struck Esslinger, by his own account, as "incredibly ugly and wasteful in production," an aesthetic failure entirely at odds with the ambitions Jobs had for the company. Esslinger's firm, soon renamed frogdesign, won the resulting commission by presenting Jobs with some forty distinct model proposals under a project internally called Snow White, named for the way its seven planned product lines echoed the seven dwarfs of the fairy tale; when Jobs saw the results, he is reported to have responded immediately and without qualification, "That's it!" Apple signed frogdesign to an exclusive contract worth roughly two million dollars a year, an enormous sum for design services at the time, and the resulting Snow White language — pale, nearly white enclosures, gently rounded edges, and rows of fine, evenly spaced ventilation slits that turned a purely functional necessity into a deliberate decorative texture — was applied across Apple's product line from the Apple IIc in 1984 through the Macintosh II and beyond, remaining the company's visual signature for the better part of a decade, well before Jony Ive ever set foot inside Apple's design studio.

The continuity between Esslinger's Snow White era and Ive's later studio is not merely a matter of historical curiosity; it establishes that Apple's obsession with industrial design as a defining corporate discipline, rather than an afterthought bolted onto engineering, predates the products and even the executive team most people associate with it. Esslinger, decades later, would describe his role bluntly, saying that he had, in effect, taught Jobs to put design first — to treat the shape and material and finish of a product as inseparable from its function rather than as a cosmetic layer applied after the engineering was already settled, the same conviction that would later drive the endless iteration and manufacturing obsession of Ive's studio. When Jobs was exiled from Apple in 1985, the Snow White language and the frogdesign relationship persisted for years under the executives who succeeded him, evidence that the design-first philosophy had, by then, become genuinely institutional rather than simply an extension of one founder's taste. What changed when Jobs returned in 1997 and elevated Ive above every other design voice at the company was not the basic premise that Esslinger had helped install fifteen years earlier — that Apple's products should look and feel like nothing else on the market — but the scale of resource, secrecy, and personal attention Jobs was now prepared to devote to it, transforming a strong design department into the sealed, revered sanctuary this chapter has described.

The design studio was, in a real sense, Steve Jobs's spiritual home within Apple, and his relationship with it and with Ive was one of the most important of his life. He visited the studio almost daily, more than any other part of the company, because it was where the thing he cared about most — the products, and their form and feel and beauty — was created. His partnership with Ive was extraordinarily close, a genuine meeting of minds and sensibilities, two men who shared an almost religious devotion to the object, to craft, to the emotional power of a beautifully made thing. Jobs called Ive his spiritual partner at Apple, gave him more power and independence than any other executive, and protected the design studio as a sanctuary where the ordinary pressures of business and engineering could not override the pursuit of the right form. And the collaboration between them — Jobs's product vision and force of will, Ive's design genius and craft — produced the objects that defined an era. But the design studio was only one part of the strange and demanding culture that made Apple work. The products were shaped there, but they were kept secret by a machine of secrecy as elaborate as anything in government, and they were made great by a discipline of focus and refusal that ran through the whole company. To understand how Apple made things, we have to understand not just how it designed them, but how it hid them, and how it said no.

Chapter 47 — Secrecy

Apple under Steve Jobs was one of the most secretive companies in the world, more secretive than many intelligence agencies, and its secrecy was not incidental but central — a deliberate and elaborate system that served the company's strategy, protected its products, and fed the theater of the launches that were among its most powerful marketing weapons. Understanding Apple's secrecy is understanding a real part of how it worked, because the surprise of a Jobs keynote, the gasp when a new product was revealed, the sense that Apple's creations descended fully formed from some hidden Olympus — all of it depended on a machinery of concealment that kept the company's work invisible until the moment Jobs chose to unveil it.

The secrecy operated at every level and was enforced with a seriousness that struck outsiders as extreme. Inside Apple, information was tightly compartmentalized, so that employees knew only what they needed to know for their own work and were kept ignorant of what other teams were doing; people working on one part of a product often had no idea how it fit into the whole, and many employees learned about Apple's new products at the same time as the public, by watching the keynote. Projects were hidden behind code names and locked doors and, in the most sensitive cases, physical barriers — rooms within rooms, teams walled off in secure areas, prototypes chained down and disguised. Employees signed strict confidentiality agreements and understood that leaking information was a firing offense and potentially a legal one; Apple pursued leakers aggressively and made examples of them. The culture of secrecy was so pervasive that it shaped how people behaved even outside work, trained not to discuss what they did, to deflect questions, to keep the wall of silence intact. To work at Apple was to live inside a system of concealment, and the company enforced it with a discipline that most organizations could never sustain.

The strategic purposes of all this secrecy were several, and they were real rather than merely obsessive. The most obvious was competitive: if rivals did not know what Apple was building, they could not copy it in advance or prepare their response, and Apple could arrive in a market with a finished, surprising product before competitors even knew it was coming, as it had with the iPhone. A second purpose was to control the narrative: by keeping products secret until launch, Apple ensured that the world learned about them in exactly the way Apple wanted, through Jobs's carefully staged presentation, rather than through leaks and rumors and premature coverage that would muddy the message and squander the impact. A third, subtler purpose was the creation of desire through mystery and anticipation; the secrecy generated an atmosphere of speculation and longing, a drumbeat of rumor and expectation that built, before each launch, into a frenzy of anticipation worth enormous amounts of free publicity. The secrecy fed the theater, and the theater sold the products. When Jobs finally revealed a device that had been hidden and speculated about for months, the revelation landed with a force that no ordinary product announcement could match, and that force translated directly into sales, coverage, and the sense that Apple's products were events rather than mere goods.

There was also, in the secrecy, an expression of Jobs's deepest instincts about control and about experience, and it connects to everything else in his philosophy. Just as he insisted on controlling the hardware and the software, the manufacturing and the retail, so he insisted on controlling the moment and manner of a product's revelation, refusing to let the experience of encountering a new Apple product be spoiled by leaks or shaped by anyone but himself. The unveiling was part of the product, the first chapter of the customer's relationship with it, and Jobs would no more surrender control of it than he would surrender control of the design. The secrecy was the whole-widget philosophy extended to information: Apple would control everything, including what the world knew and when it knew it, so that every element of the experience — including the anticipation and the surprise — could be orchestrated to perfection. It was of a piece with the theatrical genius of the keynotes, the obsessive design, the sealed products, the refusal to let anything about the Apple experience be left to chance or to others.

The most vivid illustration of both how seriously Apple guarded its secrets and how imperfect even its system could be came in the spring of 2010, in an incident that has become one of the most retold stories in the company's history. An Apple software engineer named Gray Powell, celebrating his twenty-seventh birthday at a German beer garden in Redwood City called Gourmet Haus Staudt, left behind on a barstool what looked like an ordinary iPhone 3GS disguised in a case — in fact an unreleased prototype of the iPhone 4, complete with its then-unannounced flat-sided design and front-facing camera. The device passed through another patron's hands and was eventually sold, for five thousand dollars, to the technology blog Gizmodo, whose editor Jason Chen published a detailed teardown of the phone on April 19, 2010, months before Apple was due to unveil it — an almost complete rupture of the secrecy this chapter has described as sacrosanct.

Apple's response revealed just how far the company was prepared to go to protect its unreleased work. Jobs personally telephoned executives at Gawker Media, Gizmodo's parent company, to demand the prototype's return, and within days a specialized California computer-crimes task force, acting on a search warrant, raided Chen's home at night and seized his computers — a law-enforcement response aggressive enough against a journalist that it triggered a genuine debate about press protections, and drew scrutiny from press-freedom advocates who argued the raid had crossed a line ordinary corporate secrecy should never reach. Powell, remarkably, kept his job at Apple despite having caused the most damaging leak in the company's history to that point, a small mercy suggesting that Apple's culture of secrecy, whatever its severity, was not always as punitive in practice as its reputation implied.

The episode is worth dwelling on because it complicates the picture of flawless, impenetrable secrecy that Apple's own mystique can make the company sound like it possessed. Apple's system of concealment was real, elaborate, and usually effective, but it was enforced by ordinary human beings capable of ordinary carelessness, and the company's actual history includes plenty of leaks, blurry photographs of unreleased hardware, and supply-chain rumors that turned out to be accurate. What made Apple's secrecy remarkable was not that it never failed, but that it failed so rarely relative to the number of people — designers, engineers, contract manufacturers across Asia, retail employees receiving shipments — who had to be kept in the dark for a system of that scale to work at all, and that when it did fail, as it did with conspicuous embarrassment in 2010, the company's response was swift and unmistakably meant to signal to every employee watching that a repeat would not be tolerated.

The habits forged in those years persist essentially unchanged. Apple prototypes still travel disguised in decoy cases, are still tracked by internal serial numbers and access logs, and the company still requires suppliers across its manufacturing network to sign covering agreements and submit to audits meant to prevent exactly the kind of leak that embarrassed it in 2010. Every autumn, in the weeks before a new iPhone's unveiling, a familiar ritual of blurry leaked photographs, parts leaks from the supply chain, and dueling analyst predictions still plays out online — proof that the secrecy machine, however refined since Gray Powell's birthday, has never again been either fully airtight or fully defeated, and that the tension between concealment and inevitable leakage remains as central to how Apple operates today as it was under Jobs.

Beyond the walls, the badges, and the decoy cases, Apple has long relied on a subtler and more devious technique for guarding its secrets, one borrowed from the world of counterintelligence rather than corporate security: the canary trap. The method is simple in principle and has reportedly been used by Apple in various forms for years. When the company suspects that confidential information is being leaked from a particular team, a project, or even a specific meeting, it can deliberately seed slightly different, uniquely identifiable pieces of false information to each of the suspected sources — a different fake release date here, an invented feature there, a made-up code name in one version and not another — so that if any of the false details surface publicly, Apple can trace the leak back to precisely which version, and therefore which person or small group, let it out. The technique takes its name from the same logic as its intelligence-world namesake, in which a specific, distinguishing detail planted in a document functions like a canary in a coal mine, dying — or in this case, surfacing — only if a particular pipeline has been breached, revealing the exact point of failure among what might otherwise be dozens of employees who each had access to a similar but not quite identical account of the truth. The company itself has never formally confirmed the practice in detail, in keeping with its general habit of saying essentially nothing about its own security methods, but journalists who cover Apple's supply chain and product cycles closely, and who have occasionally received demonstrably false information traceable to a narrow set of sources, have described being caught in exactly this kind of trap, publishing a detail that later proved to have been invented specifically to identify them or their source.

The canary trap illustrates something the earlier account of Gray Powell's lost prototype might understate: that Apple's secrecy operation is not merely defensive, a matter of locks and confidentiality agreements meant to keep information contained, but actively offensive, engineered to hunt down and identify the sources of leaks after the fact rather than simply preventing them beforehand. It is also, in its way, a natural extension of the same compartmentalization this chapter has already described, since a workforce that is already accustomed to knowing only fragments of the whole picture can be fed those fragments in intentionally varied forms without arousing suspicion, each employee assuming that whatever detail they were told simply reflects the ordinary, need-to-know slice of truth allotted to their role. Whether any individual case of a leak traced this way has ever resulted in a firing that the public could confirm, the persistence of the tactic across years of reporting about Apple's product cycles suggests that the company treats the identification of a leaker as being nearly as valuable, strategically, as the prevention of the leak itself — a lesson in how far a company built on surprise is willing to go to protect it.

The culture of secrecy had costs as well as benefits, and an honest account should name them. It made Apple an opaque and sometimes paranoid place to work, a company where trust was rationed and information hoarded, where the compartmentalization that protected secrets also prevented the free flow of ideas that innovation sometimes requires. It fed a culture of fear around leaks, and it contributed to the general atmosphere of intensity and pressure that made Apple both extraordinarily productive and, for many, extraordinarily stressful. And it kept Apple famously closed and uncommunicative with the outside world, a company that revealed little, explained less, and treated the press and the public with a control-freak's wariness. But the secrecy worked — it protected the products, controlled the narrative, fed the theater, and preserved the surprise that was one of Apple's most potent weapons — and it was, like so much about the company, an extension of Steve Jobs's own nature: his need for control, his instinct for showmanship, his conviction that every element of the experience must be orchestrated. The secrecy hid the products; the design shaped them; and one more discipline made them great, perhaps the most important and least understood of all. It was the discipline of refusal — of saying no to the thousand good ideas in order to do a few things perfectly — and it was, Jobs believed, the true secret of Apple, harder and rarer and more important than any act of creation.

Chapter 48 — Saying No

Steve Jobs believed that the most important discipline in making great products was not deciding what to do but deciding what not to do — that focus meant saying no, that innovation was as much about the thousand things you rejected as the few you pursued, and that the willingness to refuse was rarer and more valuable than the ability to create. "People think focus means saying yes to the thing you've got to focus on," he said. "But that's not what it means at all. It means saying no to the hundred other good ideas that there are. You have to pick carefully. I'm actually as proud of the things we haven't done as the things I have done. Innovation is saying no to a thousand things." This principle — the discipline of refusal, the pruning of possibilities, the ruthless narrowing of focus — was one of the deepest keys to how Apple worked, and it ran counter to almost every instinct of a large, successful, resource-rich company.

The clearest demonstration of the principle was the story we have already seen: Jobs's return to Apple in 1997 and his slashing of the product line from dozens of models to four, the two-by-two grid that concentrated the company's entire effort on making a few products great rather than many products adequate. But the discipline of saying no operated at every scale, not just the strategic. In the design of an individual product, it meant leaving things out — refusing to add features that would clutter the experience, even features that customers asked for and competitors offered, in the conviction that a product that did fewer things beautifully was superior to one that did more things clumsily. The original iPhone shipped without features that other phones had, and Jobs defended the omissions, because the features it had were perfect and the ones it lacked would have compromised the whole. Apple products were, characteristically, defined as much by what they refused to do as by what they did: the single button, the sealed case, the missing floppy drive, the absent ports, the features declined. This was maddening to critics and to some customers, who pointed out all the things Apple's products could not do that rivals' could — and it was central to why Apple's products felt so clean, so coherent, so easy, because every no was a subtraction of complexity, a removal of the clutter that made other products confusing and ugly.

The discipline of saying no was psychologically and organizationally difficult in a way that is easy to underestimate, and this is why so few companies manage it. Every feature that could be added has someone advocating for it; every market that could be entered has someone arguing its potential; every product that could be made has a business case. The natural tendency of any organization, especially a large and successful one with abundant resources, is toward proliferation — to say yes to more, to add and expand and enter and extend, because each individual addition seems reasonable and because saying no means disappointing someone and forgoing some possible gain. Resisting this tendency, keeping a company focused on a small number of things done superbly while saying no to the endless temptations to do more, requires enormous discipline and, often, a willingness to be the person who kills projects, disappoints advocates, and forgoes opportunities — a thankless and unnatural role. Jobs was uniquely willing and able to play it. He killed products, projects, features, and whole initiatives ruthlessly; he told people no constantly, often brutally; he kept Apple, even as it grew into the largest company in the world, astonishingly focused on a remarkably small number of products, refusing the diversification and proliferation that its resources could easily have funded. The company that could have made anything made very few things, and made them great, because its leader was willing to say no.

There is a connection between the discipline of saying no and the Zen sensibility that had shaped Jobs since his youth, and it is worth drawing out because it reveals the coherence of his whole approach. Zen prizes emptiness, subtraction, the elimination of the unnecessary, the single perfect thing over the cluttered many; it finds beauty and meaning in what is left out as much as in what is present. Jobs's discipline of refusal was, in a sense, this Zen aesthetic applied to business and product design — the treatment of subtraction as a positive act, the conviction that removing was as creative as adding, the pursuit of an essence achieved by stripping away everything inessential. The empty white space of an Apple product, an Apple store, an Apple advertisement; the single button; the refusal of clutter and complexity; the concentration on a few things — all of it was subtraction as a philosophy, the belief that greatness lay in reduction to essence rather than accumulation of features. It was the same instinct that had drawn the young Jobs to Zen and to the clean lines of good design, now operating as the organizing principle of the most valuable company in the world.

The clearest live demonstration of the discipline came only months into Jobs's return, at Apple's Worldwide Developers Conference in May 1997, in an exchange that has been replayed ever since as a case study in disciplined leadership. An audience member stood up and told Jobs, not gently, that he was "a bright and influential man" but that "it's sad and clear" that on several matters under discussion "you don't know what you're talking about," before demanding to know what, exactly, Jobs had been doing for Apple in recent years. Rather than answering the technical challenge on its own terms, Jobs used the moment to restate his whole philosophy of focus, acknowledging the questioner was probably right about some narrow point, then turning to the larger question of how any single feature fit into "a cohesive, larger vision" capable of selling billions of dollars of product a year — the discipline of subordinating any individual good idea to the question of whether it belonged among the small number of things Apple had chosen to do. The hostile crowd, which had begun the exchange ready to boo, applauded by the end of it.

The same instinct traveled well beyond Apple's own product line, and one of the clearest illustrations of it involves a company Jobs never ran. When Mark Parker became Nike's chief executive in 2006, one of his first calls was to Jobs, seeking advice on how to lead a company that had swelled into hundreds of thousands of product variations across dozens of categories. Jobs's answer was blunt: "Nike makes some of the best products in the world," he told Parker. "Products that you lust after. But you also make a lot of crap. Just get rid of the crappy stuff and focus on the good stuff." Parker later said Jobs was "absolutely right," and Nike's subsequent editing of its own product lines, combined with its partnership with Apple on the Nike+ running system, became one of the more celebrated turnarounds in the athletic-apparel business — Jobs's gospel of subtraction exported, intact, to an entirely different industry, proof that the principle was a transferable discipline of leadership rather than an idiosyncrasy of consumer electronics.

It is worth being precise about the scale of the original 1997 cut, because the story is often told in vague language about "slashing the product line" without conveying just how radical the reduction was. By the end of that year, Jobs and his team had eliminated on the order of seventy percent of Apple's existing products and projects, collapsing a catalog that had sprawled into dozens of confusing, overlapping models down toward the simple four-quadrant grid of consumer and professional desktops and portables. It is tempting, in hindsight, to treat this as an obviously correct decision that any competent manager would have made, but it required killing products that real teams inside Apple had built real careers around, canceling revenue a struggling company could ill afford to walk away from in the short term, and betting that a smaller, more focused Apple could out-earn a larger, more scattered one — a bet that took genuine courage to make while the company was still ninety days from insolvency.

The discipline has outlasted its inventor to a degree that is easy to overlook simply because it has become normal. More than a decade after Jobs's death, Apple still sells only a small handful of core product families, compared with the hundreds of variants competitors offer across their own consumer electronics lines, and its retail stores still display that same restraint — a handful of tables holding a handful of devices rather than the crowded, category-by-category sprawl of an ordinary electronics retailer. Every time a customer walks into an Apple Store today and finds the choice among products refreshingly simple rather than paralyzing, they are experiencing, without necessarily noticing it, the durable residue of a decision made under pressure in 1997, when a nearly bankrupt company chose to do far less, far better.

The clearest living ritual of this discipline, repeated inside Apple year after year, was a retreat Jobs held for what became known informally as the "Top 100" — a group of roughly one hundred employees he judged most critical to Apple's future, chosen not strictly by title or org-chart seniority but by Jobs's own private assessment of who mattered most, an assessment so idiosyncratic that senior executives were sometimes left off the list while junior engineers Jobs admired were included. At the close of these retreats, by several accounts from people who attended them, Jobs would stand at a whiteboard in front of the assembled group and ask a single deceptively simple question: what are the ten things Apple should be doing next? The room would offer up its ideas, jockeying and arguing for its own priorities, and Jobs would write each suggestion on the board in his own hand, a process that could go on for some time as the list swelled with genuinely good ideas, worthy projects, reasonable proposals that any well-run company might pursue. Then, once the list of ten had been assembled and debated, Jobs would do the thing that made the exercise Jobs's rather than anyone else's: he would cross off the bottom seven himself, on the spot, over the objections of whoever had championed them, and announce to the room that Apple could only actually do three of the ten things it had just spent an hour discussing.

The ritual was, in miniature, the entire philosophy of this chapter performed live, once a year, in front of the very people whose ideas were being killed. It was not enough for Jobs to say, in the abstract, that focus meant saying no; he staged the mechanism of refusal in front of an audience of the company's most valued people, making the discipline visible and personal rather than merely rhetorical, and ensuring that the lesson — that having a good idea was not the same as having a reason to pursue it — was absorbed not as a slogan but as a memory of watching seven perfectly reasonable proposals get crossed off a whiteboard by the man in charge. "Deciding what not to do is as important as deciding what to do," Jobs told the room on more than one such occasion, a formulation blunter and more procedural than his more famous line about saying no to a thousand good ideas, because it described an actual, repeatable act of triage rather than a general attitude. The Top 100 retreat is not run quite the same way today, and no later Apple executive has tried to reproduce its particular theater of public refusal, but the underlying test it encoded — write down everything worth doing, then ruthlessly discard all but a small fraction of it — remains, by the testimony of people who worked under both Jobs and his successors, one of the most durable habits of mind the company inherited from him.

The discipline of saying no is, finally, one of the hardest parts of Jobs's legacy to transmit, because it is a discipline of temperament and conviction rather than a technique that can be taught, and because it runs against the grain of every organizational incentive. Many companies studied Apple and tried to copy its designs, its retail, its marketing, its secrecy; far fewer managed to copy its focus, because focus requires saying no, and saying no requires a willingness to forgo, to disappoint, to resist the constant pressure to do more, that most organizations and most leaders cannot sustain. It was, perhaps, the deepest and most personal of Jobs's contributions to Apple, rooted in his own nature and his own aesthetic, and it was among the things most at risk of being lost once he was gone — the fear being that Apple, without the singular figure willing to kill projects and refuse features and keep the company brutally focused, would drift toward the proliferation that afflicts all large successful companies, would start saying yes to too many things, would lose the discipline of refusal that had made its products great. Whether Apple could maintain that discipline without Jobs was one of the central questions of the era that followed his death. But the discipline of saying no was only part of the culture Jobs built, and it was entangled with the most controversial and difficult aspect of his character and his method — the intensity, the cruelty, the strange and demanding personal force that inspired and wounded in equal measure, the phenomenon his own team had named the reality distortion field. To reckon fully with how Apple made things, and with what kind of man made Apple, we have to confront that force directly, and weigh what it created against what it cost.

Chapter 49 — The Reality Distortion Field

The phrase "reality distortion field" was coined by Bud Tribble, one of the original Macintosh engineers, borrowing a term from *Star Trek* to describe the effect Steve Jobs had on the people around him, and it has become the standard shorthand for the strangest and most important aspect of his character. Jobs, his colleagues observed, could bend other people's perception of reality — could convince himself and everyone around him that the impossible was possible, that a deadline could be met that could not be met, that a product could do what it could not do, that limits which everyone else accepted simply did not apply. In his presence, people found themselves believing things they knew to be false, agreeing to do things they knew to be impossible, and — this is the crucial and disorienting part — sometimes actually accomplishing those impossible things because Jobs had made them believe they could. The reality distortion field was not merely delusion or manipulation, though it was partly both; it was a genuine force that, at its best, expanded what people were capable of by refusing to accept the constraints they had accepted, and that, at its worst, was a form of tyranny that punished people for the failure to defy physics.

The positive power of the field was real and is worth taking seriously, because it accounts for some of Apple's greatest achievements. Again and again, Jobs refused to accept that something could not be done, and his refusal, transmitted through his intensity and charisma to his teams, produced results that everyone had believed were impossible. Told that a feature would take a year, he would insist it be done in three months, and berate and inspire and will his people until, sometimes, they found a way to do it in three months — discovering, under the pressure of his refusal to accept the timeline, capabilities and solutions they would never have found if they had accepted the "realistic" schedule. The reality distortion field was, in this aspect, a tool for transcending self-imposed limits, for pushing past the reasonable and the accepted into the extraordinary, and much of what made Apple's products great — the impossible schedules met, the features that could not be built and then were, the standards that seemed unreachable and then were reached — came from Jobs's fundamental refusal to accept the constraints that ordinary judgment took for granted. He genuinely believed that the rules did not fully apply, that reality was more malleable than people thought, that will and conviction could accomplish what conventional wisdom deemed impossible, and often enough he was right, and the being-right built a company and a body of products that would not otherwise have existed.

But the field had a dark and destructive side that this book has traced throughout and must now name plainly, because the same force that inspired impossible achievement also caused real and lasting human damage. Jobs could be extraordinarily cruel. He divided people crisply into geniuses and "bozos" and could switch a person from one category to the other without warning or mercy. He told people their work was worthless, and that they were worthless, often in front of their colleagues, with a contempt that could be devastating. He took credit for others' ideas and denied credit to the people who deserved it; he could dismiss an idea as idiotic and then, weeks later, present the same idea as his own brilliant insight, without apparent awareness of the contradiction. He was capable of astonishing callousness toward the people closest to him, most terribly in his years-long denial of his daughter Lisa, but also in countless smaller cruelties to colleagues, friends, and employees. The reality distortion field, applied to people rather than to products, meant that Jobs often refused to accept the truth about how his behavior affected others, or simply did not care, treating people as instruments to be used in the service of the work and discarding or crushing them when they failed to meet his standards. Many of the people who did the greatest work of their lives under Jobs describe the experience as the most exhilarating and the most damaging of their careers, in the same breath, and both halves of that description are true.

How should we weigh this? It is the central moral question of Steve Jobs's life, and this book does not pretend to resolve it, because it is genuinely unresolvable and because the attempt to resolve it too neatly falsifies the truth. There is a school of thought, popular in the business world and encouraged by Jobs's own self-mythology, that holds that the cruelty was the necessary price of the greatness — that only someone willing to be brutal, to demand the impossible, to reject the merely good in pursuit of the insanely great, could have built what Jobs built, and that the human damage was a regrettable but acceptable cost of world-changing achievement. There is an opposite school that holds that the cruelty was never necessary, that Jobs achieved what he achieved despite his cruelty rather than because of it, that a leader can be demanding and visionary without being cruel — as, indeed, Ed Catmull was at Pixar, building a company of extraordinary creative achievement on a culture of candor and respect rather than fear and contempt. The example of Pixar, where Jobs himself witnessed a different and gentler model of creative excellence, is the strongest argument against the necessity of his cruelty: it suggests that greatness and kindness are not incompatible, that the brutality was a feature of Jobs's particular character rather than a requirement of building great things. The truth is probably that Jobs's intensity and refusal to accept limits were genuinely essential to what he built, and that the cruelty that so often accompanied them was not — that the reality distortion field could have been maintained, perhaps, without the casual devastation of the people who fell within it, and that the human damage was real and avoidable and should not be laundered into a necessary cost of genius.

The term itself has a precise and well-documented origin worth recounting in full, because its original context sharpens what it actually meant. In February 1981, Bud Tribble, one of the earliest members of the Macintosh software team, used the phrase to explain to a newly hired engineer, Andy Hertzfeld, why an apparently impossible shipping schedule for the Mac's operating system might nonetheless be met. Tribble borrowed the term from the original *Star Trek* television series, specifically the two-part episode "The Menagerie," in which an alien race called the Talosians possess the power to project entirely convincing illusions directly into other beings' minds. Hertzfeld, who went on to chronicle the Macintosh project in loving detail on his website Folklore.org, later described the effect this way: Jobs's reality distortion field was his ability to convince himself and everyone around him of almost anything, through a mixture of charm, bravado, hyperbole, marketing, and sheer persistence, so that seemingly rational people caught within its radius found themselves suspending their own judgment about what was and was not possible.

One of the anecdotes Hertzfeld recorded illustrates, better than any abstract description, how the field actually operated in practice. Frustrated that the Macintosh took what felt like an eternity to start up, Jobs pressed the engineer responsible for the startup sequence to shave time off it. When the engineer protested that a few seconds hardly mattered, Jobs did the arithmetic aloud in front of him: if the Macintosh sold, say, five million units, and each owner waited a few extra seconds every time the machine started, that added up, across a single year of use, to millions of minutes — a figure Jobs translated into human lifetimes, spent waiting on a machine to start, that could instead be given back to the world. The engineer found meaningful time savings within a couple of weeks. It is a small story, but it captures precisely what made the field effective rather than merely delusional: Jobs was not simply insisting that the impossible be done, he was reframing an engineer's sense of what the stakes of a mundane technical decision actually were, and that reframing, however manipulative it might look from outside, produced a genuinely faster, better machine.

The phrase Tribble borrowed from a 1960s science-fiction episode has, in the years since Jobs's death, escaped its original context entirely and become a stock item of business vocabulary, applied loosely to any founder or executive whose charisma seems to bend a room's collective judgment — other Silicon Valley figures, political leaders, and, at times, ordinary demanding bosses in industries that have nothing to do with technology. Used this loosely, the term has lost much of its original precision; the specific, well-documented mechanism Hertzfeld described — the reframing of stakes, the alternation of charm and intimidation, the genuine self-belief rather than conscious deception — is usually missing from the looser modern usage, which tends to flatten "reality distortion field" into a simple synonym for bullying or hype. The original phenomenon, whatever its costs, was more interesting and more specific than the diluted cliché it became.

Few descriptions of the field's mechanics are as vivid, or as unsettling, as the one offered by Debi Coleman, who managed manufacturing for the original Macintosh team and who worked close enough to Jobs during those years to feel its full force directed at her personally. Coleman compared him, in terms she did not intend as flattering, to Rasputin, the manipulative mystic of the Russian imperial court: Jobs, she said, "laser-beamed in on you and didn't blink," fixing his attention so completely on a person that ordinary skepticism simply evaporated in his presence, so that "it didn't matter if he was serving purple Kool-Aid" — a phrase that has since become one of the more quoted shorthand descriptions of what it felt like to be on the receiving end of his conviction, evoking both the cult-like intensity of the experience and the faint, uncomfortable echo of coerced belief the word "Kool-Aid" carries in American speech. And yet Coleman's account, like so many others from people who worked closely with Jobs, refused to resolve neatly into simple condemnation. Asked what happened once a person had, in effect, drunk the Kool-Aid and agreed to attempt whatever Jobs was demanding, she offered the observation that captures the field's productive side as precisely as anything in the record: "You did the impossible, because you didn't realize it was impossible." The two halves of her testimony — the discomfort of being manipulated by a man who would not blink, and the genuine achievement that manipulation somehow produced — sit side by side in her account exactly as they sit side by side in this book's larger reckoning with him, neither canceling the other out.

Coleman's own career inside Apple suggests she was not simply a passive casualty of the field but someone who learned, over time, to operate within its distortions and even to benefit from them; she went on to run manufacturing at Apple as a vice president and later became one of the small number of women to reach senior operational leadership in Silicon Valley's technology industry during the 1980s, a trajectory that would have been unlikely without the demanding, high-visibility proving ground the Macintosh project provided. Her account matters here less as a biographical footnote about one executive's career than as first-hand testimony, from someone who managed the unglamorous, physical, deadline-bound work of actually building the machines Jobs demanded, that the reality distortion field was experienced by its subjects not as an abstract theory later applied by biographers but as a specific, bodily sensation — the feeling of being looked at without being allowed to look away, and of finding, afterward, that the thing declared impossible had somehow been done.

What is certain is that the reality distortion field, in all its creative and destructive power, was inseparable from who Steve Jobs was, and that it was, in a sense, his most personal creation — more personal than any product, because it was the direct expression of his character imposed on the world. It built Apple and it wounded the people who built Apple; it produced insanely great products and it produced human wreckage; it was a tool of transcendence and a mechanism of tyranny, and it was all of these at once, and the attempt to separate the good from the bad, to keep the visionary and discard the tyrant, founders on the fact that they were the same force. Steve Jobs was not a great man who happened to be cruel, nor a cruel man who happened to be great; he was a single, indivisible person whose greatness and cruelty flowed from the same source, and the honest reckoning with him requires holding both together, refusing both the hagiography that erases the damage and the condemnation that erases the achievement. He put a dent in the universe, and he left dents in a great many people, and the story of Apple is the story of both. He died in 2011, and the reality distortion field died with him — and the question that remained was whether the company he had built on it could survive its absence, whether Apple without its distorting genius could remain Apple, or whether the magic had been, all along, simply him. The answer would be given by a very different kind of leader, in a very different key, over the fifteen years that followed.

Chapter 50 — The Operator

When Tim Cook became chief executive of Apple in August 2011, the conventional wisdom held that he was a caretaker — a competent operations man who would keep the machine running for a while but who lacked the visionary genius that was Apple's essence, and under whom the company would inevitably decline as the magic faded. Fifteen years later, that conventional wisdom looks not merely wrong but almost comically so. Under Tim Cook, Apple did not decline; it grew, enormously, becoming far larger and more valuable than it had ever been under Steve Jobs — the first company in history to be worth one trillion dollars, then two, then three, then four. Cook ran Apple for longer than Jobs ran it in his second act, and by the ordinary measures of business he was one of the most successful chief executives in the history of the world. The story of how the caretaker became one of the great CEOs, and of what he did and did not change, is essential to understanding what Apple really is — whether it was Steve Jobs, or something more durable that Jobs had built.

Tim Cook was, in almost every respect, the opposite of Steve Jobs, and the contrast is the key to understanding him. Where Jobs was volatile, theatrical, and mercurial, Cook was calm, measured, and disciplined. Where Jobs was a product visionary who cared little for operations, Cook was an operations genius who had built the most sophisticated supply chain in the world. Where Jobs led through charisma and the reality distortion field, through inspiration and fear and force of personality, Cook led through steadiness, consensus, and quiet competence. Where Jobs was a showman who lived for the stage, Cook was reserved and private, uncomfortable with the spotlight, a man who let the products and the results speak. Cook came from a modest background in the American South — born in Alabama, the son of a shipyard worker and a homemaker — and he brought to Apple a very different temperament from the countercultural Californian intensity of its founder: methodical, ethical, understated, a manager rather than an artist. He had joined Apple in 1998, recruited by Jobs to fix the company's chaotic operations, and had spent thirteen years mastering the unglamorous but essential work of manufacturing, logistics, and supply — the plumbing that made Apple's products actually get built and delivered, at scale, profitably.

The doubt about Cook was, at bottom, a doubt about whether Apple could be led by someone who was not a product visionary — whether the company's magic was so bound up in Jobs's singular genius for products that no one else could sustain it, and whether an operations man, however brilliant at his craft, could keep Apple great. It was a reasonable doubt, and Cook answered it not by trying to be Steve Jobs, which would have been fatal, but by being himself and by understanding that his job was different from Jobs's. Cook did not pretend to have Jobs's product genius; instead, he built a structure in which others — the designers, the engineers, the executives Jobs had assembled and trained — could exercise that genius, and he provided the steady leadership, the operational excellence, the strategic discipline, and the ethical grounding that let the whole machine run at a scale Jobs had never managed. He understood, correctly, that Apple by 2011 was no longer a small company that could be the lengthened shadow of one man; it was a vast global enterprise that needed a great manager and leader as much as it needed a great products person, and that the products person's role could be distributed among the talented people Jobs had left behind. Cook's genius, if the word applies to him, was the genius of the institution-builder rather than the artist — the ability to take the extraordinary thing Jobs had created and make it durable, scalable, and sustainable, to turn a founder's company into a lasting institution.

Cook's own background is worth dwelling on, because its plainness was itself part of what made him so different from the man he succeeded. He was born in 1960 in Mobile, Alabama, the son of a shipyard worker, and grew up nearby in Robertsdale, a small town on the Gulf Coast far removed from Silicon Valley's countercultural ferment. He studied industrial engineering at Auburn University, graduating in 1982, before spending more than a decade in operations roles at IBM and Compaq — a résumé built entirely around the unglamorous disciplines of manufacturing, logistics, and inventory management that Jobs had never had much patience for and that Apple, before Cook arrived in 1998, badly needed. It was a background suited less to reinventing an industry than to running one with ruthless efficiency, and that turned out to be exactly the complementary skill Apple's visionary but operationally undisciplined founder required.

The depth of the personal bond between the two men, so often obscured by the contrast in their public styles, is captured in an episode that only became public years after Jobs's death, when it was recounted in a 2015 book on Jobs's later years. In January 2009, as Jobs's health was failing and he faced the prospect of a liver transplant, Cook had his own blood tested, discovered he shared Jobs's rare blood type, and went to Jobs to offer to donate a portion of his own liver. Jobs's reaction was immediate and furious refusal. "He cut me off at the legs, almost before the words were out of my mouth," Cook recalled. " 'No,' he said. 'I'll never let you do that. I'll never do that.'" Cook later noted that Jobs raised his voice at him only four or five times in the thirteen years they worked together, and that this was one of them. It is a story rarely mentioned alongside the more famous accounts of Jobs's cruelty, and it complicates the picture of the two men's relationship: whatever else defined it, it was not merely a functional partnership between a visionary and his operations chief, but something closer to real personal devotion, at least on the evidence of that one conversation.

The scale Cook eventually built is worth stating in plain figures, because the doubts about him in 2011 are almost impossible to credit once the numbers are laid beside them. On August 2, 2018, Apple became the first publicly traded American company in history to close a trading day valued at one trillion dollars; two years later, in August 2020, it passed two trillion; and within a few more years its value passed three trillion — figures that would have sounded like fantasy even to the Apple of Jobs's final year, when the company's valuation, already in the hundreds of billions, felt at the time like an almost unrepeatable summit. Cook did this not by discovering some new insanely great product to rival the iPhone, but largely by executing relentlessly on Jobs's existing playbook — the ecosystem, the retail experience, the premium pricing, the supply chain — at a scale and a level of operational precision that Jobs himself had never had the discipline, or perhaps the interest, to sustain for so long.

The personal discipline that let Cook run this machine at such scale is itself part of the story, and it stands in instructive contrast to the mercurial, all-hours intensity that defined Jobs's own working life. Cook has for years maintained a famously rigid and austere daily routine: he wakes before four in the morning, by his own account around three forty-five, and spends the first hour of his day not on strategy or product decisions but reading through messages from ordinary Apple customers, a habit he has described as a way of staying grounded in what the company's products actually mean to the people who buy them, before most of his own employees have even woken up. From there he goes directly to the gym, typically arriving by five and training for close to an hour, a regimen he has credited with managing the stress of running the world's most valuable company, and he has spoken publicly, more than once, about the personal satisfaction of closing all three rings on his own Apple Watch each day — a small, almost domestic detail that nonetheless captures something real about a man who leads by consistency and quiet self-discipline rather than by the theatrical unpredictability that defined his predecessor. Where Jobs's working life was organized around bursts of obsessive focus, confrontation, and improvisation, often stretching into the night and governed by mood as much as by schedule, Cook's is organized around an almost monastic regularity, the same sequence of hours repeated with little variation, year after year, a rhythm better suited to managing a global manufacturing and logistics operation spanning hundreds of suppliers across dozens of countries than to the sporadic bursts of creative intensity Jobs relied on to wring a perfect product out of his design studio.

Cook has said of his own temperament that he can "control the morning better than the evening," because the unpredictable demands of running Apple — the meetings that run long, the crises that erupt without warning, the decisions that cannot wait — tend to accumulate as the day wears on and are hardest to manage once they begin; protecting those first quiet hours before dawn, devoted to customers and to his own body, was his way of establishing at least one part of each day he could fully govern. It is a small irony worth noting that the trait most often cited by people who worked under both men — Cook's near-legendary ability to sit silently through long stretches of a meeting, absorbing information without visibly reacting, then to ask a single pointed operational question that exposed a gap no one else had noticed — descends from exactly the same instinct for control that drove Jobs's more theatrical management style, expressed instead through patience and quiet interrogation rather than charisma and volume. The two men led in opposite registers, but the underlying demand each of them made of the people around them — total command of the details, no tolerance for the unexamined assumption — was, in the end, remarkably similar.

Cook also brought to Apple a moral and social dimension that Jobs had largely neglected, and it became a defining feature of his tenure. Where Jobs had been almost entirely focused on the products and indifferent to Apple's broader social role, Cook made Apple a company that took public positions on questions beyond technology — on privacy, which he elevated into a core Apple value and a competitive differentiator, arguing that Apple's customers were not its product and that their data would be protected; on the environment, committing Apple to ambitious goals for renewable energy and carbon neutrality; on labor conditions in its supply chain, pushing (imperfectly, as we will see) to improve the treatment of the workers who built Apple's products; and on social questions, including his own decision, remarkable for the chief executive of the world's most valuable company, to come out publicly as gay, saying he considered it a gift from God and hoped his openness might help others. Cook made Apple a more socially engaged, more values-driven company than it had been under Jobs, and while critics could and did argue that some of this was branding, that the values were selectively applied and sometimes in tension with Apple's commercial interests, the shift was real and it reflected Cook's own character — the ethical seriousness of a man from a different background and a different mold than the founder he succeeded. Under Cook, Apple would face the great reckonings of its maturity — the controversies over labor, over China, over the App Store, over its sheer power — and it would do so under a leader who, whatever his limits, took the moral questions seriously. But first, before the reckonings, came the growth, and the growth rested on the thing Cook understood better than anyone alive: the supply chain, the invisible engine that turned Apple's designs into hundreds of millions of physical objects and delivered them to the world.

Chapter 51 — The Supply Chain as Art

The least glamorous and most underappreciated pillar of Apple's success is its supply chain — the vast, intricate global system that turns raw materials and components into hundreds of millions of finished products and delivers them to customers around the world — and it was Tim Cook's mastery of this system that made him indispensable, first to Steve Jobs and then to Apple itself. To most people the supply chain is invisible; you buy an iPhone and it simply exists, and you never think about the extraordinary logistical achievement required to produce that object in enormous quantities, at consistent quality, at a cost that leaves Apple its famous margins, and to have it available in stores and shipping to customers on launch day around the world. But that achievement is one of the real foundations of Apple's dominance, as important in its way as the design or the software, and it is one of the hardest for competitors to replicate.

When Cook joined Apple in 1998, the company's operations were a mess — bloated, inefficient, losing money, with too much inventory sitting in warehouses and too little coordination between what Apple made and what it could sell. Cook attacked these problems with a discipline and rigor that transformed the company's economics. He slashed inventory, understanding that unsold products sitting in warehouses were like spoiling produce, tying up cash and losing value by the day; he closed factories and warehouses, shifting Apple toward a model in which it designed products and orchestrated their manufacture by contractors rather than building them itself; he built relationships with suppliers and manufacturers, above all in Asia, that gave Apple unprecedented control and priority; and he wove the whole thing into a tightly managed system in which components flowed just in time to assembly, products flowed just in time to customers, and the enormous machine ran with a precision that competitors could not match. The financial results of this operational excellence were as important as any product to Apple's success: by mastering the supply chain, Cook made it possible for Apple to sell premium products at premium prices while keeping its costs low, generating the extraordinary profits that funded everything else and that made Apple, eventually, the most profitable company in the world.

The heart of Apple's manufacturing was, and remains, in China, and this fact — the source of enormous efficiency and, as we will see, enormous controversy — deserves to be understood in its full dimensions. Apple did not build most of its own products; instead, it contracted the assembly to enormous manufacturing partners, above all a Taiwanese company called Foxconn, which operated vast factory complexes in China employing hundreds of thousands and sometimes over a million workers, who assembled iPhones and iPads and other Apple products by hand on assembly lines of staggering scale. This arrangement gave Apple access to a manufacturing capability that existed nowhere else on earth: an immense, flexible, skilled workforce that could be mobilized at short notice, factory complexes that could ramp production up and down with astonishing speed, an entire ecosystem of component suppliers clustered together, and a cost structure that American or European manufacturing could not approach. The famous story — that when Jobs demanded a last-minute change to the iPhone's screen shortly before launch, a Chinese factory could rouse thousands of workers from their dormitories in the middle of the night to implement it immediately — captures the capability that Apple's China-centered supply chain provided: a responsiveness and scale that were simply impossible elsewhere. Cook built and managed this system, and it became one of Apple's deepest competitive advantages, a manufacturing engine of a sophistication and scale that rivals spent years and billions trying, mostly unsuccessfully, to match.

The supply chain was also, in a sense, an expression of the same whole-widget philosophy that governed everything Apple did, extended from design into manufacturing and logistics. Apple did not simply place orders with suppliers and take what it got; it involved itself deeply in how its components were made, investing in suppliers' factories and equipment, sometimes buying up the entire global supply of a critical component or a key piece of manufacturing machinery to secure priority and to deny it to competitors, dictating quality standards and processes, and integrating the whole supply chain into its own tightly controlled system. This control over manufacturing paralleled Apple's control over hardware and software; just as Apple insisted on owning the design and the operating system, so it insisted on a degree of control over its supply chain that most companies never sought, and this control was part of what let it achieve the quality, the scale, the speed, and the cost structure that made its business work. The supply chain was the whole widget extended backward into the process of making, and Cook was its master architect.

One story from Cook's first months at Apple captures the operational instinct he brought to the job better than any abstract description could. In the fall of 1998, with the original iMac selling faster than Apple's factories could ship it, Cook moved to secure roughly one hundred million dollars' worth of air freight capacity for the coming holiday quarter — buying up, in effect, almost the entire available air-cargo capacity that Apple's rivals would otherwise have used to move their own products in time for Christmas. Dell and Compaq, competing for the same scarce cargo space, found themselves unable to book it, while Apple's iMacs flowed to stores on schedule. It was a small, unglamorous, entirely characteristic Cook maneuver — not a new product, not a new design, just a ruthless, well-timed piece of logistics — and it announced the arrival, inside a company that had always defined itself by its designers and engineers, of an operations mind capable of thinking several moves ahead of the whole industry.

The scale that mind eventually built is hard to grasp except through its specific, staggering details. Foxconn's flagship complex in Zhengzhou, in central China, grew so large that it acquired its own nickname, "iPhone City" — a fenced campus of dormitories, cafeterias, and production halls that functioned as a company town in its own right, its workforce swelling from a baseline of tens of thousands to as many as two hundred thousand people in the weeks before a new iPhone's launch. The rhythm of that surge became an annual ritual: in the summer of 2024, ahead of the iPhone 16 launch, Foxconn hired roughly fifty thousand additional workers at Zhengzhou in the space of about two weeks, dangling completion bonuses worth roughly a thousand dollars to those who stayed through the crush of the launch season. By some estimates Foxconn alone assembled close to two-thirds of all the iPhones made worldwide as recently as 2024 — a concentration of production, in one company, in one country, that measures just how completely Cook's system had come to depend on a single extraordinary manufacturing ecosystem.

That dependence, however, is no longer quite what it was, which corrects a common assumption that every iPhone is still simply "made in China." Under pressure from tariffs, geopolitics, and the plain business logic of not keeping every egg in one basket, Apple spent the years after

Cook's own tenure pushing manufacturing outward from China at a pace that would have seemed implausible a decade earlier. India, which assembled only a small fraction of Apple's phones as recently as 2023, grew within a few years to account for roughly a quarter of all iPhones made worldwide, with tens of millions of units a year coming off lines run by Foxconn and by Tata Electronics, the Indian conglomerate that came to assemble even the flagship Pro models. Vietnam never assembled a single iPhone, but became the backbone of another part of the ecosystem, host to dozens of Apple suppliers and, on some estimates, the site of the majority of the world's AirPods production. China remained the core of the system and the home of its most sophisticated component clusters, but the supply chain Cook had built as a monument to concentration had itself begun, under his successors, to spread its risk across a much wider map.

The other side of that scale is the human cost that Apple has always been more reluctant to advertise. Life on Foxconn's production lines has, at various times, meant grueling hours, dense dormitory housing, and heavy reliance on temporary agency labor, and in 2010 a wave of worker suicides at Foxconn's Shenzhen facilities — eighteen deaths or attempts over the course of the year, almost all by workers jumping from factory buildings — became an international scandal that forced Foxconn to raise wages, bring in counselors, and install netting around its dormitory towers to catch anyone who jumped. Apple, which had its products assembled in those same buildings, issued a statement saying it was "saddened and upset" and sent a team to inspect the conditions, the beginning of a supplier-responsibility program that continues today. Conditions have generally improved since, but the underlying arrangement — a company that captures extraordinary profit margins from a device assembled, under considerable pressure, by workers who see a small fraction of its retail price — remains the least examined and most uncomfortable part of the supply-chain story, the shadow behind the choreography that lets a customer order a new iPhone and have it appear, days later, finished to a standard few factories on earth could match.

The same leverage that let Apple command extraordinary favors from its manufacturing partners could also, when a partner failed to deliver, be turned into something close to a death sentence, and the collapse of GT Advanced Technologies is the starkest illustration of how unforgiving that leverage could be. In November 2013, Apple signed a deal with GT Advanced, a manufacturer of sapphire crystal, to supply synthetic sapphire — a material harder and more scratch-resistant than the glass then used on iPhone screens — for future Apple products, and it backed the arrangement with hundreds of millions of dollars in prepayments, roughly five hundred seventy-eight million dollars in total, to help GT Advanced build a dedicated sapphire-growing plant in Mesa, Arizona, and staff it with hundreds of workers. The partnership went wrong almost immediately: GT Advanced struggled to get its furnaces producing sapphire at anything close to the yield rates Apple needed, reportedly achieving success rates of twenty-five percent or lower on the crystal boules it was supposed to be turning out in bulk, and when Apple launched the iPhone 6 in September 2014 without the rumored sapphire display that GT Advanced's plant had been built to supply, it became clear the arrangement had failed. Weeks later, on October 6, 2014, GT Advanced abruptly filed for bankruptcy, its own court filings accusing Apple of having imposed "oppressive and burdensome" terms on the relationship and describing the deal's continuation as no longer commercially viable, while the company was reportedly burning through roughly a million dollars a day it did not have. The Mesa plant shut down before it ever meaningfully supplied a single iPhone; roughly eight hundred ninety employees lost their jobs, and Apple, through the ensuing bankruptcy settlement, recovered its prepayments not in cash but by auctioning off between fourteen hundred and two thousand of GT Advanced's specialized sapphire-growing furnaces.

The episode is worth setting beside the celebrated stories of Apple's supply-chain mastery — the air-freight coup of 1998, the workforce mobilized overnight in a Chinese dormitory, the "iPhone City" that could scale to two hundred thousand workers on demand — because it shows the same system's underside. Apple's extraordinary purchasing power and its willingness to dictate terms, specifications, and timelines to its suppliers were the source of the speed, quality, and cost control that built its profits; but that same power meant that a supplier who could not meet Apple's exacting standards, on Apple's schedule, bore essentially all of the financial risk of the failure, even when Apple itself had helped select the technology, financed the factory, and driven the aggressive terms that made the yield problem so difficult to solve in the first place. GT Advanced was not a marginal contractor exploited at the fringes of Apple's empire; it was a company Apple had chosen, funded, and worked alongside for nearly a year, and its collapse into bankruptcy, its Arizona plant shuttered, and its workforce laid off within weeks of the iPhone 6 launch stands as a reminder that the discipline and control that made Apple's supply chain a marvel of modern manufacturing could, when a partner faltered, prove every bit as unforgiving toward a corporate supplier as toward the individual assembly-line worker.

The mastery of the supply chain is, finally, why Tim Cook was the right successor to Steve Jobs, even though — because — he was so completely different from him. Apple by 2011 was a company that sold hundreds of millions of physical products a year, and the challenge of actually making and delivering those products, at that scale, at that quality, at that cost, was as central to the company's success as the challenge of designing them. Jobs had provided the vision and the products; Cook provided the ability to manufacture and deliver them to the entire world, reliably and profitably, at a scale Jobs himself could never have managed. The two capabilities were complementary and both essential, and it was Apple's good fortune, and Jobs's wisdom, that the company had both — the visionary who created the products and the operator who could build them by the hundreds of millions. When Jobs died, Apple lost its visionary but kept its operator, and it turned out that at Apple's scale and maturity, the operator's capability, combined with the design and engineering talent Jobs had assembled, was enough to keep the company growing for another decade and a half. The supply chain that Cook had built became the engine of Apple's continued dominance, and it powered the company through a series of new products — some evolutionary, some genuinely new — that would extend Apple's reach onto people's wrists and into their ears, and that would prove, to the doubters, that Apple after Jobs could still innovate. The first of them was strapped to the wrist.

Chapter 52 — Wrist and Ear

The first entirely new product category Apple created after Steve Jobs's death was the Apple Watch, introduced in 2014 and released in 2015, and it carried a heavy burden of expectation, because it was meant to answer the question that hung over the entire Cook era: could Apple still innovate, could it still create new categories, without the singular genius who had created the Mac and the iPod and the iPhone and the iPad? The Apple Watch was Tim Cook's Apple making its case that the magic had not died with Jobs — that the company could still take an existing, unsatisfying product category (the watch, the wearable) and reinvent it in Apple's image, as Jobs had done so many times. The answer the Watch gave was nuanced and instructive, and it revealed both the strengths and the limits of Apple after Jobs.

The Apple Watch did not, at first, know quite what it was, and this uncertainty is itself revealing. In its early conception and marketing, Apple positioned the Watch heavily as a fashion and luxury object — a beautiful piece of jewelry, available in gold at extravagant prices, promoted in fashion magazines and on the wrists of celebrities, sold as a status symbol as much as a technology product. This framing reflected the influence of Jony Ive and of executives Apple had recruited from the luxury and fashion worlds, and it was, in retrospect, a misreading of what the Watch was best at. The luxury positioning largely failed; people did not, on the whole, want a very expensive gold smartwatch that would be technologically obsolete in a few years, and the fashion framing never quite fit a device whose real value lay elsewhere. Over the following years Apple pivoted, discovering through experience and customer behavior what the Watch was actually for, and the answer turned out to be health and fitness. The Watch became, above all, a health device — tracking the wearer's activity, heart rate, exercise, and sleep, nudging people to move, and eventually incorporating genuinely significant medical capabilities: the ability to detect an irregular heart rhythm, to take an electrocardiogram, to detect a hard fall and call for help, features that have been credited with saving lives. Repositioned around health, the Apple Watch found its purpose and became a major success, the best-selling watch in the world, a substantial business in its own right, and a device that many wearers came to feel they could not live without.

The second new category was the AirPods, introduced in 2016 — wireless earbuds that connected effortlessly to the iPhone and other Apple devices, small white objects that sat in the ears and, like the iPod's white earbuds before them, became an instantly recognizable cultural signifier. The AirPods, too, were initially met with skepticism and even mockery; the sight of small white pods sticking out of people's ears struck some observers as ridiculous, and there were the usual doubts about whether people wanted or needed such a thing. And once again the skeptics were wrong: the AirPods became an enormous success, one of the most popular products Apple had ever made, so ubiquitous that they, like the iPod earbuds and the Apple Watch, became a visible marker of the Apple ecosystem and a genuine cultural phenomenon. The AirPods succeeded because they did one thing so well — connecting wirelessly and seamlessly to Apple devices, with a magical ease of pairing and switching that competitors struggled to match — that they made the alternative (tangled wires, clumsy Bluetooth pairing) suddenly feel intolerable. And they were, not coincidentally, made possible and desirable partly by Apple's controversial decision to remove the headphone jack from the iPhone, another instance of Apple amputating a familiar technology to force the future, absorbing the criticism, and being proven commercially right.

The pivot to health was not merely a marketing repositioning; it was validated, again and again, by real medical outcomes that Apple could point to with more confidence than almost any other claim it had ever made about its products. In 2019, an Alabama woman who had received an Apple Watch Series 4 as a Christmas gift used its newly introduced electrocardiogram feature and found that it was registering an irregular heartbeat; she had the reading confirmed by hospital equipment, was diagnosed with atrial fibrillation, and ultimately underwent open-heart surgery to replace a faulty valve and reduce her risk of stroke — one of many such stories that circulated in the years after the ECG app's 2018 launch, and one that Apple itself came to cite as proof that a wrist-worn accessory could be a genuine instrument of preventive medicine rather than a novelty. The underlying technology held up to scrutiny: independent clinical reviews pooling multiple studies found the Watch's atrial-fibrillation detection to be roughly ninety-five percent sensitive and ninety-five percent specific, accuracy good enough that in 2024 its AFib History feature became the first digital health technology to qualify for the United States Food and Drug Administration's Medical Device Development Tools program — a regulatory milestone, rare for any consumer electronics company, that formally recognized the Watch's data as a legitimate tool in cardiac care rather than a mere wellness gimmick.

The AirPods, for their part, went on to a dominance that

made the early mockery look almost quaint in hindsight. By the end of 2024 Apple had sold more than seventy-five million pairs of AirPods and counted over one hundred million active users worldwide, a business generating on the order of twenty-four billion dollars a year in revenue; by early 2026 AirPods, even excluding Apple's Beats brand, still commanded roughly a quarter of all global shipments of wireless earbuds and — because of their premium pricing — closer to half of the entire category's revenue, a share no single competitor, from Samsung to Sony to Xiaomi, came close to matching. It is worth pausing on how completely this inverted the conventional wisdom at launch: reviewers in 2016 wondered aloud who would pay for earbuds with no wire tethering them together, joked that people would lose them constantly or that they looked absurd jutting from the ear, and treated the entire premise as a solution to a problem nobody had. A decade later, the "no wire" design that critics found strange had become the default expectation of an entire global industry, and the small white pods Apple once had to defend against ridicule had become one of the most profitable consumer electronics products in history, quietly generating more revenue on their own than many entire companies.

Nor was the ear, any more than the wrist, left as a purely audio accessory. In September 2024 the Food and Drug Administration authorized the AirPods Pro 2, through a software update, to function as an over-the-counter hearing aid for people with mild to moderate hearing loss — the first time the agency had cleared any product to work this way, and a milestone that took a pair of earbuds millions of people already owned and turned them, for a meaningful share of those users, into a substitute for a device that had traditionally cost thousands of dollars and required a visit to an audiologist. In the clinical study Apple submitted to support the feature, users who fitted the hearing aid function themselves, guided only by a short hearing test taken on the iPhone, reported benefits comparable to those who had the same underlying hardware professionally fitted by a specialist — a result that mattered less as a piece of trivia than as a demonstration of exactly the thesis Apple had been arguing since it repositioned the Watch around health: that products already in hundreds of millions of pockets and ears could, with the right sensors and the right software, be quietly repurposed into serious medical tools, at a scale and a price no dedicated medical-device company could reach.

The commercial verdict on the wrist followed a similar arc from skepticism to dominance. As early as 2019, market researchers found that Apple alone had shipped more watches — 30.7 million units that year — than the entire Swiss watch industry combined, whose collective exports were falling even as Apple's wearables division grew by double digits; the company mocked for trying to sell an overpriced gadget in gold had, within a few years of launch, become the largest watchmaker on earth by volume, eclipsing an industry with centuries of prestige behind it. It was a strange kind of victory, and an instructive one: the Apple Watch won not by beating Rolex and Omega at their own game of craftsmanship and status, but by redefining what a watch was for in the first place, so thoroughly that the comparison to Swiss watchmaking came to feel almost beside the point.

A third medical capability arrived in September 2024, extending the health strategy from the heart to an entirely different physiological system: sleep. Alongside that year's new Apple Watch models, Apple introduced a sleep apnea notification feature, cleared by the Food and Drug Administration on September 13, 2024, that used the Watch's accelerometer to detect the subtle wrist movements associated with disruptions in normal breathing during sleep — a method that required no additional sensor hardware beyond what tens of millions of existing Watch owners already had strapped to their wrists. Each night the Watch would record a measure Apple called "breathing disturbances," and once a month it would analyze the accumulated pattern and, if the data showed consistent signs of moderate or severe obstructive sleep apnea, surface a notification recommending the wearer consult a doctor — a condition that, by most public-health estimates, affects tens of millions of adults in the United States alone, the great majority of whom remain undiagnosed because a formal diagnosis has traditionally required an overnight stay in a specialized sleep laboratory wired to monitoring equipment far more elaborate than a wristwatch. Apple supported its FDA submission with a clinical validation study spanning more than fourteen hundred participants, whose results the agency judged sufficient to clear the notification algorithm against standard clinical-grade sleep testing, a bar of evidence considerably higher than what most consumer wellness gadgets are ever asked to clear.

The sleep apnea feature completed a pattern that, three separate times now, had followed the same arc: a Watch capability introduced with genuine medical stakes, validated against a large clinical dataset, and cleared by a national regulator, transforming what had begun as a fashion accessory that struggled to justify its own existence into a device capable of flagging cardiac arrhythmia, amplifying hearing, and now screening for a chronic respiratory condition, all through software updates delivered to hardware people had already bought for entirely different reasons. It was a trajectory almost nobody, least of all Apple's own early marketing team with its gold cases and fashion-magazine photo shoots, would have predicted for the product in 2015, and it mattered because it answered, in the most concrete terms available to any consumer product, the doubt that had shadowed the Watch since its introduction: not merely that people would buy it, which by then was no longer seriously in question, but that owning one could measurably change the course of a person's health, catching a hidden condition — an irregular heartbeat, a hearing loss, a night of disrupted breathing — before the wearer had any reason of their own to go looking for it. The wrist that had once been fitted for a fashion statement had become, one FDA clearance at a time, something closer to a clinic.

The verdict on Apple's post-Jobs record as an innovator is, in the end, a more interesting truth than the simple question of whether the company could still innovate. Both products were genuine successes and genuine new categories, proving that Apple could still create desirable new kinds of products and reach new markets. But both were also, notably, accessories to the iPhone — devices that orbited the phone, that depended on it, that extended the Apple ecosystem outward from the central device rather than creating a wholly independent new platform the way the iPhone itself had. The Watch and the AirPods were brilliant executions of a strategy of ecosystem extension: they made the iPhone more valuable and Apple's customers more locked in, they generated substantial revenue, and they deepened the moat around Apple's business, but they were not the kind of world-remaking, category-defining, standalone revolution that the iPhone had been. This was, perhaps, the honest measure of Apple after Jobs: a company that could still innovate brilliantly at the level of execution, that could create excellent new products and successful new categories, but that had not — at least not yet — produced a new platform as transformative as the ones Jobs had created, a new center of gravity to rival the phone. Whether that reflected the absence of Jobs's singular vision, or simply the difficulty of ever again finding a product as universal and revolutionary as the smartphone, or the reality that such revolutions come rarely in any company's history, is a question worth holding open. What is clear is that the Watch and the AirPods extended and enriched the empire the iPhone had built, and that they did so through devices strapped to the wrist and nestled in the ear — and that the real growth engine of the Cook era, the thing that drove Apple to its trillions, was increasingly not any single device but a business that had no physical form at all.

Chapter 52½ — Siri and the AI Question

Of all the questions hanging over Apple as it entered the mid-2020s, none was sharper or more consequential than the question of artificial intelligence, and none exposed more clearly the anxieties beneath the company's record valuation. For a period in which artificial intelligence became the defining technology story of the age — in which rival companies staked their futures on it and poured fortunes into it — Apple was widely perceived to have fallen behind, and the perception, fair or not, went to the heart of the doubt about whether Apple after Steve Jobs could still lead rather than follow. The story of Apple and AI is, at the time of this writing, unfinished, but it is essential to any honest account of the company's modern situation, because it is the arena in which Apple's ability to remain at the technological frontier is being most severely tested.

Apple's early move into artificial intelligence had come in 2011, in the last months of Jobs's life, with Siri — the voice assistant, built into the iPhone, that let users speak commands and questions and receive spoken answers. Siri was, at its introduction, a genuinely striking demonstration, one of the first mass-market voice assistants, and it captured the imagination as a glimpse of a future in which people would simply talk to their devices. But over the following decade, Siri disappointed. It remained limited, error-prone, and frustrating, often misunderstanding requests or failing to accomplish them, and it fell behind the voice assistants that rivals developed. Siri became, over the years, a symbol of a certain Apple weakness — the sense that the company that excelled at hardware and design and integration was not equally strong at the data-driven, cloud-based, machine-learning services that increasingly defined the cutting edge, and that its very strengths, including its principled commitment to privacy and its reluctance to harvest user data, might handicap it in a field that fed on data. The gap between Siri's early promise and its persistent mediocrity was a small but telling crack in the image of Apple as the company that always got things right.

The larger reckoning came with the explosion of generative artificial intelligence in the 2020s — the arrival of systems that could produce fluent text, images, and code, that could hold conversations and answer questions with startling capability, and that seemed to many to herald a transformation as profound as the personal computer or the internet. Rival technology companies threw themselves into this new field with enormous investment and urgency, racing to build and deploy ever more capable systems, and the AI story dominated the industry. Apple, characteristically, was quieter and slower, and its relative silence was read in two opposite ways that map onto the two readings of Apple-after-Jobs that run through this book. The critics saw a company caught flat-footed by the most important technological shift of the era, lacking the AI talent and infrastructure and urgency of its rivals, its cautious culture and privacy commitments leaving it behind, its Siri a years-long embarrassment, its promised AI features delayed and underwhelming — evidence that Apple had become a follower, brilliant at refining but no longer able to lead a genuine revolution. The defenders saw a company doing what Apple always did: waiting, letting others make the early mistakes, and preparing to enter when it could do so in a distinctively Apple way — integrated, private, on-device, human-centered — arguing that Apple had been quietly building AI into its products and its chips for years and would, in time, deliver AI that was more useful and more trustworthy than the flashy but unreliable offerings of its rivals.

Which reading is correct is, as with the Vision Pro, not yet knowable, and the honesty of a current history requires resisting a premature verdict. What can be said is that the AI question posed, more acutely than any other, the fundamental uncertainty about Apple's future. Artificial intelligence appeared likely to be the defining technology of the coming decades, the terrain on which the next great competitive battles would be fought, and Apple's ability to compete on that terrain would go a long way toward determining whether it remained one of the world's leading technology companies or slipped, gradually, into the comfortable but diminishing status of a maker of beautiful legacy devices. Apple's traditional strengths — hardware, design, integration, its own silicon capable of running AI efficiently on the device, its enormous installed base, its brand and its privacy reputation — gave it real advantages in the AI era if it could bring them to bear. Its apparent weaknesses — the Siri disappointment, the perception of falling behind, the tension between AI's hunger for data and Apple's commitment to privacy, the caution that might be wisdom or might be paralysis — gave the skeptics real grounds for doubt.

The most concrete measure of how badly the promised Siri overhaul went came in the repeated slipping of its release date. Apple first announced a dramatically more capable, more personalized Siri at its developer conference in 2024, promising deep integration with a person's own data and apps; the feature then slipped past its original window in March 2025, slipped again, and by early 2026 had missed its announced arrival often enough that industry reporters were describing it, without much exaggeration, as the company's third broken promise on the same feature, with pieces of the rebuilt assistant now scattered across a string of later software updates rather than arriving in one release as originally billed. Behind the delays lay a more structural problem than mere scheduling: over the course of 2025 Apple lost more than a dozen senior artificial-intelligence researchers to competitors, including Ruoming Pang, the executive who had led the team building Apple's own foundation models, who departed for Meta after reportedly being offered a compensation package worth some two hundred million dollars — a sum that testified, more eloquently than any speech, to how fiercely the rest of the industry was bidding for exactly the talent Apple needed to keep in-house.

The resolution Apple reached by 2026 was, in its way, the most striking admission in the whole saga, because it inverted a principle the company had followed since the earliest days of the Macintosh: rather than build the core intelligence behind the new Siri entirely itself, Apple struck a multiyear deal with Google, agreeing to pay on the order of a billion dollars a year to run a custom version of Google's Gemini model behind the scenes of Apple's own assistant. It was not the first such arrangement — Apple had already begun routing Siri's more demanding questions to OpenAI's ChatGPT for users who opted in — but the scale and the partner made the Gemini deal a different order of concession. This was Apple, the company whose entire post-Jobs identity rested on owning the whole widget from silicon to software, agreeing to rent the single most important piece of the coming decade's technology from the search company it had spent years trying to keep at arm's length on the iPhone's home screen, wrapping Google's intelligence in Apple's interface and Apple's privacy protections and calling the result Siri.

Whether that arrangement should be read as prudent humility or as a quiet capitulation is exactly the kind of question this book has repeatedly had to leave open, and it corrects a simpler myth that had circulated during the years of Siri's public struggles — the assumption that Apple, dazzled by its rivals or simply out of ideas, had abandoned building its own artificial intelligence altogether. It had not: Apple continued developing its own foundation models throughout this period, running many of them privately on its own devices and in its own data centers precisely to preserve the privacy commitments that were central to its brand, and the Gemini deal supplemented rather than replaced that effort, providing the raw conversational horsepower Apple's own models had not yet matched while Apple kept control of the interface, the hardware, and the data-handling architecture around it. Still, the fact that the arrangement was necessary at all — that the company that once refused even to let other manufacturers build accessories for its machines was now paying a rival roughly a billion dollars a year for a piece of its most important new product — marked a real and rare departure from four decades of Apple orthodoxy, one imposed not by choice but by the sheer speed at which the AI race had outrun Apple's own timetable.

The organizational chart behind Siri changed almost as dramatically as the technology itself, and the changes are worth setting down because they show how far Apple was willing to reorganize once the original plan collapsed. In March 2025, Apple stripped Siri away from John Giannandrea, the search-and-AI veteran hired from Google in 2018 to lead Apple's machine-learning effort, and handed it instead to Mike Rockwell, the engineer who had built the Vision Pro from scratch, with the newly configured Siri team now reporting up through Craig Federighi's software organization rather than through Giannandrea's AI group — a reassignment widely read, inside and outside Apple, as a verdict on Giannandrea's stewardship of the very feature his division had been created to deliver. Giannandrea himself did not last much past that demotion: by December 2025 he had agreed to leave the company entirely after eight years, staying on briefly as an adviser while Apple recruited his successor from outside its own ranks for the first time in years — Amar Subramanya, a Microsoft executive who had previously spent sixteen years at Google, much of it leading engineering for the Gemini Assistant that Apple would soon be licensing for Siri itself, an irony that seemed almost too pointed to be accidental. The reshuffling reflected a company willing to break its own usual preference for promoting from within its existing product culture when the stakes were high enough, reaching outside for AI leadership even as it reached outside for the AI itself.

The eventual product of all that turmoil arrived at Apple's developer conference in June 2026, when Federighi stood on stage to unveil what Apple was now calling, simply, Siri AI — a rebuilt assistant with its own standalone app, deep integration with the iPhone's Dynamic Island, and the ability to draw on a user's own messages, photos, and calendar to answer genuinely personal questions, running atop the customized Gemini model Apple had licensed from Google months earlier. Federighi used much of his stage time not to boast about the assistant's raw capability, which by then lagged the competition's by any honest measure, but to reassure the audience about privacy, describing in some detail how the queries that needed Google's model were stripped of identifying information before they ever left the device — an argument that only made sense in light of everything that had gone wrong before it, a company defending the trustworthiness of a system built substantially on someone else's foundation. The new Siri was bound to iOS 27, scheduled for release that autumn, meaning that even the version unveiled at the conference was, once again, a promise rather than a product in hand — a pattern so familiar by 2026 that reporters covering the keynote noted it almost in passing, as an established fact about how Apple now talked about Siri rather than as fresh news.

The language Apple and Google used to announce the

arrangement, in a joint statement issued in January 2026, was carefully anodyne, the corporate equivalent of a diplomatic communiqué: "After careful evaluation, Apple determined that Google's AI technology provides the most capable foundation for Apple Foundation Models and is excited about the innovative new experiences it will unlock for Apple users." Read plainly, it was an admission, in Apple's own chosen words, that its own artificial intelligence had lost an internal bake-off to a competitor's — a sentence that would have been almost unthinkable from the Apple of Jobs's era, which built its own operating systems, its own chips, its own maps rather than license anyone else's, and treated dependence on a rival's core technology as a kind of defeat. For the reader encountering this chapter years after it was written, the test of how the story ended will be simple enough to check: opening an iPhone and asking Siri a genuinely hard question, and noticing — or, if Apple's engineers did their job, failing to notice — that the answer may now be quietly assembled, behind an interface still unmistakably Apple's own, by a model built in Mountain View rather than Cupertino., and it was surely part of the context in which Apple's board thought about succession. The company passing from Tim Cook to John Ternus in 2026 would have, as one of its defining challenges, the task of ensuring that Apple did not miss or fumble the artificial-intelligence revolution the way it had, in some tellings, missed being first in earlier waves — the task of proving that Apple could still be a leader in a genuinely new and transformative technology rather than a fast follower. Whether Apple would rise to that challenge, whether it would find a way to make AI as distinctively excellent and desirable as it had made the phone and the tablet, or whether it would be outpaced by rivals more native to the new technology, was among the most important open questions of Apple's second half-century. It was, in a sense, the modern form of the oldest question about the company: could Apple, without the singular product genius of its founder, still see and seize the future — or could it now only follow where others led? The answer would be written in the years after this book was finished, in the products Apple did or did not ship, in the frontier it did or did not reach. The garage was fifty years gone. The question it had first posed — whether a company could keep changing the world — was still open.

Chapter 53 — Services

The most important business development of the Tim Cook era was not a device at all, and it does not appear in any of the launch-day lines outside Apple stores, but it may have done more than any single product to shape Apple's finances and its future. It was the rise of Services — Apple's business of selling digital services and subscriptions rather than physical hardware — and its growth into one of the largest and most profitable parts of the company transformed what Apple was and how it made money. Understanding the Services business is understanding the mature Apple, the Apple of the 2010s and 2020s, and understanding a strategic shift as consequential as any product launch.

For most of its history, Apple was a company that sold hardware — computers, then music players, then phones and tablets and watches — and made its money from the sale of physical objects. The problem with a hardware business, however profitable, is that it depends on people continually buying new devices, and it is vulnerable to the maturing of markets: once nearly everyone who wants a smartphone has one, and once smartphones become good enough that people replace them less often, the growth in hardware sales inevitably slows. By the mid-2010s, the smartphone market was maturing, iPhone sales were plateauing, and the question of where Apple's future growth would come from became pressing. The answer Cook's Apple developed was Services: instead of relying solely on selling people new devices, Apple would make more and more money from the enormous installed base of devices already in people's hands — from the more than a billion iPhones and other Apple products in active use around the world — by selling their owners digital services and subscriptions on an ongoing, recurring basis.

The Services business encompassed a growing range of offerings, and its breadth is part of its power. There was the App Store, taking its cut of the vast economy of apps and, especially, of the in-app purchases and subscriptions that came to dominate mobile software. There was Apple Music, the company's subscription streaming service, launched in 2015 to compete with Spotify, giving Apple a recurring monthly revenue stream from millions of subscribers. There was iCloud, the storage service that most Apple users ended up paying for as their photos and files outgrew the free tier. There was Apple Pay, the payment service that took a small slice of transactions. There was Apple TV+, the company's entry into producing and streaming original video, competing with Netflix and the other streaming services. There were the Apple Card, Apple Arcade, Apple Fitness+, and a proliferating suite of other subscriptions and services, each adding another stream of recurring revenue from the installed base. Together, these services grew into an enormous business — tens of billions of dollars a year, growing steadily, and, crucially, highly profitable, with margins far higher than hardware. Services became Apple's second great business, the growth engine that carried the company forward as hardware sales matured, and a central part of the story analysts and investors told about Apple's future.

The strategic logic of the Services business was elegant and formidable, and it rested entirely on the foundation the hardware had built. Every Apple device sold was not just a one-time hardware sale but the beginning of an ongoing, recurring revenue relationship — a device that would, over its life, generate a stream of Services income from its owner. This transformed the economics of the installed base: the more than a billion active Apple devices in the world were not just past sales but a vast, captive, recurring-revenue machine, each one a customer who could be sold subscriptions and services for years. And the Services business deepened the ecosystem lock-in that was central to Apple's strategy, because the more services a customer subscribed to, the more their digital life was bound up in Apple's world, and the harder and more painful it became to leave. A person with an iPhone, an Apple Watch, AirPods, an Apple Music subscription, iCloud storage, Apple TV+, and a library of purchased apps was enmeshed in Apple's ecosystem in a way that made switching to a competitor a wrenching disruption of their whole digital life. Services thus served two purposes at once: it generated enormous, growing, high-margin revenue, and it strengthened the moat around Apple's business, making customers ever more loyal and locked in.

By the middle of the 2020s the sheer size of the numbers involved had become almost as staggering, in its own quiet way, as anything the hardware business produced. In its 2025 fiscal year, Apple's Services division brought in a hundred and nine billion dollars, up fourteen percent from the year before, with the fourth quarter alone — the three months ending in late September 2025 — setting an all-time single-quarter record of 28.8 billion dollars, a fifteen-percent jump over the same quarter a year earlier; every quarter of that fiscal year, in fact, set a new all-time high for the segment, an unbroken run of records that hardware, subject to the ordinary cycles of upgrade fatigue and market saturation, could not match. The App Store alone, by Apple's own account, was drawing some 850 million weekly active users across its various storefronts by 2025, and the company noted that developers had collectively earned more than five hundred and fifty billion dollars through the store since its 2008 launch — a figure that, whatever one thinks of the thirty-percent commission Apple took along the way, testified to the scale of the economy that had grown up around a service originally added to the iPhone almost as an afterthought.

The clearest sign of how much strain the Services business had begun to place on Apple's legal position came from its long-running fight with the game maker Epic Games over the App Store's commission structure. After Epic deliberately triggered Apple's rules by adding its own payment system to Fortnite in 2020, the resulting lawsuit dragged on for years and, in January 2024, reached a point where the United States Supreme Court declined to hear further appeals from either side, leaving in place a lower-court order requiring Apple to let developers link out to other payment options from within their apps. Apple's initial compliance was grudging — it still charged a twenty-seven-percent fee on purchases made through those outside links and wrapped the links in discouraging warning screens — and in the spring of 2025 the federal judge overseeing the case, Yvonne Gonzalez Rogers, ruled that Apple had willfully defied her own injunction, striking down the twenty-seven-percent tax and ordering Apple to stop obstructing the very links it had been told to permit. Apple appealed, and in December 2025 an appeals court partially sided with the company, restoring its right to collect some commission on external transactions, but it pointedly noted that Apple had made those external links "as hard to use as possible," a phrase that captured, better than any amount of commentary could, the tension between Apple's stated openness and its commercial instinct to protect its toll.

Not every corner of the Services empire generated the kind of unbroken record the segment's headline numbers suggested, and two of its most visible components told a more complicated story. Apple TV+, the prestige streaming service that had won Apple its first Best Picture Oscar with *CODA* and later a Best Picture nomination for *Killers of the*

Flower Moon, remained by most outside estimates a money-losing operation years after launch — analysts in 2025 put its subscriber base at around forty-five million globally, a fraction of Netflix's audience, and its annual losses at roughly a billion dollars, even after Apple trimmed its content budget from something like five billion dollars a year closer to four and a half billion following a string of costly theatrical disappointments. Apple defended the investment as a long-term bet on prestige and on the value of video as a piece of the broader Services bundle, and unlike its streaming rivals it never introduced a cheaper, advertising-supported tier, a choice that kept the service premium but also kept it small. The Apple Card told a parallel story of a different kind: after six years in which Goldman Sachs served as the card's sole issuing bank — a partnership Goldman had once treated as a cornerstone of an ill-fated push into consumer banking, and that reportedly cost the bank more than a billion dollars in a single year alone — Apple and Goldman announced in 2023 that they would part ways, and by early 2026 Apple had lined up JPMorgan Chase to take over as issuer, absorbing tens of billions of dollars in existing Apple Card balances in a handover expected to unfold over roughly two years. Both episodes were reminders that Services, for all its record quarters, was not a uniformly profitable machine; it was a portfolio of very different businesses, some of them minting money and others still waiting, years in, to prove they belonged in it at all. Apple's own executives generally declined to break out profitability figures for individual pieces of Services in their public filings, folding Apple TV+'s losses and the App Store's outsized margins into a single reported segment, a presentation that let the enormous profitability of the App Store and Apple Music largely obscure, in the headline numbers investors saw each quarter, just how much red ink the video ambitions and other newer bets were still generating underneath. It was, in miniature, the same story that ran through the whole of Cook's Services strategy: an installed base so vast and so profitable in its most established corners that it could comfortably subsidize years of experimentation in the newer ones, patiently waiting to see whether prestige television or a banking partnership would eventually pay for itself the way the App Store and Apple Music already had.

It is worth correcting a simplification that often creeps into casual accounts of this business: Services is not, as it is sometimes shorthanded, simply "the App Store with a fancier name." By the mid-2020s the category had grown to include a genuinely diverse bundle of revenue streams — subscription income from Apple Music, Apple TV+, Apple Arcade, and Apple Fitness+; recurring iCloud storage fees; the Apple Card and Apple Pay's transaction fees; and, increasingly, a fast-growing advertising business built around the App Store's own search results and Apple's other properties, a category analysts had begun to treat as a meaningful profit center in its own right rather than a footnote. This diversification mattered strategically, because it meant Apple's second great business no longer depended on any single revenue stream remaining politically or legally untouched — a hedge that turned out to be prudent, given how much legal pressure was about to fall specifically on the App Store's commission structure.

The rise of Services also, however, sharpened the controversies that would define Apple's later years, and it connects directly to the reckonings the company would face. Much of the Services revenue came from the App Store, and specifically from Apple's thirty-percent cut of app sales and in-app purchases — the toll that developers increasingly resented and that regulators increasingly scrutinized. As Apple leaned more heavily on Services for growth, its incentive to protect and maximize that toll grew, and so did the tension with the developers who paid it and the governments that questioned it. The Services business, in other words, made Apple more dependent on exactly the kind of platform control that was becoming legally and politically contested, and it raised the stakes of the fights over the App Store, over Apple's power, over whether the walled garden had become an abusive monopoly. Apple's most important growth engine of the 2010s and 2020s was built on the gatekeeping power that would, in those same years, bring the company into conflict with developers, competitors, and regulators around the world. The Services triumph and the antitrust reckoning were two sides of the same coin, and we will come to the reckoning in its place. But the Services business also freed Apple to keep pushing its hardware into new and ambitious territory, secure in a growing base of recurring revenue, and in the early 2020s Apple made two of its boldest bets yet — remaking the very silicon at the heart of its computers, and attempting to define, as it had defined the smartphone and the tablet, the next great platform after the phone.

Chapter 54 — Apple Silicon

In 2020, Apple announced that it would stop using Intel's processors in its Macintosh computers and begin using chips of its own design — a move known as the transition to Apple Silicon — and though it sounded like an obscure technical decision of interest only to engineers, it was one of the most audacious and consequential moves of the entire Cook era, the culmination of a strategy that had been building for more than a decade, and a demonstration that Apple's whole-widget philosophy had reached all the way down to the most fundamental layer of the machine. To understand its significance is to understand how deep Apple's ambition to control everything ran, and how a decision about semiconductors became one of the company's greatest triumphs.

The story of Apple Silicon began, in a sense, with the iPhone. When Apple built the iPhone, it needed processors suited to a small, battery-powered device, and over the years it moved from buying chips designed by others to designing its own — building, chip by chip and year by year, a world-class semiconductor design capability inside Apple, staffed by some of the best chip designers in the world, producing the custom processors that powered the iPhone and iPad. These Apple-designed mobile chips, built on the energy-efficient architecture used in phones, grew steadily more powerful with each generation, until by the late 2010s they were among the fastest and most efficient processors of their kind in the world, rivaling and in some respects surpassing the chips in far larger devices. Apple had, almost without the wider world noticing, become one of the premier chip-design companies on earth, and it had done so in service of its mobile devices. The transition to Apple Silicon was the decision to take that hard-won capability and apply it to the Macintosh — to replace the Intel processors that had powered Macs since a previous transition in 2006 with chips of Apple's own design, descended from the iPhone's, custom-built for Apple's computers and integrated with Apple's software as tightly as everything else Apple made.

The results were spectacular, and they vindicated the strategy beyond what even optimists had predicted. The first Apple Silicon Macs, powered by a chip called the M1 and its successors, delivered performance and, especially, energy efficiency that stunned the industry — laptops that were dramatically faster than their Intel predecessors while running cooler, quieter, and for far longer on a battery, sometimes lasting the whole day or more on a charge in a way that had never been possible. Because Apple designed the chip and the operating system together, it could optimize each for the other, wringing out performance and efficiency that no company buying standard chips from Intel could match; the whole-widget philosophy, applied to silicon, produced computers that were simply better than what competitors using off-the-shelf processors could build. The transition, which many had feared would be painful and risky — moving the entire Mac line to a new kind of processor, requiring software to be adapted, threatening compatibility — was managed by Apple with the same discipline it had brought to earlier transitions, and it went remarkably smoothly, aided by clever software that let old programs keep running while developers adapted. Apple Silicon revitalized the Macintosh, made Apple's computers the envy of the industry, and demonstrated, once again, that Apple's willingness to control every layer of its products, down to the very chips, was a source of advantage that competitors could not easily match.

The strategic meaning of Apple Silicon extended beyond the performance of individual Macs, and it is worth drawing out. By designing its own chips for all its products — the iPhone, the iPad, the Watch, and now the Mac — Apple achieved a degree of vertical integration that no other company in the industry approached, controlling its products from the silicon all the way up to the services, every layer designed by Apple and optimized to work with every other. This freed Apple from dependence on outside chip suppliers like Intel, whose stumbles and delays had constrained Apple's Macs for years; it let Apple set its own roadmap, advancing its chips on its own schedule rather than waiting for a supplier; and it created a common technological foundation across all Apple's devices, chips descended from a common lineage running a common family of operating systems, so that the whole ecosystem shared a coherent architecture. The move also positioned Apple well for the future, giving it control over the fundamental computing hardware on which future capabilities — including the demanding computations required by artificial intelligence — would depend. Apple Silicon was the whole-widget philosophy carried to its logical conclusion: Apple now designed essentially everything in its products, from the transistors on up, and reaped the benefits of that total integration in performance, efficiency, control, and independence.

The chip that started it all deserves to be named and dated precisely, because the specifics tell their own story of ambition. Apple unveiled the M1 on November 10, 2020, and installed it first in the humblest members of the Mac lineup — the MacBook Air, the Mac mini, and the entry-level thirteen-inch MacBook Pro — rather than saving it for a flagship, a signal of confidence that the new architecture did not need to be hidden away in a showcase machine. The M1 packed some sixteen billion transistors onto a chip built on Taiwan Semiconductor Manufacturing Company's five-nanometer process, combining four high-performance cores and four energy-efficient cores with up to eight graphics cores, a dedicated neural engine for machine-learning tasks, and Apple's Secure Enclave, all fused onto a single piece of silicon in the kind of tight integration that had once seemed like a specification sheet from a mobile chip, not a desktop one — because, in a real sense, it was one, the direct descendant of the processors Apple had spent a decade refining for the iPhone and iPad. Apple's own marketing claimed the M1 contained "the world's fastest CPU core in low-power silicon," a boast that in this instance the independent benchmarks that followed largely bore out.

It is worth correcting a version of the Apple Silicon story that flattens its novelty into something more mundane than it actually was — the assumption that Apple simply took an iPhone chip, scaled it up, and dropped it into a laptop. The lineage was real: Apple's Mac chips descend from the same core architecture, the same design team, and the same instruction set as the chips in its phones and tablets, and that shared ancestry is exactly why Apple's whole ecosystem could be woven together as tightly as it was. But the M-series chips built for the Mac were their own substantial engineering undertaking, with far larger dies, dramatically more memory bandwidth, additional cores, and a "Pro," "Max," and eventually "Ultra" family of variants built for professional workloads that no iPhone chip was ever asked to handle — video editors rendering feature-length films, engineers running large simulations, developers compiling enormous codebases. Treating the M1 as merely "a big iPhone chip" understates the years of additional design work Apple's silicon team, led by veterans of the mobile chip effort, had to do to make a phone's philosophy of efficiency scale up to a professional desktop machine without losing what made it special in the first place.

The M-series lineage did not stand still after that first release, and by the middle of the 2020s Apple's chip strategy had extended well beyond the Mac to become the common thread running through nearly every major hardware bet the company made. Successive generations — M2, M3, M4, and by 2025 the M5 — pushed the same architecture to smaller manufacturing processes and higher performance with each iteration, and Apple began deploying the same silicon family into products far removed from a traditional computer: the M5 chip that Apple installed in its revamped Vision Pro headset in October 2025 was drawn from exactly the same design lineage that had first appeared in a MacBook Air five years earlier, brought to bear on rendering the demanding, twin-eye, high-resolution graphics that spatial computing required. The chip that began as a bet on the humble Mac had become, in effect, the common nervous system running through Apple's entire hardware line — a single technological asset, patiently built over more than a decade, now doing the work of powering everything from a budget laptop to the company's most ambitious and unproven new category of device.

The silicon strategy also began, in these same years, to reshape where Apple's chips were physically made, and not merely how they were designed. For its entire history, the actual manufacturing of Apple's most advanced processors had happened almost exclusively in Taiwan, at the fabrication plants of Taiwan Semiconductor Manufacturing Company, the contract manufacturer whose extreme-ultraviolet lithography machines were the only ones on earth capable of producing chips at the scale Apple's designs required. That geographic concentration became, amid the trade tensions and supply-chain anxieties of the 2020s, a strategic vulnerability in its own right, and TSMC responded by building a vast new manufacturing complex in Arizona, eventually envisioned as a cluster of six fabrication plants and two advanced-packaging facilities, backed by a total investment on the order of a hundred and sixty-five billion dollars — the largest foreign direct investment in the history of the United States. Apple, as TSMC's largest customer, was widely understood to be the anchor tenant of the whole undertaking, and mass production of Apple chips began at the Arizona site in January 2025, with Apple announcing the following year that it intended to purchase more than a hundred million chips from the Arizona fabs in 2026 alone, part of a five-hundred-billion-dollar pledge of domestic investment the company made amid political pressure to bring more of its supply chain onshore. Even so, the most advanced Apple Silicon designs remained, for the time being, tied more closely to Taiwan than to Arizona, since the newest manufacturing processes reached the Arizona site only after they had already been proven on the original production lines a generation or two ahead of it — a reminder that reshoring a supply chain as intricate as advanced semiconductor fabrication took years even for a company with Apple's resources and urgency.

Apple's chip ambitions extended, in this same period, beyond the processors that ran its devices and into the radios that connected them to cellular networks, a project with its own long and difficult history. For years Apple had depended on Qualcomm for the modem chips that let an iPhone talk to a cell tower, a dependency it had fought bitterly in court even while it could not yet do without it, and in 2019 Apple acquired the bulk of Intel's struggling modem business in an attempt to build its own replacement. That effort took far longer than expected — five years of development, missed internal deadlines, and, by some accounts, serious doubts inside Apple about whether it could be done at all — before Apple's first in-house cellular modem, called the C1, finally shipped inside the iPhone 16e in 2025. It was a quieter milestone than a new M-series chip unveiled on a keynote stage, but a significant one all the same, extending Apple's now-familiar logic of owning the whole widget into a component the company had never before dared build itself, and setting up an expectation among industry analysts that Apple could eliminate its reliance on Qualcomm's modems from its lineup entirely within a few more years.

, and it says something important about what Apple became after Jobs. It was not a flashy new consumer product that people lined up to buy; it was a deep, patient, technically formidable achievement, years in the making, that transformed Apple's products from within — exactly the kind of thing that a disciplined, long-term, operationally excellent company led by an operator rather than a showman would produce. Steve Jobs had set the strategy of controlling the whole widget and had begun the chip-design effort that made Apple Silicon possible; Tim Cook's Apple carried it through to its full realization, executing a transition of enormous technical difficulty with patience and precision, and producing one of the great engineering successes in the company's history. It demonstrated that Apple after Jobs could still do things that no other company could do, could still take enormous, patient, integrated bets and win them — even if those bets were now more likely to be deep technical achievements than flashy new devices. But Apple's ambition was not only to perfect the products it had; it was still, even in its maturity, chasing the dream of defining the next great platform, the successor to the iPhone, the next revolution in how humans interact with computers. In 2023 and 2024 it made its boldest attempt at that dream, strapping a computer to people's faces and declaring the dawn of a new era of computing — an attempt whose outcome remained genuinely uncertain, and which posed, more sharply than anything else, the question of whether Apple could still, without Steve Jobs, invent the future rather than merely refine it.

Chapter 55 — Spatial Computing

In 2023, Apple unveiled the Vision Pro, and in early 2024 it went on sale — a headset that a person wore over their eyes, that displayed digital content overlaid on or replacing their view of the real world, and that Apple declared to be the beginning of a new era of computing it called "spatial computing." The Vision Pro was Apple's boldest bet since the iPhone, its most ambitious attempt to define a new platform, and it posed, more directly than any other product of the Cook era, the central question of Apple after Jobs: could the company still create a revolutionary new category, a new paradigm of computing to succeed the smartphone, or had that particular kind of magic died with its founder? The answer, as of the writing of this book, is genuinely unresolved — and the honesty of an up-to-date history requires saying so plainly rather than pretending to a certainty that does not yet exist.

The Vision Pro was, as a piece of technology, extraordinary, and even its skeptics acknowledged the achievement. It was the product of years of work and enormous investment, a dense concentration of advanced technology: ultra-high-resolution displays that put a sharp digital image before each eye, an array of cameras and sensors that tracked the user's eyes, hands, and surroundings with precision, and the processing power to render convincing digital objects that appeared to exist in the space around the wearer. It could immerse the user entirely in a virtual environment, or overlay digital screens and objects onto their view of the real room, controlled by looking at things and pinching fingers together, without any physical controller. The experience, by many accounts, was genuinely impressive, a glimpse of a kind of computing that had long been imagined but never so well realized — screens that floated in your space, digital content woven into the physical world, an interface controlled by eye and hand. It represented, in engineering terms, a real achievement, a demonstration that Apple could still push the frontier of what was technologically possible, and it embodied Apple's characteristic strengths: the integration of hardware and software, the obsessive design, the willingness to make an enormous long-term bet.

But the Vision Pro also faced formidable obstacles, and its early reception was far from the immediate triumph of the iPhone. It was extremely expensive — priced at thousands of dollars, far beyond the reach of most consumers, positioning it as a product for enthusiasts and developers and the wealthy rather than a mass-market device. It was heavy and, for many users, uncomfortable to wear for extended periods, and there was something inherently isolating and awkward about a device that covered the user's face and separated them from the people around them, a social barrier that the iPhone and the Watch and the AirPods, for all their ubiquity, never imposed. And, most fundamentally, it was not clear what the Vision Pro was for — what the compelling, must-have use was that would drive ordinary people to buy and wear it, the way music had driven the iPod and communication and apps had driven the iPhone. The device was a remarkable answer to a question that many people were not sure they were asking, a solution whose problem remained to be defined, and its early sales were modest, its adoption limited to a small population of enthusiasts. It was, in these respects, reminiscent less of the iPhone's instant triumph than of some of Apple's slower-burning or uncertain products, and it left open the question of whether spatial computing would follow the iPhone's path from initial skepticism to world-conquering ubiquity, or whether it would remain a niche, a technically brilliant product that never found the mass purpose that would make it revolutionary.

Tim Cook himself, in the months after launch, was candid about exactly what kind of product the Vision Pro was and was not. Asked directly about its steep price, he said plainly: "At $3,500, it's not a mass-market product. Right now, it's an early-adopter product. People who want to have tomorrow's technology today — that's who it's for. Fortunately, there's enough people who are in that camp that it's exciting." It was an unusually frank admission from a company that had built its reputation on products that, at launch, redefined an entire mass market almost immediately — the iPhone did not need to be described as a niche device for early adopters — and it set expectations that the subsequent sales figures would, if anything, undershoot.

Those figures, once they arrived, told a sobering story. Apple shipped roughly 390,000 Vision Pro units in 2024, respectable for a three-and-a-half-thousand-dollar headset but a rounding error next to the tens of millions of iPhones or Apple Watches Apple moved in a single quarter; by the 2025 holiday quarter, shipments had fallen to an estimated 45,000 units, a decline steep enough that Apple's manufacturing partner in China, Luxshare, reportedly paused production lines early in the year, and that Apple itself pulled back digital advertising for the device by more than ninety-five percent in major markets like the United States and the United Kingdom — a retreat in marketing spend that read, to many observers, as an unmistakable signal about how the company itself had come to view the product's near-term prospects. Apple did not abandon the device outright: in October 2025 it released an updated Vision Pro built around the newer M5 chip, with a longer battery life and a redesigned headband meant to address the comfort complaints that had dogged the original, evidence that the long-game reading of the product still had institutional backing inside Apple. But the refresh did not move the sales needle in any way that became publicly visible, and direct sales of the device, more than two years after launch, remained confined to a baker's dozen of countries — a far cry from the instant, worldwide, line-around-the-block rollout that had greeted the iPhone.

It would be a mistake, though, to read this as proof that Apple had quietly given up on spatial computing, a misconception that understandably follows from headlines about production halts and advertising cuts but that overstates what actually happened. Apple kept shipping new hardware, kept updating the software platform it called visionOS, and kept its developer tools active — the behavior of a company still funding a long-term bet, even a chastened one, rather than one preparing to declare defeat and walk away. What the weak sales numbers demonstrate for certain is only that the transition from expensive, niche, first-generation hardware to the kind of ubiquitous, taken-for-granted product the iPhone became — if it happens at all — was, by the middle of the 2020s, still years away rather than imminent, and that the most audacious bet of the Cook era remained exactly what it had been at launch: unresolved.

Apple's own subsequent decisions about where to point its spatial-computing roadmap offer perhaps the most honest evidence of how the company itself had come to weigh the Vision Pro's prospects. For a time, Apple was reported to be developing a lower-cost headset, sometimes called the Vision Air, that would have stripped out some of the original's most expensive components — its dual micro-OLED displays chief among them — in pursuit of a price closer to two thousand dollars than three and a half. By 2026, however, that cheaper headset had been quietly shelved: reporting in the spring indicated Apple had paused the project, and further reporting that May indicated the company had canceled it outright, with the display work Apple had commissioned from Samsung for the cheaper model winding down entirely by that summer. In its place, Apple appeared to be redirecting much of its spatial-computing energy toward a different form factor altogether — smart glasses without any built-in display, closer in concept to the camera-and-microphone-equipped glasses Meta had already brought to market in partnership with Ray-Ban, and reportedly a priority Tim Cook pursued personally in hopes of beating Meta to a genuinely wearable, all-day alternative to the headset. Meanwhile the existing Vision Pro found a narrower but more durable niche than its original consumer marketing had promised, adopted by hospitals for surgical training, by airlines and flight schools for simulation, and by architecture and design firms for walking clients through spaces that did not yet exist — specialized, high-value uses where the price could be justified by professional return rather than by mass consumer appeal, a use case closer to the industrial workstation Apple built decades earlier than to the iPhone. Set against Meta, the rival Apple had most explicitly hoped to leapfrog, the contrast in strategy was almost total: Meta's Quest headsets sold in the hundreds of dollars rather than the thousands, sacrificed display quality and finish for volume, and had, over several product generations, achieved a real if still modest foothold among gamers and fitness enthusiasts that the Vision Pro, for all its technical superiority, had not come close to matching in sheer numbers of units in people's homes. That divergence forced an uncomfortable comparison for Apple, a company accustomed to defining a new category by simultaneously being both the most advanced and, within a few product cycles, the most popular option — a combination the iPhone and the iPad had each achieved and that spatial computing, years into the experiment, had not yet delivered from either competitor, let alone from Apple specifically. Whether that gap would close as prices fell and the technology matured, or whether it reflected something more fundamental about the appetite for face-worn computing, remained exactly the kind of question that only the passage of years, not the launch of any single new model, would be able to answer.

, and it is worth resisting the temptation to render a premature verdict in either direction. The optimistic reading is that the Vision Pro is a first-generation product, expensive and imperfect as first-generation products always are — the iPhone, too, was costly and limited at launch — and that Apple is playing its familiar long game, establishing a platform that will improve, cheapen, and find its purpose over years, until spatial computing becomes as natural and universal as touching a screen, and the Vision Pro is remembered as the crude but pioneering ancestor of a new computing era. The pessimistic reading is that the headset is a solution in search of a problem, that the fundamental social and physical awkwardness of a face-worn computer is not a first-generation flaw but an inherent limitation, that spatial computing may remain forever a niche rather than a successor to the phone, and that the Vision Pro reveals an Apple that can still engineer brilliantly but can no longer reliably intuit what people actually want — that the product genius that was Steve Jobs's singular gift has, in fact, not been fully replaced. Both readings are defensible on the current evidence, and which one history will vindicate is not yet knowable. What the Vision Pro demonstrates for certain is that Apple, more than a decade after Jobs's death, was still willing to make enormous, risky bets on defining the future, still reaching for the next revolution rather than merely refining the last one — and that the question of whether it could still succeed at that highest level of ambition, the level of creating a genuinely new platform, remained the great open question of its post-Jobs existence. That question, and the company that must answer it, would soon pass into new hands, for the leader who had guided Apple through the entire era since Jobs's death was, in 2026, preparing to step aside — and the numbers he would leave behind were almost be-yond comprehension.

Chapter 55½ — The Spaceship

Steve Jobs's last product was not a device but a building, and it is fitting that a man so obsessed with design and craft and the making of beautiful objects should have devoted his final energies to the creation of a monument that would house the company he loved. Apple Park — the vast, ring-shaped headquarters in Cupertino that opened in 2017, six years after Jobs's death but conceived and championed by him in his final years — is his architectural testament, an expression in glass and steel and landscape of everything he believed about design, and a window into both his genius and his excess.

Jobs presented the plans for the new campus to the Cupertino city council in June 2011, just months before he died, in one of his last public appearances, already visibly ill. The design was audacious: an enormous circular building, a single continuous ring nearly a mile in circumference, four stories high, clad in the largest panels of curved glass ever manufactured, set in a landscape of thousands of trees meant to restore the site to something like the orchards of the old Valley of Heart's Delight. Jobs described it as looking "a little like a spaceship landed," and the nickname stuck; Apple Park became known as the spaceship, a gleaming ring of glass in the California landscape, visible from the air as one of the most distinctive structures on earth. It was designed to house thousands of Apple employees in a single continuous space, to foster the collaboration and serendipitous encounter that Jobs believed drove innovation, and to embody, in its every detail, the values that governed Apple's products.

And the details were pursued with exactly the obsessive perfectionism that Jobs brought to everything, extended now to architecture at enormous scale and cost. The stories of Apple Park's construction became legend, and they are recognizably the same stories told about Apple's products: the fanatical attention to elements most people would never notice, the insistence on perfection in the invisible as well as the visible, the willingness to spend vast sums and to redo work to achieve the exactly right result. The wood used inside had to be a specific grade, cut at a specific time of year. The door thresholds had to be perfectly flat, with no transition a person would feel underfoot, because Jobs believed that entering a building should not require a distracting physical adjustment. The signage, the elevators, the handles, the ventilation, the curve of every piece of glass — all of it was subjected to the standard of insanely great, held to tolerances more common in the manufacture of precision devices than in construction. The building reportedly cost around five billion dollars, making it one of the most expensive corporate headquarters ever built, and every element of that cost reflected the same conviction that had built Apple's products: that the details matter, that craftsmanship lives in the parts no one sees, that a thing should be perfect because it can be and because the people who use it will feel the difference even if they cannot name it.

Apple Park is, therefore, a perfect physical expression of Steve Jobs's philosophy, and like everything about him, it can be read two ways, and both readings are true. On one reading, it is a magnificent achievement, a beautiful and thoughtful building that embodies Apple's values, that treats the workplace with the same care Apple treats its products, that will stand for generations as a monument to design excellence and to the company Jobs built — his father's lesson about the hidden craftsmanship of the cabinet, rendered at the scale of a mile-wide ring. On another reading, it is an act of extravagance and even hubris, a five-billion-dollar temple to a single man's aesthetic obsessions, a perfectionism carried past the point of reason into the realm of the pharaonic, a monument as much to ego as to design — the kind of grand headquarters that companies have often built at the peak of their power and just before their decline, a warning sign as much as an achievement. Both readings have merit, and the truth, as usual with Jobs, includes both: Apple Park is genuinely beautiful and genuinely excessive, a real embodiment of admirable values and a real monument to the perfectionism that shaded into obsession, the finest and the most self-indulgent expression of the same sensibility.

The choice of architect was itself a decade in the making and reveals how early Jobs began imagining the building. He recruited Norman Foster — the British architect responsible for some of the world's most admired modern structures — as early as 2009, two years before he stood before the Cupertino city council to present the finished design, and the two men worked together over that time to translate Jobs's instincts about materials, light, and openness into something an architect could actually engineer and build. The finished campus, when it opened, covered some 2.8 million square feet and was designed to hold around twelve thousand employees inside a single, unbroken ring, with roughly eighty percent of the surrounding 175-acre site given over not to parking lots or plazas but to green space, planted with drought-resistant species native to the valley — a landscaping decision as deliberate and as costly as anything inside the building, meant to return the site of the old Hewlett-Packard campus closer to the orchards that had once covered the Santa Clara Valley before Silicon Valley existed.

Public building permits filed during construction later allowed outside observers to reconstruct, with unusual precision, exactly where the famous five-billion-dollar figure went. The main ring building — the "spaceship" itself — accounted for something over four hundred and twenty-seven million dollars of that sum on its own, driven overwhelmingly by its glass: the structure's walls were built from roughly eight hundred curved panels, each some forty-five feet tall, individually fabricated to Apple's specifications as the largest curved sheets of glass ever manufactured for a building anywhere. The adjoining Steve Jobs Theater, the sleek, glass-cylinder auditorium where Apple would hold many of its future product launches, cost upward of a hundred and seventy-nine million dollars by itself — a separate nine-figure building constructed for the sole purpose of unveiling new products to the world — while the parking structures ringing the site added roughly another hundred and thirteen million dollars, an eye-watering sum for garages that testified to just how thoroughly the campus's design values extended even to the buildings visitors would spend the least time inside.

It is worth correcting one assumption that Apple Park's nickname sometimes encourages: that the ring is simply the largest office building on earth, a superlative that does not, in fact, belong to it. Older and larger single structures, like the Pentagon, still dwarf Apple's headquarters in raw square footage; what makes Apple Park distinctive is not sheer size but the totality of the design control exercised over every element within that size, the same insistence — carried from products into architecture — that no detail was too small to specify personally, whether that detail was the flatness of a threshold or the curvature of forty-five feet of glass. Today the ring remains Apple's working headquarters, visible from the air as one of the most recognizable corporate structures on the planet, still hosting the product announcements that carry Jobs's old showmanship forward inside a building he never got to walk through himself.

The ring's sustainability credentials, pursued with the same perfectionism as its glass and its thresholds, made it in a literal sense the largest building of its kind in North America to earn the highest LEED Platinum certification, the rating system's top tier. A seventeen-megawatt rooftop solar installation, spread across the curve of the ring and its parking structures, was designed to supply roughly three-quarters of the campus's power on a good day, backed by four megawatts of biogas fuel cells supplied by Bloom Energy for the hours the sun alone could not carry the load, the whole system stitched together by a microgrid sophisticated enough to sell surplus power back to the public grid when the campus's own demand dropped. Natural ventilation, drawn through the building by its own design rather than by mechanical air-conditioning for much of the year, was projected to cut the ring's energy use for heating and cooling dramatically compared with a conventional office tower of the same size, and a dedicated water-recycling system was built to reclaim tens of millions of gallons that would otherwise have been drawn from the municipal supply, redirecting it to irrigation and to the toilets of the twelve thousand people working inside. None of this was invisible marketing; it was infrastructure, buried in mechanical rooms and rooftop arrays that almost no visitor would ever see, which made it, in its own way, the purest expression of the philosophy Jobs had preached about the cabinetmaker's unseen backboard — care lavished on the parts of the building that existed only to work, not to be admired. Not every employee who actually worked inside the ring shared the architects' enthusiasm for it, and the building's most persistent internal criticism concerned the very quality Jobs had prized above almost all others: openness. The vast, largely undivided floors that were meant to encourage chance encounters and cross-team collaboration struck a number of engineers, in the years after the move, as noisy, distracting, and short on the private space that focused technical work sometimes required, prompting some employees to retreat to the campus's stairwells or outdoor pathways simply to take a phone call in something resembling quiet — a mundane, human complaint that sat awkwardly beside the building's five-billion-dollar ambitions, and a reminder that even the most meticulously engineered spaces cannot fully anticipate how the people inside them will actually want to work. Jobs, characteristically, would likely have shrugged off such complaints as the price of a vision worth holding to; he had never designed for the comfort of the crowd so much as for the standard he believed the crowd would eventually come to appreciate, whether the crowd in question was buying a computer or simply reporting for work each morning inside the ring he had built for them.

, tells us something about how he understood his own legacy. He was building not just a headquarters but a home for the institution he hoped would outlast him, a physical embodiment of the culture and values he wanted Apple to preserve after he was gone, a monument that would remind future generations of Apple employees, every day as they entered the ring, of the standards their company was meant to hold. He would not walk its halls; he died before it opened. But he had shaped it as he had shaped everything, down to the flatness of the thresholds, and it stands now in Cupertino as his last and largest work — a beautiful, extravagant, perfect, excessive ring of glass, housing the company he built twice, a fitting final product from a man who believed to his last days that the details mattered and that the making of beautiful things was worth any amount of effort and expense. He had put a dent in the universe, and then he had built, on the site of the old orchards, a spaceship for the people who would carry the work on without him.

Chapter 56 — Trillions

The numbers that Apple posted during the Tim Cook era are so large that they defeat the ordinary human capacity to grasp them, and it is worth pausing to try, because the sheer scale of what Apple became is itself a historical fact of the first importance — the emergence of the largest concentration of corporate value the world has ever seen. In August 2018, Apple became the first publicly traded American company in history to reach a market capitalization of one trillion dollars — a valuation so vast that it exceeded the entire economic output of most countries. It did not stop there. In 2020, Apple crossed two trillion dollars. In late 2022 it touched three trillion dollars in intraday trading, and in 2023 it closed above that mark. And in 2025, Apple reached four trillion dollars — a figure that would have seemed like science fiction not just in 1997, when the company was ninety days from bankruptcy, but even in 2011, when Steve Jobs died and Apple, already the most valuable company in the world, was worth a fraction of what it would become.

To measure the achievement, set it against the starting point. When Tim Cook took over as chief executive in August 2011, Apple was worth roughly three hundred and fifty billion dollars — already an enormous and successful company, the most valuable in the world. Over the following fifteen years, under Cook, that value grew more than tenfold, to four trillion dollars. The caretaker who was supposed to preside over Apple's inevitable decline had instead multiplied its value more than ten times over, adding trillions of dollars of worth, presiding over the greatest sustained creation of shareholder value in the history of capitalism. Whatever one thinks of Cook's product record compared to Jobs's — the absence, so far, of a new platform as revolutionary as the iPhone — the financial record is beyond dispute: by the measure that markets use, Tim Cook was one of the most successful business leaders who has ever lived, and the company he ran became the most valuable enterprise that has ever existed. The doubt that had greeted his succession, the assumption that Apple was Steve Jobs and would fade without him, had been answered by fifteen years of growth so enormous that it dwarfed everything the company had achieved under its founder.

What do the trillions actually mean, beyond their power to astonish? They mean, first, the extraordinary profitability of the iPhone and its ecosystem — the fact that Apple, selling premium devices at premium prices to more than a billion customers, wrapped in a sticky ecosystem generating growing streams of Services revenue, had built a money-making machine of unprecedented efficiency and scale. They mean the success of Cook's operational and financial management, which turned that machine's output into staggering profits and returned enormous sums to shareholders through dividends and buybacks. They mean the durability of the thing Jobs had built — the brand, the ecosystem, the loyalty, the design and engineering culture — which continued to generate value long after its creator was gone. And they mean, more broadly, a particular moment in economic history, in which a handful of technology companies came to dominate the global economy to a degree without real precedent, and Apple sat at or near the summit of them all, its four-trillion-dollar valuation a monument to the concentration of wealth and power in the technology industry of the early twenty-first century. Apple held cash reserves larger than the treasuries of nations; its decisions moved markets; its products shaped the daily lives of a substantial fraction of humanity; its power, economic and cultural, rivaled that of governments.

The trillions also, inevitably, provoked their own reckoning, and the scale of Apple's success became, in these years, a source of scrutiny and criticism as much as admiration. A company so vast, so dominant, so profitable, controlling platforms on which whole industries depended, inevitably attracted the attention of those who worried about concentrated corporate power — regulators, legislators, competitors, and critics who asked whether Apple had become too powerful, whether its control of the App Store and its ecosystem had crossed from excellence into monopoly, whether the four-trillion-dollar colossus was extracting more than it created, whether its power over developers and customers and markets had become the kind of dominance that the law exists to check. The very scale that measured Apple's success also measured the concern it provoked, and the trillions that testified to Cook's achievement testified equally to the size of the questions Apple now faced about its power and its responsibilities. Success at this scale is never merely celebrated; it is interrogated, and Apple, in the years of its greatest valuation, faced interrogation from many directions at once.

It is worth tracing the milestones in order, because the pace of the climb tells its own story about acceleration. Apple crossed one trillion dollars in market value in August 2018, reached one and a half trillion within about a year, and cleared two trillion in 2020 before finishing that same extraordinary year above two and a half trillion — a company that had needed forty-two years to reach its first trillion adding another half-trillion in a matter of months. The climb was not uninterrupted: in 2022, amid a broad technology-sector downturn, Apple's value slid back from nearly three trillion to a little under two trillion dollars, a reminder that even the most dominant company in history remained subject to the ordinary gravity of markets. But the recovery came quickly, and by the middle of 2023 Apple's shares had risen enough to push its value to roughly three trillion dollars again, and by 2025 the company had reached four trillion. Here a common assumption deserves correcting: Apple was not the first company to reach that particular milestone. Nvidia, riding the artificial-intelligence boom that had exposed some of Apple's own vulnerabilities, and then Microsoft, both crossed four trillion dollars before Apple did, making Apple only the third company in history to join that club rather than, as it had been at one, two, and three trillion, the very first. It was a small but telling asterisk on an otherwise unbroken record of being first to every previous milestone, evidence that even in the measure where Apple's post-Jobs success was least disputable, the technology-industry landscape it operated in had itself changed, producing rivals capable of outpacing even Apple at the specific game of raw valuation.

None of which diminishes the scale of what Cook's Apple ultimately built. By the summer of 2026, with the leadership transition to John Ternus already underway, Apple's market capitalization stood at roughly four and a half trillion dollars — a sum that, translated into the more tangible language of nations, exceeded the annual economic output of every country on Earth except a handful of the very largest, and that made Apple's shareholders, collectively, wealthier from their holding in a single American technology company than the entire population of most member states of the United Nations was from the whole of their national economies. The company that had once needed Michael Dell's mocking suggestion to shut down and give the money back to shareholders had, thirty years later, become one in which giving money back to shareholders — through the dividends and buybacks that were now a routine and enormous feature of Apple's financial calendar — was itself one of the largest capital-return programs any company had ever run, a scale of wealth transfer so large that the numbers, taken in isolation, risk obscuring the human institution that produced them: engineers, designers, factory workers, and executives whose collective labor, across five decades, had built something that the raw arithmetic of trillions can describe but never quite explain.

Much of that value flowed back to shareholders through a capital-return machine of its own staggering scale, and no shareholder benefited more visibly, or spoke about it more instructively, than Warren Buffett. Apple reinstated a dividend and began repurchasing its own shares in 2012, and by the mid-2020s the buyback program alone had retired more than eight hundred billion dollars of Apple stock since its inception — reducing the number of shares outstanding by well over two-fifths and, in the process, quietly increasing the ownership stake of every investor who held on, Berkshire Hathaway among them. Buffett began buying Apple shares for Berkshire in 2016, eventually accumulating more than a billion shares at an average cost of well under forty dollars apiece, and Apple grew into the largest single holding in Berkshire's entire portfolio, at one point worth more than the rest of the conglomerate's stock holdings combined. Buffett was characteristically blunt about why he liked the buybacks in particular, explaining that a shrinking share count raised Berkshire's claim on Apple's businesses "without any cost to us" — a mechanism, he noted, that worked purely to the advantage of investors patient enough to keep their shares while the company retired everyone else's. That patience was not universal even at Berkshire: in 2024, in a move that startled markets, Buffett trimmed roughly thirteen percent of the position ahead of an announced hundred-and-ten-billion-dollar Apple buyback, and by early 2026 he had sold off the large majority of Berkshire's original stake entirely, redirecting the proceeds elsewhere — a reminder that even the investor most publicly associated with Apple's rise, the "Oracle of Omaha" who had helped cement Apple's reputation as a haven for conservative long-term capital, ultimately treated the stock as a position to be managed rather than a marriage to be honored, and that the trillions, however durable they looked from the outside, remained, in the end, ordinary shares that even their most famous holder was willing to sell. Berkshire's exit did nothing to slow the buybacks themselves, which continued at a pace few other companies on earth could sustain, funded by the same enormous, recurring cash generation that made Apple's stock so attractive to a value investor like Buffett in the first place — a self-reinforcing loop in which the company's own profits steadily shrank the pool of shares those profits had to be divided among, lifting the value of each remaining share regardless of whether any particular famous investor chose to stay for the ride. The dividend told a quieter version of the same story: modest by the standards of some older industrial companies, raised most years by only a few cents a share, but compounding steadily enough over more than a decade that it, too, had become one more small, reliable proof that the company Michael Dell had once suggested liquidating was instead in the business of returning wealth to its owners on a scale that made the phrase "shareholder value" feel almost too bloodless for what had actually occurred.

The trillions are, finally, the answer to one version of the question this book has been asking — could Apple survive without Steve Jobs? — and the answer, by the measure of value, is emphatic: not only did Apple survive, it thrived, growing far beyond anything Jobs had achieved, becoming the most valuable company in history under the leadership of the operator he had chosen. But the trillions are not the whole answer, because the question was never only financial. The deeper question was whether Apple could remain Apple — whether it could keep the qualities that had made it special, the design, the focus, the willingness to make revolutionary bets, the capacity to define the future rather than merely refine the present — or whether it would become, for all its value, a different and lesser kind of company, a magnificent machine for monetizing the installed base that Jobs had built, coasting on his legacy while losing his spark. The Vision Pro's uncertain reception, the absence of a new platform to rival the iPhone, the growing reliance on Services and on the toll of the App Store, gave the skeptics material for their case even amid the record valuations. Apple was, by 2026, both the most valuable company in history and a company facing hard questions about its power, its future, and its soul — and those questions came into sharp focus in the shadows the great success had cast. For the four trillion dollars had been built on foundations that many found troubling: on the labor of workers in distant factories, on a dependence on a China that was becoming a geopolitical fault line, on a control of the App Store that courts and governments were beginning to challenge, and on a walled garden whose walls, once the source of Apple's excellence, were increasingly seen as the instrument of its dominance. To understand Apple fully, we must turn from the light of its triumph to the shadows it cast.

Chapter 56½ — Maps and Missteps

Apple's post-Jobs history is usually told as a story of triumph — the trillions, the growth, the enduring dominance — and that story is largely true, but it omits the failures, and an honest history must include them, because they reveal that Apple, even at its most successful, remained a fallible company capable of ordinary blunders, and because how it responded to those failures says something about what it had become. The company that could do no wrong did, in fact, do plenty wrong, and cataloging some of its missteps is a useful corrective to the myth of infallibility that Apple's success tends to generate.

The most spectacular stumble of the early Cook years was Apple Maps. In 2012, Apple replaced Google's mapping service, which had been the default on the iPhone, with its own Apple Maps, a product it had rushed to build in order to reduce its dependence on Google, an increasingly direct competitor. Apple Maps launched badly — very badly. It was riddled with errors: misplaced landmarks, distorted satellite imagery, towns in the wrong locations, directions that led travelers astray, bridges that appeared to melt and buildings that appeared to collapse in its three-dimensional views. For a company whose entire brand rested on things that just worked, whose products were held to a standard of polish that competitors could not match, shipping a broken, error-strewn core application was a humiliation, and the public mockery was intense and sustained. The failure was severe enough that Tim Cook took the extraordinary step of issuing a public apology — a letter acknowledging the product's failings, apologizing to customers, and, remarkably, recommending that they use competitors' mapping apps until Apple fixed its own. It was a striking admission of failure from a company unaccustomed to admitting any, and it had consequences: Scott Forstall, the senior executive who led iOS software and was seen as a possible eventual successor to Cook, reportedly refused to sign the apology and was pushed out of the company shortly after, one of the most significant executive departures of the era. Apple eventually repaired Maps over years of quiet, patient work, and it became a decent product, but the launch remains a landmark failure, proof that Apple could ship something broken and pay for it.

Apple Maps was the most famous but not the only misstep, and the others form a pattern worth noting. There was "Antennagate," in 2010, still in Jobs's time: the iPhone 4, for all its acclaim, had an antenna design that could lose signal when held in a certain way, gripping the phone's metal band in a "death grip" that degraded reception. The problem was real, the criticism was loud, and Jobs's initial response — suggesting that users were simply holding the phone wrong — became infamous as a rare instance of Apple arrogance backfiring, before the company offered free cases to mitigate the issue. There was "Bendgate," when a later, thinner iPhone proved susceptible to bending under pressure in pockets. There was "Batterygate," a genuinely damaging controversy in which Apple was found to have quietly slowed the performance of older iPhones as their batteries aged — Apple explained this as a measure to prevent unexpected shutdowns, but many customers saw it as evidence of planned obsolescence, a deliberate degrading of old phones to push people toward new ones, and the episode led to lawsuits, regulatory fines, and a real blow to Apple's trustworthiness. There were product missteps and dead ends — a wireless charging mat that was announced and then canceled before it ever shipped, a redesigned keyboard for its laptops that proved unreliable and had to be abandoned, various services and features that underwhelmed or were quietly discontinued.

These failures matter not because they were catastrophic — none of them seriously threatened Apple, and the company's overall trajectory through the period was one of enormous success — but because of what they reveal and what they puncture. They puncture the myth of Apple as a company of unbroken perfection, reminding us that even at the height of its dominance it was run by fallible human beings who shipped flawed products, made bad calls, and paid the price. They reveal, in Apple's responses, both its strengths and its weaknesses: the willingness, in the case of Maps, to apologize and to fix the problem over years of patient work, showing a company that could learn from failure; and the defensiveness, in cases like Antennagate and Batterygate, that showed a company sometimes too proud or too commercially motivated to handle its failures well. And they complicate the simple narrative of the Cook era as pure triumph, showing that the growth and the trillions came alongside real stumbles, that Apple's success was not the frictionless execution of infallible genius but the messier reality of a very good company that also, regularly, got things wrong.

The Batterygate affair, in particular, deserves a closer look at how it was actually resolved, because the number involved is instructive about the gap between reputational damage and financial consequence at Apple's scale. In November 2020, Apple agreed to pay 113 million dollars to settle claims brought by a coalition of more than thirty state attorneys general, who alleged that Apple had concealed the battery problems behind its 2016 decision to throttle the performance of aging iPhones and had misled consumers about what the software update was actually doing. It was, by any ordinary corporate standard, a serious regulatory rebuke — the kind of multistate settlement usually reserved for genuine corporate wrongdoing — and Apple agreed as part of it to be more transparent going forward about how software updates might affect battery life and performance. And yet 113 million dollars, spread across dozens of states, amounted to something close to a rounding error for a company whose quarterly profits alone ran into the tens of billions; the settlement punished the behavior without meaningfully denting the balance sheet, an asymmetry that critics of Apple's power would return to again and again in later, larger fights over the App Store.

Apple Maps, for its part, offers the more encouraging half of this chapter's pattern — proof that a genuine, patient fix was possible even after the most humiliating launch of the Cook era. By the middle of the 2020s, Apple had rebuilt Maps essentially from the ground up, sending its own fleet of mapping vehicles to gather fresh imagery and data rather than relying on licensed information, and adding a "Detailed City Experience" of photorealistic buildings and custom landmarks to several dozen cities worldwide. The rebuilt product earned genuine praise for its cleaner visuals, its tighter integration with the rest of the iPhone, and its comparatively strict approach to user privacy — though it never caught Google Maps in raw scale, holding something on the order of a tenth of the global navigation-app market against Google's roughly seventy percent. It is worth correcting the assumption, common among people who remember only the 2012 debacle, that Apple Maps remains the broken, embarrassing product it was at launch; more than a decade of quiet engineering had turned a punchline into a genuinely competent piece of software, even if it never became the dominant one — a smaller, less dramatic vindication than Apple usually seeks, but a vindication all the same.

The largest and longest-running of Apple's abandoned projects never became a public product at all, which makes it a different kind of misstep — not a launch that embarrassed the company but a decade of investment that produced nothing anyone outside Apple ever got to touch. Beginning around 2014 under the internal name Project Titan, Apple poured enormous resources into the development of an electric, ultimately autonomous automobile, at its peak assigning several thousand employees to the effort and cycling through repeated changes of direction — first toward a full self-driving vehicle with no steering wheel, later toward something closer to a conventional electric car that a person would actually drive. None of it converged into a product Apple felt ready to sell, and in February 2024 the company quietly told the team that the entire project was being shut down, with roughly two thousand remaining employees reassigned to other divisions, especially the burgeoning generative-AI effort, or laid off outright; Apple formally surrendered its road-testing permit with California regulators later that year, closing the book on a undertaking that had cost, by outside estimates, tens of billions of dollars over its lifetime without ever producing a single car for sale. Two smaller misfires from the same stretch of years rounded out the pattern in more concrete terms: AirPower, the ambitious charging mat Apple unveiled onstage in 2017 that was meant to charge an iPhone, a Watch, and AirPods simultaneously anywhere on its surface, proved impossible to build without the device overheating, and Apple canceled it in 2019 without ever shipping a single unit, an admission of engineering defeat rare enough to be startling from a company so allergic to acknowledging failure; and the butterfly-mechanism keyboard that replaced traditional scissor switches in MacBooks starting in 2015, prized for its thinness, proved so prone to sticking and repeating keys from ordinary dust and debris that Apple eventually abandoned the design entirely in 2019 and, years later, agreed to a fifty-million-dollar class-action settlement to reimburse customers who had paid for repairs. What unites the car and the charging mat and the keyboard, despite their very different scales, is that each was killed by Apple itself rather than by a competitor or a regulator — proof that the company retained, even in its most institutionalized and process-driven years, the discipline to walk away from a project that was not meeting its own standard, however painful and however costly the years already sunk into it, rather than ship something merely adequate under a name that was supposed to mean more than that. It was a discipline that cut both ways, however: the same willingness to walk away that spared customers a mediocre car or a charging mat prone to overheating also meant that a decade of Project Titan's engineering, and untold billions of dollars behind it, simply vanished from public view, absorbed into other divisions or written off entirely, leaving outsiders to guess at what exactly had been built and why none of it, in the end, had been judged good enough to sell.

The missteps also connect to the larger question of Apple's character after Jobs, and they can be read, like everything in this period, in two ways. The optimistic reading is that a company that makes as many products as Apple, at such scale and ambition, will inevitably have failures, and that Apple's failures were relatively minor and well-handled, the ordinary cost of pushing boundaries, and that its ability to recover from Maps and to keep succeeding showed institutional resilience. The pessimistic reading is that the missteps — especially Batterygate, with its whiff of planned obsolescence, and the various abandoned products — suggested a company that had grown somewhat complacent, somewhat too focused on protecting its business and pushing its upgrade cycle, somewhat less magically sure-footed than it had been under Jobs at his peak. Both readings capture part of the truth. What is certain is that Apple after Jobs was neither the infallible genius of its myth nor a company in decline, but something more ordinary and more human: a very successful, very powerful, very capable company that also, regularly, failed, apologized, recovered, and moved on — a company, in other words, that had become, for all its extraordinary success, somewhat more like other companies than the singular, myth-wrapped Apple of the Jobs era had been. And that, perhaps, was the deepest change of all: not decline, but the slow normalization of the extraordinary, the settling of a revolutionary company into the successful maturity of an institution.

Chapter 57 — Foxconn

The beautiful objects that Apple sold, designed in the sunlit studios of California and unveiled in the theatrical glow of the keynotes, were assembled by human hands in enormous factories on the other side of the world, and the conditions of that assembly are the first and most human of the shadows that Apple's success cast. Behind every gleaming iPhone lay a supply chain that ran through the vast manufacturing complexes of China, and behind the miracle of Apple's operational efficiency lay the labor of hundreds of thousands of workers whose lives were very far from the aspirational imagery of Apple's advertising. To tell the history of Apple honestly is to include those workers, and the controversy over how they were treated, because the story of the world's most valuable company is also the story of the people who physically built its products, and their story is not a comfortable one.

The center of the controversy was Foxconn, the Taiwanese company that operated the giant factories in China where much of Apple's assembly took place, employing at its peak more than a million workers across its facilities, in complexes so large they were effectively cities, with their own dormitories, cafeterias, and services. In 2010, these factories became the focus of international attention and alarm when a cluster of workers at a major Foxconn complex died by suicide, several of them jumping from the buildings, in a wave that drew the world's attention to the conditions inside. Investigations and reporting in the following years painted a troubling picture: long working hours, sometimes far exceeding legal limits, especially during the intense production ramps before major product launches; monotonous, grueling assembly-line work performed at high speed under strict discipline; low wages by the standards of the wealthy countries where the products were sold; crowded dormitory living; and a general atmosphere of pressure and regimentation that critics described as harsh and, in the accounts of some workers and observers, dehumanizing. Foxconn's response to the suicides — which included, notoriously, installing nets around the buildings to catch jumpers — became a grim symbol of the whole situation, and the image of the world's most desirable consumer products being made in factories that needed suicide nets was a powerful and damaging counterpoint to Apple's carefully cultivated image of enlightened, humane design.

Apple's responsibility for these conditions was, and remains, a genuinely complex question, and it deserves to be reckoned with honestly rather than either excused or sensationalized. Apple did not own the Foxconn factories; they were operated by a contractor, and the conditions in them reflected the broader realities of Chinese manufacturing, the pressures of the global electronics industry, and choices made by Foxconn and by the workers themselves, many of whom sought these jobs as a path to a better life. Apple could and did argue that it was not directly responsible for a contractor's practices, that conditions at its suppliers were often better than at other Chinese factories, and that it was working to improve them. And Apple did take real steps in response to the criticism: it published its supplier lists and audit findings, established codes of conduct for its suppliers, conducted audits, pushed contractors to reduce excessive overtime and improve conditions and safety, and cut ties with some suppliers that violated its standards. These efforts were real and produced real improvements, and Apple became, in some respects, a leader among technology companies in supply-chain transparency and accountability. But critics argued, with considerable force, that Apple's responsibility went deeper than it acknowledged — that as the dominant customer, wielding enormous power over its suppliers, Apple set the prices and the timelines and the pressures that shaped conditions in the factories, and that a company earning the greatest profits in the history of business, with hundreds of billions in cash, could have done far more to ensure that the workers who made its products were treated well, had it chosen to prioritize that over its margins.

The Foxconn controversy poses, in its sharpest form, a moral question that hangs over the whole of modern global capitalism and that Apple embodies more visibly than almost any other company: the question of the human cost of the cheap, abundant, beautiful goods that the wealthy world enjoys, and the responsibility of the companies and consumers who benefit from that cost. Apple's products were affordable and profitable in part because they were assembled by workers earning a fraction of what workers in wealthy countries would earn, under conditions those workers would not accept, in a country whose labor system gave workers little power. This was not unique to Apple; it was the model of nearly the entire consumer-electronics industry and much of global manufacturing. But Apple's extraordinary visibility, its enormous profits, and its self-presentation as an enlightened, humane, values-driven company made the gap between its image and the conditions in its supply chain especially stark, and made it a lightning rod for the broader unease about the human foundations of the global economy. The company that sold objects of such beauty and that spoke so much about its values was also a company whose products were made possible by the hard labor of distant, poorly paid workers, and holding those two facts together is part of the honest reckoning with what Apple is.

Terry Gou, the founder and chairman of Foxconn, met the crisis of 2010 first with defiance and then with a scramble of remedies that, taken together, told the whole story of how the company understood the problem. At a press conference convened as the death toll mounted, Gou insisted that Foxconn was "certainly not running a sweatshop," a claim meant to reassure the world but that only underscored how far the public conversation had moved past reassurance. Behind the denial, Foxconn moved quickly on the practical front: it raised wages substantially for its Shenzhen workforce, installed the now-infamous netting along the dormitory buildings to physically prevent further jumps, brought in Buddhist monks to conduct prayer ceremonies on the factory grounds, and had workers sign pledges promising not to take their own lives. It was a strange and telling combination of remedies, at once financial, architectural, spiritual, and contractual, and it reflected an institution treating a crisis of despair as a problem to be managed rather than a symptom to be understood. Life inside Longhua, the sprawling complex at the center of the story, gave the despair its context: shifts stretching past ten hours, a single day off in a week that was itself often eroded by mandatory overtime, a shop-floor culture in which idle talk between workers was discouraged or forbidden outright, and dormitories where a dozen young migrants from the countryside might share a single room, sleeping in bunks stacked to the ceiling, with little to mark the boundary between one exhausting day and the next. Apple's own public response was brief and carefully calibrated — a statement saying the company was "saddened and upset by the recent suicides at Foxconn" — the sort of language that acknowledged tragedy without conceding fault, and that would recur, in only slightly different phrasing, whenever future controversies over supplier conditions arose.

The most sensational chapter in the whole affair, and the one most often misremembered, involved not a journalist but a monologist. In early 2012, the radio program

This American Life broadcast an excerpt of a one-man stage show by Mike Daisey called "The Agony and the Ecstasy of Steve Jobs," in which Daisey described his own visit to the Foxconn gates and recounted meeting underage workers and a man whose hand had been mangled making iPads. The piece became the most downloaded episode in the program's history and supercharged the public outcry against Apple, but within weeks it unraveled: a reporter tracked down Daisey's Chinese interpreter, who disputed key details, and confronted with the discrepancies, Daisey admitted he had fabricated or embellished several of his most vivid claims. *This American Life* retracted the episode outright in a program titled, starkly, "Retraction." It became fashionable afterward, especially among Apple's defenders, to treat the retraction as proof that the entire Foxconn story had been invented by a dishonest performer looking to sell tickets — but that inference did not survive contact with the independent evidence. Around the same time as the Daisey scandal, and for reasons unrelated to it, Apple had already invited the Fair Labor Association, an independent monitoring group, to audit its Chinese suppliers, and the FLA's investigators — who were given real access to the Foxconn floor and even let ABC News film inside the plants — did not find the specific horrors Daisey had invented, but they did describe an environment that was, in their own words, mind-numbingly monotonous, and they documented genuine violations of legal overtime limits and other labor standards. The lesson was not that the critics of Foxconn had been vindicated in every particular, nor that Apple's defenders were right to dismiss the whole affair; it was that a fabulist's lies and a factory's real problems could exist side by side, and that the retraction of one dishonest storyteller's account did nothing to retract the underlying reality that outside auditors, using their own eyes rather than a playwright's imagination, had independently confirmed.

The dependency that the suicides and the audits exposed did not disappear with better wage scales or improved dormitories; it migrated, in the years that followed, into a strategic vulnerability that Apple would spend the 2020s trying to manage. The Zhengzhou complex that Foxconn built in China's Henan province grew so vast that it became known simply as "iPhone City," a single campus, at its peak, responsible for producing the large majority of all iPhones sold anywhere in the world. That concentration became impossible to ignore in the autumn of 2022, when strict pandemic lockdowns at the Zhengzhou plant triggered worker unrest, mass walkouts, and clashes with security personnel just as Apple was racing to fulfill holiday-season demand for its newest phones — a vivid demonstration that a single facility, in a single country, under a single government's public-health policy, could interrupt the flow of Apple's most important product worldwide. In the years since, Apple pushed harder than ever to diversify the geography of its assembly, encouraging Foxconn and its other manufacturing partners to expand production in India, where by some industry estimates Apple aimed to have roughly a quarter of all iPhones built within a few years, and in Vietnam, where Foxconn poured hundreds of millions of dollars into new industrial parkland. It was, in its own way, a continuation of the very same reckoning that had begun with the suicides and the nets: an acknowledgment, however belated and however driven by self-interest rather than conscience, that a business built on the labor of workers half a world away could not simply take that labor, or the political and human conditions surrounding it, for granted.

The pattern of documented violations did not end with the 2010s reforms, and later investigations showed that some of the oldest abuses in the supply chain had simply taken new forms. China Labor Watch, the advocacy group whose earlier reporting had helped force Apple's supplier-monitoring programs into being, published a report in 2023 describing a vocational-school internship program at a Foxconn plant in Chengdu in which students were placed on the same production lines and the same overtime schedules as full-time workers, under instructors who reportedly threatened that refusing the assignment would cost them their diplomas — an arrangement that, whatever euphemism it traveled under, functioned as a supply of compelled labor and that ran afoul of China's own rules governing student internships. Subsequent investigations into Foxconn facilities producing later iPhone models documented workers logging as many as sixty-five hours a week during slow periods and closer to ninety during the run-up to a new phone's launch, figures that, if accurate, exceeded China's own statutory overtime limits several times over and suggested that the underlying pressures of Apple's launch calendar — the same annual rhythm that gave the keynote its theater and the App Store its holiday spike in Services revenue — continued to translate, at the far end of the supply chain, into exactly the kind of grinding schedules that had first drawn global attention back in 2010. Apple's standard response to such reports had by then become a familiar script: an audit, a promise to investigate, occasional confirmation that a supplier had broken the rules, and a public commitment to corrective action, a cycle that critics increasingly read less as accountability than as a predictable and almost ritualized cost of doing business, absorbed and repeated every few years without altering the deeper economics that produced the pressure in the first place. What had changed since 2010 was less the underlying reality on the factory floor than the machinery built up around it — the auditors, the codes of conduct, the advocacy groups with their own institutional interest in finding and publicizing new violations — a whole apparatus of accountability that made each fresh report easier to document and harder for Apple to simply deny, even as it did comparatively little to change the seasonal crush of overtime that a global consumer-electronics calendar, with its single make-or-break holiday quarter, imposed on the workers at the very end of the chain. The vocational-student cases, in particular, exposed a specific vulnerability that ordinary labor law was not well designed to catch: interns, unlike full employees, sat in a legal gray zone between education and employment, and it was precisely that gray zone that had let Foxconn and its recruiting partners funnel young people into what amounted to full production shifts under the cover of a school-sponsored program, a loophole regulators and monitors had to be taught to look for anew each time a fresh version of it surfaced.

There is no comfortable resolution to the Foxconn question, and this book will not manufacture one. Apple was neither the uniquely evil exploiter that its harshest critics portrayed nor the responsible, blameless actor that its own accounts suggested; it was a company operating within, and profiting enormously from, a global system of manufacturing whose human costs were real and whose moral weight it bore a significant share of, and it responded to criticism with a mixture of genuine improvement and self-protective minimization. The workers who assembled the iPhones were real people whose labor made Apple's success possible and who shared very little in the trillions of dollars of value that success created, and their story is a permanent part of Apple's story, however much the keynotes and the advertising left them out. And the Foxconn controversy was, in another dimension, a symptom of a deeper dependency that would become, in the geopolitics of the 2020s, one of the greatest strategic vulnerabilities and moral entanglements of Apple's entire business: its profound reliance on China, not just as a place to make its products but as a market, a partner, and a power whose interests Apple could not ignore. That dependency is the next shadow, and it runs deeper than any factory.

Chapter 58 — The Walled Garden on Trial

The App Store, which had turned the iPhone into a platform and become one of Apple's greatest sources of profit and lock-in, became in the later Cook years the target of the most serious legal and regulatory assault Apple had ever faced — a global reckoning over whether Apple's control of the software that ran on its devices, and the toll it charged for that control, had crossed the line from a legitimate business model into an abusive monopoly. The walled garden that Steve Jobs had built, and that had made Apple's products so seamless and secure and profitable, was put on trial, in courtrooms and legislatures around the world, and the outcome would reshape the terms on which Apple operated and would test the limits of the control that had been central to its success.

The core of the dispute was Apple's absolute control over the iPhone's software and the thirty-percent commission it took on app sales and in-app purchases. To run software on an iPhone, a developer had to distribute it through Apple's App Store; there was no other way to install an app, no alternative store, no ability for a user to install software directly as they could on a traditional computer. And for digital goods sold within apps — subscriptions, game items, and the like — developers were required to use Apple's payment system and to pay Apple its thirty-percent cut, with no ability to direct customers to cheaper alternatives outside the app. For years, developers had chafed at this arrangement — at the toll, at the rules, at Apple's power to reject apps and dictate terms — but Apple's control had seemed unchallengeable, the price of access to Apple's lucrative customers. Then, in 2020, the maker of a wildly popular game, Epic Games, deliberately violated Apple's rules by offering its own payment system inside its app, was expelled from the App Store, and sued Apple, arguing that Apple's control of the App Store was an illegal monopoly that harmed developers and consumers. The lawsuit, Epic Games v. Apple, became a landmark, dragging Apple's practices and its internal communications into open court and putting the whole model of the walled garden before a judge and the public.

The arguments on both sides were substantial, and an honest account should present them fairly rather than assuming Apple was simply a villain or simply within its rights. Apple's defense rested on several claims: that its control of the App Store was what made the iPhone secure and reliable, protecting users from malware, fraud, and privacy violations by vetting every app; that the thirty-percent commission was in line with what other digital platforms charged and paid for the enormous value Apple provided in distribution, tools, and access to its customers; that Apple had created the platform and had the right to set the terms for the business it had built; and that its control benefited consumers by delivering a safe, curated, high-quality experience. The critics' arguments, advanced by Epic and by many other developers, regulators, and competitors, were equally forceful: that Apple's control was not about security but about profit and power; that the thirty-percent toll was an excessive tax extracted through a monopoly on iPhone software distribution; that Apple used its control to disadvantage competitors and to prevent developers from even telling customers about cheaper options; and that a company controlling access to more than a billion devices, on which entire industries and livelihoods depended, wielded a gatekeeping power that had become a genuine monopoly requiring legal restraint. The dispute was, at bottom, about the double nature of the walled garden that this book has traced throughout: the same control that produced excellence also produced power, and the question before the courts was whether that power had become abuse.

The legal and regulatory results were mixed, evolving, and consequential, and they marked a real erosion of the total control Apple had long enjoyed. In the Epic case, courts reached a split verdict, largely rejecting the claim that Apple was an unlawful monopolist under American antitrust law while nonetheless finding that some of Apple's practices — particularly its prohibition on developers telling customers about alternative ways to pay — were anticompetitive and had to change. More sweeping challenges came from outside the United States, especially from the European Union, which enacted new laws aimed squarely at the power of the dominant technology platforms and used them to force Apple to open its ecosystem in ways it had always resisted — to allow alternative app stores, to permit developers to use other payment systems, to loosen the walls of the garden. Around the world, regulators, legislators, and courts increasingly moved to constrain Apple's control, and Apple, fighting a rearguard action, was compelled to make concessions it had long refused, cracking open, bit by bit, the closed system that Jobs had built and that had been so central to Apple's business. The walls of the garden did not fall, but they were breached, and the era of Apple's absolute, unchallenged control over its platform came, gradually and grudgingly, to an end.

When the ruling in Epic Games v. Apple finally arrived in September 2021, from Judge Yvonne Gonzalez Rogers of the federal court in Oakland, it was widely reported in the press as a split decision, and in the narrowest technical sense it was: Apple prevailed on nine of the ten claims Epic had brought, and the judge explicitly declined to find that Apple was an illegal monopolist under federal antitrust law. But the popular memory of the case, in the years since, has tended to compress that split verdict into a simple story of Apple winning and Epic losing, and that compression obscures what was, in practical terms, the most significant single check on Apple's App Store power in its history. On the tenth claim, brought under California's unfair competition law, Judge Gonzalez Rogers ruled against Apple's practice of forbidding developers from telling their own customers, inside their own apps, that cheaper ways to pay might exist elsewhere. "The Court concludes that Apple's anti-steering provisions hide critical information from consumers and illegally stifle consumer choice," she wrote, and she ordered Apple, nationwide, to stop enforcing the rule. It was a narrow legal opening, but through it developers began, for the first time, to communicate directly with customers about alternatives to Apple's payment system, and the myth that Epic had simply lost its long fight against Apple has never quite survived the fact that Apple spent years afterward trying, and repeatedly failing, to comply with that single sentence of the ruling to the courts' satisfaction — a fight that dragged on so long that by 2025 a federal judge had found Apple in willful violation of her own injunction and referred the matter for possible criminal contempt, and by 2026 Apple was asking the Supreme Court itself to intervene.

Even as the American courts wrestled with the narrower question of anti-steering, the more sweeping transformation of Apple's walled garden was arriving from Brussels. The European Union's Digital Markets Act, aimed at curbing the power of a short list of "gatekeeper" platforms, forced Apple in March of 2024 to do something it had resisted since the iPhone's introduction: to let iOS users in the European Union install apps from outside its own

App Store. With the release of iOS 17.4, Apple built the technical scaffolding for alternative app marketplaces and reworked its commission structure for the region, cutting its standard cut on qualifying transactions roughly in half while introducing, in its place, a new per-install fee on developers whose apps proved unusually popular — a fee structure that critics immediately denounced as Apple's attempt to preserve, in a different form, the economics of the tollbooth it had just been ordered to open. The changes were real, and they cracked open a door that had been welded shut for a decade and a half, but they did not end the fight; within weeks, the European Commission had opened formal non-compliance investigations against Apple, arguing that its new rules for uninstalling apps, changing default settings, and steering users to competitors still fell short of what the law required, a reminder that regulatory victories over a company as practiced in resistance as Apple were rarely won in a single legislative stroke.

The American government, watching Brussels succeed where its own courts had moved more cautiously, brought its own reckoning in March of 2024, when the Department of Justice and sixteen state attorneys general filed a sweeping antitrust complaint against Apple in federal court in New Jersey, alleging that the company had illegally maintained a monopoly over the smartphone market itself, not merely over its App Store. Assistant Attorney General Jonathan Kanter, announcing the suit, offered a description of Apple's conduct that might have served as a thesis statement for this entire chapter: "For years, Apple responded to competitive threats by imposing a series of 'Whac-A-Mole' contractual rules and restrictions that have allowed Apple to extract higher prices from consumers, impose higher fees on developers and creators, and to throttle competitive alternatives from rival technologies." The complaint argued that each individual restriction Apple imposed — on cloud gaming services, on cross-platform messaging, on third-party smartwatches and digital wallets — might look defensible in isolation, but that together they built what the government's lawyers called a moat, protecting not the security of users but the durability of Apple's profits. A federal judge allowed the core of that case to proceed toward trial, ensuring that the reckoning over Apple's control of its platform, which Epic had begun in a courtroom in Oakland and Brussels had continued through legislation, would carry on for years yet in New Jersey, with the full weight of the United States government now arrayed against the garden wall.

The pressure on Apple's control of its platform was, by the middle of the 2020s, no longer a story confined to Brussels and Washington, and the spread of similar laws to other major markets showed how thoroughly the European approach had become a template rather than an isolated exception. Japan enacted its own Mobile Software Competition Act in 2024, designating Apple and Google as regulated "specified software operators" and, once the law took full effect in December 2025, requiring both companies to permit alternative app marketplaces and outside payment systems on their platforms — while notably permitting Apple to charge a smaller, five-percent core-technology commission on sales made through those alternative channels, a narrower toll than the one European regulators had accepted but a toll all the same. The United Kingdom moved down a parallel track through its Digital Markets, Competition and Consumers Act, which took effect in 2024 and empowered the country's Competition and Markets Authority to designate firms with "Strategic Market Status" and impose tailored conduct requirements without needing to prove a monopoly case in court first, a lower evidentiary bar than the traditional antitrust route the Justice Department was still grinding through in New Jersey. Efforts to pass comparable legislation in South Korea and India, by contrast, ran into a different kind of obstacle entirely: reporting indicated that American trade negotiators, in the course of broader tariff and trade discussions with both governments, made the shelving of proposed app-store legislation an implicit condition of goodwill in those talks, a reminder that the fight over Apple's walled garden had become entangled with great-power trade diplomacy in ways that had little to do with antitrust law as such, and that geopolitics, not just courtrooms, was now shaping where and how far the garden's walls would come down. The cumulative effect, across Brussels, Tokyo, London, and the American courts all moving at once, if not always in concert, was that Apple by 2026 found itself managing not one regulatory fight but a patchwork of overlapping obligations that varied meaningfully by country — different commission rates, different sideloading rules, different disclosure requirements — an outcome that itself undercut one of the walled garden's original selling points, the promise of a single, uniform experience for developers and users regardless of where in the world an iPhone happened to be sold. Ironically, the very complexity of complying with a dozen overlapping regimes at once gave Apple a new argument of its own, one it made increasingly often to legislators weighing further rules: that a fragmented, country-by-country patchwork of app-distribution requirements was itself a burden on small developers, who now had to master an entirely different set of obligations depending on where their software was downloaded, a burden regulators had originally set out to lift from developers' shoulders rather than add to them.

The trial of the walled garden is the sharpest instance of the great irony that runs through Apple's entire history, and it is worth stating one final time in its fullest form. Apple was founded by two young rebels who built a device to defy a monopoly — Wozniak's and Jobs's blue box, made to steal from the telephone monopoly that dominated their world. The company they created defined itself, in the "1984" ad and the "Think Different" campaign, as the rebel against the dominant power, the champion of the individual against the monolith, the insurgent against the establishment. And over fifty years, that rebel became the establishment — became one of the most powerful and controlling gatekeepers in the history of commerce, a monopolist (or near-monopolist) in the eyes of many, sued by smaller companies and constrained by governments for exactly the kind of dominating control that its founders had once existed to defy. The company that began by breaking into a monopoly's network ended by building a walled garden that governments had to pry open. This is not hypocrisy exactly; it is something more like the natural trajectory of success, the way the insurgent who wins becomes the incumbent, the way the rebel who conquers becomes the thing rebels rebel against. But it is the deepest irony of Apple's story, and the trial of the App Store made it impossible to ignore. And the walled garden's dependence on one country, above all, made it vulnerable to a shadow larger than any lawsuit — the shadow of geopolitics, and of Apple's entanglement with China.

Chapter 59 — Made in China

Apple's relationship with China is one of the most consequential and fraught aspects of its modern existence, a dependency so deep that it shaped the company's products, its politics, and its vulnerabilities, and that became, in the geopolitics of the 2020s, one of the greatest strategic risks Apple faced. China was, for Apple, three things at once — the place where its products were made, a huge and growing market where its products were sold, and a rising authoritarian power whose government could, through its control of both the factories and the market, exert enormous leverage over the world's most valuable company. This triple entanglement gave China a hold over Apple that no other external force possessed, and it forced Apple into compromises and accommodations that sat uneasily with its professed values and that exposed the limits of even a four-trillion-dollar company's independence.

The manufacturing dependency was the foundation. As we have seen, the overwhelming majority of Apple's products were assembled in China, in a supply chain that had taken decades to build and that could not be quickly or easily moved. This gave the Chinese government real leverage, because Apple's entire business depended on the continued smooth operation of its Chinese manufacturing, and anything that disrupted it — political tension, regulatory pressure, labor problems, or the government's displeasure — threatened the company at its core. Apple could not afford to antagonize the Chinese state, because the Chinese state held the factories on which everything depended. Over the 2020s, as tensions between China and the United States grew and as the risks of concentrating manufacturing in a single, increasingly rival country became more apparent, Apple began, cautiously, to diversify — shifting some production to India, Vietnam, and elsewhere, seeking to reduce its dependence on China. But the shift was slow and partial, because the Chinese manufacturing ecosystem was so vast, so skilled, and so deeply established that it could not be replaced quickly, and Apple remained, deep into the decade, profoundly reliant on China to make its products, and therefore profoundly exposed to the risks that reliance entailed.

The market dependency compounded the manufacturing one. China was not only where Apple made its products but one of the largest places it sold them — a huge and, for years, growing market of hundreds of millions of consumers, many of whom prized the iPhone as a status symbol and a desirable object, and which generated an enormous share of Apple's revenue. This gave the Chinese government a second lever, because it could threaten not only Apple's ability to make its products but its ability to sell them, through regulation, through encouragement of domestic competitors, through the myriad ways an authoritarian state can favor or disfavor a foreign company in its market. Apple's dependence on China as both workshop and marketplace meant that the Chinese government held two of the most important variables in Apple's business, and that Apple had powerful incentives to keep that government satisfied.

The consequences of this dependency were visible in the compromises Apple made, and they sat in sharp tension with the values-driven image Tim Cook had cultivated.

Apple, which under Cook championed privacy as a fundamental right and human dignity as a core value, made accommodations to the demands of the Chinese state that critics found difficult to reconcile with those principles. It removed apps from its Chinese App Store at the government's demand, including apps used to evade censorship and apps offering news the government disliked. It stored the data of its Chinese users on servers in China, subject to Chinese law and, critics feared, to the government's access, in a way that sat uneasily with its privacy rhetoric elsewhere. It complied with Chinese regulations and censorship in ways that it would have loudly resisted in other countries, and it generally avoided public criticism of the Chinese government's human-rights record, even as it spoke out on social issues at home. The company that presented itself as a principled defender of privacy and human dignity behaved, in China, like a company that could not afford to offend its host — because it could not. The gap between Apple's professed values and its conduct in China was one of the sharpest contradictions of the Cook era, and it revealed the limits of corporate values when they collided with the imperatives of business and the power of a state that held a company's supply chain and market in its hands.

The full depth of the accommodation was not visible at the time it was made, and it took years of reporting to bring even part of it into public view. In December 2021, the technology publication The Information reported that Cook had personally negotiated and signed a sweeping, previously secret agreement with Chinese officials back in 2016, at a moment when Apple's business in the country was faltering and regulators were making life difficult for the company in myriad small ways. Under the arrangement, said to run for roughly five years, Apple committed to investing many billions of dollars beyond what it already spent in China — on new retail stores, on research and development centers, on renewable-energy projects, and on partnerships with Chinese universities —

and pledged to expand its use of components from Chinese suppliers, to sign agreements with Chinese software companies, and even to make direct investments in Chinese technology firms. In exchange, Apple's operations were said to be spared some of the more onerous regulatory scrutiny that Beijing routinely applied to foreign companies. Whatever the precise terms, the broader shape of the deal captured something true about the relationship: Apple bought a measure of goodwill and stability from the Chinese state, and it paid for that goodwill not merely in dollars but in deference.

That deference showed up most visibly, and most uncomfortably, in the App Store. In 2017, amid a broader government crackdown on tools that let Chinese citizens evade the Great Firewall, Apple removed hundreds of VPN applications from its Chinese storefront at Beijing's insistence — reporting at the time put the number in the many hundreds — stripping ordinary users of one of their few remaining ways to reach the unfiltered internet. When American senators wrote to Cook to ask why Apple had cooperated so readily, the company's answer was a version of an argument it would repeat for years: that Apple could do more good for free expression by remaining engaged in China, working within the country's laws, than by refusing to operate there at all. Two years later, during the mass pro-democracy protests that convulsed Hong Kong in 2019, Apple pulled a crowdsourced mapping app called HKmap.live from its store after it had briefly become one of the territory's most downloaded apps; the app let protesters and ordinary residents alike track police movements, road closures, and clashes in real time, and Apple's stated reason — that it violated guidelines and ran afoul of unspecified local laws — satisfied almost no one on either side of the debate, while Beijing's state media had, not coincidentally, denounced the app just before its removal. Taken together, the VPN purge and the HKmap.live takedown were small acts by the standards of a company that size, single line items in a vast App Store catalog, but they were also unmistakable signals of where the balance of power in the relationship actually lay.

It would be a mistake, though, to read Apple's China predicament as simply a story of cheap labor exploited and easily replaced once the politics turned inconvenient, and the years after 2018 tested that assumption directly. As trade tensions between Washington and Beijing hardened into tariffs, export controls, and mutual suspicion, and as American policymakers pressed companies to "de-risk" their China exposure, Apple did begin, in earnest, to build a second manufacturing base in India, working with Foxconn and, increasingly, with the Indian conglomerate Tata Group, which acquired a struggling Wistron assembly plant and expanded rapidly into iPhone production. By the mid-2020s the shift had real momentum: India's share of global iPhone assembly climbed from a small fraction to roughly a quarter of Apple's worldwide output, with tens of millions of iPhones a year rolling off Indian assembly lines, and Tata's share of that Indian production rising fast enough that some analysts expected it to rival Foxconn's within a few years. Yet the diversification did not mean an unwinding of the China relationship so much as a hedging of it: the components inside an Indian-assembled iPhone still traced back, overwhelmingly, to Chinese suppliers and Chinese-trained engineering expertise, and China remained by far the larger and more sophisticated manufacturing base even as India's role grew. The popular notion that Apple was simply "leaving China" for India missed the more complicated truth — that Apple was distributing risk rather than eliminating it, adding a second dependency without fully escaping the first.

The market side of the China relationship, meanwhile, delivered its own sobering lesson in how quickly deference to Beijing could fail to insulate Apple from Beijing's own homegrown competition. Huawei, the Chinese telecommunications giant that American export controls had crippled by cutting off its access to advanced chips and to Google's Android services, engineered a startling comeback in the mid-2020s, releasing phones built on chips manufactured domestically in China that restored much of its earlier competitiveness and unleashed a wave of patriotic buying that Apple could do little to counter. The numbers were stark: Apple's iPhone shipments in China fell by roughly a quarter in the first months of 2024 alone, the steepest such decline the company had ever recorded in the market, while Huawei's own shipments surged by more than sixty percent over the same stretch — the first time since the American sanctions first hit that Huawei had managed to outsell Apple again on its home turf. By early 2025, Apple had slipped to third place among smartphone makers in China, trailing not only Huawei but the domestic budget brand Xiaomi, with its market share cut roughly in half from where it had stood barely a year earlier. Analysts attributed the collapse to a combination of forces: the resurgent appeal of a homegrown champion at a moment of rising Chinese nationalism, aggressive pricing and feature competition from Xiaomi and other domestic manufacturers, and, pointedly, Apple's own inability to bring its newest Apple Intelligence features to Chinese customers at all, since deploying generative AI inside the country required a locally licensed partner and government approval that had not yet arrived — leaving Chinese iPhone buyers, for a time, without access to the very features Apple was promoting most heavily to the rest of the world. It was a vivid illustration of the deeper argument this chapter has made: that Apple's dependence on China cut in both directions, and that a government capable of enabling Apple's manufacturing miracle was equally capable of nurturing the domestic rivals that would erode Apple's position in its own showcase market. Apple's response was, by its own recent standards, unusually aggressive for that single market: steep, repeated discounting on iPhone prices within China, expanded trade-in programs, and a wave of new retail openings, all deployed in an attempt to defend share against rivals whose products, by the mid-2020s, closed much of the hardware gap that had once made an iPhone worth its premium price to a Chinese buyer regardless of the patriotic appeal of the alternative. The episode complicated the tidy story, popular among some Western commentators, that Chinese consumers were turning away from Apple purely out of nationalist sentiment stoked by the government; the more mundane truth was that Huawei, Xiaomi, and their peers had simply gotten good enough, fast enough, that price and features alone were doing a great deal of the work that patriotism was often credited with, a distinction that mattered because it suggested Apple's China problem was, at bottom, a competitive one rather than a purely political one — and therefore, in principle, one that better products could still address.

The China entanglement is, finally, a story about the limits of power, and it provides a revealing coda to the tale of the world's most valuable company. Apple was, by 2026, worth four trillion dollars, richer and more powerful than most nations, seemingly answerable to no one. And yet it was, in a fundamental way, not free — bound by its dependence on China to accommodate a government whose values it did not share, unable to act on its stated principles where they conflicted with its access to Chinese manufacturing and markets, exposed to a geopolitical risk it could not quickly escape. The most valuable company in the history of the world discovered that its wealth did not translate into independence, that it had built its empire on a foundation controlled by a rival power, and that even it had masters. This vulnerability — the dependence on a single, authoritarian, increasingly antagonistic country for both the making and much of the selling of its products — was, as Apple entered its second half-century, perhaps the greatest strategic risk it faced, greater than any competitor or lawsuit, and it was the price of the very supply-chain mastery that had helped make Apple so successful. The efficiency that Tim Cook had built by concentrating manufacturing in China was also a chain that bound Apple to China, and unwinding it would be one of the central challenges of the era to come — an era that would begin under new leadership, for in 2026 Tim Cook, having led Apple through fifteen years of triumph and reckoning, prepared to hand the company to a successor. The privacy, repair, and environmental questions that also shadowed Apple's success deserve their own accounting first, and then we can turn to the succession, and to what, in the end, Steve Jobs and the company he built had wrought.

Chapter 60 — Privacy, Repair, and the Planet

Three further shadows fall across Apple's success, and they are worth gathering together because each involves a genuine tension between the company's professed values and its commercial interests, and because each shows Apple as it really is — better than its harshest critics allow, worse than its own marketing claims, a company navigating real trade-offs in which principle and profit pull in different directions. They concern privacy, the right to repair, and the environment, and in each Apple has been both leader and laggard, admirable and self-serving, sometimes in the same breath.

Privacy became, under Tim Cook, one of Apple's defining public values, and here Apple's record is genuinely strong, though not without its complications. Cook made a strategic and, it seems, sincere decision to position Apple as the technology company that protected its users' privacy, in explicit contrast to competitors like Google and Facebook whose businesses depended on collecting and monetizing personal data. "You are not our product," was the essence of Apple's argument: because Apple made its money selling devices and services rather than advertising, it had no incentive to harvest and sell its users' data, and it could therefore be trusted to protect it. Apple built privacy protections into its products — encryption that even Apple could not break, features that limited apps' ability to track users, a general design philosophy that minimized data collection — and it made privacy a selling point and a matter of principle. In one celebrated episode, Apple refused a demand from the American government to help unlock the iPhone of a terrorist, arguing that building a way to bypass its encryption would endanger all its users' security, and it fought the government in a public standoff over the principle that strong encryption protected everyone. On privacy, Apple was, by and large, as good as its word, and better than its rivals, and this was a real and creditable difference. Yet even here there were tensions and contradictions — the accommodations to China, where Apple's privacy principles bent to the state's demands; the enormous payments Apple accepted from Google to make Google's data-hungry search engine the default on the iPhone, a deal that sat awkwardly with Apple's privacy rhetoric. Apple's privacy leadership was real and its privacy purity was not, and both are part of the truth.

The right to repair is a shadow where Apple's record is far less admirable, and where its interests and its stated values pulled sharply apart. Apple designed its products to be difficult for users or independent shops to repair — sealing devices with special screws and glues, refusing to sell parts or provide repair manuals, using software to prevent unauthorized repairs, and generally channeling all repairs through Apple's own expensive service or its authorized providers. Critics — a growing "right to repair" movement of consumers, independent repair shops, and legislators — argued that this was a deliberate strategy to control the lucrative repair business, to force customers toward expensive Apple repairs or toward buying new devices rather than fixing old ones, and that it was wasteful, anti-consumer, and environmentally destructive, generating mountains of electronic waste as repairable devices were discarded. Apple defended its approach on grounds of safety, security, and quality, arguing that unauthorized repairs with inferior parts could harm users and compromise its products. But the defense was widely seen as self-serving, a rationalization of a policy whose real purpose was control and profit, and the right-to-repair movement won growing public sympathy and, eventually, legislation in various places requiring companies to make repair more accessible. Under pressure, Apple made some concessions, launching programs to provide parts and manuals and to allow more independent repair — but grudgingly, partially, and clearly in response to external force rather than internal conviction. On repair, Apple was, fairly plainly, on the wrong side, defending a closed, controlling, wasteful model against the interests of its own customers and the planet, and being dragged toward openness only by law and public pressure.

The environment is a shadow of a more mixed and evolving character, where Apple made real commitments and real progress while remaining, inescapably, a company whose business model was the sale of ever more physical devices. Under Cook, Apple made ambitious environmental pledges — to power its operations with renewable energy, to become carbon neutral across its entire business and supply chain, to use recycled materials, to reduce its environmental footprint — and it made genuine progress toward these goals, becoming, in some respects, a leader among large corporations on climate and sustainability. These commitments were real and creditable, and Apple's scale meant that its efforts to green its supply chain had significant effects. Yet there was an unavoidable tension at the heart of Apple's environmental posture, which no amount of renewable energy could resolve: Apple's business was selling hundreds of millions of new devices every year, encouraging customers to replace their phones and computers and watches on a regular cycle, and this fundamental model — the continual production and consumption of new physical goods — was itself environmentally costly, no matter how green the factories that made them. A company whose profits depended on people continually buying new devices, and whose repair policies discouraged keeping old ones, could green its operations but could not escape the environmental logic of its own growth. Apple's environmental leadership was real, and the environmental cost of its business model was also real, and the two coexisted in a tension the company's sustainability marketing tended to obscure.

The clearest demonstration of what Apple's privacy stance actually cost its rivals came in the spring of 2021, when Apple introduced a feature called App Tracking Transparency in iOS 14.5. The change was, in mechanical terms, modest: apps would now have to ask a user's explicit permission before tracking that user's activity across other companies' apps and websites for advertising purposes, using a device identifier that had previously been harvested more or less by default. In practice the change was seismic, because it threatened to sever the data pipeline that powered the entire targeted-advertising industry, and no company depended on that pipeline more than Facebook, soon to rename itself Meta. Facebook fought back in the most public way it could, taking out full-page advertisements in major American newspapers arguing that Apple's change would crush small businesses that relied on precisely targeted ads to reach customers affordably, and framing itself as standing up for the little guy against a trillion-dollar gatekeeper. The campaign largely backfired, seen by much of the press and even some of Facebook's own employees as a transparent defense of Facebook's own advertising business dressed up as populism, and it only sharpened the contrast Apple wanted drawn between a device maker that sold hardware and a platform that sold its users' attention. Facebook's own later disclosures to investors made the stakes explicit, estimating that Apple's change would cost the company billions of dollars in lost advertising revenue — a rare, concrete measurement of what "You are not our product" was actually worth in dollars, and of how much of the internet's economy had been built on the very tracking Apple now made optional.

On repair, Apple's story did not end where the earlier reckoning left it, and the company's later reversal complicates the simpler narrative of pure obstruction. Having spent years resisting right-to-repair legislation around the country, Apple changed course in 2022, launching a Self Service Repair program that let ordinary customers order genuine parts, tools, and manuals to fix iPhones and, eventually, some Mac models themselves rather than routing every repair through Apple or its authorized network. A year later the shift became more than a marketing gesture: in 2023, Apple threw its public support behind California's SB 244, the state's Right to Repair Act, with the company writing to the bill's author that it backed the legislation "because it includes requirements that protect individual users' safety and security, as well as product manufacturers' intellectual property." The bill passed the state senate unanimously and was signed into law that October, and Apple's endorsement — from the company that had spent a decade lobbying against similar bills in statehouse after statehouse — was widely read as a recognition that the legislative tide had turned decisively enough that resistance was no longer the more profitable strategy. It would be too generous to call this a conversion of principle; it was, more precisely, a company reading the room and deciding that shaping favorable repair legislation from the inside beat losing the fight on someone else's terms. But the practical effect for consumers and independent repair shops was real, even if the motive behind it remained mixed.

The environmental side of the ledger likewise deserves a fuller accounting than the broad brush allows, because Apple's efforts there were neither pure marketing nor a complete answer to the problem. Under Lisa Jackson, the former head of the U.S. Environmental Protection Agency whom Cook hired in 2013 to lead Apple's environmental and policy efforts, Apple reached 100 percent renewable energy across its own global operations in 2018 and then committed, in 2020, to making its entire business — including its manufacturing supply chain and the full life cycle of its products — carbon neutral by 2030, a goal the company pursued by cutting emissions and only then offsetting what remained through verified nature-based projects. Some of the more tangible symbols of that effort were the disassembly robots Apple built to recover materials from old devices: Daisy, introduced in 2018, could take apart twenty-three different iPhone models at a rate of roughly two hundred units an hour, separating components with enough precision to recover materials — including cobalt, rare earths, and other elements — at a purity that conventional shredding-based recycling could never match, feeding Apple's parallel push toward using only recycled and renewable materials in its products. By its own later accounting, Apple estimated that shifting to lower-carbon materials, including recycled content, helped it avoid millions of metric tons of greenhouse gas emissions in a single recent year. None of this erased the fundamental tension at the heart of Apple's environmental posture — that its business still depended on selling hundreds of millions of new devices annually — but it was a more serious and more measurable effort than a company merely burnishing its image would have needed to make, and it placed Apple, however imperfectly, ahead of most of its industry peers on the specifics rather than only in the marketing.

Privacy's most instructive controversy, in fact, was not a case of Apple failing to protect its users but of Apple trying to protect a different and more vulnerable group and discovering how sharply that goal could collide with its own encryption principles. In 2021, Apple announced a suite of child-safety tools that included a system for detecting known child sexual abuse material within a user's iCloud Photos library, a technique designed to compare images against a database of previously identified illegal material using cryptographic matching performed partly on the device itself before anything was uploaded. The backlash was immediate and came from directions Apple had not fully anticipated: security researchers, the Electronic Frontier Foundation, the former NSA contractor turned privacy exile Edward Snowden, and even some of Apple's own employees warned that building any on-device scanning capability, however narrowly targeted, created an infrastructure that authoritarian governments could someday compel Apple to repurpose for searching devices for other kinds of content entirely — dissent, political speech, anything a state wished to find. Apple first delayed the rollout, then, in December 2022, abandoned the iCloud-scanning proposal altogether, effectively conceding that the tool it had built to protect children could not be reconciled with its broader promise never to weaken encryption for anyone, even for a cause as morally unambiguous as fighting child exploitation. The retreat did not end the matter: Apple was later sued for more than a billion dollars by plaintiffs who argued that abandoning the tool had allowed harmful material to keep circulating unchecked on its platform, a case that posed, in stark and uncomfortable terms, the question of whether a company can simultaneously be blamed for building surveillance infrastructure and for declining to build it — a genuine dilemma, without a clean resolution, that captured better than almost any other episode how privacy absolutism, however principled, was not free of costs measured in something other than dollars. Apple's alternative, less invasive child-safety features — on-device warnings when a minor's account sent or received a sexually explicit image, and expanded guidance built into Siri and search — survived the retreat and remained part of its software, a narrower and more defensible middle path than the abandoned scanning system, but one that critics on the child-safety side still considered a poor substitute for the detection capability Apple had walked away from. The episode is worth holding up against Apple's better-known privacy triumphs, like its public refusal to help the government unlock a terrorist's iPhone, because together the two cases show that Apple's encryption stance was not a selectively applied marketing position but a genuinely load-bearing principle, one the company held to even when doing so meant abandoning a tool built for an unimpeachable purpose and absorbing years of criticism, and even litigation, as the price of consistency.

Taken together, these shadows — the labor of the factories, the trial of the walled garden, the entanglement with China, and the tensions over privacy, repair, and the planet — do not diminish Apple's genuine achievements, but they complicate them, and they are essential to an honest reckoning with what the company became. Apple was, by its second half-century, a company of enormous power and genuine excellence that was also implicated in the harder realities of global capitalism, corporate power, and environmental cost, and that navigated the tensions between its values and its interests as all great companies do — sometimes admirably, sometimes self-servingly, always with an eye to both principle and profit. The beautiful objects and the trillions of dollars were real, and so were the shadows, and the mature judgment of Apple requires holding all of it together: the design and the labor, the excellence and the power, the values and the compromises, the light and the shadow, which were never separable and never will be. And it was this whole, complicated Apple — triumphant and troubled, beloved and criticized, the most valuable company in history and the subject of lawsuits and reckonings around the world — that Tim Cook, in 2026, prepared to hand to the next person to lead it, in a succession that would close one long era and open another, and that invites us, at last, to ask what Steve Jobs and the company he built had finally wrought.

Chapter 61 — Succession

In April 2026, Apple announced that Tim Cook would step back from the role he had held for nearly fifteen years, becoming executive chairman of the company's board, and that a new chief executive would take his place: John Ternus, the company's senior vice president of hardware engineering, effective September 1, 2026. The announcement, made through Apple's own newsroom and described as the culmination of a thoughtful, long-term succession process approved unanimously by the board, marked the second great leadership transition in Apple's modern history — the first being the handoff from Steve Jobs to Cook in 2011 — and it invited, inevitably, the same question that had greeted Cook's ascension: could Apple continue to thrive under yet another leader, in yet another key, as it moved further and further from the founder whose vision had defined it?

The choice of John Ternus was, in its way, both a continuation and a statement. Ternus was, like Cook before him, an insider — a twenty-five-year veteran of the company, a mechanical engineer by training who had risen through Apple's hardware-engineering organization to oversee the physical development of the company's most important products: the iPhone, the iPad, the Mac, the Apple Watch, the AirPods, and the Vision Pro. In selecting him, Apple's board chose continuity and deep institutional knowledge over an outside disruptor, and it chose, notably, an engineer and product person rather than an operations executive — a signal, perhaps, that after fifteen years under the operator Cook, Apple wished to return its leadership closer to the making of products, to the hardware and engineering that had always been its foundation. Ternus, at fifty-one, was younger than Cook and represented a generational handoff to leaders who had spent their entire careers inside the Apple that Jobs and Cook had built, who had never known the company in its garage days or its near-death, who had come of age professionally in the era of the iPhone. He was, in the accounts that emerged, respected as a capable and grounded leader, steeped in the products, well-prepared by years of increasing responsibility. Whether he possessed the particular genius that Apple's greatest successes had required — the product vision of Jobs, or even the operational mastery of Cook — was, as with every succession, something only time and results could reveal.

The transition was designed, in characteristic Apple fashion, to be smooth and controlled. Cook would not vanish; he would remain as executive chairman, staying on through the summer to work closely with Ternus on the handover and continuing, in his new role, to engage with matters including the company's relationships with governments around the world — a significant role at a time when Apple's entanglements with regulators, with China, and with the geopolitics of technology were among its greatest challenges. The arrangement kept Cook's experience and relationships available to the company while transferring operational leadership to Ternus, a carefully managed passing of the torch rather than an abrupt break, reflecting the same disciplined, long-term planning that had characterized Cook's whole tenure. It was, in its orderliness, a testament to the institution Apple had become — a company mature and stable enough to plan its leadership transitions years in advance and execute them without drama, a far cry from the boardroom coups and desperate rescues of its earlier history.

The succession also arrived at a genuinely pivotal moment for Apple, and the challenges Ternus would inherit were formidable and worth naming clearly, because they define the questions that hang over Apple's future. He would take command of a company at the summit of global business, worth four trillion dollars, but facing questions on every side: whether it could produce a new platform as revolutionary as the iPhone, or whether the Vision Pro's uncertain reception signaled that the era of Apple-defined revolutions had passed; whether it could navigate the erosion of its App Store control as courts and regulators pried open the walled garden; whether it could reduce its dangerous dependence on China without crippling its supply chain; whether it could compete in the emerging technologies, above all artificial intelligence, where some observers judged Apple to have fallen behind rivals; and whether it could sustain its growth as its core smartphone market matured. Ternus would lead Apple not in the heroic mode of the founder building something from nothing, nor even in the mode of Cook scaling and perfecting Jobs's creation, but in the harder, less glamorous mode of stewarding an aging empire through the challenges of maturity, competition, and change — the mode in which the real test is not creating greatness but sustaining it, not building an empire but keeping one from decline.

The 2026 handoff to Ternus depended, at every turn, on the precedent and the memory of the first and far more improvised succession the company had undergone, fifteen years earlier, when Jobs himself, dying and running out of strength, told Apple's board in his final weeks that Cook should take his place. Jobs formally resigned as chief executive on August 24, 2011, in a letter to the board that recommended, in essence, its own succession plan and named Cook as the man to execute it; the board acted on his recommendation that same day, and Arthur Levinson, a director since 2000 and by then chairman, helped steer the company through the changeover alongside fellow board members that included former Vice President Al Gore. What was remembered less often, in the retellings of that moment, was Jobs's own account of why he had chosen Cook, an account he gave to his biographer Walter Isaacson not long before his death: "He had the same vision I did, and we could interact at a high strategic level, and I could just forget about a lot of things unless he came and pinged me." It was not the language of a man settling for a caretaker; it was the language of a man who believed he had found a partner capable of running the parts of Apple he no longer needed to think about.

That nuance is easy to lose beneath the caricature that grew up around Cook in the years after he took over — the idea, repeated so often it hardened into folk wisdom, that he was merely an operations man installed to keep the trains running while the company coasted on Jobs's designs. The caricature drew real fuel from Jobs himself, who told Isaacson, in the same set of interviews, that "Tim's not a product person." Isaacson later acknowledged that he had, if anything, softened some of Jobs's harsher private judgments for the finished book, and that in unguarded moments, frustrated and often in physical pain, Jobs said sharper things about colleagues than made it to the page. But the "not a product person" line, quoted endlessly out of context in the years since, obscures the plainer truth of the succession: Jobs did not hand Apple to Cook despite their difference in gifts but in some sense because of it. He had spent a decade watching Cook's operational discipline free him to obsess over products, and he judged, correctly as it turned out, that the same discipline could hold the company together once he was no longer there to obsess.

Cook's leadership, once he held the position outright, diverged from Jobs's in ways visible to anyone who had watched the company under its founder. The theatrical unveilings continued, but the persona onstage was quieter, less prone to withholding praise or credit, more inclined to share the microphone with the executives — Craig Federighi in software, Jony Ive in design, and later engineers like John Ternus — who had built whatever was being shown. Decision-making broadened; Apple under Cook pushed further into services and subscriptions and into wearables such as the Apple Watch and AirPods, categories that did not exist, or barely existed, when Jobs was alive, and that came to generate a growing share of the company's revenue without depending on a single visionary's next great idea. Cook made a different kind of history in October 2014, when he wrote a personal essay for Bloomberg Businessweek disclosing that he was gay — "I'm proud to be gay, and I consider being gay among the greatest gifts God has given me," he wrote, adding that the experience of being part of a minority had made him "more empathetic" and given him "a richer life." He became, by most accounts, the first sitting Fortune 500 chief executive to come out publicly while still in office, a fact with no precedent in Jobs's more guarded, private era of the company and one that reshaped, at least a little, what the public imagined an Apple chief executive could be.

The clearest sign that Cook was building not just a successor culture but an actual bench came in 2019, when Jony Ive, the designer who had partnered with Jobs on the iMac, the iPod, and the iPhone and who remained the last prominent figure from Apple's founding-era creative core, announced he was leaving to start an independent firm called LoveFrom, with Apple retained as its first client. Cook's internal message to employees called Ive "a friend" and credited him with a role in "Apple's revival" that "cannot be overstated." Ive's departure fed a wider anxiety, voiced by critics and analysts for years afterward, that Apple could no longer produce the kind of radical, category-defining design it had under Jobs and the young Ive — an anxiety this book has already traced through the

Vision Pro's uncertain reception and the slower cadence of true surprises at Apple's keynotes. But it also cleared space, however painfully, for the next generation of leaders to take on visible responsibility rather than remain in a legend's shadow, and the hardware and software organizations that Federighi and Ternus went on to run in Ive's absence became, in time, precisely the proving ground from which the company would draw the leader named to succeed Cook himself.

Ternus was not the only name on Apple's own list, and understanding who else stood near the top of it clarifies what the board was actually choosing between. Cook had, for years, kept a small bench of internal candidates visibly seasoned for the possibility of succeeding him, among them Craig Federighi, the charismatic head of software engineering; Eddy Cue, the longtime services chief who had helped build the App Store, iTunes, and Apple's media businesses; Greg Joswiak, the head of worldwide marketing; and Deirdre O'Brien, who oversaw both retail and human resources — along with Jeff Williams, Apple's chief operating officer and Cook's closest operational deputy for years, who retired from the company in early 2026 shortly before the announcement, removing from contention the executive whose own career path had most closely mirrored Cook's own rise from operations to the top job. That Ternus emerged from this group rather than Federighi, in some ways the more natural public face of the company after years of confident keynote appearances, reflected a specific bet by the board about where Apple's next decade of competition would actually be fought: not primarily in the App Store's software ecosystem or in the services subscriptions that had powered so much of Cook's own tenure, but in the harder engineering problem of fusing hardware and silicon tightly enough to run demanding on-device AI and to support new wearable categories like the Vision Pro and whatever smart-glasses product followed it. Ternus's own track record made him a plausible answer to that specific bet: he had coordinated the hardware side of the Intel-to-Apple-Silicon transition, had overseen Vision Pro's physical development from prototype to shipping product, and had built, by most accounts, an unusually close working relationship with Federighi himself, a partnership the board seemed to be gambling would let the new chief executive lean on his internal rival's strengths rather than compete with them — much as Cook himself had once depended on partnerships with Jony Ive and Federighi to cover the ground his own gifts did not reach. Cue and Joswiak, older than Ternus and each identified for years mainly with a single function — media and services in Cue's case, marketing in Joswiak's — never emerged in press coverage as serious front-runners in the way Federighi and Ternus did, a fact that itself said something about how narrowly the board's real deliberation had come to focus on the hardware-software axis of the company rather than on the commercial and communications side that Cook's own tenure had done so much to build up. Deirdre O'Brien's name surfaced more as a marker of the board's seriousness about internal diversity of experience than as a genuine contender for the very top job, her portfolio spanning retail and people rather than the product-facing disciplines the other candidates shared — a reminder that even a carefully cultivated bench does not guarantee every strong internal executive an equal chance at the chair itself.

The deeper significance of the 2026 succession, for the story this book has told, is what it says about the question that has run through the whole of it: whether Steve Jobs built something that could outlast him. When Jobs died in 2011, the skeptics believed Apple was Jobs, that it would fade without him, that no company so bound to one man's vision could survive his loss. Fifteen years later, Apple has not merely survived but grown enormously, has weathered one leadership transition and is executing a second, has become the most valuable company in history under a leader who was not its founder, and is passing to a third leader who never worked directly under Jobs at all. By this measure, Jobs's greatest creation was not any product but the company itself — the institution, the culture, the design and engineering capability, the ecosystem, the brand, the set of principles and people that could continue to produce and thrive without him. He had built, the second time, not just insanely great products but an insanely durable institution, one robust enough to outlive its creator and to keep succeeding under leaders of very different gifts. Whether that durability would extend indefinitely, whether Apple could remain great through the challenges Ternus inherited and the leaders who would follow him, no one could say. But the mere fact that Apple in 2026 was thriving, transitioning smoothly to its third era of leadership, richer and larger than ever, was itself an answer of sorts to the question of what Jobs had wrought — and it invites the final reckoning of this book, the attempt to say, across the whole fifty-year arc from the garage to the four-trillion-dollar succession, what Steve Jobs and Apple finally meant.

Chapter 62 — One More Thing

Steve Jobs had a habit, at the end of his product launches, of pausing as if he were finished, letting the audience begin to relax, and then turning back to the podium with a small smile and the words: "But there's one more thing." What followed was usually the real climax — the product or the announcement he had held back for maximum effect, the surprise that sent the audience home electrified. The phrase became one of his signatures, a piece of theater so associated with him that its mere utterance could quicken the pulse of an Apple audience. And it makes a fitting title for the end of this book, because the question of what comes next — the one more thing, the next revolution, the future that Apple and the technology it pioneered are carrying us toward — is the question that Jobs's whole life poses, and that his death left open.

What, in the end, did Steve Jobs and Apple change? The answer is: an enormous amount, more than almost any individual and company of their age, and in ways so woven into ordinary life that they have become invisible. Consider the world before and after. Before Jobs and Apple, computers were tools for experts and businesses, intimidating machines that ordinary people did not own or understand; Apple, more than any other company, made the computer personal, friendly, and human, and put it into homes and schools and lives. Before the iPod and iTunes, music lived on physical discs and the digital future was chaos; Apple reorganized the whole industry and taught the world to carry its music in its pocket. Before the iPhone, the mobile phone was a clumsy device for calls and texts; Apple turned it into a pocket computer that has become the single most important and ubiquitous technology on earth, carried by billions, mediating work and love and news and knowledge and attention and nearly every other aspect of modern life. The design language Apple pioneered — the clean, simple, human-centered aesthetic, the marriage of technology and beauty — reshaped not just computers and phones but the whole material culture of the digital age, influencing how nearly every object and interface is designed. The way a modern person interacts with technology — touching glass, tapping icons, carrying a networked computer everywhere, living inside apps and ecosystems — was, to a remarkable degree, defined by Apple. Few individuals have left so deep and pervasive a mark on the texture of daily human life.

But the honest reckoning that this book has tried to sustain requires setting the achievement alongside its costs and its ambiguities, and refusing the simple story of the visionary who made the world better. Jobs and Apple gave the world tools of extraordinary power and beauty, and those same tools have costs that grow clearer with time. The smartphone that Apple perfected has connected humanity and also fractured its attention, colonized its waking hours, and reshaped its psychology in ways we are only beginning to understand and that many find alarming. The ecosystems Apple built are seamless and also confining, walled gardens that lock people in and give a single company enormous power over the software, the commerce, and the digital lives of billions. The beautiful objects were made by distant workers under hard conditions, sold at prices that generated the greatest fortune in history, and designed to be replaced rather than repaired, at real cost to the planet. And the man himself was, as this book has insisted throughout, not the saint of the eulogies but a complicated and often cruel human being, whose genius and whose damage flowed from the same source, and whose story is falsified by the hagiography as much as by the condemnation. The full truth of Steve Jobs and Apple is neither the inspirational fable nor the cynical exposé, but the harder thing that includes both — the genuine world-changing achievement and the genuine costs, the beauty and the power, the light and the shadow, held together without collapsing either into the other.

There is a lesson in Jobs's life that transcends technology and business, and it is worth stating plainly, because it is the thing that draws people to his story and that his story genuinely earns. It is the lesson of the second act — that failure is not final, that being cast down is not the same as being defeated, that the wilderness can be the making rather than the unmaking of a person. Jobs was thrown out of the company he founded, humiliated, written off; he wandered for a decade through expensive failures; and he came back and did the greatest work of his life. He built Apple, lost it, and built it again, better. The years everyone counted as his failure — NeXT, Pixar, the wilderness — turned out to be the years that made him capable of his triumph, that gave him the operating system that would run his empire, the studio that taught him to lead, the humility and patience and seasoning that the young prodigy had lacked. That arc — the fall, the wilderness, the return, the vindication — is one of the oldest and most powerful stories human beings tell, and Jobs lived it in fact, and it is a large part of why his story resonates far beyond the world of technology. It says that a life is not over when it seems over, that the interruption may be the prologue, that what looks like the end may be the middle.

The version of Jobs that most of the world carries in its head was shaped decisively by a single book: Walter Isaacson's authorized biography, published within three weeks of Jobs's death and built on more than forty interviews with Jobs himself, conducted over the last two years of his life, alongside conversations with family, friends, rivals, and colleagues. It became the dominant lens through which the public understood him, and it earned that place honestly, refusing the easy hagiography that a company-sanctioned tribute might have produced. Yet even that unsparing portrait, Isaacson later admitted, was gentler than the man in the room. He said he had, if anything, softened some of Jobs's harshest private judgments for the finished book, and that in unguarded moments, frustrated and often in physical pain during their final interviews, Jobs said sharper and crueler things about the people around him than made it onto the page. The common assumption is that the Isaacson biography is the harsh corrective to the mythology, the warts-and-all antidote to the reality-distortion field; the truer picture is that even the corrective pulled some of its punches, which means the real Steve Jobs, in his hardest moments, was harder still than the book that defined him for history.

What has not faded, in the years since, is the ritual of memory that Jobs's death set in motion. Every October, as the anniversary of his passing approaches, Apple pauses, however briefly, to look backward. Tim Cook has marked the date most years with a public tribute, writing in one of them that "Steve saw the future as a bright and boundless place, lit the path forward, and inspired us to follow." At Apple Park, the auditorium where the company unveils its newest products was named the Steve Jobs Theater and opened, fittingly, with a product launch of its own; Cook has said plainly that "not a day goes by that we don't think of him," adding that "it was only fitting that Steve should open his theater." In 2022, on the eve of the eleventh anniversary of his death, Cook, Jony Ive, and Jobs's widow, Laurene Powell Jobs, appeared together on a conference stage to talk about him at length, a rare joint public reckoning by the three people who had perhaps known him best in his final years. Alongside that conversation, Powell Jobs launched the Steve Jobs Archive, an online project meant to preserve his letters, speeches, and ideas for future generations, saying she hoped it would be "a place to draw inspiration from Steve's life and work, spurring new generations to make their own contributions to our common future," and that Jobs himself had possessed "a boundless sense of possibility and a belief in the power of individuals to make an enduring contribution to humanity."

These are not merely sentimental gestures; they mark an unusual and continuing negotiation between a company that must keep moving and a memory it has chosen never quite to let go of. As Apple grew, in the years after Jobs's death, from a company worth a few hundred billion dollars into one valued at several trillion — one of the most valuable enterprises human beings have ever built — the temptation to treat Jobs as a closed chapter, a founder-myth safely retired to the history books, must have been real. Instead, the company kept naming buildings and rooms after him, kept marking the anniversary, kept inviting the people who loved him back on stage to speak of him in the present tense. Every new product unveiling, whether or not it says so, is still measured, consciously or not, against the ghost of his stagecraft; every "one more thing" moment, wherever it appears, recalls the man who invented the gesture and made ordinary retail theater feel like revelation. That tension — between honoring an irreplaceable founder and building a future that does not depend on him — is itself one of the truest measures of what Jobs left behind, because a legacy strong enough to be worth wrestling with in public, year after year, on conference stages and anniversary posts and the naming of theaters, is a legacy that has clearly outlived the man.

Hollywood, characteristically, arrived at its own reckoning with Jobs's contradictions well before this book did, and the two attempts it made within a few years of each other reveal, by their very disagreement, how unsettled the public understanding of the man remained. The first, a 2013 film simply titled *Jobs*, starred Ashton Kutcher and traced a fairly conventional arc from his years as a Reed College dropout through the launch of the iPod, and it leaned toward the founder-genius version of the story, the young rebel vindicated by history. The more ambitious attempt came two years later: *Steve Jobs*, directed by Danny Boyle from a screenplay by Aaron Sorkin, structured the entire film not as a chronological biography but as three extended backstage sequences set in the minutes before three separate product launches — the original Macintosh in 1984, the NeXT computer in 1988, and the iMac in 1998 — using the tense, high-pressure minutes before each unveiling to dramatize Jobs's relationships with his daughter Lisa, with Steve Wozniak, and with the executives around him. Sorkin drew on his own interviews with people who had known Jobs, including some who had declined to speak with Isaacson, and the resulting portrait, played by Michael Fassbender, was considerably less flattering than Kutcher's, giving full weight to the cruelty and the denial that this book has also insisted belong in any honest account. Notably, the film's costume designer later acknowledged that the real Jobs had not actually worn his signature black turtleneck at any of the three launches the film dramatized, and Fassbender himself said the choice to put him in it anyway, in the final act, was deliberate — a piece of visual shorthand meant to signal the moment the character had fully become the icon the public remembers, even at the cost of literal accuracy. That two prestige films, released within twenty-four months of each other and drawing on much of the same source material, could arrive at such different Jobs — one closer to hagiography, one closer to indictment — says something about how large and how contested his image had already become within a few years of his death, and it is a small piece of evidence for the same argument this book has made throughout: that the true Jobs, cruel and visionary in equal and inseparable measure, resists compression into either the flattering myth or its cynical opposite. Both films, tellingly, kept returning to the same handful of scenes — the garage, the ouster from his own company, the triumphant return — because those beats were simply the load-bearing structure of the story itself, the parts no dramatist could omit and still be telling the tale of Steve Jobs at all; where the two films parted ways was in how much they were willing to let the man's cruelty toward the people around him sit, unresolved and unredeemed, beside his gifts, and that difference in nerve, more than any difference in the underlying facts, is what separated a competent biopic from the more uncomfortable and more lasting one.

And so we come to the one more thing, which is the future, and which neither Jobs nor this book can know. Apple continues, into its second half-century, under new leadership, facing the challenges of its maturity — the question of the next platform, the reckoning over its power, the entanglement with China, the race in artificial intelligence, the eternal problem of sustaining greatness after the founder is gone. The technologies that Jobs and Apple set loose in the world continue to reshape human life in ways no one fully controls or foresees, for better and for worse. Whether Apple will remain great, whether it will produce another revolution or coast on Jobs's legacy toward eventual decline as all empires do, whether the next great transformation of human life will come from Cupertino or from somewhere no one is yet watching — these are the open questions, the one-more-things that the future holds and that we cannot yet see. What we can say is that a college dropout who was given up at birth and thrown out of his own company nonetheless managed, in fifty-six years, to change the daily life of most of humanity, to build the most valuable company in the history of the world, and to leave behind an institution that outlived him and a set of objects and ideas woven so deeply into modern existence that we no longer notice them. He wanted, he said, to put a dent in the universe. He did. The dent remains, and so do the shadows it casts, and the story —

his, and Apple's, and ours — goes on. There is always one more thing.

Epilogue: The Dent in the Universe

Walk into any room in the developed world today and count the Apple products. The phone face-down on the table, its owner's whole life inside it. The white stems of earbuds in the ears of the person across from you. The watch on a wrist, counting heartbeats and steps. The silver laptop open on a desk, glowing. The tablet a child holds, absorbed. These objects are so ordinary now, so woven into the fabric of the everyday, that we have stopped seeing them, and it is worth, at the end of this story, making the effort to see them again — because every one of them descends, in a direct and traceable line, from two young men in a suburban garage in 1976, and from the strange, brilliant, difficult man who was the more famous of the two.

That is the astonishing fact at the center of this book: that so much of the material texture of modern life — the way we communicate, work, listen, watch, navigate, remember, and pay attention — was shaped to a remarkable degree by a single company, and that company was shaped to a remarkable degree by a single person who did not, in the technical sense, invent almost any of it. Steve Jobs did not invent the personal computer, or the graphical interface, or the mouse, or the MP3 player, or the smartphone, or the tablet, or any of the underlying technologies. What he did — the thing he was uniquely great at, the thing that was his real genius — was to see, before others, what these technologies could become; to insist, against every pressure to compromise, that they be made beautiful and simple and human; to combine them into products that ordinary people could love; and to will those products into existence through a force of vision and character that could inspire greatness and inflict cruelty in the same gesture. He was not the inventor of the modern world. He was its editor, its designer, its impresario — the one who took what was possible and made it desirable, who turned the raw material of the digital age into objects that people wanted to hold.

The dent he put in the universe is real, and it is permanent, and it is double. On one side is everything good: the empowerment of ordinary people with tools of extraordinary capability, the democratization of creativity and communication and knowledge, the sheer beauty and pleasure of well-made things, the demonstration that technology need not be cold and ugly and hostile but can be warm and simple and human. On the other side is everything troubling: the colonization of human attention, the walled gardens and concentrated power, the fractured focus and the anxious dependence, the hidden labor and the environmental cost, the transformation of billions of people into users locked inside ecosystems they do not control. Both sides of the dent are Steve Jobs's legacy, and both are Apple's, and the honest measure of the man and the company requires seeing both — refusing the temptation to remember only the beauty or to see only the shadow.

Steve Jobs died believing that Apple's brightest days lay ahead of it, and by the measure of the fifteen years since his death, he was right — the company grew beyond anything he had achieved, into the most valuable enterprise in history, and passed smoothly into new hands, proving that his deepest creation was not any product but the institution itself. Whether he will be right forever, whether Apple can remain great through the long future, whether the dent will deepen or fade, no one can know. Empires rise and fall; even the greatest companies eventually decline; and the technologies Jobs set loose are still reshaping the world in ways that will not be understood for generations. But the story told in these pages — of a boy given up at birth, raised by a machinist who taught him that craftsmanship lives in the parts no one sees; of a partnership between a salesman and an engineer that began by defrauding the phone company; of a company built and lost and built again; of a wilderness that turned out to be a prologue; of a second act unmatched in the history of business; of a man who changed the daily life of most of humanity and died at the summit, at fifty-six — that story is finished, even as its consequences are not.

The numbers alone tell part of the story of what came after. In August 2018, Apple became the first American company in history to close a trading day worth $1 trillion, a threshold that had sounded, a decade earlier, like a rounding error in a work of speculative fiction rather than an achievable line on a balance sheet. It did not stop there. Two years later, in the pandemic summer of 2020, with much of the world confined indoors and buying phones and laptops to work and study and stay in touch with people they could no longer see in person, Apple doubled that valuation to $2 trillion — again the first American company to do so — in an odd, unplanned demonstration of how completely its products had become the infrastructure of ordinary life rather than a luxury layered on top of it. By the summer of 2023 the company closed above $3 trillion, a mark it would clear again and again through the following year, trading at times above $3.5 trillion, a scale of corporate value that no American company had ever before reached, doubled and redoubled within less than a decade of the founder's death, on a foundation he had spent much of his career insisting would remain fragile, one great product away from irrelevance. He was, in this respect as in so many others, both right and overtaken by events: the culture of paranoid craftsmanship he built into the company outlasted the fragility he feared, and turned Apple into something closer to a permanent institution of American life, more akin to a utility than a startup, its quarterly results a small weather system that moves markets around the world.

The products that carry the Jobs-era ambitions forward have had a more complicated reception than the era itself. In June 2023 Apple unveiled the Vision Pro, a mixed-reality headset that the company pitched, in the unmistakable vocabulary of its founder, as the start of "spatial computing," a wholly new category to sit alongside the Mac, the iPhone, and the iPad. It shipped in February 2024 to admiring reviews of its engineering and its price tag, which put it out of reach of the mass market that had always been the point of Jobs's designs, and it sold in the hundreds of thousands rather than the tens of millions — a niche, expensive, unmistakably impressive object still waiting for the software and the moment that might turn it into something people actually needed. A year later, in the summer of 2024, Apple made its long-delayed entry into the generative-AI race with a set of features it branded Apple Intelligence, folding large-language-model writing tools, image generation, and a more capable Siri into iPhones, iPads, and Macs — an announcement met not with the operatic unveiling energy of the old product keynotes but with a more sober question, asked openly across the technology press, of whether the company that had always insisted on shipping only when a thing was ready had, this once, promised more than it could deliver on schedule, as a more conversational version of Siri slipped from its original release date into the following year. It was a small, telling reversal: the company built on the principle that Apple ships nothing before it is insanely great, learning in public what it costs to compete in a field it did not invent and does not yet clearly lead.

None of this settles the argument about what Steve Jobs actually built, or what it will mean in the long run. Retrospectives written in the years after his death have tended to split along the same fault line this book has traced throughout: admiration for a man who married engineering to taste more successfully than anyone in the history of consumer technology, set against unease at the world of glowing rectangles and algorithmic attention-capture that his products did so much to usher in, whether or not he intended it. Tim Cook, the operations man Jobs chose as his successor over more visionary candidates precisely because Apple no longer needed another Jobs, has now run the company for longer than Jobs ran it after his return in 1997, presiding over its transformation from an insurgent maker of beautiful objects into one of the largest financial entities on Earth, a services-and-hardware conglomerate now navigating antitrust scrutiny in Washington and Brussels alike. Jobs would likely have found parts of this present unrecognizable and other parts entirely predictable. He always said he wanted to build a company that would outlast him, one whose values were, in his own phrase, imprinted so deeply that they would survive any single leader, including its founder. By that test, whatever else is said about the trillion-dollar valuations, the antitrust suits, and the AI features arriving a year behind schedule, Apple had already succeeded beyond what almost anyone, including Jobs himself, thought possible in the bleak years of 1997, when the company was ninety days from bankruptcy and no one outside Cupertino would have bet on any of this.

He wanted to make a dent in the universe, and to do it with a small band of pirates rather than the navy, and to make things insanely great, and to leave the world different than he found it. He did all of it. The universe is dented. The pirates won. And somewhere in the world, right now, someone is picking up one of the objects he willed into being, and holding it, and using it, without a thought for the strange and difficult and extraordinary man who made sure it would exist. That is, perhaps, the truest measure of what he built: that it has outlived him, and become invisible, and gone on. There is always one more thing.

Timeline

1955 — February 24: Steven Paul Jobs is born in San Francisco and adopted by Paul and Clara Jobs.

1971 — Steve Jobs meets Steve Wozniak; the two begin building and selling illegal "blue boxes."

1972 — Jobs enters Reed College; drops out after one semester but stays on, auditing classes including calligraphy.

1974 — Jobs works at Atari; travels to India in search of enlightenment.

1975 — The Homebrew Computer Club holds its first meeting; Wozniak designs the Apple I.

1976 — April 1: Apple Computer Company is founded by Jobs, Wozniak, and Ronald Wayne. Wayne sells his 10% stake for $800 within two weeks. The Apple I goes on sale in July at $666.66.

1977 — January 3: Apple Computer, Inc. is incorporated, with Mike Markkula's backing. The Apple II is launched at the West Coast Computer Faire.

1978 — Jobs's daughter Lisa Brennan is born; he denies paternity for years.

1979 — VisiCalc, the first spreadsheet, ships for the Apple II. Apple engineers visit Xerox PARC.

1980 — December 12: Apple's initial public offering makes Jobs and many others wealthy.

1983 — The Apple Lisa launches and fails commercially. John Sculley is recruited from PepsiCo as CEO.

1984 — January 22: the "1984" Super Bowl ad airs. January 24: the Macintosh 128K is launched.

1985 — After a power struggle with Sculley, Jobs is stripped of authority and resigns in September; he founds NeXT.

1986 — Jobs buys the computer-graphics division of Lucasfilm for ~$5 million and renames it Pixar.

1988 — The NeXT Computer is unveiled.

1990 — Tim Berners-Lee builds the first web browser and server on a NeXT machine at CERN.

1991 — Jobs marries Laurene Powell.

1993 — NeXT abandons hardware to focus on software. Apple ships the Newton; Sculley is ousted.

1995 — November: *Toy Story* is released; Pixar's IPO makes Jobs a billionaire.

1996 — December: Apple agrees to buy NeXT (~$429 million); Jobs returns to Apple as an adviser.

1997 — Jobs becomes interim CEO ("iCEO"); announces the Microsoft investment and patent truce; launches "Think Different"; cuts the product line to four machines.

1998 — The iMac G3, designed with Jony Ive, is released and returns Apple to profitability.

2001 — Mac OS X ships. The first Apple Retail Stores open. October 23: the iPod is introduced.

2003 — The iTunes Music Store opens. Jobs is diagnosed with a pancreatic neuroendocrine tumor.

2004 — Jobs delays and then undergoes cancer surgery.

2005 — Jobs delivers the Stanford commencement address ("Stay hungry, stay foolish").

2006 — Disney buys Pixar for ~$7.4 billion; Jobs joins the Disney board.

2007 — January 9: the iPhone is unveiled. June 29: it goes on sale. The company is renamed Apple Inc.

2008 — July: the App Store opens.

2009 — Jobs undergoes a liver transplant; takes medical leave.

2010 — April: the iPad is released. Apple surpasses Microsoft in market value.

2011 — August 24: Jobs resigns as CEO; Tim Cook succeeds him. October 5: Steve Jobs dies at age 56.

2012 — September: the iPhone 5 launches alongside a redesigned Maps app; inaccuracies in Apple's own mapping data provoke a public backlash, and Tim Cook issues a rare open letter of apology.

2012 — October: Scott Forstall, the executive who led iOS development and refused to sign the Maps apology, is forced out of Apple; Tim Cook consolidates the company's design and software teams under Jony Ive.

2013 — June: Apple unveils a radically redesigned, cylindrical Mac Pro at WWDC.

2013 — September: the iPhone 5s, introducing the Touch ID fingerprint sensor, and the lower-cost iPhone 5c are released.

2014 — May: Apple acquires Beats Electronics and Beats Music from Dr. Dre and Jimmy Iovine for roughly $3 billion, its largest acquisition to date.

2014 — September: the Apple Watch is unveiled alongside the iPhone 6 and 6 Plus, and Apple Pay is introduced as a mobile payment service.

2014 — October: Tim Cook publicly comes out as gay in a Bloomberg Businessweek essay, becoming the first openly gay CEO of a Fortune 500 company.

2015 — The Apple Watch and Apple Music are launched.

2015 — November: the first iPad Pro is released, expanding the iPad line toward professional users.

2016 — February: Apple publicly resists a federal court order to help the FBI unlock an iPhone used by a shooter in the San Bernardino attack, setting up a high-profile standoff over encryption and privacy.

2016 — September: the iPhone 7 ships without a headphone jack.

2016 — AirPods are introduced.

2017 — Apple Park, the ring-shaped headquarters, opens.

2017 — September: the iPhone X is unveiled, introducing Face ID and an edge-to-edge OLED display on the iPhone's tenth anniversary.

2018 — February: the HomePod smart speaker is released.

2018 — Apple becomes the first company to reach a $1 trillion market capitalization.

2019 — June: Jony Ive announces he will leave Apple after nearly 30 years to found his own independent design firm, LoveFrom.

2019 — August: Apple Card, a credit card issued in partnership with Goldman Sachs, launches.

2019 — November: Apple TV+ and Apple Arcade launch, marking Apple's move into subscription video and gaming services.

2020 — June: Apple announces at WWDC that Mac computers will transition from Intel processors to Apple's own custom "Apple Silicon" chips.

2020 — Apple reaches $2 trillion; the transition to Apple Silicon (the M1 chip) begins.

2021 — April: Apple releases AirTags, a Bluetooth item-tracking device, alongside iOS 14.5's App Tracking Transparency feature, which requires apps to obtain explicit permission before tracking users across other companies' apps and websites.

2021 — The verdict in *Epic Games v. Apple* is issued, a split decision on the App Store.

2022 — April: Apple launches the Self Service Repair program, allowing customers to buy genuine parts, tools, and manuals to repair their own iPhones and Macs.

2022 — September: the Apple Watch Ultra, aimed at athletes and outdoor use, and the iPhone 14, with Emergency SOS via satellite, are released.

2022–2023 — Apple reaches $3 trillion (intraday in 2022; closes above in 2023).

2023 — June: Apple unveils the Vision Pro, a mixed-reality headset, at WWDC — its first new major product category since the Apple Watch.

2023 — September: the iPhone 15 becomes the first iPhone with a USB-C port, replacing Lightning in compliance with a new European Union regulation.

2024 — The Apple Vision Pro ships.

2024 — February: Apple cancels "Project Titan," its decade-long effort to build an electric, self-driving car.

2024 — March: the U.S. Department of Justice and sixteen state attorneys general file a sweeping antitrust lawsuit accusing Apple of illegally monopolizing the smartphone market.

2024 — June: at WWDC, Apple announces Apple Intelligence, a suite of generative-AI features for iPhone, iPad, and Mac.

2024 — October: Apple Intelligence begins rolling out with iOS 18.1, marking Apple's most significant entry into consumer AI.

2024 — Apple's market capitalization climbs above $3.5 trillion, the highest valuation any public company had ever reached.

2025 — Apple reaches $4 trillion in market value.

2025 — Facing the European Union's Digital Markets Act, Apple begins permitting alternative app marketplaces and sideloading on iPhones sold in the EU.

2025 — Apple postpones a significantly overhauled, more conversational version of Siri, originally expected in 2025, to 2026 amid struggles to deliver on its Apple Intelligence promises.

2026 — April: Apple announces that Tim Cook will become executive chairman and John Ternus will become CEO, effective September 1.

Who's Who

Steve Jobs (1955–2011) — Co-founder of Apple, its visionary and public face; CEO 1997–2011. The protagonist of this book: the editor and impresario of the digital age.

Steve Wozniak (b. 1950) — "Woz." Co-founder of Apple; the engineering genius who designed the Apple I and Apple II. Left day-to-day involvement in the 1980s; celebrated for his generosity and modesty.

Ronald Wayne (b. 1934) — The third co-founder, who drew Apple's first logo and wrote its partnership agreement, then sold his 10% stake for $800.

Mike Markkula (b. 1942) — Apple's early investor and second chairman; author of the one-page "Apple Marketing Philosophy" (empathy, focus, impute).

Mike Scott — Apple's first president/CEO ("Scotty"), installed to bring order to the young company; clashed with Jobs.

Regis McKenna — The marketing strategist who shaped Apple's early public image.

Jef Raskin (1943–2005) — Originator of the Macintosh project, later displaced by Jobs.

Bill Atkinson, Andy Hertzfeld, Burrell Smith, Susan Kare — Core members of the original Macintosh team (graphics software; system software; hardware; fonts and icons).

John Sculley (b. 1939) — Recruited from PepsiCo to be Apple's CEO (1983–1993); won the 1985 power struggle that forced Jobs out.

Gil Amelio — Apple CEO (1996–1997) who bought NeXT and was then replaced by Jobs.

Bill Gates (b. 1955) — Co-founder of Microsoft, Jobs's great rival, and, in 1997, the source of a $150 million investment that helped save Apple.

Ed Catmull (b. 1945) — Computer scientist and co-leader of Pixar; architect of its candor-based creative culture.

John Lasseter (b. 1957) — Animator and creative leader of Pixar; director of *Toy Story*; champion of story over technology.

Jony Ive (b. 1967) — Apple's chief designer; Jobs's "spiritual partner"; designer of the iMac, iPod, iPhone, and much else.

Tim Cook (b. 1960) — Operations chief recruited in 1998; CEO 2011–2026; builder of Apple's supply chain and the leader under whom Apple reached $4 trillion. Executive chairman from 2026.

John Ternus (b. c. 1974) — Longtime head of hardware engineering; named CEO of Apple effective September 1, 2026.

Tony Fadell — "Father of the iPod" and a key iPhone engineer.

Scott Forstall — Led iOS software; left Apple in 2012 after the flawed launch of Apple Maps.

Laurene Powell Jobs (b. 1963) — Jobs's wife (married 1991); philanthropist and founder of Emerson Collective.

Lisa Brennan-Jobs (b. 1978) — Jobs's first daughter, denied for years and later reconciled; author of the memoir *Small Fry*.

Paul and Clara Jobs — Steve Jobs's adoptive parents. **Mona Simpson** — his biological sister, the novelist, discovered in adulthood.

Ross Perot — Businessman and investor whose funding of NeXT he later called one of his worst investments.

Bob Iger (b. 1951) — The Disney CEO who negotiated the 2006 purchase of Pixar, making Jobs Disney's largest individual shareholder.

Eddy Cue (b. 1964) — Apple's SVP of Services and Health, at the company since 1989; built the online Apple Store, the iTunes Store, and the App Store, and remains one of the last executives from the Jobs era still serving under Cook.

Craig Federighi (b. c. 1969) — SVP of Software Engineering; came to Apple through the NeXT acquisition, left for a decade, then returned in 2009 to run macOS and, after Scott Forstall's 2012 exit, iOS as well. Known on stage for his self-deprecating humor, he later took charge of Apple Intelligence and the overhaul of Siri.

Phil Schiller (b. 1960) — Apple's marketing chief from Jobs's 1997 return through 2020, credited with shaping the messaging around the Mac, iPod, iPhone, and App Store. In 2020 he became an Apple Fellow, handing marketing to Greg Joswiak while continuing to run the App Store and Apple's product events.

Greg Joswiak (b. c. 1963) — "Joz," a marketer at Apple since 1986 whose nickname blends the surnames of Steve Jobs and Steve Wozniak. He succeeded Schiller as SVP of Worldwide Marketing in 2020 and became the public face of iPhone and Mac product launches.

Angela Ahrendts (b. 1960) — Former CEO of Burberry,

recruited by Cook in 2014 to lead Apple Retail; reimagined Apple Stores as community "Town Squares" before departing in 2019, when Deirdre O'Brien took over the role.

Deirdre O'Brien (b. c. 1966) — A 35-plus-year Apple veteran who became SVP of Retail and People in 2019, overseeing both the company's stores and its internal culture; she resumed the combined role in 2024 after a brief split.

Jeff Williams (b. 1963) — Apple's chief operating officer from 2015 to 2025, and before that the operations chief who ran the supply chain and oversaw creation of the Apple Watch. Long seen as a possible successor to Cook, he retired in November 2025 and was succeeded as COO by Sabih Khan.

Lisa Jackson — Former Administrator of the U.S. Environmental Protection Agency (2009–2013); joined Apple as VP of Environment, Policy and Social Initiatives, driving its renewable-energy programs and the "Apple 2030" carbon-neutrality pledge before announcing her retirement in 2026.

Katie Cotton (1965–2023) — Apple's VP of Worldwide Communications from 1996 to 2014 and one of Jobs's most trusted advisers; architect of the company's famously tight-lipped "anti-PR" media strategy.

Art Levinson (b. 1950) — Former longtime CEO of Genentech; joined Apple's board in 2000 and became its chairman in 2011, steering the board through the succession after Jobs's death. He also leads Calico, Alphabet's life-extension research venture.

Al Gore (b. 1948) — Former Vice President of the United States and Nobel Peace Prize–winning climate activist; served on Apple's board from 2003 until his mandatory retirement at age 75 in 2024.

Terry Gou (b. 1950) — Founder of Foxconn (Hon Hai Precision Industry), the Taiwanese contract manufacturer that assembles the great majority of the world's iPhones. He won Apple's manufacturing business in the late 1990s and built Foxconn into the world's largest electronics assembler, including the vast Zhengzhou complex nicknamed "iPhone City."

Judge Yvonne Gonzalez Rogers — U.S. District Judge for the Northern District of California who presided over *Epic Games v. Apple*; her 2021 ruling largely favored Apple on antitrust grounds but barred its anti-steering rules, a decision substantially upheld on appeal to the Ninth Circuit and left standing by the Supreme Court.

Walter Isaacson (b. 1952) — Journalist and biographer; former editor of *Time* and CEO of CNN. His 2011 authorized biography *Steve Jobs*, drawn from more than forty interviews with Jobs himself in his final years, became the definitive account of his life.

Glossary

Terms, products, and concepts used in this book.

Products and platforms

Apple I — Apple's first product (1976): a single-board computer, sold for $666.66, requiring the buyer to add a case, keyboard, and power.

Apple II — The 1977 mass-market computer, with color, sound, and expansion slots, that built Apple's early fortunes.

VisiCalc — The 1979 spreadsheet program, the first "killer app," which drove Apple II sales.

Lisa — Apple's 1983 graphical computer, named (secretly) for Jobs's daughter; a costly commercial failure.

Macintosh (Mac) — The 1984 computer that brought the graphical interface to the mass market and defined Apple's design ethos.

NeXTSTEP — The advanced operating system built by Jobs's company NeXT; later the basis of Mac OS X and every modern Apple OS.

Mac OS X / macOS — Apple's Unix-based operating system, derived from NeXTSTEP, introduced in 2001.

iMac — The 1998 all-in-one computer that returned Apple to profitability; the first product of the Jobs–Ive partnership.

iPod — The 2001 music player ("a thousand songs in your pocket").

iTunes / iTunes Store — Apple's music software and its 2003 online store, which reshaped the music industry.

iPhone — The 2007 multi-touch smartphone that became the defining device of the age.

iOS — The operating system of the iPhone and iPad, descended from Mac OS X.

App Store — The 2008 marketplace for third-party iPhone apps, which created a new global software economy.

iPad — The 2010 tablet computer.

Apple Watch (2015), AirPods (2016), Apple Vision Pro (2024) — Apple's wearables and its spatial-computing headset.

Apple Silicon (M-series) — Apple's own processors for the Mac, introduced in 2020, descended from iPhone chips.

Apple Services — Apple's business of digital subscriptions and services (App Store, Apple Music, iCloud, Apple TV+, Apple Pay, and others).

Face ID / Touch ID — Apple's biometric authentication systems: Touch ID (2013) reads a fingerprint, while Face ID (2017) maps the face with an infrared depth sensor and largely replaced it on the iPhone.

LiDAR scanner — A laser-based depth sensor, added to Pro-model iPhones and iPads starting in 2020, that measures reflected light to map a room for augmented-reality apps.

Neural Engine — The dedicated machine-learning processor built into Apple Silicon chips, used for tasks such as Face ID, computational photography, and on-device AI features.

Unified memory architecture — The Apple Silicon design in which the CPU, GPU, and Neural Engine share one pool of high-speed memory rather than separate dedicated memory banks.

Find My network — A crowdsourced system that uses nearby Apple devices to help locate lost hardware, or (via AirTag trackers) other items, without revealing the finder's identity.

visionOS — The operating system of the Apple Vision Pro headset, built around spatial computing.

Apple Intelligence — Apple's suite of generative-AI features, introduced in 2024 across iOS, iPadOS, and macOS, including writing tools, image generation, and a redesigned Siri.

MagSafe — A magnetic attachment and charging system, first used on MacBook power cords in 2006 and revived in 2020 for iPhone wireless charging and accessories.

ProMotion — Apple's adaptive high-refresh-rate display technology (up to 120Hz), introduced on the iPad Pro in 2017 and later brought to the iPhone.

StandBy — An iPhone display mode, introduced in 2023, that turns a charging, sideways-facing phone into a bedside clock, photo display, or widget screen.

Continuity — The features that let Apple devices work together across a single Apple ID — Handoff, Universal Clipboard, AirDrop, and answering calls or texts from another device.

Concepts and terms

Graphical user interface (GUI) — A way of using a computer through windows, icons, menus, and a pointer rather than typed commands.

Bitmapped display — A screen on which every pixel is individually controllable, allowing any image or font.

Multi-touch — The finger-gesture input system (tapping, swiping, pinching) central to the iPhone.

Killer app — A program so useful that people buy the hardware just to run it (e.g., VisiCalc).

Blue box — An illegal device that generated tones to make free long-distance phone calls; Jobs and Wozniak's first product.

Phone phreaking — The subculture of exploiting the phone network's control tones.

Whole widget / vertical integration — Apple's philosophy of controlling both hardware and software (and later chips, retail, and services) to deliver an integrated experience.

Walled garden — Apple's tightly controlled ecosystem, in which software must come through the App Store and Apple sets the rules.

Reality distortion field — The Macintosh team's term for Jobs's ability to convince himself and others that the impossible was achievable.

Impute — Markkula's principle that people judge a product by the signals a company sends about it, so presentation matters.

"Insanely great" — Jobs's phrase and standard for a transcendent product.

Skunkworks / pirates — A small, secret, elite team operating outside normal bureaucracy (the original Macintosh group).

Post-PC era — Jobs's term for the age in which smartphones and tablets displace the personal computer as the center of digital life.

Reality of the supply chain — The global manufacturing system, centered on contractors like Foxconn in China, that assembles Apple's products.

Right to repair — The movement opposing Apple's restrictions on repairing its devices.

Market capitalization — The total market value of a company's shares; Apple crossed $1 trillion (2018) to $4 trillion (2025).

App Tracking Transparency (ATT) — A privacy feature introduced in iOS 14.5 (2021) that requires apps to obtain explicit user permission before tracking their activity across other companies' apps and websites for advertising.

Digital Markets Act (DMA) — European Union legislation, in force from 2023, that designates large platforms including Apple as "gatekeepers" and compels them to permit sideloading, alternative app stores, and other competition Apple had previously barred.

Sideloading — Installing an app on a device from outside its official app store; long forbidden on iOS, it was opened to users in the European Union under the Digital Markets Act.

Anti-steering — App Store rules that once barred developers from telling users about cheaper ways to pay outside the app; the *Epic Games v. Apple* litigation forced Apple to loosen them.

Self Service Repair — An Apple program, launched in 2022, that sells consumers genuine parts, tools, and manuals to repair their own iPhones and Macs.

App Store commission ("Apple tax") — The percentage, historically as high as 30%, that Apple takes on paid apps and in-app purchases sold through the App Store; a central grievance in antitrust cases including *Epic v. Apple*.

Antitrust — Laws aimed at preventing monopolies and anticompetitive conduct; the legal framework behind *Epic Games v. Apple*, the U.S. Department of Justice's 2024 suit against Apple, and the EU's Digital Markets Act.

Carbon neutral / Apple 2030 — Apple's pledge to make its entire business — including its supply chain and the full life cycle of its products — carbon neutral by 2030.

Daisy — Apple's robot for disassembling used iPhones to recover cobalt, aluminum, and other materials for recycling; successor to an earlier robot, Liam.

Foxconn / EMS (electronics manufacturing services) — Foxconn (Hon Hai Precision Industry) is Apple's largest contract manufacturer; "EMS" describes the industry of firms that assemble electronics on behalf of brands that do not operate their own factories.

Notarization (macOS) — An Apple security check in which developers submit Mac software for automated scanning before macOS will run it without warning, intended to catch malware distributed outside the App Store.

Secure Enclave — A separate, isolated processor within Apple chips that stores fingerprint, face, and payment data, keeping it inaccessible to the main operating system.

Differential privacy — A mathematical technique, adopted by Apple, for gathering aggregate data about user behavior while adding statistical noise that prevents any individual's data from being identified.

Mail Privacy Protection — An Apple Mail feature, introduced in 2021, that hides a user's IP address and preloads message images so senders cannot reliably track whether or when an email was opened.

USB-C transition — Apple's 2023 shift of the iPhone from its proprietary Lightning connector to the industry-standard USB-C port, made under a European Union mandate for a common charging standard.

Spatial computing — Apple's term for computing that blends digital objects with the physical environment, as with the Vision Pro headset.

Further Reading

For readers who wish to go deeper, the following books and sources informed this history and reward direct study. They are grouped roughly by subject.

The life of Steve Jobs

- Walter Isaacson, *Steve Jobs* (2011). The authorized biography, written with Jobs's cooperation and extraordinary access; the essential single-volume life, panoramic and personal.
- Brent Schlender and Rick Tetzeli, *Becoming Steve Jobs* (2015). A corrective to Isaacson that emphasizes Jobs's growth and reads the NeXT and Pixar years as the making of the mature leader.
- Lisa Brennan-Jobs, *Small Fry* (2018). His daughter's luminous, painful memoir; indispensable for the human cost.
- Jeffrey S. Young, *Steve Jobs: The Journey Is the Reward* (1988). The first book-length biography, covering Jobs's rise at Apple through his 1985 ouster.
- Jeffrey S. Young and William L. Simon, *iCon: Steve Jobs* (2005). An unauthorized biography of Jobs's return and reinvention of Apple, its title punning on both "icon" and "con man."
- Randall E. Stross, *Steve Jobs and the NeXT Big Thing*

(1993). A skeptical, contemporaneous account of the NeXT years, written when Jobs's fortunes were at their lowest.

The early company and the Macintosh

- Michael Moritz, *The Little Kingdom* (1984), reissued as *Return to the Little Kingdom* (2009). The earliest serious Apple history, written with access in the founding years.
- Andy Hertzfeld, *Revolution in the Valley* (2004). Insider anecdotes of the original Macintosh team, drawn from the folklore.org archive.
- Steven Levy, *Insanely Great* (1994). A cultural history of the Macintosh; also Levy's *The Perfect Thing* (2006) on the iPod.
- Owen Linzmayer, *Apple Confidential 2.0* (2004). A dense chronicle of Apple's triumphs and blunders.
- Jim Carlton, *Apple: The Inside Story* (1997). The near-death years of the 1990s.
- John Markoff, *What the Dormouse Said* (2005). How 1960s Bay Area counterculture, psychedelics, and hobbyist computing shaped the industry that produced Apple.

Pixar

- David A. Price, *The Pixar Touch* (2008). The definitive account of Pixar's rise, essential for the exile years.
- Ed Catmull with Amy Wallace, *Creativity, Inc.* (2014). Catmull's account of building Pixar's creative culture.

Design, the iPhone, and modern Apple

- Leander Kahney, *Jony Ive* (2013) and *Tim Cook* (2019). The design and the operations halves of modern Apple.
- Ken Kocienda, *Creative Selection* (2018). How the iPhone's software was actually built, from inside the room.
- Tripp Mickle, *After Steve* (2022). Apple in the Cook-and-Ive era, after Jobs.
- Fred Vogelstein, *Dogfight: How Apple and Google Went to War and Started a Revolution* (2013). The iPhone-Android rivalry, told from inside both companies.
- Adam Lashinsky, *Inside Apple* (2012). A reporter's account of Apple's secretive internal culture and management practices under Jobs and the early Cook years.
- Yukari Iwatani Kane, *Haunted Empire: Apple After Steve Jobs* (2014). A skeptical look at Cook's early leadership and whether Apple could sustain Jobs's vision without him.
- Brian Merchant, *The One Device: The Secret History of the iPhone* (2017). A ground-up account of the iPhone's invention, from its engineers to the mines and factories behind its parts.

Primary and reference sources

- Steve Jobs, **Stanford Commencement Address** (2005) — "Stay hungry, stay foolish"; a primary text worth watching in full.
- The **Macworld keynotes**, especially 1997 (the Microsoft deal) and 2007 (the iPhone unveiling) — filmed primary sources.
- **Apple Newsroom** (apple.com) — official product launches, financial results, and the 2026 Cook–Ternus succession announcement.

- **Britannica** entries on Apple Inc., Steve Jobs, Tim Cook, and John Ternus.
- **Wikipedia** articles "Steve Jobs," "History of Apple Inc.," "Apple Inc.," "Tim Cook," and their many linked sub-topic pages, which provided the chronological skeleton.
- **U.S. court records** in *Epic Games v. Apple* (N.D. Cal., 2021) and related antitrust proceedings, and **Apple's SEC filings (10-K)**, for the App Store dispute and the financials.
- *Triumph of the Nerds* (PBS, 1996) and *Steve Jobs: The Lost Interview* — filmed primary sources on the early industry.
- *Steve Jobs: The Man in the Machine* (2015, dir. Alex Gibney). An unsparing documentary portrait, drawing on archival footage and interviews with those closest to Jobs.
- *Steve Jobs: Billion Dollar Hippy* (BBC, 2011). A British television documentary on Jobs's rise, with interviews including Steve Wozniak and John Sculley.
- *Steve Jobs* (2015), dir. Danny Boyle, screenplay by Aaron Sorkin. A dramatization, not a documentary, adapted from Isaacson's biography and built around three product launches, with Michael Fassbender as Jobs.

A Note on Sources and Acknowledgments

This is a work of popular history, written for the general reader, and it makes no claim to original archival research. Its purpose is synthesis: to tell the whole fifty-year arc of Apple and Steve Jobs in one readable narrative, drawing on the substantial body of journalism, biography, memoir, and public record that others have built, and to weigh the famous stories against the available evidence rather than simply repeating them.

Its spine is the standard literature listed in the Further Reading, above all Walter Isaacson's authorized biography for the life, Brent Schlender and Rick Tetzeli for the reappraisal of the exile years, Andy Hertzfeld and the folklore.org archive for the Macintosh, David Price for Pixar, and Leander Kahney, Ken Kocienda, and Tripp Mickle for the design culture and the modern company. For the chronology and the factual scaffolding — dates, figures, product specifications, and the sequence of events — this book leaned on the detailed and well-sourced Wikipedia articles on Steve Jobs, the history of Apple, Apple Inc., Tim Cook, and John Ternus, and on the Britannica entries for the same subjects, cross-checked where possible against primary sources such as Apple's own newsroom announcements and financial filings and the public record of the *Epic Games v. Apple* litigation.

Several matters in this book are recent enough that they fall after the settled historical record and were verified by direct research in mid-2026: Apple's rise to a four-trillion-dollar market valuation in 2025, and the April 2026 announcement that Tim Cook would become executive chairman and John Ternus would become chief executive effective September 1, 2026. These facts are drawn from Apple's own newsroom and from contemporary reporting, and readers consulting this book at a later date should bear in mind that the story of Apple's most recent years is still unfolding as these pages go to press.

This book has tried throughout to observe a discipline it calls, in its own pages, holding the legend against the ledger: to separate, wherever the evidence allows, the mythologized Steve Jobs from the man who actually lived, and to resist both the hagiography that erases his cruelty and the debunking that erases his achievement. Where accounts conflict — and around Jobs they conflict constantly, with different witnesses remembering the same events in incompatible ways — the book has tried to note the disagreement rather than to paper over it, and to flag where a beloved story is uncertain or embellished. Any errors of fact or interpretation that remain are the author's own.

Finally, a word of gratitude. This book was written in admiration not only of Steve Jobs but of the many people whose work the cult of the founder tends to erase — Steve Wozniak, who built the machines and gave the designs away; Mike Markkula, who wrote the philosophy; the Macintosh pirates; Ed Catmull and John Lasseter, who taught even Jobs a gentler way to make great things; Jony Ive, who gave the vision its form; Tim Cook, who made it endure; and the countless engineers, designers, and workers, named and unnamed, in California and across the world, whose labor made the objects real. The story is usually told as the tale of one extraordinary man. It is truer, and better, as the tale of the many hands that swung the hammer.

— *E.B Cohen, 2026*

www.ingramcontent.com/pod-product-compliance
Lightning Source LLC
LaVergne TN
LVHW100132061126
851857LV00010B/55
9798233960116